IN THE POWER OF THE GOVERNMENT

The Rise and Fall of Newsprint in Ontario, 1894–1932

For forty years, historians have argued that early twentieth-century provincial governments in Canada were easily manipulated by the industrialists who developed Canada's natural resources, such as pulpwood, water power, and minerals. With *In the Power of the Government*, Mark Kuhlberg uses the case of the Ontario pulp and paper industry to challenge that interpretation of Canadian provincial politics.

Examining the relationship between the corporations that ran the province's pulp and paper mills and the politicians at Queen's Park, Kuhlberg concludes that the Ontario government frequently rebuffed the demands of the industrialists who wanted to tap Ontario's spruce timber and hydro-electric potential. A sophisticated empirical challenge to the orthodox literature on this issue, *In the Power of the Government* will be essential reading for historians and political scientists interested in the history of Canadian industrial development.

MARK KUHLBERG is an associate professor in the Department of History at Laurentian University.

In the Power of the Government

The Rise and Fall of Newsprint in Ontario, 1894–1932

MARK KUHLBERG

UNIVERSITY OF TORONTO PRESS
Toronto Buffalo London

© University of Toronto Press 2015
Toronto Buffalo London
www.utppublishing.com
Printed in the U.S.A.

ISBN 978-1-4426-4663-6 (cloth)
ISBN 978-1-4426-1453-6 (paper)

Printed on acid-free, 100% post-consumer recycled paper with vegetable-based inks

---

Library and Archives Canada Cataloguing in Publication

Kuhlberg, Mark, 1966–, author
In the power of the government : the rise and fall of newsprint in Ontario, 1894–1932 / Mark Kuhlberg.

Includes bibliographical references and index.
ISBN 978-1-4426-4663-6 (bound). – ISBN 978-1-4426-1453-6 (pbk.)

1. Newsprint industry – Government policy – Ontario.   2. Newsprint industry – Ontario, Northern – History.   3. Paper industry – Government policy – Ontario.   4. Paper industry – Ontario, Northern – History.   5. Ontario – Politics and government – 1867–.   6. Industrial policy – Ontario – History.   I. Title.

HD9839.N43C36 2015   338.4'7676286   C2014-907134-5

University of Toronto Press acknowledges the financial assistance to its publishing program of the Canada Council for the Arts and the Ontario Arts Council, an agency of the Government of Ontario.

 **Canada Council Conseil des Arts
for the Arts du Canada**

 **ONTARIO ARTS COUNCIL
CONSEIL DES ARTS DE L'ONTARIO**
an Ontario government agency
un organisme du gouvernement de l'Ontario

University of Toronto Press acknowledges the financial support of the Government of Canada through the Canada Book Fund for its publishing activities.

To Cindy, for all your love and support

Contents

Section IV. "The chief is the whole show": The Conservatives, 1923–1932   191

Maps, Charts, and Figures

Maps

Charts

Figures

Acknowledgments

I never intended to write *this* book. As a young and much shaggier doctoral student, I set out to produce a sequel to H.V. Nelles's *The Politics of Development* and determine if the paradigm of "government as a client of industry" applied to the period after the Second World War. In my quest for archival materials from the province's pulp and paper makers, I ended up on the third floor of Francis H. Clergue's stately turn-of-the-century office building in Sault Ste Marie, which sits a stone's throw from the site on which he built northern Ontario's first pulp and paper mill. There, hidden among a generous scattering of mice turds and dead bats, smashed filing cabinets, and decades of practically undisturbed layers of dust, were the initial signs of a story left untold for nearly one century: namely, the degree to which conflict marked the relationship between the provincial government and many of Ontario's newsprint makers. It was a paper trail that presented me with a perplexing dilemma. I could ignore it, proceed full steam ahead with my original project, and complete it – hopefully! – within a reasonable time. Conversely, I could pick up the scent I had found and see where it led; it was immediately apparent that this path would involve challenging the venerable "Nelles's thesis." While the prospect of delaying my exit from graduate school was most unenticing, my conscience would not let me write the sequel to an epic after I had unearthed solid grounds for questioning its very foundation. It was for this reason that I began writing *this* book.

This decision proved exponentially more costly than I could ever have imagined. It consumed an inordinate amount of my time, left me without a thesis supervisory committee, and repeatedly raised profound questions about what it meant to be a historian; I would also like to blame it for my present state of follicle-challengedness. Nevertheless, I feel the project was worth it, and hopefully the reader will share this perspective. Although I have done my best to get the story straight, I accept full blame for all errors and omissions.

Considering I spent nearly twenty years researching and writing this book, it is hardly surprising that I have many persons to thank for their contributions to it. Many years ago, when my doctoral dissertation project was derailed, the late Jack T. Saywell stepped out of retirement to get the project back on track. By that time, he – and Suzanne – had already become dear friends to both me and my wife; we will never forget the many fun times we shared up at Tupper's farm. Successfully lobbying to have an area that I and some friends had re-greened at York University named in his honour was one way of expressing my gratitude to him; ensuring that this book saw the light of day is another. Professors Craig Heron, Richard Hoffman, and John Warkentin also stepped up to the plate to ensure that I had completed my thesis. So, too, did the late Peter Oliver, who was completely supportive of my work even though it presented a direct challenge to his own. Ian Radforth agreed to be the outside examiner, and I thank him for all his help and friendship over the years. Economist Mark Mueller also kindly read my manuscript and offered insightful feedback.

Over the last two decades, a string of individuals across the continent have taken time to help me both understand woodlands and access the documentary evidence to write about our interaction with them. Foremost among them is Ken Armson. From the first time I called him as a nervous MA student, he has offered unfailing and generous support for my work; over the years he has become a great friend and mentor to me and my family. Likewise, from the moment I began "eating dirt" – as Charlotte Gill so eloquently put it – as a treeplanter in northern Ontario, a number of persons offered their insights into the biotics and politics of our forests. Gary McKibbon was the first, way up in Red Lake, and he was followed by Malcolm "Mac" Squires, Paul Poschmann, Bill Smith, and Tom Ratz at the Lakehead. In the northeast, Marc Dube, when he was Woodlands Manager at St Mary's Paper in the Soo in the mid-1990s, was truly awesome to me. He believed in my ability to clean and organize that mill's archival collection, which now sits in the local public library archives as one of the best forest history fonds in the country. More importantly, he offered words of encouragement as my energy for heading up to the third floor of that office building (it had twenty-foot ceilings after all!) reached its low ebb. Thanks also to Rick

Telfer for taking me fishing for "specks." When Paul Krabbe and the late Kent Virgo were working in Kapuskasing, they went to great lengths to help me review documents held there. Mike Innes, formerly with Abitibi-Consolidated, did the same with regard to materials in the possession of his company, and he also shared his profound understanding of forestry and forest history with me. George Stanclik and Rob Tomchick in Iroquois Falls did the same.

Some remarkable archivists and individuals far and wide have gone way above the call of duty in facilitating my research. In terms of the former, I would like to say thanks to all of the ones who work at the institutions listed in the back of this book. I must make special mention of my friends at the University of Toronto Archives and the Archives of Ontario, and John Mekitiak at the Ontario Ministry of Natural Resources office in Peterborough. Dr Tory Tronrud, curator of the Thunder Bay Historical Museum Society's archives at the Lakehead, has assisted me for longer than I can remember. His thoughtfulness in advising me of the discovery of the Hogarth-Little correspondence in the mid-1990s was probably the TSN Turning Point in my project. Julie Latimer at the Ron Morel Memorial Museum in Kapuskasing and Betty Brill at the Nipigon Museum were most helpful in responding to my requests for germane photos. The staffs at the Bancroft Library at the University of California at Berkeley, the New York Public Library Archives in New York City, and the Wisconsin Historical Society in Madison were also particularly helpful. My friends on the board of directors at the Forest History Society, based at Duke University in Durham, North Carolina, also deserve mention for their willingness to share their knowledge and insight with me; the staff at the FHS's archives was also fantastic in helping me review records. In terms of accessing private/company records, I received enormous assistance. In particular, the good folks who were in senior positions with Avenor and Abitibi (particularly Mike Innes) many years ago permitted me to review documents in Thunder Bay (Fort William), Iroquois Falls, and Montreal; most recently both Paul Poschmann and Tom Ratz helped me identify potential photographs at the Lakehead. The president of Seaman Paper Company, George D. Jones III, was most gracious in permitting me to review his firm's old minute books.

In addition, I owe a double debt of gratitude to the great folks at the University of Toronto Press; my excitement over publishing my last book caused me to overlook thanking them for their aid on that occasion! Len Husband has been exemplary in offering gentle words when required and blunt ones when needed, and luckily he enjoys doing so over delicious ales. The other staff at UTP have also been fantastic, especially Frances Mundy. James Leahy was most helpful in editing this book. I would also like to thank the readers who reviewed my manuscript – twice no less! One of them, let's call her Reader A, offered some of the most constructive feedback I have ever received on my work, and for that I am most grateful.

My friends also deserve so much for having stuck by me on this journey; without their help I never would have made it this far. Special mention is merited by Steve G. Cooke, my accomplice on so many wild and wacky outings when we were growing up; he has remained true and never forgotten what matters in life. It is the same with Sean Sleeth and Lisa Douglas, who have not only offered great friendship over the years but also proofread this manuscript when I submitted it to complete my PhD; Lisa also provided invaluable legal insight when asked. Mike Sherwin in Peterborough repeatedly offered me a place to lay my weary head when I was researching in his bailiwick. He did so at a time when I did not have the resources to sleep at even the cheapest motel and his own life was already overflowing with activity. I am so thankful for all the support and kindness (and maple syrup!) that he – and his family – have shown and given me from the day we first met. Likewise, during my twenty seasons as a treeplanter and project supervisor, I met some of the greatest people in the world who made working in the bush a true pleasure … most of the time. They include Darren Brown, Scott Andrew Johnson, Claire Walker, Joe Shouldice, Andrea Mueller, Murray Richardson, Dan Nelson, Geoff and Mike Bodnar, Julie Ash, and Devlin Fernandes. In Sudbury, our new friends have welcomed us with open arms and helped us adjust to life "up north." In particular, Doug, Fiona, and Cam Maki have shared their fishing "hot spots," firewood, moose meat, fireworks, and, most importantly, their lives with us. Similarly, Bob and Janey Hall have truly spoiled us with their generosity and thoughtfulness, and Bob has been a superb proofreader to boot. Finally, Kath Salidas and Normand Dubé have been great friends to my wife and me, and enrich our kids' lives in so many special ways.

I also wish to thank Laurentian University, my home institution, for having supported this undertaking. It provided me with two LU Research Fund grants, one to create digitized maps and the other to defray the cost of publishing the book. Léo Larivière is a map-maker extraordinaire; he is also a wonderful fellow and friend.

Finally, the most important thanks are due to my immediate family. Marce, my mother, devoted much of her adult life to raising my sister and me essentially alone. Now that I have a family of my own, I marvel at how she succeeded in getting through those trying years; why she did not throw me over the balcony for my insufferable behaviour as a troubled youth will forever remain one of life's greatest unsolved mysteries! Marce, please know that I will never forget what you did for me, and hopefully you will recognize my commitment to seeing this project through to completion as proof positive that your son has learned most of the lessons you tried to teach him. My kids – Carling and Nolan – have brought me more joy than I ever thought possible. I did not believe in miracles until I saw them being born, and every day since I have marvelled at the astounding range and depth of emotions they cause me to feel. May they know that their presence in my life reminds me of the constant need to separate work from life, and never lose sight of which one is of primary importance. Cindy, what can I say? You have watched this project from its genesis to its conclusion and have faithfully ridden with me the roller coaster of good times and bad that connected those two points without ever questioning whether the trip was worth it. I thank you for all the love and kindness you have shown over the years, and I hope you are up for continuing the excursion – fingers crossed that it will be a more tranquil one! – for many more. For all that you have done, this book is dedicated to you.

IN THE POWER OF THE GOVERNMENT

The Rise and Fall of Newsprint in Ontario, 1894–1932

Introduction

As the twentieth century dawned, a few sage Ontarians recognized the awesome industrial potential of the province's northern forests and water powers. Although there was little accurate information about the extent of these resources, the few existing oral accounts and written reports exuberantly described their bountiful nature and their as-yet-untapped value to pulp and paper producers, specifically newsprint manufacturers. Thomas Southworth, the Ontario government's Clerk of Forestry, was one such visionary. Commenting on the future he envisaged for "New Ontario," he proclaimed in 1897 that it "requires no prophetic eye to see the time now near at hand when this part of the Dominion of Canada will be the seat of a great [newsprint] paper making industry ... With the great supply of raw material to be found in the district, and almost unlimited water powers this result can not [sic] fail to be achieved."[1] In many ways it was. Paper mills began springing up in northern Ontario in the mid-1890s, and by 1916 Ontario was the largest producer of newsprint in Canada, a title it held for roughly the next decade. By the late 1920s, however, the industry was experiencing significant difficulty, and by 1932, practically every firm in the province was in receivership. This book traces the establishment, extensive growth, and decline of the pulp and paper industry in northern Ontario during this period, and the central role the provincial state played in these developments. In doing so, it contends that the Ontario government generally gave the paper makers a lukewarm reception at best, kept them under very strict control, and did comparatively little to assist them in establishing and expanding their operations.

Delving into the history of the forest industry in any part of Canada is not a novel exercise. We have historically mythologized our lumberjacks and river drivers, espoused a deep love for the beauty and bounty of our forests, chosen a leaf for our national symbol, and staked our international reputation on our ability to excel at playing a game that – at least in the good old days – required a wooden stick to play. Moreover, professional and amateur historians alike have chronicled our nation's colonial timber trade and pre-Confederation lumber industry. The product has been a rich literature that speaks to everything from "the staples thesis" and "metropolitanism" to historical geography and folkloric tales of our days spent acting as little more than simple "hewers of wood."[2]

At the same time, however, Canadian historians have shown a surprising lack of interest in writing about certain aspects of our interaction with our woodlands, specifically the "modern" staples industry of manufacturing pulp and paper. The most conspicuous lacuna in the literature is a comprehensive history of the pulp and paper industry on either a provincial or national scale.[3] Several decades ago, Ian Radforth bemoaned the tendency to ignore or downplay the industry's importance, and Michael Bliss pointedly wrote that "the Canadian pulp and paper industry still awaits its historian." Barry Boothman recently suggested that this topic "has represented the equivalent of a toxic spill for Canadian historians, a controversial and complicated subject best avoided. Despite its economic importance, analyses of the evolution of the industry have been surprisingly few because many records have been destroyed or scattered across less accessible locations."[4]

The few who have ventured into this realm have, by and large, focused their attention on the political economy of the pulp and paper industry. The starting point for this subject in Canada in general and Ontario in particular is H. Vivian Nelles's groundbreaking *The Politics of Development*, which looked at the Ontario government's handling of the paper makers in the four and a half decades before the Second World War. Nelles argues that, in general, the state devised policies and established an administration to oversee the exploitation of Crown resources in order to promote this activity instead of regulate it, thereby sacrificing what could generally be defined as "the public interest." This behaviour, Nelles claims, meant that "the politics of development ... resulted in a reduction of the state, despite an expansion of its activities, to a client of the business community." Despite the myths about the pioneering efforts of "self-made, self-sufficient" entrepreneurs who brought the newsprint industry to Ontario, Nelles contends that the birth and growth of the pulp and paper sector was throughout a "joint public and private venture," with the provincial government playing the role of "a far from silent partner in the enterprise."[5]

Practically every historian who has written in this field since Nelles published his epic accepted his interpretation and built upon it, and this is especially true of the literature that deals with Ontario. In his biography of G. Howard Ferguson, whom historians have most closely identified with the rise of Ontario's newsprint industry during this period, Peter Oliver argues that this premier eagerly befriended the paper makers in an effort to maximize the growth of their enterprises. In Oliver's view, "since his days as a Hearst minister [1914–19], Howard Ferguson had believed it to be to the mutual advantage of the people of Ontario and the pulp and paper producers that the industry be provided with an assured supply of raw material and that large units of production be encouraged in the interests of conservation, stability, and permanence."[6] Economic historians, and those whose expertise lies in the field of northern development, arrive at the same conclusion. In examining the province's economy between 1867 and 1939, Ian M. Drummond argues that, with regard to the pulp and paper industry, "the major purpose was to promote growth ... In order to attain th[is] goal the Ontario government was willing to sacrifice revenues and to enter into a very close relationship with business interests."[7] Authors who have examined the history of the province's forest policy also concur with this view, as do those who studied the development of Ontario's bureaucracy.[8]

This same perspective defines the literature that deals with the early development of the pulp and paper industry in other parts of North America. This is true of authors who have examined its early history in the Pacific Northwest and the Maritimes, although most of them have added a corollary to this concept. They argue that a particular government's subordinate status vis-à-vis industry was the practically ineluctable end point in a story of "dependent development."[9] The general histories of Canada concur with Nelles's thesis. In summarizing the provincial governments' relations with the paper producers during the crucial 1920s, John Herd Thompson and Allan Seager assert that "what happened in the paper industry ... was that businessmen and provincial politicians became partners in development. The relationship between politicians and developers was intimate; it bordered in many cases on what might today be considered scandalous."[10]

Finally, the foregoing viewpoint also resonates with that presented by authors in the field of political economy whose gaze has been international in scope and whose subject has been economic development policies in general. Ha-Joon Chang and Dani Rodrik have been most compelling in this regard. They demonstrate the degree to which the conscious decision made by developed countries to pursue policies of "selective" or "smart" globalization was in large part responsible for the prosperity these nations now enjoy. This strategy involved charting the "middle way" between the polarities of unmitigated free trade and an autarkic system. Under this regime, these governments retained some barriers to the free movement of capital, goods, and workers, namely those they saw as benevolent, and removed others that they viewed as obstacles to their interests. In other words, Chang and Rodrik argue that an interventionist industrial policy, not free-market laissez-faire, is the best way to develop.[11]

In attempting to start cleaning up the "toxic spill" – to borrow Boothman's analogy – as far as the pulp and paper industry in Ontario is concerned, this study casts its net broadly in terms of methodologies and research. With regard to the former, this book is basically a study in political economy. Its structural framework is built upon the period's political history, with divisions falling naturally around the four administrations – the Liberals, the Conservatives, the United Farmers, and the Conservatives again – that served during the years which saw the pulp and paper industry arrive in northern Ontario, grow by leaps and bounds, and then slump. This tale is also infused with a strong dose of business history, both domestic and international. It devotes significant attention to examining how industry framed the issues it sought to address in its dealings with the provincial state, and how American businesses aimed to access – with varying degrees of success – government-controlled resources in a foreign land. At the same time, the study pays homage to the import of the burgeoning historical subfield of environmental history by dropping the assumptions that have often underlain earlier studies of resource development in Canada, namely that the bestowal of large grants of things such as trees by government was inherently tantamount to an extravagant gift to industry. By examining the particular nature of the forest tracts in question, for example, and the size of waterways and the cascades that punctuated them, this study aims to focus a sharper light on the transactions it examines. In terms of research, this investigation taps a well of new sources and reassesses ones that have previously been examined in both the United States and Canada. Most notable among them is the remarkable correspondence between Donald Hogarth and James A. Little that is housed at the Thunder Bay Historical Museum Society's archives. These two political insiders at the Lakehead had a ringside seat to the machinations between politicians and the forest industry during much of this period. Their candid insights had remained hidden – safely concealed in a tin box under the eaves of a house owned by one of Little's allies in Port Arthur – until they were found in the late 1990s by workmen doing repairs.

The product of combining this methodology with this investigative approach is a story that provides grounds for reconsidering the crucial concepts that have defined the existing literature in this field: namely, that the nature of government relations with the pulp and paper industry can be explained in terms of the "client" state and "dependent development." On the contrary, it is argued here that in Ontario between 1894 and 1932 the provincial government demonstrated a consistent aversion to granting the pulp and paper industry's wishes even though the newsprint makers would quickly become the most important economic users of the province's trees.

The departure point for this reinterpretation is a grasp of the general factors affecting industry–state relations in the resource sector during this period. A government that is responsible for administering Crown timber, hydro powers, and minerals faces a number of challenges and constraints. It is presumably interested in facilitating economic development, but there are as many different strategies it can pursue to achieve this goal as there are resources to exploit. In considering which path it will follow, a government must first determine the cost of doing so. It is easiest to facilitate development when the exploiter of the resource places minimal demands upon the state; it is far more difficult to do so when a supplicant makes major requests of the government.

There are also several variables that affect the potential power the state can exercise in dealing with requests for resources. The government's strength in its relations with industry is directly related to the number and value of assets it has available to develop, and the number of parties who want to develop them. Of course, the state is left almost prostrate when it has only a few resources of minimal value under its control, or when merely one party is interested in exploiting them. A government that has a multitude of natural riches at its disposal and a string of suitors for them can deal from a position of strength.

In addition, allocating forest tracts and hydro powers is a contest in which there are ultimately winners *and* losers; in the vernacular of the political scientist, this is the classic "zero sum game." With only a finite quantity of resources to dispense, when the state handed some of them to one interest it usually meant that it was denying them to another. Clearly, a faulty assumption underlies the contention that the state could become merely a client of business, for it suggests that there was one monolithic business to which it could cater, which was rarely, if ever, the case. This book will demonstrate that in Ontario during this period the various players within an industry, as well as the different industries, competed – often intensely – with each other for resources.

Furthermore, during the 1894–1932 period, "government," a term which will be used in a broad sense to encompass both elected politicians and appointed bureaucrats, underwent many significant changes in Ontario, but power remained squarely in the hands of the elected officials. Provincial policymaking became an increasingly complex affair, and to assist the politicians in making informed choices the state hired trained experts and advisers who formulated recommendations based upon examinations of the relevant facts. Elected officials were under no compulsion to act on this advice, however, and political expediency often made it irresistibly tempting for them not to do so. In fact, historians generally agree that patronage considerations – not sound advice – drove Canadian politics prior to the Second World War.[12] The following chapters demonstrate that this often resulted in illogical, disconnected decisions that bore little resemblance to a "policy."

Bearing these considerations in mind, we turn to Ontario in the mid-1890s, just as the pulp and paper makers were arriving in the province's northern reaches. By this time, Ontario had long boasted the country's strongest and most diversified economy. Not only was it founded on the basis of a prosperous commercial agricultural sector, but the province's guiding lights believed that Ontario's future vitality depended upon expanding its agrarian frontier.[13] But a few hurdles lay in the way of achieving this aim. The allure of the Canadian prairie was drawing farmers away from Ontario, and soon its attractiveness would have the strength of a magnet on steel. In addition, there were grave doubts about the feasibility of farming on the vast swathe of central and northern Ontario that had yet to be settled. Faced with this crisis that challenged its national ascendancy, the province's political masters saw populating "New Ontario" as their only salvation, the sole means, as one MPP put it, whereby "the Province could retain its present foremost position in the Dominion."[14] The goal thus became peopling the province's hinterland, with practically any means justifying the end. Although the government propagandized the notion that commercial farming was possible in northern Ontario, it never lost sight of the fact that attaching homesteaders to the hinterland would involve – above all else – creating the best market possible for the settlers' first and most valuable crop, the spruce pulpwood they cut from their lots and the local forests. And long before Ontario boasted its own pulp and paper mills, American plants were eager buyers of this timber. The provincial politicians thus recognized – both at this time and even after the industry was well established in the province – the crucial function pulpwood exporters would play in helping the state achieve its primary aim – settlement – in the hinterland, and befriended the exporters as a result.

Also by the turn of the twentieth century, the lumbermen were deeply entrenched as the dominant player in the province's forest industry. They had lorded over Ontario's woodlands for decades, but their traditional supplies of white and red pine were receding at this time. Their industry was thus in a state of flux, whereby some of its members were recalibrating to begin harvesting other species and manufacturing new products from them. For a variety of reasons, the lumbermen had also long enjoyed the cosiest of relationships with the provincial government, a bond that produced a string of benefits for both parties.

It was into this milieu that the pulp and paper makers began moving, and the odds were stacked against them receiving a warm embrace from the Ontario government upon their arrival. For starters, they asked the provincial state for rights, privileges, and resources of unprecedented scope and magnitude, an imposition the lumbermen and pulpwood exporters never made on the government. Moreover, if the provincial state had responded favourably to the requests that the pulp and paper makers made of it, doing so would have directly conflicted with its primary goal in northern Ontario, namely populating the hinterland, and the interests of the existing users of the Crown forests, namely the pulpwood exporters and the lumbermen.

By the time the pulp and paper industry had established itself as a major presence in northern Ontario soon after the First World War, a host of new factors had arisen to join the aforementioned ones in preventing the provincial government from rushing to link arms with the paper makers. A few decades of dealing with this new breed of industrialist, for example, who sought timber holdings larger than some of the states in the Union, had taught Ontario's politicians that it could often be detrimental to acquiesce to the paper makers' applications for resources. For their part, the paper makers seemed to trust that, as the provincial state matured, so, too, would its approach to administering Crown resources. While the pulpwood exporters and lumbermen were well attuned to the fact that the provincial government had always allocated the timber and water powers it controlled based almost strictly upon patronage considerations, and would continue to do so, the pulp and paper makers, by and large, were not. Their business model was based on modern concepts such as scientific management and long-term planning, and it drove them to seek access to Crown resources by fostering ties with the new cadre of professional bureaucrats whom the provincial state employed. Although this coterie of expert administrators was largely sympathetic to the pulp and paper makers' progressive ideas, decision-making power rested in the hands of the elected officials, with whom the new industrialists were seldom able to forge intimate and favourable bonds. This inability was occasionally a function of the personal enmity that developed between the paper makers and the politicians, but most often it reflected the latter's decision to conceptualize the industrialists within the framework of realpolitik. In the minds of the elected officials, the fundamental question was not what they could do for the mills, but what the mills could do for them. For these and other reasons, the Ontario government was, by and large, cool to the pulp and paper industry between 1894 and 1932 and retained practically complete control over it, and the industry itself was responsible for much of its early growth and development.

In some ways, these findings are congruent with those presented by a significant body of literature – whose focus has been both international and Canadian – that has examined the degree to which political states have exercised independence in their dealings with business interests. Perhaps most notable in this regard are Michael E. Porter and Claas van der Linde. They forcefully argue that when a government exercises significant autonomy in its relations with industry the results can be beneficial to industry in the long run.[15] Similarly and much more recently, Dimitry Anastakis effectively demonstrates that Canadian policymakers were not tools of the "Big Three" car makers during the 1970s and 80s. Instead, they formulated a fairly independent policy for the automotive sector that often drew them into conflict with private capital.[16] These authors – and others – lay plain the various advantages that result when the state retains its liberty vis-à-vis industry.

In this case study of Ontario's pulp and paper makers, it is certainly true that the provincial government's decision to retain its autonomy in dealing with these businessmen in particular and its approach to administering the province's hinterland in general produced several benefits. First and foremost, the provincial state was able to achieve its primary aim in the north, namely peopling the hinterland. While it is a moot point the extent to which northern Ontario's population would have grown had the state pursued a different approach, the data speak for themselves. Between 1891 and 1931, northern Ontario's population exploded. It grew from roughly 55,000 in 1891 (or under 3 per cent of the province's total) to over 360,000 forty years later (or about 10.5 per cent of the total). Moreover, the provincial government knew full well that it had significant latitude in dealing with the pulp and paper industry. It rightfully surmised that the competitive advantages accruing from establishing and operating a newsprint-making facility in northern Ontario transcended the need to respond to the mills' every desire. A capitalist who was willing to invest millions in such ventures was not simply going to fold and run when the government refused, for instance, to provide him with the volume of pulpwood he sought. The story that follows bears out the wisdom of the provincial state's perspective in this regard.

Nevertheless, the manner in which the Ontario government administered Crown timber and water powers during this period in general and its handling of the pulp and paper industry in particular had more downsides than upsides, the likes of which have become glaringly apparent in recent times. During the 1894 to 1932 period, the Ontario government did not implement a coherent strategy to address the decline of the traditional lumber industry and the rise of the new pulp and paper industry, and instead dealt with this process in a pell-mell fashion. Time and time again, politicians sustained lumber mills not because they were run efficiently or located near large supplies of economical timber, but because their owners were "government patrons." Likewise, the provincial state frequently insisted upon dictating to the newsprint mills when and how they expanded their operations, and rarely provided them with secure and sufficient resources to do so. The upshot in the short term was an industry operating on an unstable footing, and in the long term one that faced a grossly inefficient allocation of precious fibre supplies.

Finally, the fact that the story told here has remained undocumented for so long speaks to the dichotomy that has come to define Canadians and issues involving their "public" forests. As Canada became increasingly urbanized during the twentieth century, Canadians' first-hand contact with and rational understanding of the woodlands decreased at the same time as their view of the forest became increasingly romanticized, elevated to a higher spiritual level the less Canadians saw of it. Growing public pressure for the government to set aside recreational and wilderness areas caused the lumberjack to fall abruptly out of favour, transformed from an honourable and celebrated folk hero to someone who was engaged in one of the most vilified occupations in the country. Admittedly, the forest industry has had an ignominious history as far as woodland stewardship is concerned and has been rightly condemned for its past transgressions. At the same time, however, historians reinforced the impression of the industry as being inherently evil through their standard portrayal of the politicians as having "sold out" long ago to the tree cutters, especially the pulp and paper makers. What is more, the public – especially those in academia – has accepted practically unquestioningly this interpretation, as if it intuitively knew the story before anyone even ventured to the archives. The evidence presented here indicates that the fundamental premise that lies at the heart of this understanding of how things work in the forest – that the provincial government has historically been allied with the pulp and paper makers – is unfounded, at least in Ontario between 1894 and 1932.

A few explanatory words will help make sense of both the terms used in this story and the reasons for its format. As far as the former is concerned, the body that administered Ontario's Crown resources changed its name over time. It went from being the Department of Crown Lands (1867–1905) to the Department of Lands, Forests and Mines (1905–20) to the Department of Lands and Forests (1920–72). Likewise, prior to 1905, the elected official who headed this arm of the bureaucracy was known as a Commissioner, whereas after this date he was known as a Minister. For simplicity's sake, department and minister are used in the text to refer to the minister of lands and forests and the department which he headed. In addition, the pulp and paper industry processed pulpwood, and it was measured in *cords*. One cord equalled a pile of four-foot logs stacked four feet high by eight feet wide. Finally, original spellings – such as Nepigon – and Americanisms have been preserved where appropriate.

The format for the story is relatively simple. In an effort to highlight the continuity and change each newly elected government faced in Ontario vis-à-vis the pulp and paper industry, and how it reacted to these situations, the tale is told in four sections. The first outlines the political and natural setting for the story and the case that will be made, and it analyses the approach the Liberals took between 1894 and 1905. The following three sections assess the strategies pursued by the successive administrations, namely the Conservatives (1905–19), the United Farmers of Ontario (1919–23), and the Conservatives again (1923–32). Each of these is introduced by brief synopses of the state of Ontario's and North America's pulp and paper industry at the time, and the major actions that each government took towards the forest industry in general and the paper makers in particular during its tenure. Finally, because most of the documentation from the years before 1915 has been destroyed, the sections that deal with that period are relatively and regrettably brief.

SECTION I

The Setting and the Liberals, 1894–1905

1 The Natural and Political Landscapes

While it is axiomatic that trees are at the root of any story about the forest industry, woodlands have long been a unifying thread that have woven their way through Ontario's social, political, and economic fabric. In many respects, the development of the province, especially in its nascent stages, has been dictated by the nature of its forests. Even today, with scant evidence in the southern part of the province – where the overwhelming majority of Ontarians live – of the rich woodlands that once covered this region, many residents of this area remain intimately connected to the province's forests through their dependence on them for their livelihood, not to mention their recreational pursuits. From the construction firm in Oakville that orders two-by-fours from Nairn Centre to the newspaper publisher in Toronto whose newsprint is produced in Kapuskasing, and from the heavy machinery manufacturer in Mississauga whose equipment is sold to bush workers in Ear Falls to the civil servants in the employ of the Ministry of Natural Resources in Peterborough, southern Ontarians – indeed all urban-dwelling Canadians – continue to look to the woods to varying degrees for their economic vitality. As a result, tracing this inextricable link between the province's people and its forests is an invaluable exercise that reveals much about our history.

The departure point for this enlightening journey is the pre-Contact period, a time when a description of the province's forest cover could truly begin in the area most Ontarians call home. At this time, woodlands covered almost the entire province and were highly diversified as a result of differences in local site, soil, and climatic conditions. They changed gradually but dramatically as one travelled from the Canadian shore of Lake Erie to the tidewaters of Hudson Bay, with practically pure stands of hardwoods in the south and softwoods in the north serving as neat bookends on this voyage. At any point in between, a wide array of permutations was possible.

Ontario's forest cover is demarcated into four regions, although nature did not, of course, delineate them as neatly as the map makers (Map 1). Starting in the far south, the Deciduous Forest Region hugs the Canadian side of Lakes Ontario and Erie in a narrow belt that winds its way up to the southern tip of Lake Huron. The area's preponderant rich soils and favourable climate support a truly astounding range of deciduous species, with the poorer sites often defined by pine and cedar. Subtle changes are noticeable as one heads north to the Great Lakes–St Lawrence Forest Region, and these are largely a function of a cooler climate and shallower and poorer soils. This region forms an interrupted strip across the province, and its rugged, undulating terrain is better known as the landmark Canadian Shield. A variety of coniferous and deciduous species grow in this region. On the extensive sandy plains and rocky outcrops, stands of white and red pine predominate, while the deeper soils are often covered with stands of yellow birch, red maple, and red oak. The Boreal or Taiga Forest Region forms the province's and the country's largest forest type, and endures an extreme climate. For the most part, shallow soils cover its subterranean mountains of rock, and water pools in its myriad bogs, lakes, and rivers. Several major pockets of deep, poorly drained clay are interspersed in this area, and two of the largest ones are found in northeastern Ontario (much more will be said about them later). Black spruce dominates the boreal, and it is accompanied by roughly one-half dozen other species found in different arrangements. Finally, beginning at about 50° latitude the Coastal Plain makes up the upper reaches of the Boreal Forest Region, and its muskeg landscape represents the limits of commercially exploitable trees.

Several crucial factors must be kept in mind when we consider all forests. The most important is the extent to which woodlands are defined by change. Nature provides ample agents of disturbance – insect predators, disease, and lightning, to name a few – to ensure that the forest's composition is continually in flux. For example, the spruce budworm that periodically visits Ontario feeds primarily on balsam fir and white spruce, and attacks of sufficient intensity and duration cause corresponding degrees of mortality. If lightning then strikes these dead and dying trees during a warm-weather thunderstorm, the highly combustible dry wood ignites. Depending on conditions, the resulting blaze

Map 1. Forest Regions of Ontario

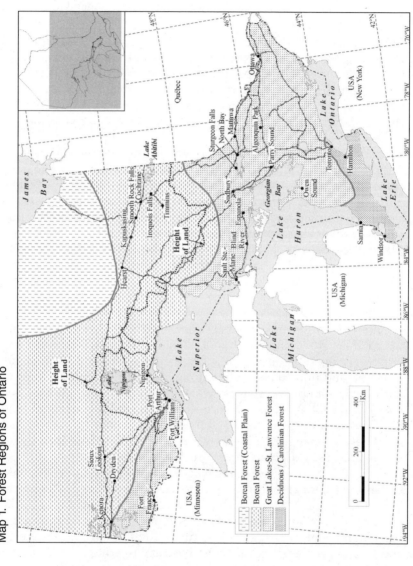

can spread to several hundred square miles or be contained to a few acres. Soon after the conflagration, a new crop of trees either seeds or "suckers" into the freshly created opening in the forest, and nature's cycle begins anew. Although the specifics may change – it could be the hemlock looper instead of the budworm – the phenomenon never has. The upshot is a quilted patchwork of tracts within a forest area, with each uniquely sized and asymmetrical piece of the whole composed of trees of varying ages and species, each having been burned, eaten, and attacked by disease, pests, and weather at different times. Long before humans ever altered the province's woodlands, then, nature had taken steps to ensure that its fingerprint was unmistakably etched on the "untouched" forest.

The second critical point to remember about the pre-Contact forest is the occasional and inconsistent homogeneity of its composite parts. Some of the patches of the quilt, particularly the farther one headed north of the upper Great Lakes and deeper into the boreal forest, consisted of enormous stretches of only one species. These extensive, pure stands of either black spruce or jack pine were the product of large fires. While it will be seen that industrialists had good reason to wistfully – yet often incorrectly – assume that northern Ontario's forest was all composed of such highly valuable groves, the lesson here is that, at times, Mother Nature was the first practitioner of "monoculture" forestry.

Ontario's forests are intimately connected to the watersheds upon which they grow, and the rivers, streams, and lakes divide easily into two categories. Those south of the height of the land are moderate in length and punctuated by many rapids and waterfalls. Except for those in the far northwest, these watersheds flow into either the Great Lakes or the Ottawa–St Lawrence Rivers. Beyond the height of land, the rivers flow north, or west and then north, to the Arctic watershed. Relatively speaking, they are very long and, although defined by numerous cascades, drain territory which is generally flat.[1]

While the Natives used the woodlands of pre-Contact northern Ontario, the pace at which the commercial exploitation of these – and indeed the world's – forests proceeded was determined largely by distance from population centres. Commodities such as spices, furs, and precious minerals were highly concentrated and, relative to their weight and volume, very expensive. Their physical properties more than compensated for the added expense of transporting them great distances. In sharp contrast, forest products are bulky and cheap relative to their weight and volume. As a result, the location of the trees to be harvested and the attendant cost of delivering them in their processed form to market has been the critical factor in determining the economic viability of exploiting particular forests. Woodlands closest to markets were, other things being equal, harvested first.

Ontario's location relative to the world's major markets for wood products thus shaped the pace at which its forest industries developed. Great Britain's need to maintain and expand the Royal Navy when it was at the height of its global dominance made it a prodigious purchaser of pine and oak. While it initially tapped nearby supplies of these trees in Scandinavia, the artificial stimulant of war – specifically Napoleon's blockade of Europe in the early 1800s – drove the British government to protect wood sourced from within the empire with preferential tariffs. This made it cost effective to shift its harvesting operations to British North America, and soon large quantities of Upper Canada's pine trees – largely from the Ottawa Valley and what would become eastern Ontario – were being felled, squared, and shipped to England. The domestic market also created a strong demand for a wide variety of wood products, adding further impetus to the development of the forest industry. Although Britain ended its protectionist policy in the mid-1800s, serendipity had already smiled on harvesters of Upper Canada's pine by presenting them with the chance to process their logs into a new product, lumber, for a new market, the United States.[2]

From that point until the turn of the twentieth century, Ontario's lumber industry boomed, thereby becoming the province's most important industrial activity and the hinterland's economic backbone. The sawmillers had pushed northward in pursuit of the receding supplies of white and red pine, their journey expedited by the construction of numerous longitudinal railways. By the time of Confederation, they had pushed through central Ontario and hit the shores of Georgian Bay, and over the next few decades their operations became the engines of economic growth in a string of northern communities spread from one side of the province to the other. In the far northwest, for instance, the soon-to-be-named town of Kenora boasted seven large sawmills by 1890, while in the northeast James M. Austin and George Nicholson operated a lumbering fiefdom consisting of five mills scattered along the Canadian Pacific Railway (CPR) and centred on the town of Chapleau. The scope of these operations varied widely, with John R. Booth representing one end of the spectrum. Based in Ottawa, his operation produced well over 100,000,000 board feet of lumber annually (about enough wood to frame 50,000 houses), controlled more than 7,000 square miles of timber limits, employed thousands of workers each year, and was reputedly the largest enterprise of its kind in the world. Operating in Booth's long shadow were hundreds of large to tiny sawmillers of both Canadian and American heritage, and numerous other "timber contractors" and "jobbers" who simply procured wood the mills required but did not operate the processing plants. These robust activities meant that most of the towns along the CPR in northern Ontario that would become major pulp and paper centres owed their genesis to the lumber industry, and the owners of these sawmills had already laid claim to significant swathes of Crown forests in the environs of their enterprises long before the paper makers arrived.[3]

Participating in the lumber business was an intensely complex political affair because, after 1867, the Ontario government controlled the province's natural resources. The principle of Crown ownership of land, water, and timber was one of Ontario's colonial legacies. It had been established largely because the province's first rulers had recognized that, for two distinct reasons, these assets held immense potential value. The government could administer Crown resources – considered "the people's wealth" – for the benefit of all in the realm, occasionally selling portions of them to raise funds to finance projects for the advantage of the province's citizens. The government could also manage Crown resources in a manner that primarily benefited the resource extractors and the elected officials who controlled access to them. On these occasions, the politicians viewed administration of these assets as, first and foremost, an invaluable instrument they could ply to reward themselves and their friends, and only secondarily as a fiduciary duty.[4]

The system by which the government dispensed Crown assets varied for each resource. For example, the state either granted farmland or sold it outright for a nominal sum under a system of freehold tenure, and these transactions were usually accompanied by contracts that outlined settlement duties. The government required a certain amount of development – such as clearing a specified acreage and erecting permanent structures – from the settler-cum-farmer in exchange for the deed to the land, which presumably represented the agriculturist's incentive to invest time and money in the venture. The execution of the land deed, however, severed the dependent relationship that previously existed between the farmer and the state. Subsequently, the government could not influence how the arable land was operated, whether it produced to its potential, how much or which crops were grown, or whether the farm was well maintained or left derelict.

The government administered the Crown forest in a fundamentally different manner. It sold only a licence to cut a specified area or quantity of wood in the public woodlands, retaining for itself ownership of the land on which the timber grew. Whereas the farmer was freed from his liabilities to the state once he received title to his land, the government gave Ontario's forest industry timber licences that initiated a landlord-tenant relationship between it and the tree harvesters. These contracts required licensees to perform a number of duties to maintain their agreements in good standing, such as paying annual fees and respecting regulations pertaining to the size and species of trees they could fell. While enforcement of these rules was admittedly lax, the harvesting of Crown woodlands proceeded only at the pleasure of the government, in whose hands rested potentially immense power over the forest industry. The provincial politicians could dictate how much of each species would be cut annually, how the harvesting took place, and which products (e.g., masts, lumber, etc.) were made from the trees.

The timber licensing system that developed in Upper Canada before Confederation and continued in Ontario thereafter reflected the government's primary goal during this period, namely to extend the province's farming base. This had been the aim of successive administrations since the colony was originally established in 1791, when the state first offered free land to settlers in an effort to entice them into colonizing the southern reaches of the province. Normally, these pioneers first had to clear the trees from their lots, and the government endeavoured to facilitate this process by permitting the forest industry to cut the valuable standing timber from soon-to-be-settled tracts. By granting the harvesters only a licence to extract the wood and not a deed to the land on which the trees grew, the state furthered its agrarian agenda because the settler could move onto the partially cleared tract that the lumbermen would gladly surrender. Thomas Southworth, Ontario's clerk of forestry, explained near the turn of the twentieth century that the provincial government had traditionally viewed a lumberman simply as "the precursor of the settler" because "Ontario was regarded as a purely agricultural country, adapted only to agriculture in which timber was not considered a profitable crop." This was why the licensing system was aimed "at clearing ground for farming" but in doing so "to first dispose of the most valuable timber to the best advantage. In all this," Southworth emphasized, "it is plain that the ... framers of [timber] legislation looked to the future rural population of Ontario to be solely farmers and not foresters."[5]

Generally speaking, both the lumbermen and the provincial government supported this licensing system – and the landlord-tenant dynamic upon which it rested – because they saw it as being mutually beneficial. From the lumbermen's perspective, the state kept Crown stumpage charges (i.e., fees paid based on the volume of wood cut) relatively low compared with the rising price of lumber. Furthermore, the lumbermen had little interest in gaining control over the land under the trees they cut because they did not foresee the next crop maturing for the better part of a century. As long as they could precede the settlers into the forest to clear the pine from a tract, they were only too glad to return the pine stumps and "weed" species to the Crown for dispensing to homesteaders. For the government, this system achieved its goals because, first and foremost, it facilitated settlement. Furthermore, it sustained the health of the provincial treasury. During the first four decades after Confederation, the stumpage dues the sawmillers paid each year for the privilege of cutting Crown timber accounted for roughly one-third of Ontario's revenues. In addition, the sawmillers provided tens of thousands of jobs each year, most of which went to pioneers who were realizing that farming on the province's frontier could not be a full-time occupation; the only way they could survive was by cutting wood during the winter. Last, and perhaps most important, the politicians relished their control over licences to Crown timber because it gave them an enormously valuable tool they could use for patronage purposes, particularly at a time when dispensing public resources to friends and partisan supporters was the de facto law of the land.[6]

In fact, political control over timber limits – and the conjunction of interests it fostered between the lumbermen and the elected officials – created a situation in which, by the turn of twentieth-century Ontario, the line separating the two groups essentially disappeared. Dozens of office-holding provincial and Dominion officials listed "lumbering" as their occupation during these years, and Erskine H. Bronson personified them. He was the president of one of Ontario's largest lumber firms and a prominent member of the Liberal provincial cabinet during the early 1890s. The Opposition Tories excoriated Bronson for exploiting his seat on the executive council to further his business interests; the same cabinet to which he belonged had sanctioned providing him with at least twenty-eight timber licences under egregiously favourable terms. Instead of taking action to prevent such abuses in the future, the Liberals reacted in a manner that spoke volumes about their allegiance to the "Forest Compact," this patronage system of doling out timber. They executed a statute in 1894 to confirm that holding timber licences would not disqualify persons from sitting in the Ontario Legislature. For at least the next several decades, a string of lumbermen would hide behind the aegis provided by this legislation to enhance their timber holdings.[7]

The story of the Georgian Bay Lumber Company (GBLC) exemplifies these various themes, namely the extent and importance of the saw-millers' operations and their intimate association with the period's decision makers. Anson G.P. Dodge, a scion of a wealthy New York family of lumbermen, purchased, built, and renovated eight sawmills on the Georgian Bay shore over the course of 1869–70 and incorporated them into GBLC in 1871. The firm was inextricably linked to the fledgling Dominion's leading lawyers and politicians – its inaugural board of directors included John Beverly Robinson and D'Alton McCarthy, and the company's officials openly admitted that they enjoyed a tight relationship with Frederic W. Cumberland, the MPP and MP for the local riding of Algoma. Over the next few decades, the GBLC was the raison d'être for a number of towns and rural communities in central Ontario, and it gained control over an ever-expanding realm of forest to support its enterprise. By the early 1900s, prominent local resident William J. Sheppard had taken over the firm, and although he was notoriously parsimonious, he had no qualms about spending money when it was politically expedient. Jim Angus notes that Sheppard simply saw it as good business to offer "cash in a ... direct way to influence the outcome of [an] election."[8]

Even though the Ontario government was profoundly committed to its settlement agenda, the politicians' intimate alliance with the lumbermen compelled the former to protect the latter's interests when they clashed with the state's agrarian agenda. By mid-century, the arable land in southern Ontario had been taken up, prompting a search for a new farming frontier. While some saw the Red River valley as the solution, those who wished for the province to retain its sons and daughters believed that pushing the fringes of settlement into the central part of Ontario – districts such as Muskoka and Parry Sound – would answer their prayers. To facilitate this process, the provincial government began offering free land for settlement in these areas, which also supported fine stands of pine. This move thus drew the lumbermen's ire, because the approach of homesteaders was anathema to their enterprise. Settlers often used fire to raze the brush and non-pine timber from their land, and these blazes frequently spread uncontrollably through the lumbermen's adjacent timber stands. In addition, the lumbermen feared the infamous pseudo-settlers, who capitalized on the government's willingness to hand out free land to potential homesteaders to acquire tracts of prime pine, strip them of their trees, and then abandon them. Not only did this undermine the lumbermen's control of the pine lumber market, but it also decreased the size of their potential labour pool. The widespread use of the timber pirates' ruse during the last few decades of the nineteenth and early twentieth centuries led to a flood of complaints from the lumbermen and bona fide settlers alike.[9]

The provincial state, however, did endeavour to obviate the potential clashes between colonizing and lumbering in a variety of ways. Immediately after Confederation, for example, it executed legislation that authorized it to grant free land in the hinterland to pioneers but only those tracts that it "considered suitable for settlement and cultivation, and not being … Pine Timber Lands." It also enacted statutes that reserved for the lumbermen's future use all pine on settlers' land and restricted homesteaders to cutting only the small quantity of pine required to construct their dwellings, thereby helping assuage the lumbermen's concerns about "bogus settlers." In addition, as the wave of colonization lapped into the hinterland towards prime stands of pine, the government auctioned them off at the insistence of the lumbermen, who asked that they be sold before the homesteaders arrived.[10] Furthermore, in the event that a settler applied to buy a lot that was covered by a timber licence, the Ontario government asked the licensee whether he approved of the sale, permission that was rarely forthcoming. Finally, the state established a series of forest reserves in which pine predominated and from which it prohibited settlement. Within short order, it had safeguarded roughly 10,000 square miles of Ontario's remaining pineries in this way.[11]

These initiatives eased but did not eliminate tensions between the lumbermen and settlers; Richard Lambert and Paul Pross aptly describe the continuing battle as "the never-ending guerrilla warfare between the land and forest interests." As the value of pine timber rose and the mature and easily accessible supply dwindled, the incentive to acquire tracts of it under the guise of settlement grew increasingly difficult to resist. Likewise, the relatively puny bureaucracy that administered the vast domain that was northern Ontario in the late nineteenth century virtually guaranteed that a cunning timber pirate could "cut and run" with impunity. The wave of settlement had also pushed well north of the French River and into the Rainy River District by the turn of the twentieth century, locating settlers amid some of the province's richest remaining tracts of pine.[12]

By this time, however, dark clouds were threatening the future of both lumbering and homesteading in northern Ontario. The sawmillers faced the spectre of ever more remote supplies of white and red pine. Although their migration deeper into the hinterland to tap these new supplies temporarily reinvigorated their industry, many of these pine trees were widely scattered among other species, rendering them expensive to harvest. The government's policy of extending the province's agricultural base into northern Ontario was simultaneously languishing. Although it had achieved notable success in establishing farming communities in the 1890s in the environs of Lake Temiskaming and far-off Dryden, these were the sole beacons of light in an otherwise benighted undertaking. Not only were the geography and climate of northern Ontario largely unsuited to farming wheat on a commercial scale, the settlers' plight was exacerbated because they were unable to subsidize their income by selling the pine timber found on their uncleared plots, for it was either already licensed to or reserved for the lumbermen. Compounding the problem was the growing allure of the Canadian prairies, a situation which the province's commissioner of Crown lands continually lamented.[13]

And then, Providence intervened in the form of the North American pulp and paper industry, specifically newsprint. While it temporarily takes the story ahead a bit, it is helpful at this point to explain the basic processes involved in manufacturing paper from wood at the turn of the twentieth century. In addition to enormous quantities of clean water, converting trees into pulps and/or papers required large amounts of energy that was derived from either power or chemicals. *Groundwood* was the most common pulp manufactured at the turn of the century. It was produced by using immense amounts of energy to break down logs into their fibrous components. This pulp is relatively weak because it retains the waste elements of the wood that are unfit for paper but are not eliminated from the concoction. For this reason, one cord of pulpwood produces roughly one ton of groundwood pulp. This mix is relatively cheap, making it ideal for use in high-consumption papers such as newsprint. Because there are no chemicals added to groundwood pulp to brighten or strengthen it, the colour and quality of the wood fibre used in its manufacture are critical. The whitest and strongest fibre comes from spruce, specifically black spruce.

A variety of other pulps are manufactured using chemicals and heat instead of friction to break down logs into pastes. They are more expensive to produce, but are superior in quality (i.e., stronger and finer than groundwood) because the non-fibrous waste material is eliminated from the mixture through a cooking process. This explains why one cord of pulpwood produces only about one-half ton of chemical pulp. *Sulphite* pulp was the most popular chemical pulp produced during this period, and like groundwood pulp, the species best suited to making it was black spruce. In contrast, *sulphate* pulp can be made from resinous conifers such as jack pine, which gives the product its distinct brown colour. The kraft (Swedish for strong) paper made from sulphate is used in products – such as cardboard packaging – where strength and not colour is the most important consideration. *Soda* pulp is often made from poplar, a deciduous species, and it is primarily used to produce fine paper for books and glossy magazines.

Pulp and paper mills could be configured in several ways. Some plants specialized in processing raw wood into one type of pulp, other "conversion" mills started with pulp as their raw material and transformed it into paper, while still others began with raw wood and processed it first into pulp and then into paper, an arrangement that required several different lines within the mill. Newsprint, for example, was made from four parts groundwood pulp and one part sulphite pulp, thereby requiring three separate but integrated lines of production: one large one for groundwood pulp, a much smaller one for sulphite pulp, and one to mix the two together to make the final product.

North America's newsprint industry underwent dramatic changes in the last half of the nineteenth century. In the mid-1800s, paper was made from rags, and four factors influenced where producers had located their mills. Most important was the availability of a large power supply, which was needed to grind the raw material into pulp and reformulate this mixture into newsprint. Because the technology to transmit electricity long distances was still several decades away, and large volumes of clean water were needed to make pulp and paper, these mills were constructed on rivers whose hydraulic energy could be harnessed to drive machinery. It was also necessary to locate mills near urban centres both to ensure a readily available supply of rags and to minimize shipping costs to the cities and towns in which newsprint was sold. This explains why the continent's first producers were located along the major rivers in the heavily populated American northeast, principally in New England and New York State. By the 1880s, the hearty population growth in the Midwestern United States, and the strong demand it had created for newsprint far from the traditional production centre back east, had precipitated the construction of newsprint plants at the many rapids that partitioned the rivers of the Great Lakes states, principally those in Wisconsin.[14]

It was only *after* these mills had been established that timber supplies became the pressing concern for North American newsprint makers. Beginning in the 1860s, they slowly began replacing rags with wood as the basic raw material from which they made newsprint. Mills were still relatively small, however, and the few hundred cords of pulpwood needed to supply the one- or two-ton paper plants which predominated during the 1880s could easily be produced by a handful of local farmers over the course of the winter. As the patent rights to the machinery that processed wood instead of rags expired in the 1880s and 1890s, the newsprint makers' use of timber became practically universal. During the same period, American consumption of newsprint soared. Mills expanded in response, and plants that produced 40 tons of paper per day and annually consumed thousands of cords of wood, primarily spruce, were common as the twentieth century dawned.

Virtually overnight the value of spruce skyrocketed. Heretofore perceived as a "weed species," thereafter it became the most sought-after tree in northeastern North America. Officials with the Ontario government repeatedly commented on this unexpected turn of events. In October 1892, Aubrey White, the deputy minister, reported that "the cutting of spruce and other softwoods suitable for manufacture into pulp [and paper] has recently assumed large proportions in the Province, particularly in the newer portions thereof." Only a few years later, the department noted that, although black spruce had previously been regarded as "being destitute of commercial worth," it now rivalled the august white pine in value. This dramatic metamorphosis inspired an articulate forester years later to appositely name black spruce "the Cinderella Species."[15]

The newsprint industry's sudden conversion to spruce abruptly recast its priorities. Maurice L. Branch explains that, after 1890, "wood supply became the *sine qua non* of development and growth for the [American] industry in general and the Lake States industry in particular." The forests that surrounded the mills in Wisconsin, Michigan, and Minnesota were dominated by hardwoods and pine that were best suited to supporting the traditional lumber industry, prompting American paper makers to look to northern Ontario for their spruce. They sought the province's most accessible (i.e., cheapest to harvest) pulpwood, specifically that along the north shores of Lakes Huron and Superior and principally in the Thunder Bay District.[16]

For the Ontario government, these developments were tantamount to divine intervention. Spruce occurred throughout northern Ontario and in patches in central Ontario, the very areas into which the provincial state had been pushing homesteading. Furthermore, settlers on the hinterland desperately needed an income to sustain their efforts as they pursued their dreams of carving farms out of the forest, and now cutting pulpwood could address this need. Most importantly, in sharp contrast to pine, spruce became valuable at a time when there was no entrenched interest in Ontario that sought to hoard and protect it from the settlers. In fact, quite the opposite was true. The politicians – and the sawmill owners – had a compelling reason to encourage homesteaders to raze all the spruce they could get their hands on, as this would ease the settlers' drive to cut the lumbermen's cherished pine. Not only did spruce's new value spell a potential end to the sawmillers' conflict with the settlers, it was also seen as a lifesaver for Ontario's badly flailing colonization effort.

At the outset (and for at least the next seven decades), American mills were major buyers of the province's spruce. There were no pulp and paper mills in northern Ontario prior to the mid-1890s, and only a few for the next several decades, and the handful of spruce-processing plants in southern Ontario were relatively tiny. They could obtain the small volumes of timber they needed from either the nearby forests or those in south-central Ontario. In sharp contrast, for reasons that have been explained, the dozens of mills in the Great Lake states were eager to obtain spruce from northern Ontario, and they had begun doing so in the late nineteenth century. While newsprint makers across the northeastern United States had already been frantically snapping up tracts of Canadian spruce in an effort to cope with their own fibre shortages, those in Wisconsin obtained roughly half their pulpwood supplies from northern Ontario just after the turn of the century, paying as much as $14 per cord at a time when newsprint sold for roughly $40 per ton.[17]

These factors compelled the Ontario government to conceive of spruce's value within a narrow framework on the eve of the twentieth century, and for years after. First and foremost, the politicians in Ontario

– as so many provincial governments did across the country[18] – saw cutting pulpwood in the north as the panacea to their floundering colonization efforts. It would tie these pioneers to a part of the province they eagerly sought to populate even if farming turned out to be, as it almost inevitably did, unviable. To deliver the maximum benefit (i.e., the highest price) to the settlers from the sale of their spruce, the government committed to creating the most robust market possible for their timber, which necessitated nurturing the export trade. Even after mills were built in northern Ontario, American purchasers had the freedom to compete for pulpwood right across the province, whereas practical limitations – such as the locations of plants relative to railroads and the direction in which rivers flowed – prevented domestic paper makers from doing so. The corollary to this policy was a world in which the Ontario government did not see pulpwood as a precious resource that warranted careful consideration in order to realize the development of a "home-grown" pulp and paper industry. Spruce was far too important for that, and the early reports about the virtually limitless supply of it in the province – the government trumpeted in 1900 that its hinterland held nearly 300,000,000 cords of pulpwood – made such measures appear completely superfluous. Although these inaugural data were quickly shown to be preposterous overestimates, this realization did not effect a fundamental shift in approach.[19]

Naturally, the homesteaders came to share the state's perspective in terms of fostering a highly competitive market for their pulpwood. Settlers who had tried to make a go of it on the hinterland quickly realized that their survival, ninety-nine times out of a hundred, depended upon being able to sell the spruce they cut from their land or that they found in the vicinity of their homestead. An editorial in *Pulp and Paper Magazine of Canada* succinctly captured this point. "Pulpwood constitutes the politics, the war talk and the religion, so to speak, of the average settler of New Ontario," the piece declared. "It is the one theme in which he is interested and concerned above all others."[20]

As much as pulpwood had become the settlers' manna by the early 1890s, so, too, had it become the bread and butter for a new class of businessmen in northern Ontario: the pulpwood exporters. These middlemen were needed to bridge the gap between the American mills on the one side of the border and the homesteaders on the other. Likewise, aspiring timber contractors recognized that often the best money to be made lay in acquiring pulpwood tracts from the Ontario government, harvesting the spruce, and selling it to interests from the United States.

Figure 1. Living the Dream in New Ontario: Transforming northern Ontario's woodlands into commercial farmland was nearly impossible, but provincial politicians of all stripes continued to promote this chimerical notion well into the 1930s. This shot from the turn of the century is entitled "settler's shack." It highlights the back-breaking work a homesteader faced in simply trying to clear an opening within the forest into which he could erect a home. It also speaks to the critical importance of having a market for the timber the settler cleared in the process, specifically the scattered spruce trees in this photograph (LAC, PA-043197).

Not surprisingly, by the early 1890s the Ontario government was annually receiving dozens of applications for pulpwood-cutting privileges on the watersheds that drained into the upper Great Lakes from entrepreneurs intent upon exporting their harvest.[21]

The most important force involved in the incipient pulpwood exporting business in Ontario was the American paper makers themselves. They sought, as did all newsprint mills, stable, long-term fibre sources. They also realized that the development of Ontario's pulp and paper industry would both cut into the quantity of fibre available for export as well as create a string of competitors north of the border. American mills thus had good reason to establish branch timber companies in the province, both to broker deals with the settlers who were cutting spruce, and directly harvest and export pulpwood for the paper makers in the US from timber limits they acquired from the Ontario government. This latter practice would establish an all-important prior claim to spruce that one of their potential newsprint-making rivals in Ontario might one day desire.

Achieving this aim involved overcoming one major obstacle, however, and the American interests did so expertly. Exporting unprocessed natural resources was intensely controversial in the context of late-nineteenth-century Canada. American newsprint makers were sensitive to the potential unpopularity of their activities in Ontario, and so practically from the very beginning they established a distinct modus operandi. They offered financial support to Ontarians who would co-operate with them in arranging access to the province's fibre on at least a semi-permanent basis. To provide their operations with an acceptable facade, they incorporated subsidiaries to which they gave names that bore no resemblance to the American parent company and instead identified the new enterprises with a leading local son or landmark. To head the newly created "Canadian" firm they hired the area's most prominent entrepreneurs or politicians, who were often one and the same. This gave the exporting business the appearance of having the blessing of the northern region in which it operated, and provided the prominent clique of locals involved in the venture with a vested interest in ensuring the continued flow of pulpwood-laden booms, barges, and rail cars across the border.

A few individuals personified Ontario's pioneering pulpwood exporters. James Conmee was one. He sat as the Liberal MPP from northern Ontario for most of the late 1800s and early 1900s, and it was said that he ruled his constituency – which initially stretched nearly 500 miles from about present-day Wawa to Ontario's western boundary – like a fiefdom. He and James Whalen, his son-in-law, practically cornered the market on timber limits in this zone, and pulpwood sold for export was their most lucrative commodity. In the early 1890s the Port Huron Sulphite Company, with pulp and paper mills in Michigan, incorporated the aptly named North Shore Timber Company to procure pulpwood from the Ontario side of Lake Superior. Although the Americans owned and controlled North Shore Timber, Whalen was its figurehead in Ontario. Similarly, transplanted Detroit lawyer Walter H. Russell was another baron in this trade at this time and over the next few decades. A prominent Conservative, he represented Northern Island Pulpwood Company in the province, which purchased and harvested pulpwood for another group of American mills, principally Detroit Sulphite Pulp and Paper Company. Later, Russell established an eponymous firm. Frank H. Keefer was also a well-known Tory lawyer and principal player in the early days of the Lakehead's pulpwood exporting business.

Not only did tight personal ties connect many of Ontario's elected officials to the exporters, but these bonds were forged regardless of the latter's political stripe. What mattered above all else was the exporters' willingness to champion the party in power, as long as it continued to promote their operations. As a result, during the period in question (1894–1932), even though the balance of power in the Legislature swung among Liberals, Conservatives, and United Farmers, the quantity of pulpwood exported from Ontario steadily rose. Throughout, control over this remunerative business was concentrated in the hands of a tightly knit group based largely at the Lakehead. This was "the old non-partisan 'Timber Ring.'"[22]

The provincial government was so friendly to the exporters' cause by the 1890s that it was difficult to tell whether the colonization effort was designed to assist the colonists or the exporters. American mills were naturally intent upon procuring pulpwood in Ontario at the lowest possible price. While they purchased large quantities of settlers' spruce, this source could be unpredictable and, depending upon local competition, costly. Alternatively, prior to 1900 exporters could simply purchase licences to tracts of Crown forest from the government. While a few of them did so, this drew unwanted attention to a practice that was a potential public relations liability for the government. It also entailed the payment of Crown dues and other ancillary licensing charges, all of which cut into profits. The Ontario representatives of the American mills thus often simply harvested spruce illegally, confident that they were operating – just like the lumbermen – in a vast wilderness that was patrolled by only a handful of government officials.[23]

Far more enticing to the exporters were two cunning schemes they had devised by the 1890s, both of which prevailed only because of the provincial government's complicity. In 1892 James Conmee succeeded in amending Ontario's mining legislation in a manner that authorized the party who staked a claim to harvest the pulpwood from the tract for purposes that had nothing to do with extracting minerals. This cost the "bogus miners" only a nominal administrative fee and made it an extraordinarily remunerative venture.[24] The pulpwood exporters' other main ruse was hardly new, as they simply adopted the time-honoured subterfuge of posing as "bogus settlers." These "pulpwood pirates" flagrantly abused homesteading legislation to obtain tracts of land for pennies on the acre, clear them of their spruce, export it free of Crown dues, and then simply abandon the territory.

And so, by the late nineteenth century, the Ontario government's need for the pulpwood exporters had allowed them to become, like their lumbermen brethren, tightly integrated into the period's "Forest Compact." To be sure, the exporters' operations were still relatively small and concentrated in certain areas. But these enterprises had already ensconced themselves into the province's political, social, and economic milieu, most importantly because of their intimate association with the state's push to colonize the hinterland. The evidence attests to the strength of their activities in the 1890s and the political support for them. The Ontario government unabashedly reported at the time, for example, that spruce cut from "the Temiskaming country" near the province's border with Quebec, and the rivers flowing into Lakes Huron and Superior, was exported "in considerable quantities ... to the paper factories of the United States."[25]

The pulp and paper industry's switch to spruce in the 1880s and 1890s not only drew American pulpwood exporters to Canada, but it also resulted in an increase in the number and size of the Dominion's pulp and paper plants. Whereas previously mills had been built throughout North America at sites that provided ample power, now an equally significant precondition for locating paper plants became the proximity to a sufficient supply of spruce. Initially, the bulk of the industry's capacity in Canada was concentrated in Quebec, which was well endowed with both pulpwood forests and harnessable rivers and was near the traditional major newsprint market in the northeastern United States. It also boasted numerous ports that were directly accessible to ocean-going vessels and thus overseas buyers. The sparse data from the turn of the twentieth century indicate that these early mill ventures proved highly profitable despite the existence of the American tariff on newsprint, which remained in effect until 1913.[26] This no doubt explains the industry's rapid growth during these years, whereby the total value of pulp exported from Canada rose from under $170,000 in 1890 to over $4,000,000 some twenty years later.[27]

A number of factors allowed northern Ontario to share in the Canadian newsprint industry's robust growth. Newsprint was composed of roughly four parts groundwood and one part sulphite pulp, and the prerequisites for producing it inexpensively were abundant cheap power derived from harnessing the hydroelectric potential of large rivers and prodigious stands of spruce; the boreal forest that covered most of the province's hinterland was blessed with large quantities of both. By the eve of the twentieth century, northern Ontario was also an attractive location in which to establish newsprint mills because of its proximity to the rapidly growing market in the American Midwest. It was roughly $5 per ton cheaper to transport paper by rail from Sault Ste Marie or Kenora to Chicago than from Quebec or the American northeast to the same city. Moreover, northern Ontario and many of the major markets in the Midwestern states fronted on the Great Lakes, making it possible to deliver paper by water instead of rail and resulting in further savings of nearly $4 per ton. Locating a newsprint mill on the Great Lakes also made it relatively cheap to import raw materials, such as sulphur, which the paper makers required.[28]

Drawn by these forces, a number of interests built mills across northern Ontario between 1895 and 1924, almost all of which were initially designed to produce newsprint.[29] They were established in four main geographical regions. The first developments occurred just north of Lakes Huron and Nipissing, where, around the turn of the century, mills were built in Sault Ste Marie, Espanola, and Sturgeon Falls respectively. By the eve of the First World War, George H. Mead, an American paper maker from Ohio, had gained control over these three plants and consolidated them into the Spanish River Pulp and Paper Mills Company; the region in which these mills were located will thus be referred to as the "Spanish River" territory.

The Thunder Bay District is another region, and five mills were built there between the mid-1910s and mid-1920s. Provincial Paper, an American-owned fine-paper maker with converting mills in southern Ontario, constructed the first in Port Arthur in 1917, and three more were built in quick succession after the First World War. Local interests established the Kaministiquia Pulp and Paper Company in Port Arthur, which was soon taken over by newsprint makers from Wisconsin, who renamed it the Thunder Bay Paper Company. Around the same time, Mead and Spanish River erected a branch plant in Fort William, which they named Fort William Paper Company. The third mill that was erected in 1920–1 stood in Nipigon, and it was initially owned by an amalgam of local interests and Wisconsin pulp and paper industrialists.

Figure 2. How Great Are the Lakes: Industrialists at the turn of the twentieth century recognized the numerous advantages that accrued from building pulp and paper mills in northern Ontario, particularly if they located their plants on the shores of the upper Great Lakes. These plants would enjoy much lower shipping costs for both their outgoing product and incoming supplies. This photograph of Fort William Paper's mill in the early 1920s captures this reality; the cargo ship is docked at a slip at which incoming sulphur was offloaded and stored (Thunder Bay Historical Museum Society, 984.1.564a).

Map 2. Pulp and Paper Mills Established in Northern Ontario, 1895–1924

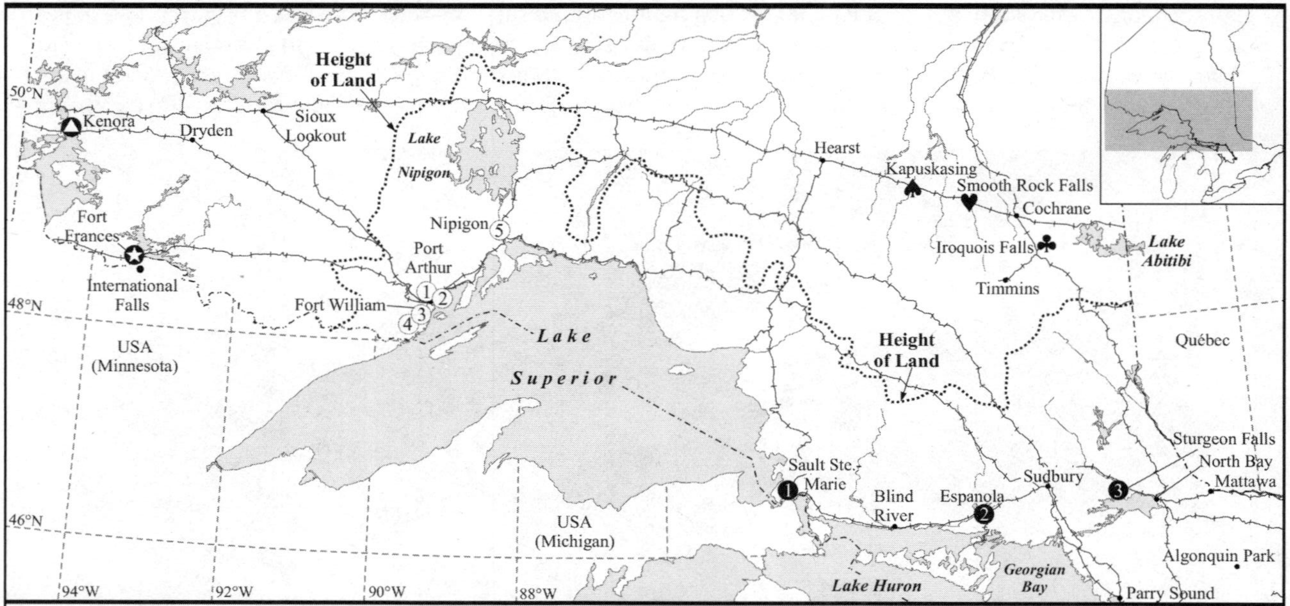

SPANISH RIVER TERRITORY		
Location	Company/Owner	Date
Sault Ste. Marie	Francis H. Clergue	1895
Espanola	Spanish River	1903
Sturgeon Falls	Imperial Paper Mills	1902

NORTHWESTERN ONTARIO		
Location	Company/Owner	Date
Fort Frances	E. W. Backus	1914
Kenora	E. W. Backus	1923

THUNDER BAY DISTRICT		
Location	Company/Owner	Date
① Port Arthur	Port Arthur Pulp	1917
② Port Arthur	Kam Pulp	1920
③ Fort William	Fort William Paper	1921
④ Fort William	Great Lakes Paper	1924
⑤ Nipigon	Nipigon Fibre	1920

NORTHERN CLAY BELT		
Location	Company/Owner	Date
♣ Iroquois Falls	Abitibi	1914
♣ Smooth Rock Falls	Mattagami Pulp	1917
♣ Kapuskasing	Spruce Falls	1922
	(Kimberly-Clark)	

0   200   400
Km

Chart 1. Pulp and Paper Companies with Interests in the "Spanish River" Territory

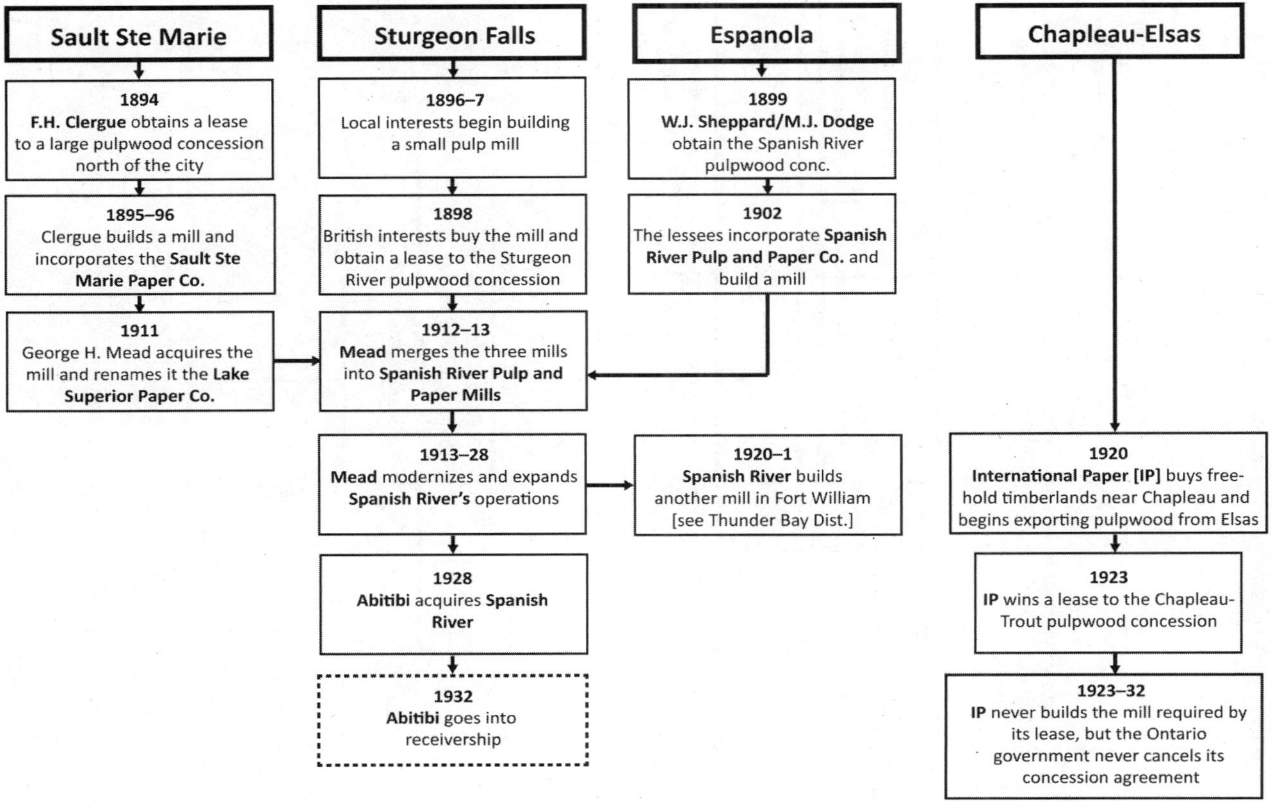

Sault Ste Marie

1894
F.H. Clergue obtains a lease to a large pulpwood concession north of the city

1895–96
Clergue builds a mill and incorporates the Sault Ste Marie Paper Co.

1911
George H. Mead acquires the mill and renames it the Lake Superior Paper Co.

Sturgeon Falls

1896–7
Local interests begin building a small pulp mill

1898
British interests buy the mill and obtain a lease to the Sturgeon River pulpwood concession

1912–13
Mead merges the three mills into Spanish River Pulp and Paper Mills

1913–28
Mead modernizes and expands Spanish River's operations

1928
Abitibi acquires Spanish River

1932
Abitibi goes into receivership

Espanola

1899
W.J. Sheppard/M.J. Dodge obtain the Spanish River pulpwood conc.

1902
The lessees incorporate Spanish River Pulp and Paper Co. and build a mill

1920–1
Spanish River builds another mill in Fort William [see Thunder Bay Dist.]

Chapleau-Elsas

1920
International Paper [IP] buys free-hold timberlands near Chapleau and begins exporting pulpwood from Elsas

1923
IP wins a lease to the Chapleau-Trout pulpwood concession

1923–32
IP never builds the mill required by its lease, but the Ontario government never cancels its concession agreement

Chart 2. Mills Established in the Thunder Bay District

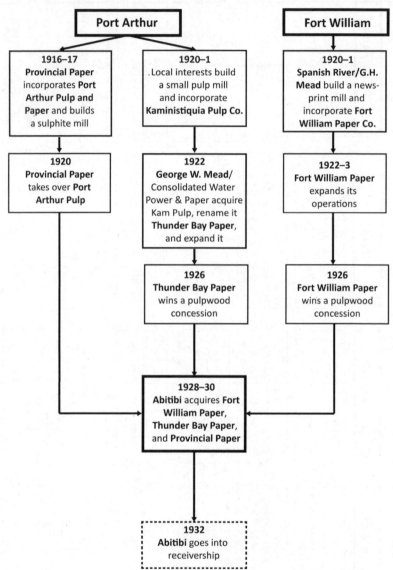

Chart 2 *(continued)*

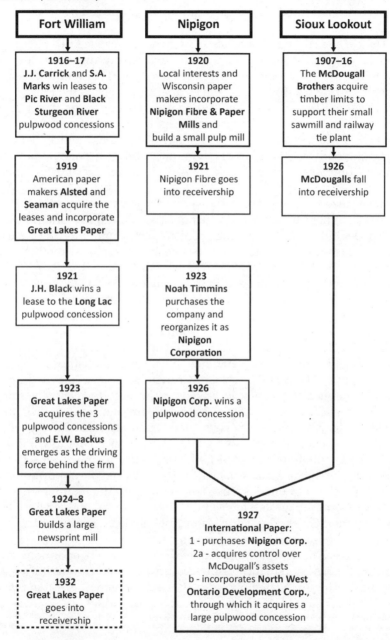

Fort William	Nipigon	Sioux Lookout
1916–17 **J.J. Carrick** and **S.A. Marks** win leases to **Pic River** and **Black Sturgeon River** pulpwood concessions	**1920** Local interests and Wisconsin paper makers incorporate **Nipigon Fibre & Paper Mills** and build a small pulp mill	**1907–16** The **McDougall Brothers** acquire timber limits to support their small sawmill and railway tie plant
1919 American paper makers **Alsted** and **Seaman** acquire the leases and incorporate **Great Lakes Paper**	**1921** Nipigon Fibre goes into receivership	**1926** **McDougalls** fall into receivership
1921 **J.H. Black** wins a lease to the **Long Lac** pulpwood concession	**1923** **Noah Timmins** purchases the company and reorganizes it as **Nipigon Corporation**	
1923 **Great Lakes Paper** acquires the 3 pulpwood concessions and **E.W. Backus** emerges as the driving force behind the firm	**1926** **Nipigon Corp.** wins a pulpwood concession	
1924–8 **Great Lakes Paper** builds a large newsprint mill		
1932 **Great Lakes Paper** goes into receivership	**1927** **International Paper:** 1 - purchases **Nipigon Corp.** 2a - acquires control over McDougall's assets b - incorporates **North West Ontario Development Corp.**, through which it acquires a large pulpwood concession	

Great Lakes Paper Company built the Thunder Bay District's fifth mill in Fort William in the mid-1920s, and it was controlled by Edward W. Backus.

The two remaining regions also saw five mills erected between 1914 and the mid-1920s. Backus dominated activity in northwestern Ontario. He built two mills there, one in Fort Frances in 1914 and another in Kenora during the mid-1920s. The northern Clay Belt is the fourth and final region. Kimberly-Clark, a leading American pulp and paper company, built a mill in Kapuskasing in the early 1920s. Just east of this enterprise stood another mill in Smooth Rock Falls, which Duncan Chisholm built in 1916–17 under the banner of the Mattagami Pulp and Paper Company. Finally, Frank H. Anson, a Montreal businessman, constructed a newsprint plant in Iroquois Falls just before the Great War and organized it as the Abitibi Power and Paper Company. From 1928 to 1930, Abitibi established a hegemonic position in the Ontario pulp and paper industry by acquiring Spanish River's four mills (the three in the "Spanish River" territory and the one in Fort William) and the individual plants owned by Provincial Paper and Thunder Bay Paper (both in Port Arthur) and Mattagami Pulp (in Smooth Rock Falls).

Like the lumbermen and pulpwood exporters, the new pulp and paper industry was forced to negotiate with the provincial government to secure access to Ontario's Crown resources. The newsprint makers' requirements and the demands they placed upon the state, however, were radically different from those of these other forest industries in several crucial ways. One was the scope of Crown timberlands they required. The lumbermen, for example, asked for licences to relatively small tracts of woodlands (few topped 100 square miles in size), which often sustained their operations for considerable periods. Likewise, the pulpwood exporters, although they sought long-term access to Ontario's pulpwood, gratefully accepted both the chance to purchase settlers' wood to take care of their immediate fibre needs and the opportunity to buy settlers' lots of uncut spruce to meet their future requirements. In both cases, the requests were limited in scope, and the government could grant them at minimal risk and cost, making it relatively easy for the politicians to meet these industries' wishes.[30]

Conversely, newsprint mills required comparatively enormous volumes of fibre. Although turn-of-the-century paper mills were still small, manufacturing in the neighbourhood of 40 tons of newsprint per day, they still consumed 48 cords of spruce daily (roughly 1.2 cords of pulpwood were needed to manufacture one ton of newsprint). As a

Chart 3. Mills Established in Northwestern Ontario

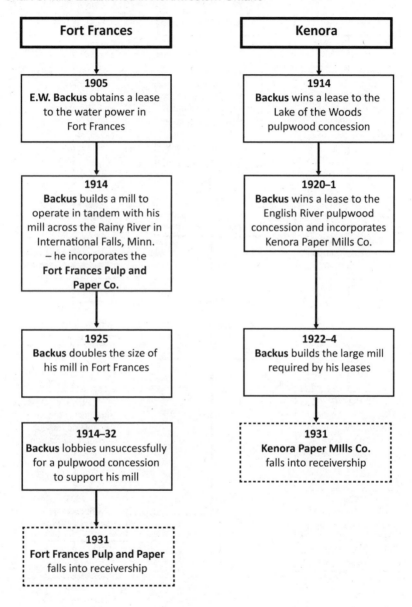

Fort Frances

1905
E.W. Backus obtains a lease to the water power in Fort Frances

1914
Backus builds a mill to operate in tandem with his mill across the Rainy River in International Falls, Minn. – he incorporates the **Fort Frances Pulp and Paper Co.**

1925
Backus doubles the size of his mill in Fort Frances

1914–32
Backus lobbies unsuccessfully for a pulpwood concession to support his mill

1931
Fort Frances Pulp and Paper falls into receivership

Kenora

1914
Backus wins a lease to the Lake of the Woods pulpwood concession

1920–1
Backus wins a lease to the English River pulpwood concession and incorporates Kenora Paper Mills Co.

1922–4
Backus builds the large mill required by his leases

1931
Kenora Paper Mills Co. falls into receivership

Chart 4. Mills Established on the Northern Clay Belt

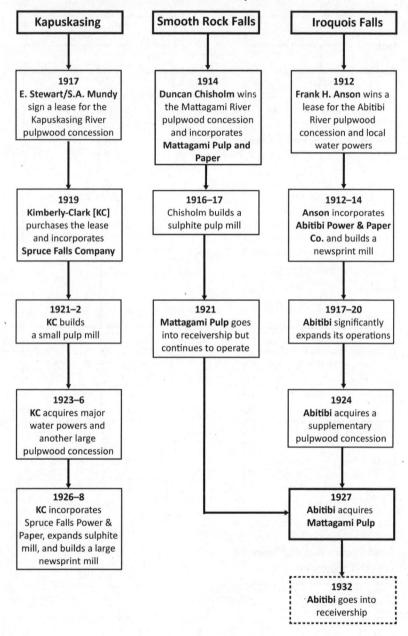

result, over the course of a standard 300-day operating year for a mill (which allowed for down time and Sunday closings), a 40-ton mill would consume 14,400 cords of pulpwood. Considering that the forest which blanketed northern Ontario generally averaged between ½ to 10 cords of merchantable spruce pulpwood per acre, harvesting 14,400 cords could require annually between 28,800 acres of forest (45 square miles) if it averaged only a ½ cord per acre and 1,440 acres (roughly 2¼ square miles) if it averaged 10 cords. Rapid technological advances during the first few decades of the twentieth century compelled plant owners to expand their operations to remain competitive. Consequently, mills of 300 tons were common by the early 1920s, and they required nearly 110,000 cords per year. If the forest from which the mill was harvesting averaged only a ½ cord per acre, it would take 216,000 acres (337½ square miles) to procure *merely one year's* supply of fibre. If it averaged 10 cords per acre, 10,800 acres (about 17 square miles) of woodlands would still be needed to provide the same quantity of pulpwood. In no uncertain terms, the pulp and paper makers required forest tracts of previously unfathomable proportions.

As important as the size of a concession was the volume and location of the spruce pulpwood found on it. Most valuable was a limit which contained dense stands of spruce – those previously mentioned homogeneous patches of the quilt, which were conducive to concentrated, low-cost logging operations. Because river driving was the primary method of delivering wood from the bush to the mill during this period, pulp and paper companies sought concessions on watersheds which flowed past their plants because this would further minimize expenses.

The newsprint men also brought a fundamentally different perspective to the woodlands they leased from the government. Lumbermen generally sought large trees (upwards of ten inches in diameter) because their sawmills were designed to process pine with wide trunks and could do little with small logs. In contrast, although newsprint makers benefited from cutting wide-diameter spruce because it lowered their harvesting and transportation costs, their mills could process logs which were as small as a few inches across. Their crucial consideration was the availability of an abundant supply of spruce, not the diameter of each tree.

This caused the pulp and paper industry to place a novel value upon those sections of its timber limits which it had not yet harvested *and* those that it had cut. It was widely believed throughout the first three

Figure 3. Food for the Mill: The capacity of pulp and paper plants grew by leaps and bounds during the early twentieth century, and this created a need for unprecedented quantities of spruce pulpwood. This photograph illustrates the mountainous "log pile" outside the mill in Kapuskasing in the early 1920s (Ron Morel Memorial Museum, Kapuskasing, Ontario).

Figure 4. Size Did Not Matter: Pulp and paper makers brought an entirely new perspective to Ontario's forests. Unlike the lumbermen, who had sought large-diameter pine, the new breed of industrialists could process spruce logs of virtually any size; what mattered to them was the availability of an abundant volume of fibre, not the girth of each tree. This photograph shows stacked piles of spruce pulpwood ready for shipment to the United States at T.S. Woollings's operations near Timmins in the 1930s (Archives of Ontario, F4624, B848104, "Porcupine Bridge," Rbr – Rondell).

decades of the twentieth century that it would take roughly sixty years for a new spruce crop to regenerate itself from seed to merchantable size (considered to be six inches in diameter), and about thirty years for the young trees which were left standing after the initial harvest to reach this same stage. Conversely, it was understood that it would take at least one century for a new stand of pine to regenerate itself to the large size the lumbermen required. As a result, the lumbermen had gladly returned to the government areas which they had cut over, but the pulp and paper industrialists sought to retain these cutovers, as their mills could process virtually any sized tree and they hoped that they could reharvest their cutovers in as little as one generation. In 1899 the *Report of the Royal Commission on Forestry Protection in Ontario* touched upon this matter, observing that "owing to the small[er] size required for pulp wood than lumber" and the fact that the former could "be cut in much quicker rotation, pulp mills could obtain a continuous supply of raw material." This compelled paper makers to seek long-term control over their timber limits.[31]

So, too, did other factors. By and large, the operations of other resource developers in Ontario were relatively short-term affairs. Lumbermen and pulpwood exporters worked the areas the government allotted them and then moved on to the next prime timber site. In contrast, permanence characterized the pulp and paper industry. Constructing a fully integrated newsprint mill, and usually a major power-generating station to provide the energy to run it, cost millions of dollars; these were not enterprises that could be simply torn down and rebuilt in a new location if local pulpwood supplies ran out. The pulp and paper makers, then, were engaged in northern Ontario's first resource-extracting business whose firms had a sustained vision for their operations. This was reflected in the paper companies' "modern" management structure, whereby they employed ranks of administrators whose job it was to apply scientific principles in formulating long-range plans to maximize efficiency. Their responsibilities included designing far-sighted harvesting strategies that were predicated on the mills obtaining permanent tenure to woodlands they leased from the government.[32]

Unlike lumbermen and pulpwood exporters, newsprint mills also sought assured access to significant Crown water powers. During the industry's pioneering phase in the 1890s and early 1900s, its energy needs were merely minor, and contemporary technology dictated that mills be located at the source of the water power. Within a few decades, however, it became possible to transmit electricity significant distances, freeing mills to locate somewhere other than at waterfalls. The larger mills also had much greater energy requirements, causing them to become intensely concerned over the extent of their water power privileges. As with their fibre supplies, they sought exclusive control over these hydroelectric assets.

The mills required access to Crown resources for these practical reasons, but they needed particular types of leases to their timberlands and water powers because they hoped to use these contracts to raise capital for their ventures. A select handful of lumbermen had been able to offer their timber licences as collateral, but generally they had done so only in the fall to arrange short-term bank loans to pay for their winter's harvesting operations and not capital expenditures. Lumbermen also operated almost exclusively as private companies, not publicly traded corporations, and did not sell securities to finance their business activities. In contrast, the immense expense involved in constructing, operating, and constantly upgrading a multi-million-dollar newsprint mill usually necessitated interesting outside investors in the enterprise. To convince financiers that they should provide the large sums required to erect and run a mill, pulp and paper makers initially had, except for the hope of future profits, only their Crown leases to offer as collateral. These agreements, then, were potentially the mills' first assets.[33]

This meant that the paper companies had their work cut out for them. Prior to their arrival, Canadian banks had accepted timber licences as collateral only in the few situations outlined above; the country's financial institutions were dubious about the worth of these contracts. Cruise reports, which detailed the quantity and type of timber on a tract, were notoriously unreliable (especially before the advent of the airplane in the 1920s), and if the lumberman was unable to repay the loan the bank was left with a licence to a woodland that was a difficult commodity to liquidate, especially when its value was in doubt. Although documents relating to the relationship between financial institutions and the forest industry are rare, one surviving relic describes the manager of the Canadian Bank of Commerce informing a lumber interest in British Columbia in 1909 that "as a rule we do not consider a timber licence a tangible security."[34]

To gain the financiers' faith and confidence, pulp and paper mill developers asked for three specific elements in their Crown contracts: reasonable terms, a perpetual supply of resources, and secure tenure. In terms of the first element, they accepted that the state had every right to demand that the lessees fulfil a series of obligations in exchange for receiving permission to exploit a substantial Crown resource, but mills asked only that these conditions be logical. Second, mill developers asked for sole access to a perpetual supply of resources. Financiers were averse to mills securing cutting privileges that permitted other operators – such as lumbermen – to cut on the paper makers' limits. In addition, bankers wanted the reassurance that the mill had access to a permanent supply of pulpwood. By the time of the Great War, it was recognized throughout the newsprint industry that each 100 tons of mill capacity required roughly 2,250,000 cords of pulpwood and 10,000 horsepower to support it on a continuous basis.[35] The third and pre-eminent element sought by mill developers in their contracts with the state was secure tenure; in Gordon Hak's words, "the importance of security of timber tenure for financing companies cannot be overestimated."[36] As a result, the paper makers aimed to acquire privileges which approximated, as closely as possible, absolute ownership. As one representative of an American pulp and paper maker explained in the early 1900s while he was negotiating with the Ontario government for a timber supply in the province, his New York financiers were chary of investing their money in any venture that would depend on a contract with elected officials. "They are [thus] very strong believers in acquiring freehold rights where they are apt to spend two to three million dollars in the construction of a factory," the Yankee industrialist emphasized.[37]

The extent to which paper mill executives were able to enshrine these three features in their contracts with the Crown dictated their strength in negotiating with their financial backers. Newsprint companies that were able to convince the government to embody all these elements in their contracts for Crown resources acquired highly prized commodities that permitted them to deal with their financiers from a position of strength. They would be able to negotiate favourable interest rates on their bonds and enjoy practically complete freedom in charting how their firms operated. The financiers would also likely deem this type of contract sufficiently valuable such that the mill property itself would not be included in the mortgage that secured the sale of bonds that paid for the mill's construction. Contracts that were weak in terms of these three elements, however, greatly undermined the mill's position vis-à-vis its backers. The mill property itself would be included in the mortgage guaranteeing the securities, and the firm was vulnerable to becoming beholden to its bondholders, who could insist that they have both strong representation on the company's board of directors and significant influence over all aspects of its activities.

Clearly, there were vast differences between the requirements of the paper mills and those of the lumbermen and pulpwood exporters, but nothing set them apart more than the former's need for secure tenure. Despite the provincial state's profound allegiance to the lumbermen and pulpwood exporters, their businesses were still subject to the vicissitudes inherent in a political system that saw Ontarians vote for a new government roughly every four years. A lumberman's sawlog supply could run out, for example, if his champion in Queen's Park lost at the polls in the next election. Despite the tenuous nature of their grip on their wood supplies, the lumbermen and pulpwood exporters were remarkably comfortable with this arrangement. Their industries were highly mobile and easily adaptable to sudden changes in government or policy, and they proved particularly adept at befriending newly elected administrations.

It was precisely this element of unpredictability that the pulp and paper industry wanted to eliminate from its relationship with the Ontario government. Its need for stable, long-term planning necessitated establishing permanence in its dealings with the state, such that its access to Crown resources would not be dramatically affected by changes in government or resource development strategies. The pulp and paper companies had developed their own managerial structures, and in negotiating with the state, they demonstrated a natural inclination towards cementing strong relationships not with Ontario's politicians, whose terms lasted only a few years, but rather with the state's own management team, namely its bureaucracy.

And in many ways, this approach seemed timely. Although the provincial civil service was comparatively tiny in the few decades after Confederation, the Department of Lands and Forests had been the largest government body in terms of staff and, most important, in terms of function. It administered the dispensation to settlers of the province's most valuable asset, land, and the sale of Ontario's most valuable northern crop, timber. The Ontario government thus viewed it, in the words of J.E. Hodgetts, as "*the* revenue department."[38] The bureaucrats who staffed the department's ranks, however, initially lacked formal, specialized training and were political appointees, meaning their jobs often lasted only as long as the party which had designated them remained in power.[39] As New Ontario was opened up beginning in the late nineteenth century and increasingly thereafter, the department dramatically expanded the spatial and jurisdictional sphere of its activities. The unprecedented demands placed upon its fledgling bureaucracy combined with the prevailing faith in the efficacy of scientific management to create a glaring need for a new kind of "expert" civil servant, one who would – theoretically – not be the traditional government clerk at the beck and call of his political masters. Instead, he would be a university-educated, career civil servant, hired to investigate issues, uncover the germane facts, and present program options – both short and long range – to the politicians based upon an objective assessment of the data and irrespective of partisan considerations. For the pulp and paper industry, here were its brothers-in-arms. As Anders Sandberg and Bill Parenteau assert, the paper producers thus sought to "rigidly avoid getting caught up in local politics ... companies investing such enormous amounts in mills and forest holdings could not afford to face the implications of the changes in government which often had a significant impact on local owner-operators ... [The paper makers' ultimate goal was to end up in] a situation where the state, independent of what political party is in power, supplies long-term and stable support for private corporations. The nature of such support is developed by a professional civil service employed on a permanent basis."[40]

These, then, were the circumstances that faced the Ontario government in the mid-1890s at the time of the newsprint industry's arrival in the province. The state's attention was firmly fixed on expanding Ontario's agricultural base northward, and it had also developed symbiotic relationships and tight alliances with the lumbermen and pulpwood exporters. Into this environment stepped the pulp and paper industry, and with it a host of novel demands on the provincial state and a revolutionary approach to operating a business in the hinterland. Under this set of circumstances, the question naturally arises: how did the Ontario government react?

From the outset, many factors mitigated against the state embracing the pulp and paper industry and responding favourably to its requests. Consider what this industry asked of the government. The pulp and paper makers, following the lead of the province's other resource industries, requested what they thought they required in order for their enterprises to succeed. They failed to recognize, however, how the exceptional nature of their requests – colossal tracts of Crown woodlands and supplies of water powers, perpetual tenure, and practically inviolable privileges – represented significant and previously unknown impositions on the provincial state.

Furthermore, the pulp and paper industry's requests clashed with the Ontario government's agrarian agenda in northern Ontario. Paper makers were supportive of this effort to people the north (after all, they required workers and spruce timber for their operations and hay from local homesteads for their horses), but they sought exclusive control over the pulpwood concessions, for example, which they leased from the government. In contrast, the provincial state favoured opening townships within pulpwood concessions to settlers in an effort to entice them into taking up a quarter section in the hinterland. Moreover, the newsprint mills sought perpetual supplies of timber, thereby making them self-sufficient in this regard. In contrast, the government hoped to foster the strongest demand possible for settlers' spruce, and while facilitating the export trade helped achieve this goal, so did depriving the province's mills of the quantity and/or quality of fibre they requested. To the state, the industry's development was primarily a means of populating the north. As G. Howard Ferguson, the individual most closely identified with Ontario's newsprint industry during these years, explained to a Royal Commission investigating the forest industry in 1940, "the general underlying principle in all … [pulpwood] agreements … was making it possible for settlers to get in and live there [in northern Ontario]." For such politicians, the mills' desire to create the strongest possible business enterprises was very much a secondary concern. A situation in which the government saw the arrival of the new industry as a means to an end, and the industry saw it as an end unto itself, presented certain grounds for misunderstanding and conflict.[41]

The pulp and paper makers' requests also interfered with the business of the lumbermen, a group that already had the provincial government squarely in its corner. Having thrived for decades on a diet composed almost exclusively of large-diameter white and red pine, the sawmillers were faced at the turn of the twentieth century with the grim reality that they had cut many of their best stands. To sustain their enterprises, most diversified their activities. For those lumbermen whose businesses remained geared towards harvesting white and red pine, they were compelled to operate in forests in which these trees were widely scattered among spruce and other species. This approach was far more costly and produced far less pine per acre than previous operations. These lumbermen thus became dependent upon harvesting pulpwood in the process of taking out pine, and used the sale of the former to subsidize their specialization in the latter. Other sawmillers turned to harvesting large-diameter white and black spruce and jack pine, which they processed into lumber and railway ties respectively, and their businesses also only survived because of their ability to market as pulpwood the small-diameter spruce they cut. As a result, the lumbermen came to covet pulpwood as much as the paper makers. *Pulp and Paper Magazine of Canada* identified this trend in the early 1900s, remarking how it was "interesting to note that power to handle … pulp-wood appears in almost all the recent incorporations of lumber companies [in Ontario]." In this competition for spruce, the provincial state remained loyal to its long-standing ally, the lumbermen.[42]

It was a similar story for the pulpwood exporters, who also eyed the same spruce as the province's pulp and paper mills. Fortunately for them, the state's predominant consideration in the north remained colonization, and integral to this effort was ensuring that settlers received the highest possible price for their pulpwood. This gave the government a compelling reason to bolster the operations of the pulpwood exporters, even if this involved blatantly breaking the spirit and sometimes the letter of a provincial law intended to prohibit their activities. Tellingly, when the government announced in 1913 that the first two newsprint mills would be built on the northern Clay Belt along the recently completed National Transcontinental Railway, its excitement sprang not so much from the fact that these new industries would provide a ready market for the local farmers' spruce but the expectation that as soon as the railway began running trains regularly "outside buyers of pulpwood will come in and widen out the market for settlers' timber."[43]

There was one overriding consideration that undermined the Ontario government's interest in granting the requests the pulp and paper industry made of it, namely the politicians' steadfast adherence to the patronage system of dispensing Crown resources. The paper makers' arrival had introduced an entirely new set of factors into the resource development equation, as did rapidly evolving attitudes towards forest management during the 1894–1932 period. These circumstances desperately cried out for a new approach to administering Crown timber and water powers. The politicians had at their disposal sophisticated experts who recognized that changes, some of them dramatic, were needed to bring the government's handling of the hinterland's natural bounty into the new century. They did not propose pursuing a strategy that would provide for the pulp and paper makers' every want, but rather a plan that would incorporate the "new staples industry" into a general policy of northern development that equitably addressed the requirements of all who sought access to the region's resources. But, as numerous studies have demonstrated, the province's elected officials consistently chose either to reject or ignore the advice Ontario's bureaucrats proffered during this period, and instead ensured that patronage remained the lifeblood of their polity, especially when Crown resources were involved. In this environment, local "political bosses" – not well-schooled bureaucrats – were the cornerstones of strong cabinets and political longevity. And, as far as our story is concerned, it was the lumbermen and pulpwood exporters who were generally ensconced within the provincial patronage network, not the pulp and paper makers.[44]

Most of the latter were extraordinarily slow in coming to grips with this reality, and few ever did. In many ways, this makes perfect sense. The imperatives that ruled this new staples industry were fundamentally incompatible with the patronage considerations that largely determined government behaviour towards resource-extracting enterprises during this period. In negotiating for Crown resources, the paper makers formulated management plans that appealed to the bureaucrats because the former felt that the latter spoke their language. But the politicians were the ones who retained control over the crucial decision-making process, and to them the paper makers were literally speaking a foreign tongue; the proof of this communication gap peppers the pages that follow.

Finally, even as circumstances changed dramatically from the mid-1890s to the early 1930s as the pulp and paper industry reached maturity, the politicians remained cool to it. Elected officials quickly came to understand the perils presented by appearing to cosy up to the growing industry. And whereas the pulp and paper makers had clear and rational ideas about how to develop their enterprises most effectively, the decision makers in office saw that they could realize enormous political dividends by instead dictating to the mills when and how the latter ran their businesses.

Thus, a variety of factors coalesced to make the Ontario government averse to embracing the pulp and paper industry. Of these, the politicians' commitment to the patronage system of dispensing Crown resources was pre-eminent, but the others were also critical. Consequently, instead of eagerly inviting the paper makers to set up shop in Ontario, the provincial state often responded reluctantly to their overtures, agreeing to assist a select few of their projects and often only to limited degrees, all the while making it clear that the state's assistance was never guaranteed. The result was a pattern of behaviour in which parties and politicians mattered. In the absence of a rational policy designed to establish a strong modern staples industry within the framework of a long-term strategy of northern development, the government implemented ad hoc measures to deal with the pulp and paper makers that were often unfavourable to them and not conducive to their sound growth and stability.

There were, however, several glaring exceptions to this rule. The government befriended a few players within the province's pulp and paper industry, but only when exceptional circumstances made it politically expedient to do so. Most often, these involved instances in which the parties who stood behind a mill project were temporarily able to penetrate the patronage system of dispensing Crown resources. On these rare occasions, they succeeded in mixing oil and water: they established a modern enterprise by speaking the old language of resource business in Ontario.

The state's generally lukewarm approach to the pulp and paper industry had a manifold impact upon its development. This treatment caused Ontario to become home to a series of paper plants largely because of industry's initiative and effort, not government inducements, and numerous newsprint mills operated in the province despite and not because of the state's policy.[45] Second, most of Ontario's newsprint makers were left with few options as far as financing their enterprises was concerned. Although H.V. Nelles writes that no newsprint "company could incur long-term obligations without being able to prove conclusively that it owned or held exclusive rights to a permanent supply of raw materials," the pages that follow reveal that he was correct but not in the way he intended.[46] These firms only rarely received these rights which they so desperately sought, a state of affairs that left them on shaky ground and contributed to the difficulties they experienced during the late 1920s and early 1930s.

Most importantly, the state's method of dealing with the pulp and paper industry created a remarkable set of paradoxes. The lumbermen and pulpwood exporters enjoyed favourable relations with the government, which helped them to meet their needs and granted them a remarkable degree of freedom from regulatory constraints. The paper makers, on the other hand, remained supplicants of the Ontario government and its lowest priority in terms of administering northern Crown resources. Collectively they held this status even though their industry grew by leaps and bounds between 1894 and 1932 to emerge by the mid-1920s as the province's most important manufacturing activity in terms of wages, capital invested, and labour employed. Moreover, the state felt compelled to keep the industry on a tighter leash – "in the power of the government," as one insider put it – than other resource users in the hinterland. In administering northern Crown timber and water powers during this period, then, the Ontario government's approach was least responsive to the industry that became the most important user of these resources.

2 "Intent upon getting grain-growing settlers upon the new land": The Liberals, 1894–1905

A number of forces made northern Ontario a highly attractive place to construct a pulp and paper mill by the mid-1890s, and its attributes in this regard attracted the attention of a string of industrialists from both the New World and Old. The region's prodigious supplies of readily accessible spruce pulpwood and water power, the construction of new railway lines into the hinterland, the rapid rise in the demand for newsprint in the nearby Midwestern United States, and the opportunity to build mills on the Great Lakes all drew the interest of paper makers to the province's northern reaches. In 1899 alone, these enticements elicited no fewer than forty supplicants asking the Ontario government to sell them pulpwood limits and water powers literally across the province's backcountry to support their mill projects; the next few years saw requests for resources located in remote areas that railways had not yet rendered accessible. So intense was this interest that it prompted one enthusiast to recommend that the provincial government invite the American Association of Pulp and Paper Manufacturers to hold its 1901 annual meeting in Toronto.[1]

While it was obvious that the arrival of this new industry would produce economic benefits for the province, the Ontario government faced several challenges in addressing its needs and wants. The Liberals were the first party to confront this situation, specifically during the late nineteenth and early twentieth centuries under premiers Oliver Mowat (1872–96), Arthur S. Hardy (1896–9) and George W. Ross (1899–1905). At the same time as the Grits were literally being bombarded with requests for Crown resources from the new staples industrialists, the province's governing party was acutely aware that it had a pre-existing set of priorities for New Ontario. Foremost among them was populating the north, ideally by expanding the province's farming frontier. Although many argued that realizing the latter goal was a chimerical dream, everyone understood that achieving the first would necessitate fostering the greatest possible market for the pulpwood the settlers cleared from their homesteads. It thus became incumbent upon the government to support the pulpwood exporting trade, which had already established a foothold in northern Ontario. Those engaged in this business would not rely solely on buying settlers' spruce, however, and they eagerly sought control over their own pulpwood limits.

In addition, the government had to consider a host of other factors in dealing with the pulp and paper makers. For one, the lumber industry had been a huge concern for the government long before the new breed of industrialists had appeared on the scene. The sawmillers had deep roots in Ontario's political economy, and during the period in question, their industry was undergoing a major transformation. It was harvesting in mixed stands from which it was extracting non-traditional species and processing them into new products. And just as with the pulpwood exporters, the lumbermen's interests were brought into conflict with those of the pulp and paper industry. Finally, the government had assisted myriad other parties, whose activities predated those of the paper makers, in using northern resources for their own purposes.[2] The Liberals – and the parties that succeeded them – thus faced a situation fraught with conflict; acquiescing to the requests of the pulp and paper industry would damage their ability to realize one of their other priorities in northern Ontario.

Fortunately, the provincial state had a few experts at its disposal who offered sound advice about how to reconcile these clashing claims. This group of counsellors did *not* include the individuals who acted as commissioner of Crown lands during the Liberals' tenure. Considering that their department had always been seen strictly as a generator of revenue for both the public purse and the governing party's coffers, it was hardly surprising that they had little insight to offer on the subject. Elihu J. Davis was typical. A farmer from King City and a nearly twenty-year veteran Grit MPP, during his term as commissioner (1899–1904) he gained notoriety not for implementing coherent policies but rather for serving as both an integral cog in the provincial Liberal political machine and one of its most outspoken defenders.[3] Far more helpful was a cadre of departmental officials, foremost among them being Aubrey White. A native of Northern Ireland, he had come to Canada in 1862 at the age of seventeen and begun working as a timber cruiser for a leading lumber concern on Georgian Bay. In 1876, the Department of Crown Lands hired him as a woods ranger, and within roughly one decade he had risen to assistant commissioner (i.e., deputy minister), a post he would hold until his death in 1915.[4] While undoubtedly White was, as Paul Pross and Richard Lambert contend, a "capable, powerful administrator so essential to the smooth running of the Department," the evidence presented in the pages that follow calls into question the traditional view of him as someone who was both profoundly committed to "keeping the lumber companies satisfied" and opposed to radical initiatives. Instead, he repeatedly endorsed dramatic departures in how the elected officials administered Crown timber.[5]

But White's words – and those of his enlightened colleagues – fell on deaf ears. Certainly, the Grits were willing to assist the industry in establishing a foundation in northern Ontario. Three mills were built – and several projects were well underway – when the Ross government fell in the 1905 election; their stories illustrate the myriad obstacles they confronted during the lengthy process involved in laying out a new staples industry in the province's hinterland. The Liberals did not help just any old paper maker, however. They reached out selectively to leading lumbermen or members of the ruling party who had heretofore enjoyed the traditional patronage connections to the provincial state; this marked the only time in Ontario's history when this critical linkage existed, and the paper makers benefited accordingly. Nevertheless, the government still dealt with the pulp and paper enterprises in a manner that subordinated their interests to its pre-existing priorities in New Ontario, primarily settlement but also the pulpwood exporters, lumbermen, and sundry other parties in the north. Indeed, the politicians quickly learned that this approach had its advantages. Overall, this chapter helps clarify our understanding of how the industry came to be established in the province's northern reaches during this period, particularly how the Ontario government reached out to the nascent pulp and paper industry but only in a highly selective and restrained manner.

Francis Hector Clergue was the first to lease a pulpwood concession in northern Ontario from the provincial government, and his experience became the general archetype for the pulp and paper makers' relations with the state and illustrates the various hurdles to success such new ventures faced. An American lawyer and business promoter from Maine, Clergue was on his way westward through Sault Ste Marie in the early 1890s when he was struck by the town's industrial potential.

He was so enthusiastic about the opportunity that he and a fellow American, E.V. Douglas, purchased the rights to the Canadian portion of the water powers on the St Mary's River from the municipality of Sault Ste Marie. Intent on expanding the local generating station, Clergue and Douglas set out to develop a wide array of industries – including a paper mill – to consume this power at "the Soo." To assist him in the endeavour, Clergue allied his enterprise with James Conmee, a key provincial Liberal whose far-flung influence in exploiting northern Ontario's resources has already been discussed. Likewise, Clergue quickly manoeuvred himself into the upper echelon of Canadian business and was soon on intimate terms with Wilfrid Laurier.[6]

These connections assisted Clergue in obtaining a pulpwood lease from the provincial Liberal government in November 1894. The agreement he signed, which became a template for such contracts in Ontario, was patterned after the model Ottawa had adopted in 1872 in selling timber on Dominion lands (Ontario executed a very different form of licence with the province's lumbermen, and it will be discussed shortly). Each deal Ottawa had brokered had been a basic quid pro quo, whereby the government bound the lessee to build and operate a mill of a certain size in exchange for cutting privileges that were to run for twenty-one years; the term of the contract was presumably based upon the common law doctrine known as "the rule against perpetuities."[7] In Clergue's case, he was obligated to erect a pulp and paper mill in the Soo within roughly one year, spend at least $200,000 on the project, and employ 300 hands for ten months in each year of the contract. An equal amount was to be spent on expanding the enterprise over the next year and hiring an additional one hundred hands. In exchange, Clergue was authorized to cut for twenty-one years pulpwood above a six-inch diameter from "rivers flowing into Lake Superior and West of Sault Ste Marie, as convenient to the said mills as shall be consistent with the public interest and having regard to where spruce may be found." Within that area, Clergue was permitted to select a fifty-square-mile tract from which he was to harvest one-twenty-first of the pulpwood he needed each year, thereby liquidating the spruce on this block over the duration of his contract. At the same time, the government agreed to provide Clergue annually with a permit "to cut elsewhere than on the said fifty miles at places to be agreed upon ... so many cords per annum as may be necessary, to keep the mills running." In other words, Clergue's mill would be able to select one fifty-square-mile tract plus many smaller ones within a vast area north of Sault Ste Marie; his cutting privileges did not apply to this entire territory. By the end of 1895 Clergue had incorporated the Sault Ste Marie Pulp and Paper Company, through which he had built and was operating a ground-wood mill that was completed on schedule and was twice as large as its intended size. Four years later the enterprise produced its first paper, but in 1902 a fire destroyed the paper mill. Although the groundwood mill continued to operate, the economic downturn of 1903 spelled an end to the growth years at the Soo.[8]

Soon after the plant had first opened its doors its owners expressed deep concerns about its wood supply. Spruce, particularly black spruce, was the best species for making newsprint, and it predominated in the Boreal Forest Region. Most of the southern part of Clergue's conces-sion, however, was located within the Great Lakes–St Lawrence Forest Region (Map 3). Its river valleys certainly supported a smattering of black spruce stands, but it was covered by a forest in which most of the species were useless for making newsprint. This situation had become glaringly apparent during the plant's inaugural harvesting operations, when Elihu J. Davis, Ontario's commissioner of Crown lands, explained that Clergue's cutters had only been able to locate "spruce scattered in small bunches" near the mill.[9]

This news came as a shock to Clergue, and for good reason. Prior to building his mill, he had every reason to believe that there was enough pulpwood in the local woods to supply his paper plant forever. As was customary prior to the advent of the airplane, his timber cruisers had relied on the best technology of the day – canoes – to traverse the pulp-wood concession the government had given his mill. Their travels were thus almost entirely confined to waterways, areas in which, coinciden-tally, stands of black spruce naturally flourished and which were also most resistant to burning because of their relatively high moisture re-gimes. These woodsmen had thus assumed that the seemingly endless thickets of black spruce past which they had paddled each day were representative of the woodlands which covered the entire timber limit they were investigating, and thus reported their results on this basis. Herein lay the problem. Although this was a quick and inexpensive means of surveying forests, it was most unreliable. Beyond the horizon of those in the canoes lay a very different woodland, one defined by vast expanses, such as rocky outcrops, swamps, and large burns, which were barren of valuable timber. Bernhard E. Fernow, North America's pioneer forester and first dean of the University of Toronto's forestry school, explained in the early 1900s why this type of estimating was

Map 3. Pulp and Paper Mill Projects and Pulpwood Concessions, 1894–1905

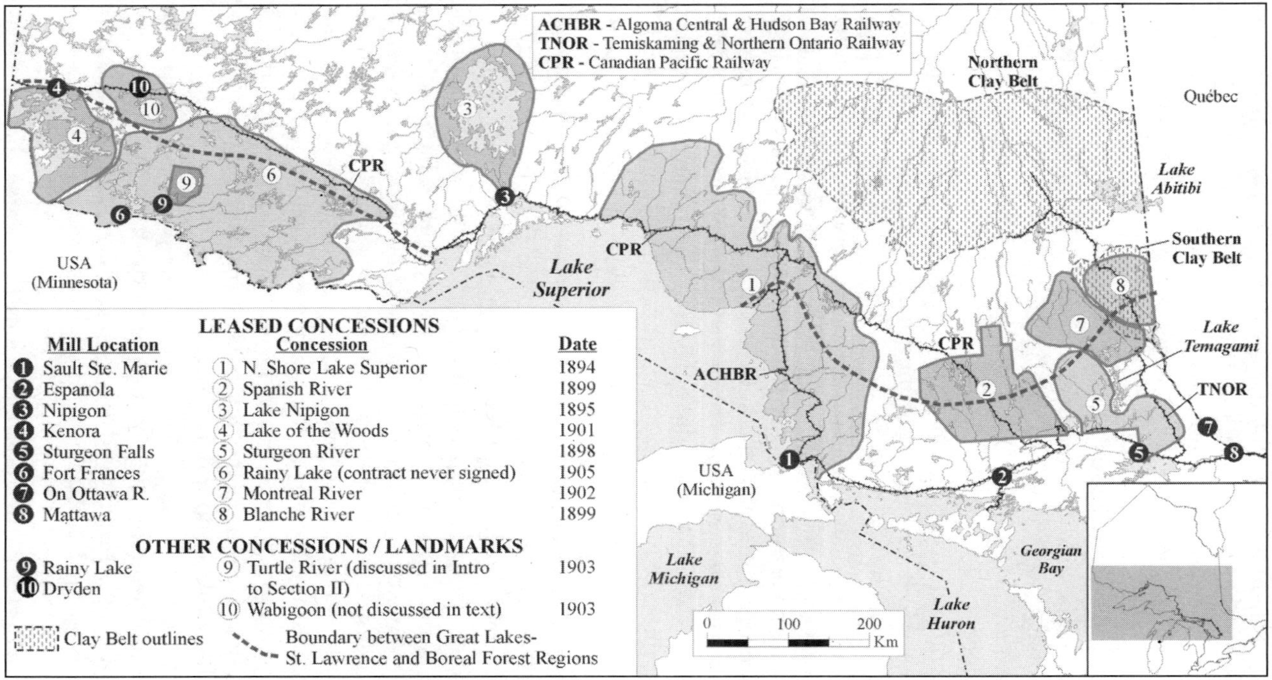

ACHBR - Algoma Central & Hudson Bay Railway
TNOR - Temiskaming & Northern Ontario Railway
CPR - Canadian Pacific Railway

LEASED CONCESSIONS

Mill Location	**Concession**	**Date**
① Sault Ste. Marie	① N. Shore Lake Superior	1894
② Espanola	② Spanish River	1899
③ Nipigon	③ Lake Nipigon	1895
④ Kenora	④ Lake of the Woods	1901
⑤ Sturgeon Falls	⑤ Sturgeon River	1898
⑥ On Ottawa R.	⑥ Rainy Lake (contract never signed)	1905
⑦ Fort Frances	⑦ Montreal River	1902
⑧ Mattawa	⑧ Blanche River	1899

OTHER CONCESSIONS / LANDMARKS

⑨ Rainy Lake	⑨ Turtle River (discussed in Intro to Section II)	1903
⑩ Dryden	⑩ Wabigoon (not discussed in text)	1903

▨▨▨ Clay Belt outlines

Boundary between Great Lakes-
–·–·– St. Lawrence and Boreal Forest Regions

Quebec

Lake Abitibi

Northern Clay Belt

Southern Clay Belt

Lake Temagami

TNOR

Georgian Bay

Lake Huron

CPR

ACHBR

USA (Michigan)

Lake Michigan

Lake Superior

CPR

CPR

USA (Minnesota)

0   100   200   Km

faulty. "There are," he noted, "as a rule, no descriptions given which may allow surmises as to the commercial character of the timber, nor how far the conditions observed from the canoe may be surmised to exist beyond the vision of the observer. The probability is that the sheltered river valleys exhibit the best development [of spruce]."[10] Consequently, it was only after Clergue's bush workers had actually begun exploring the forest beyond the stream and river banks on his pulpwood concession that they grasped its deficiencies, a realization that would soon cause similar problems for a number of other mill developers in the province.

Clergue devised a creative means of supplementing his pulpwood supply. He began lobbying the Liberals to grant him large tracts of Crown land as a subsidy to support a railway that he proposed building due north of the Soo to tap the pulpwood-rich boreal forest. Moreover, Clergue's railway would own – not lease – the tracts it would select to make up its roughly 1,500,000 acres of land grants in this prime spruce area; the mill's "freehold" cutting privileges in these woodlands would thus be perpetual. The fact that the Liberals approved Clergue's Algoma Central and Hudson Bay Railway project both reflected their recognition of his spruce-deficient concession and seemingly assured his mill a large supply of pulpwood (cut from soon-to-be granted private land) far into the future.[11]

Clergue's paper mill in the Soo stood as a shining beacon to the potential of the new modern staples industry in northern Ontario for nearly one decade, but in 1903 its light went out. In that year, Clergue's corporate web of enterprises came undone. When he was unable to pay several thousand of his workers, they rioted, taking out their frustration by trashing Clergue's main office building and wreaking havoc throughout the city. The local militia was unable to contain the uprising, which was quelled only after a large contingent of soldiers arrived from Toronto. Moreover, the town was saved from the abyss of financial ruin only when the provincial government stepped in to act as Clergue's guarantor, thereby reassuring his creditors and employees that he would honour debts owed.[12]

For the provincial government and potential investors in northern Ontario's fledgling pulp and paper industry, this episode served as a compelling lesson in the dangers inherent in such endeavours. The politicians learned that being intimately associated with new paper mills on the hinterland was a double-edged sword. Ribbon cuttings served as wonderful partisan opportunities to trumpet the crucial assistance

Figure 5. The Perils of Association: The Ontario government quickly learned that being associated with pulp and paper enterprises in the hinterland – by providing access to Crown resources – was a knife that cut two ways. For example, the ruling Liberals could claim that their wisdom in providing Francis H. Clergue's industrial empire in Sault Ste Marie with pulpwood and land grants around the turn of the twentieth century was manifest in his thriving business. But when it crumbled in 1903 and he was unable to pay his bush workers, they took out their anger on his office building (note the broken windows); only the intervention of the local militia – supported by reinforcements from Toronto – restored the peace. In these instances, elected officials were sullied with the same brush as the industrialists and rendered themselves vulnerable to intense public criticism (Sault Ste Marie Public Library – 994.3.18).

the state had afforded the enterprise in question. If the undertaking tanked, however, as Clergue's had in the early 1900s, the party's political fortunes were apt to sink as quickly as the company's. Likewise, for the entrepreneurs who had been keen to erect new paper mills in Ontario, the financial collapse in the Sault delivered a stern warning that success in the hinterland was far from assured. Not surprisingly, Clergue's difficulties dampened enthusiasm for such risk taking for at least the next few years.

Long before this time, the Liberals had already begun facilitating several other pulp and paper projects, but only those which were backed by friends of the government. Typical were a pair of undertakings that involved John R. Barber, the Grit MPP for Halton and leading first-generation Canadian paper maker. The first of these occurred roughly one hundred miles east of Sault Ste Marie at a site that would become known as Espanola. There, a group led by Barber and the district's prominent lumbermen and Liberals, including Marshall J. Dodge and William J. Sheppard, acquired freehold rights to develop the water power near the mouth of the Spanish River; in 1899 the Liberals executed a deal to provide the enterprise with spruce. In exchange for building a mill, the government permitted the entrepreneurs to harvest pulpwood from the Spanish River watershed under conditions practically identical to those outlined in Clergue's lease (Map 3). Almost immediately, the new Spanish River Pulp and Paper Company began developing its water power rights, and by 1902 its pulp mill was operational. Its activities were deleteriously affected by Clergue's demise and the general economic dislocation of 1903, so the Liberals extended the deadline by which the firm was to build its paper mill.[13]

Farther west, the Liberals assisted Barber in undertaking another pulp and paper venture at one of the best sites in the country for building such a facility, namely the Lake Nipigon basin in the Thunder Bay District. Not only does the lake form a massive natural reservoir, it is drained by a short river that is punctuated by a few precipitous waterfalls that were ideal for generating large quantities of cheap hydroelectricity. This enormous watershed also supported forests in which spruce generally predominated, and these pulpwood stands would be inexpensive to harvest and deliver to a mill because they were mostly located along the shores of the lake and its tributaries. Furthermore, this area was ideally situated to serve the growing newsprint market in the American Midwest because it was both close to this region and capable of being served by Great Lakes freighters (which would be much cheaper than rail).

These attributes made the Nipigon basin one of the first areas in Ontario to be staked by newsprint mill developers, but Barber was not initially involved in the effort. In 1895, a group fronted by James Whalen, the prominent pulpwood exporter and son-in-law of the region's political chieftain, James Conmee, had negotiated a pulpwood concession lease with the Liberals for the local watershed that obliged it to construct a small pulp and paper mill along the Nipigon River (Map 3). Difficulties in securing permission to develop a power site delayed the project for several years, however. Whalen then teamed up with Barber and Newton W. Rowell, another leading Liberal – among others – to form another syndicate, which made a similar agreement with the Ontario government in 1900. In return for building a mill, the Liberals granted the enterprise a twenty-one-year lease to cut spruce, poplar, and jack pine six inches in diameter from the watershed of Lake Nipigon and the river that drained it. Whalen and Barber incorporated the Nepigon Pulp, Paper and Manufacturing Company to carry out the venture and began clearing a site at Cameron's Pools on the Nipigon River where they intended to build their generating station. Nepigon Pulp also augmented its pulpwood supply by obtaining permission from the Liberals to construct a railway north from the town of Nipigon to tap additional timber. The project's charter included land grants on either side of its line, territory that would make up the mill's freehold fibre supply. When Nepigon Pulp ran into problems arranging for clear title to its hydroelectric site, the government granted it extensions on its pulpwood concession obligations. It was ready to begin construction in the spring of 1905, but the election of the Conservative government intervened before it could do so.[14]

The tale of another project that involved a leading lumberman of the day poignantly demonstrates how those without direct access to the Liberals' inner sanctum could still gain admission to it but how doing so could be costly and tenuous. At the turn of the century, the soon-to-be-named town of Kenora near Ontario's newly defined border with Manitoba boasted over a half-dozen sawmills, and John Mather's Keewatin Lumber and Manufacturing Company towered over them. Mather was *the* local lumber and business baron, and was intimately connected to the halls of power in Ottawa through his forest company and flour-milling business. His partner in the former venture had been William H. Brouse, Liberal senator (1878–81), and in the latter enterprise he had teamed up with the legendary Sir William Van Horne and Donald A. Smith of the Canadian Pacific Railway, both of whom enjoyed tight ties to the Conservatives. In the 1890s, Mather sought to diversify his holdings in the resource sector, but he lacked a strong conduit to the Liberal government in Toronto to realize this aim. Consequently, after he allied with some of the Ottawa Valley's most prominent lumbermen to organize the Keewatin Power Company in 1893, they agreed to the price the provincial Grits set on the lease to a water power at the outlet of Lake of the Woods which Mather and his cronies sought. For a "donation," as Mather put it, of $1,333.34 to "the Ontario election fund," a toll he continually lamented paying, the contract was theirs. Keewatin Power began constructing a hydroelectric generating station to tap the energy, but the effort's progress was plagued by delays when Mather's partners refused to ante up their share of the funds needed to complete it.[15]

Mather then began looking for a solution to the impasse, one that would again end up with him offering alms to the provincial power brokers. At the same time as he searched for a means of selling his stake in the venture, he sought a market for the power the plant would generate once it was up and running. He determined that one means of addressing the second issue would be to build a paper mill. And so he again offered his moral and pecuniary support to the Liberals in exchange for a twenty-one-year lease to a pulpwood limit in the Lake of the Woods watershed that would be the fibre supply for the 100-ton newsprint mill he now intended to erect in Kenora (Map 3). Immediately thereafter, Mather obtained technical advice about his project and began calculating the competitive advantage he would enjoy in selling his product to the prairie newspapers because of his proximity to them. As part owner of the *Winnipeg Free Press*, he knew that it had been buying its paper from E.B. Eddy, an arrangement that had forced it to pay a hefty premium for shipping its newsprint all the way from Hull, Quebec.

While Keewatin Power was anxious to break ground, it soon realized that it faced several significant challenges, and now that circumstances had changed, the Liberals proved unwilling to resolve either one. The first and most important involved Keewatin Power's pulpwood. In planning its enterprise, its goal had been to acquire enough spruce to run its operation for at least three decades (i.e., a 100-ton newsprint mill would need roughly 1,350,000 total cords). After Mather's woods rangers thoroughly investigated the timber on the concession Keewatin Power had leased from the Ontario government, however, they tallied fewer than 1,000,000 cords. This finding seriously impeded the firm's ability to interest investors in the project, particularly after the Liberals refused to grant the firm a supplementary tract of spruce; the government reasoned that it could hardly afford to be associated with assisting another pulp and paper mill project at the height of the debacle over Clergue's floundering industrial enterprise in the Soo. Keewatin Power also argued that the uncertainty that characterized its pulpwood lease made it practically impossible to interest financial support for the endeavour. "Capitalists do not care at all for this arrangement," Keewatin Power's appeal to the government for a longer term on its pulpwood lease explained,

> claiming that an initial outlay of one million dollars for machinery and buildings should be secured in raw material for at least thirty years, as twenty years will be altogether too short a time. They also claim that instead of having to look yearly for liberty to cut so many cords for the current year, that districts should be selected and set apart as near the mills as possible containing the necessary quantity. They could then go on without any doubt or want of confidence in that regard. We claim that this arrangement could do no harm in any way to the progress of settlement as the lands set aside would be wet and unfit for settlement as spruce timber grows only on such lands ... There can be no reason why this method should be condemned as without a security of an ample supply of raw material no capitalists will undertake such an enterprise.

Transportation issues also delayed Keewatin Power's paper mill project, and again the Ontario government refused to help the firm out. Although Kenora was located near newsprint buyers in the Midwestern United States, in the late 1890s no railway line directly linked the two areas. This compelled the interests who were keen to back Keewatin Power's undertaking – Itasca Paper Company of Grand Rapids, Minnesota – to plan on selling the paper initially produced in Kenora in the distant northeastern United States. The company's representatives argued that this would greatly add to their freight costs, and so they asked the Ontario government to reduce the stumpage dues it charged them on the pulpwood they harvested from the concession they leased. The politicians refused Keewatin Power's request, as did the railways that it had approached about lower freight rates. As a result, the mill in Kenora was still on the drawing board when the Liberals went down in the 1905 election.[16]

The Grits' behaviour towards another pulp and paper interest underscored how the lack of a strong connection to the traditional patronage network hindered such enterprises, and also the extent of uncertainty that surrounded a mill's fibre supply during these early days. Businessmen and local politicians from the Huntsville area had begun building a small pulp mill in Sturgeon Falls, about 100 miles east of Espanola, in 1896 – aptly naming it the Sturgeon Falls Pulp Company – after securing freehold rights to develop the water power near the mouth of the Sturgeon River. In 1898, the British firm Jenckes Machine Company purchased the company's assets and signed an agreement with the government for harvesting privileges on the Sturgeon River pulpwood concession (Map 3). Like the other contracts of this type, this one required $1,000,000 to be spent within three years on the construction of a paper plant to complement the existing pulp mill. Although these concessionaires followed Clergue's lead insofar as they applied for land grants to support a railway they intended to build up the Sturgeon River valley to Lake Temagami, their plans got bogged down during hearings before the Canadian Senate's Railway Committee and were never realized.[17]

The project endured several larger challenges, the first of which reinforced the shockwaves that Clergue's difficulties had sent through the province's fledgling pulp and paper industry. Edward Lloyd, Limited, was a major English newsprint manufacturer that had been looking for a Canadian paper supplier. Lloyd was so desperate to make an acquisition – newsprint consumption had exploded in the United Kingdom during the Boer War – that the firm had purchased in 1900 the assets of the Sturgeon Falls Pulp Company sight unseen and against the advice of its local representative. Immediately thereafter, Lloyd took legal action against the mill's previous owners on the grounds that they had misrepresented the value of the enterprise's assets, specifically by grossly overstating the volume of pulpwood available to the mill. The defendants denied the charge and emerged victorious after having demonstrated the veracity of the data they had supplied Lloyd, and they ended up retaining possession of the Sturgeon Falls Pulp Company. For northern Ontario's trailblazing pulp and paper makers, however, it was a pyrrhic victory. Financiers in the United Kingdom and the United States had been spooked by the mere suggestion that parties were presenting false estimates of the volume of pulpwood available to support a new mill venture in the province's vast, unknown hinterland. The fact that North American and British business publications, especially the *Paper Trade Journal*, gave the legal proceedings high-profile coverage only exacerbated the situation, a grim reality the Toronto dailies despairingly noted.[18]

Nevertheless, the protracted litigation only slightly delayed the Sturgeon Falls Pulp Company from fulfilling its obligations as set out in its original 1898 concession agreement. Recognizing the difficulty the firm was facing, the Ontario government in 1902 gave it a twelve-month extension on the deadline by which it was to have completed its paper mill. By the next year, the enterprise had been renamed Imperial Paper Mills of Canada (in order to distance it from the "foul odour" – as George Carruthers puts it – of the Sturgeon Falls Pulp Company), and it was producing both groundwood and newsprint for sale in the United States, Great Britain, and Australia. Not only had Imperial constructed mills that greatly exceeded the size required under its Crown agreement, but it planned on significantly increasing its newsprint capacity and building its own sulphite mill in the near future.[19]

Imperial's newly expanded mill required greater quantities of energy, but the Ontario government chose to meet the interests of the north's fledgling tourist industry instead of the paper maker's. To increase Imperial's power supply, the firm planned on damming Lake Temagami. Imperial could then use the extra water it held back to ensure a greater volume and consistency of flow through its generating station on the Sturgeon River, which drained the lake. The Liberals agreed in December 1902 to allow the company to proceed, but only on two conditions. Imperial first had to gain the government's approval for its plans for the dam, and it could not hold back any water in Lake Temagami until the lake had dropped to a "summer level" after the spring freshets. Imperial agreed to abide by these directives, but then it constructed the dam at the lake's southern outlet – and another one at the northern end of the lake – without government approval, and it raised the lake's level above the maximum point to which it had agreed. When vacationers on Lake Temagami complained about the flooding in the summer of 1903, the government dispatched an inspector, who blew up both dams. Undaunted, Imperial soon devised an alternative means of increasing its power supply. In the fall of 1903, it announced plans to build an additional power station and adjoining sulphite mill at Smokey Falls, about a dozen miles upriver from the town of Sturgeon Falls. Although it began building the new mill, its application for the hydro lease was still pending when the Liberals lost the 1905 election.[20]

By this date, Edward Wellington Backus was on the cusp of breaking ground on his pulp and paper enterprise in northwestern Ontario, and his dealings with the Grits provide the departure point for understanding how a change in government could spell ruin for a mill developer.

Born in New York State in 1860, Backus became northwestern Ontario's most renowned industrialist. Having begun his ascent in the late 1800s in the lumber business in northern Minnesota near its border with Ontario, around the turn of the century he teamed up with local senator William F. Brooks to form the Backus-Brooks Company. They soon organized the Rainy River Lumber Company to operate on the Canadian side of the international boundary in the town of the same name. To facilitate their dealings with the provincial Grits, they included Douglas C. Cameron, the local Liberal MPP, in their new venture.[21]

Backus was the engine behind the enterprise, and he initiated an aggressive campaign to create a fully integrated forest products empire. One of his first major ambitions was to build newsprint mills in International Falls, Minnesota, and Fort Frances, Ontario, towns which straddled the Rainy River (Map 3). A major impetus driving this plan was his knowledge that these paper plants would enjoy much cheaper freight rates than their eastern competitors in delivering their wares to newspaper publishers in cities such as Omaha and Minneapolis, a fact that Backus's financial backers graphically publicized to the investing public.[22] But the Rainy River divided Canada from the United States and Minnesota from Ontario, so carrying out this plan would be a complex matter. It would require permission from the national and local governments in both countries that had jurisdiction over international trade and natural resources respectively. After purchasing large tracts of pulpwood in northern Minnesota and the rights to develop the American side of the Rainy River near International Falls, Backus asked the Ontario government for leases to local supplies of pulpwood and water power.[23]

By late 1904 it appeared he had acquired both, but not for long. The Liberals initially drafted an agreement which gave Backus a lease to develop power near Fort Frances on the Canadian side of the Rainy River *and* to harvest the pulpwood on the Rainy Lake watershed. In exchange Backus was obliged to immediately construct hydro stations and pulp and paper mills. Just before signing the contract, however, Backus had asked that the government revise it. He planned to sell all the newsprint he produced in Fort Frances in the Midwestern states and had begun building a railway from Bemidji, Minnesota, northward to International Falls, to connect his Ontario operation directly to the railways that ran through the American heartland. Because it would take him a few years to complete his line, Backus asked and the provincial government agreed to separate his pulpwood concession and water power leases, whereby he would be obliged to undertake the hydro development immediately and delay the mill project for a few years. While he signed the power lease on 9 January 1905, he had not executed the agreement for the pulpwood on the Rainy Lake watershed prior to the election two weeks later in which the Liberals were defeated. This turn of events would cost Backus's project title to this fibre supply at the time and for roughly the next forty years.[24]

Undeniably, during the late 1890s and early 1900s the Grits had facilitated the establishment and development of the pulp and paper industry in northern Ontario. They had leased pulpwood concessions, and water powers when necessary, to mill builders across the province's hinterland. They had also often provided the entrepreneurs with leases to these resources that would be valuable collateral in financing their ventures. To achieve this end, the Liberals confirmed all pulpwood concession agreements – and any amendments to them – by resolution of the Legislature, for example. The government also recognized that the value of a Crown lease was greatly diminished if it included ambiguous terms that could cause the lessee to forfeit all privileges in the event of a trivial transgression. In reviewing a draft of Backus's 1905 water power lease, for instance, Alexander G. MacKay, Ontario's commissioner of Crown lands, pointed out that there was "a clause in the contract providing that in default of the observance of *any* of the terms or conditions of the contract the Government may cancel the franchise" (emphasis added). While it was axiomatic that the government ought to be empowered to force the lessee to fulfil his obligations, MacKay argued that the state must distinguish between substantive and nominal violations. Otherwise, the government's powers significantly weakened, if not ruined entirely, the collateral value of the lease because "purchasers of the Company's securities would be endangered by reason of the default of a comparatively minor point in the contract." MacKay explained that such uncertainties in agreements of this kind would "seriously interfere with the sale of ... bonds if it be left open for all time to come whether or not the purchasers are complying with this clause." Consequently, he amended Backus's contract in a manner that addressed these concerns.[25]

To benefit the mills the government also expanded the size of the pulpwood concessions they leased. The agreements initially confined the concessionaires' harvesting activities to relatively limited areas because it was assumed that they would need only small tracts to sustain their operations. Clergue's mill in the Soo, for example, was originally permitted to cut in a mere fifty-square-mile block and in other sections of a very large territory if his block proved inadequate for his needs. His (and his fellow mill owners') experience(s) had quickly demonstrated that this premise was faulty. While granting concessionaires railway building rights (and the attendant land grants) was one means of addressing this problem, the Liberals also took another step in this direction. Beginning in 1899 the government allowed lessees to cut within their entire concessions and not merely small isolated sections of these tracts; for the concessionaires whose agreements predated this novel departure, the implication was that this benefit was now extended to them as well.

The Liberals responded to the pulp and paper industry's needs in these ways because nearly all these entrepreneurs were close friends of the government who were acutely aware of the patronage system of allocating Crown resources. From Clergue in the Soo to Conmee and Rowell in Nipigon, and from Barber in Espanola to Mather and Backus in Kenora and Fort Frances, respectively, the list of Ontario's inaugural pulpwood concessionaires reads like a "Who's Who" of Ontario's leading lumbermen and Liberals. For the government, it also seemed natural to assist their long-time allies, the lumbermen, in diversifying their activities in the face of declining supplies of their traditional white and red pine sawlog timber.[26]

Nevertheless, in reaching out to the province's pulp and paper makers the government made one thing clear: its highest priority in northern Ontario was not facilitating their mill projects. There were many reasons for the government's decision to take this approach, not the least of which was the substantial risk involved in being perceived as indulging the new staples industry. The pulp and paper makers sought exclusive and perpetual access to timber limits of unprecedented proportions. Moreover, although many of the new industrial ventures were associated with veteran lumbermen, most of whose operations were family-run, they were increasingly led by the new breed of "big business" interests that typified the turn of the century's shift to corporate capitalism. As a result, any politician who dared grant the privileges the paper makers sought immediately rendered himself vulnerable to being portrayed as someone who had sacrificed "the public interest" to the ruthless "barons of industry." And even though it will be seen that the Liberals did not meet the paper makers' needs in terms of pulpwood cutting privileges, the Opposition Conservatives still pounced on the deals as prime fodder for denouncing the government, particularly during election campaigns.

The Tories' attack on the leasing in 1902 of the 1,800-square-mile Montreal River pulpwood concession in northeastern Ontario speaks to this issue (Map 3). The Conservative leader, James P. Whitney, repeatedly blasted the Liberals for having entered into the agreement even though nearly all his allegations were unfounded. In particular, Whitney criticized the Grits for having given away "monopoly pulpwood rights" to "the large corporation" and denounced the transaction as "a gigantic public robbery" and "public crime." In particular, he stressed that the timber tract the government had granted in this instance was "larger than some of the independent nations of Europe, was larger than Algonquin Park, was larger than the counties of Stormont and Glengarry, and larger than the Province of Prince Edward Island." Even though the Liberals endeavoured to set the record straight, it was practically impossible to defend against the barrage. Accusing the government of selling out to big business was a charge that resonated in the public consciousness.[27]

In terms of explaining why the Ontario government did not meet all the pulp and paper makers' needs, the most important reason was the fact that doing so would have interfered with achieving its pre-eminent goal in the hinterland, namely furthering colonization. By the late 1800s, the provincial state's campaign to people northern Ontario was languishing just as the attraction of the Canadian prairies was intensifying. To rectify this distressing state of affairs, the Liberals funded an extensive but cursory survey of the area above the height of land. After the investigation "discovered" a northern Clay Belt (the much smaller southern Clay Belt near Lake Temiskaming was already being settled), the government both zealously boasted that this confirmed its belief that commercial wheat farming would be possible in "New Ontario" and established a Colonization Branch within the Department of Crown Lands whose sole function was to propagandize this notion. The crusade to settle Ontario's hinterland was reborn, and its lifeblood would be ensuring that homesteaders could sell their pulpwood.[28]

As a result, when the Liberals executed the province's first pulpwood concession agreements, they repeatedly stressed not only that the deals would *not* impede the revivified colonization effort but that the contracts would instead promote it. The Grits achieved this aim by inserting into every contract a clause that authorized the government to open any part of the newly leased pulpwood tracts to homesteaders. In essence, this made pulpwood concessions the location of choice for settlers in northern Ontario. "Indeed, one of the main objects in working for the establishment of these pulp mills is to impart an impetus to settlement," *The Globe* noted in an editorial in the spring of 1902. The paper pointed out that a settler who was "contemplating homesteading in new Ontario ... would prefer to locate on the territories assigned to one of these pulp companies, provided it was good land, because then he would have the assurance that the pulpwood that for older Ontario was only in the way, and was got rid of by setting the match to it, will in the new lands be convertible into ready cash." For settlers who had previously depended on selling their pulpwood to exporters, the Liberals emphasized that establishing mills in these locales had actually expanded the range of buyers to whom they could peddle their spruce.[29]

The story of the Blanche River Pulp and Paper Company provides insight into how the government envisioned its plan would work, much to the paper makers' chagrin. In 1899 the government had leased to the firm a pulpwood limit at the north end of Lake Temiskaming, and the contract had included the standard clause reserving to the Crown the right to open any part of the tract to settlement (Map 3). The project seemed destined for success. It was backed by the *New York World*, a large American newspaper, and was thus guaranteed a market for its newsprint. In addition, after protracted negotiations with the Quebec government, the firm secured a water power lease on the Ottawa River. But the company had little choice but to give up the venture after it realized that hundreds of colonists had begun clearing homesteads on its pulpwood limit. While the Ontario government jubilantly rejoiced that the firm's decision to throw in the towel reflected the fact that "the settlers now control the timber," *Pulp and Paper Magazine of Canada* lamented the fact that homesteaders had "invaded the region" after the Liberals had signed the concession agreement and had thus spelled the project's ruin.[30]

The Liberals pushed this approach even though the province's pulp and paper makers found it anathema to their interests. In a lengthy appeal in 1905 for the Ontario government to grant them a measure of protection "from the inroads of farm-clearing, brush-burning settlers," they asked that the provincial state

feel bound to do one thing which its agreements with the present concessionaires do not oblige it to do ... to protect them in the enjoyment of their cutting rights during the twenty-one year period or other time of tenure specified in the lease ... [and] keep land clearing settlers off the tract conveyed. Th[is was] a most important consideration for the pulp and paper industry. Under the present agreements the pulp and paper companies are helpless against the Government. It can throw their lands open to settlement without a moment's notice, and five years after the occupation has begun the land may be producing agricultural crops instead of spruce … In that case the expensive pulp and paper mills will be left standing, a relic of the country's departed forest days. From such a fate the enterprise of pulp and paper manufacturers should be protected. While the Blanche River Pulp and Paper Company was looking for capital to go on with its building operations, settlers were over-running its limits and carving homes thereon. Soon almost the whole tract was inhabited, and the company had to abandon its project. Investors will be slow to put their money in concessions of the type now existing, for the reason that the main security – possession of an adequate source of pulpwood supply – is precarious. This matter of making permanent provision for the pulp and paper industry is one that has received too little consideration from either political party in Ontario. Both are intent upon getting grain-growing settlers upon the new land to give due attention to the needs and possibilities of the pulpwood tracts.[31]

While the province's fledgling pulp and paper industry thus generally loathed the Liberals' colonization policy, the mills in the Great Lakes states – and the pulpwood exporters upon whom they depended – welcomed it. They all recognized that the Ontario government's push to populate its hinterland rested on its ability to create the greatest market possible for the homesteaders' pulpwood, one in which their participation was vital. Their favourite means of achieving their ends was to abuse the province's colonization and mining laws to acquire at very little cost spruce-bearing lands whose arboreal cover they could harvest and export, but near the turn of the twentieth century these ruses posed potential problems. Shipping Canada's raw materials to the United States for processing had become a highly contentious issue, and the call for an end to this practice was reaching a crescendo.[32]

The Liberals devised a brilliant plan for dealing with this issue, and although the story has been told elsewhere, recounting a condensed version of it here underscores how the Grits' decision to extend the manufacturing condition to pulpwood was never intended to halt the flow of spruce heading south from Ontario. From the outset, the Liberals' enactment in 1898 of the manufacturing condition on pine was aimed at fostering indigenous industry. Not only did they devote significant resources to rigorously enforcing the measure, but they had already prevented mining interests and settlers from cutting pine on the land these interests acquired; thus, the only pine available in commercial quantities in the province was that which grew on Crown land.

In sharp contrast, the Ontario government never enforced the manufacturing condition on pulpwood. It also applied only to timber cut from Crown lands, whereas much of the spruce being cut for export was coming from private lands. At the same time, the Liberals doubled the dues on pulpwood cut from Crown lands without explanation, thereby giving the province's own pulp and paper mills even more reason to buy from settlers instead of cutting their own supplies.[33] Most importantly, the Liberals implemented the manufacturing condition on pulpwood coincidentally in the same year – 1900 – as they launched their reinvigorated colonization plan, and they stressed that the former would give the latter an immense boost by drastically increasing the value of the settlers' timber. As Newton Rowell, a senior Grit, explained at the time, "under the [manufacturing condition] regulation the settlers were the only persons entitled to export or sell [pulpwood] for export, and the necessary effect must be to greatly improve the conditions for the settler. As the supply was lessened and the American demand increased, the settlers, and they only, would reap the benefit."[34]

Ultimately, the provincial government knew it had little choice in the matter. It was obvious that prohibiting the export of spruce would have been inimical to its goal of maximizing the market for settlers' pulpwood. Moreover, during the raucous and heated debate that engulfed this question around the turn of the twentieth century, the homesteaders let all sitting and aspiring politicians know that they would take down any party that dared restrict their ability to sell their collective spruce crop, referred to by one of their impassioned brethren as "the poor man's harvest," to whomever they chose.[35] Finally, both Liberals and Conservatives alike were involved in the early years of the export trade and its illustrious – or infamous – history thereafter. Tellingly, the Grits openly admitted in 1900 that the very legislation they had enacted to implement the manufacturing condition on pulpwood exempted a firm that operated near the Lakehead from its provisions on the grounds that there was such strong bipartisan support for doing so.[36]

Thereafter, the Liberal government did enormous work on behalf of the exporters. It continued to wink at their continued, blatant abuse of Ontario's mining and settlement legislation to further their business interests and created new, even more attractive opportunities for them in this domain. In the midst of the Boer War, the Liberals introduced legislation to give veterans of the present and past conflicts free land in northern Ontario. Although a noble cause to be sure, the manner in which the government implemented the measure was most ignoble.

Not only did it interpret "veteran" in such a broad manner that it im-
bued the word with a new meaning, nearly all the townships it set aside
for these grants were as unsuited to farming as they were ideal for harvesting pulpwood, located as they were in remote sections of the boreal
forest. Predictably, almost overnight, a frenzied market developed in
"scrip" to these tracts, whereby savvy exporting interests hired barris-
ters to solicit the land certificates from those eligible to receive them in
exchange for what was often a nominal fee. A few insightful and courageous observers, one of whom was Aubrey White, the deputy minister,
pointed out these flagrant problems with this colonization law – and
the others – and offered remedies to them, but the government turned
a deaf ear to these ideas. Instead, within short order, hundreds of thousands of acres of prime spruce-bearing lands were under either the direct or indirect control of American pulp and paper makers, having
been acquired for mere pennies on the cord.

Thus, the government's ostensible embargo on pulpwood actually
facilitated the export of spruce in the early 1900s and for at least the following half-century. Many exporters expanded the scope of their operations in Ontario under the Liberals and then their successors. Moreover,
American paper makers were often left controlling greater volumes and
more valuable tracts of the province's spruce than Ontario's own mills.

In dealing with the advent of the pulp and paper makers to Ontario
at the turn of the century, the Grits also placed the interests of Ontario's
lumbermen ahead of those of the new industrialists. The Liberals delivered their message by granting the lumbermen and the pulp and paper
industry fundamentally different cutting privileges. When the government licensed the lumbermen to cut a particular timber tract, it gave
them "the right to take and keep *exclusive* possession of the lands so
described [and] … all rights of property whatsoever in all trees, timber
and lumber cut within the limits of the licence during the term thereof"
(emphasis added). In practical terms, this meant that the government
would prohibit settlement, mining, or any other activity on a timber licence until the lumbermen had abandoned it.[37] The provincial state
took the obverse approach in dealing with the pulp and paper makers.
Not only did it give them leases that left their pulpwood concessions
completely open to settlers and mining prospectors, but in 1896 the
Liberals added a clause to the Crown Timber Act which stated that
the mill owners did not have exclusive rights to *any* of the timber on
their limits, not even the pulpwood. The new provision also absolved
the government of responsibility for "the inability of any person with

whom a prior [pulpwood concession] agreement was made to obtain a sufficient supply thereof during the whole period for which the agreement is to run," and fixed at twenty-one years the maximum period for such leases. The statute thus implicitly recognized the pulp and paper industry's need for exclusive access to a perpetual supply of pulpwood but explicitly released the state from being held accountable for meeting these needs. Not only was this legislation probably the impetus behind the mills' offers to build hinterland railways in exchange for land grants and the freehold pulpwood supplies they held, but it likely explains much of the difficulty many of the mill builders experienced in securing financial backing for their projects.[38]

The degree to which the government gave the lumbermen supremacy over the pulp and paper industry was best illustrated by the "pine priority clause," which the Liberals inserted into every lease they executed with a mill developer. This term prohibited the pulpwood concessionaire from harvesting in any part of its limit in which "green merchantable pine is available for lumbering purposes or which may be considered by the Government to be pine bearing lands." The government argued that this clause was necessary to prevent pulpwood cutters from operating near stands of pine, as this might cause fires that would endanger the sawlog timber.

The government was repeatedly advised that the pine priority clause was an immense impediment for many pulp and paper makers, but it ignored this counsel. True, this restriction was inconsequential in areas such as the northern Clay Belt, where there was practically no white or red pine. It had enormous ramifications, however, in the Great Lakes–St Lawrence Forest Region within which present and future papermaking towns – such as Sturgeon Falls, Espanola, the Soo, Kenora, and Fort Frances – were located. Pine was interspersed with spruce throughout the forests in these areas, meaning the existence of the pine priority clause rendered much of the pulpwood off-limits to the paper mills. Thomas Southworth, Ontario's director of forestry, began warning the government about this problem in 1901. In reference to the mill in Sturgeon Falls, he pointed out that enforcing the pine priority clause "would practically prohibit [the mill] from operating ... till after the pine is cut ... This provision might lead to misunderstanding and I would suggest that if possible a new agreement be made with the [mill] to the effect that ... they be allowed to cut subject to [other] regulations." Not only did the Liberals reject this recommendation, they ensured that the pine priority provision also appeared in various forms in mining and settlement legislation, thereby forbidding those interests from cutting all but nominal quantities of pine from their properties. This meant that the government had reserved practically every pine tree in northern Ontario for the lumbermen's use, whereas it refused to grant the province's pulp and paper mills even exclusive access to the spruce on the concessions they leased from the state.[39]

Finally, while the government implemented the manufacturing condition on spruce primarily to support both its colonization program and the pulpwood exporters whose activities were inextricably linked to furthering settlement, it had also done so to assist the lumbermen. Faced with dwindling supplies of white and red pine, many of them had begun harvesting and processing significant quantities of large-diameter white and black spruce, trees that the pulp and paper makers also coveted. If the "embargo" on pulpwood had been intended to foster the development of the province's pulp and paper industry, it should have required that all pulpwood be made into either pulp or paper in Ontario. After all, the legislation that prohibited exporting un-processed pine was clearly aimed at assisting Ontario's lumbermen by requiring that this species be "manufactured into sawn lumber." But the manufacturing condition on pulpwood included no such narrow restriction. Instead, it declared that "spruce and other conifers" must be made "into merchantable pulp or paper, or into sawn lumber ... or other articles."[40]

The Liberals had certainly not catered to the pulp and paper makers in the decade prior to their defeat in 1905, but they had overseen the founding of this industry in northern Ontario. Their efforts had led to the establishment of three pulp and paper mills, and plans for several more plants were nearing fruition. The progress of these latter projects had been hindered by a variety of genuine difficulties, many of which – such as the encroachment of settlers onto pulpwood limits – have already been discussed. Not only did the government's decision to facilitate such homesteading incursions make investors wary of sinking their money into mill projects in the province, but the financial panic of 1903, the general recession that followed, the failure of Clergue's enterprise in the Soo in the same year, and the litigation that had plagued the mill in Sturgeon Falls in the early 1900s exacerbated this uncertainty and further delayed the mill builders' plans in Ontario.[41]

Nevertheless, the steam rising from the new pulp and paper plants that had been built in Sault Ste Marie, Espanola, and Sturgeon Falls, and the other ventures that were nearing their construction phase, provide just cause for reconsidering the standard accounts of this period. Historians have dismissed the deals the Liberals signed with the mill developers as "speculative shams," and castigated the Grits for having aided and abetted "rampant speculation" in pulpwood limits during their time in office. Granted, Ontario's pulp and paper industry was still in its earliest stages. Its few mills were small, the industry still relatively minor, and there were only architects' drawings and engineers' surveys to show for many projects.[42] But the industry had established a firm basis in northern Ontario upon which it would build in the future. Furthermore, the Grits had moved decisively to prevent a wildcat market from developing in pulpwood concessions after problems had arisen when the Sturgeon Falls Pulp Company had sold its half-finished mill and 1898 Crown concession agreement to Edward Lloyd, Limited. Fearing that the mill owners might use their pulpwood contract with the government to squeeze an unduly generous price from the prospective buyers of the plant, the Liberals had taken immediate action. Thereafter, they had begun inserting a new clause into pulpwood concession agreements that prohibited a lessee from disposing, assigning, or transferring his "franchise, rights and privileges ... under the said agreement ... to any person or persons, corporation or corporations whatever until the mills and machinery as provided in said agreement ... are completed and in running order." In other words, the Crown pulpwood contracts executed by the Liberals were worthless to speculators.[43]

Facilitating the development of the pulp and paper industry was not the Liberals' top priority in northern Ontario, however. Their main aim in this region was to further colonization, and they also placed the interests of the lumbermen and pulpwood exporters ahead of the needs of Ontario's pioneering paper makers. The upshot was a set of pulpwood concession leases that fell far short of meeting the paper makers' wants, particularly in terms of secure tenure. As an editorial in *The Globe* pointed out in 1902 regarding the industry's contracts, "the Government (not this Government alone, but any Government who may succeed them) maintains complete control over the whole situation ... It is virtually a power of confiscation which the companies leave in the hands of the Government." In this particular regard, the Liberals had set the template for relations with the pulp and paper makers which successive administrations in the province would follow for at least the next thirty years.[44]

SECTION II

"Large tracts of land are not necessary for the business of any company": The Conservatives, 1905–1919

The Conservatives under James Pliny Whitney defeated the Liberals in the 1905 provincial election, and their victory held the promise of a new age in Ontario. A major plank in the Tory platform was a commitment to correct the deficiencies which they argued had pervaded the Grit administration of Crown resources, particularly timber. This task fell to a trio of ministers of lands and forests: Frank Cochrane (1905–11), William H. Hearst (1911–14), and G. Howard Ferguson (1914–19).

This triumvirate shared a few traits. Considering they held the portfolio that dealt with the province's northern reaches, it was only natural that they represented constituencies outside the south's major urban centres. Cochrane was from Sudbury, Hearst from Sault Ste Marie, and Ferguson from rural eastern Ontario. All three would also graduate from the minister's office and go on to achieve greater glories. Robert Borden would call Cochrane to Ottawa to sit in his cabinet after the 1911 Dominion election, Hearst would succeed Whitney as premier in 1914, and Ferguson would become leader of the Ontario Tories in 1920 and serve as the province's premier for nearly one decade (1923–30).

Most importantly, Cochrane and Ferguson – and Hearst to a lesser extent – were acutely aware of the spoils that came with office and were squarely focused on keeping patronage as the engine that drove the government's administration of Crown resources. To be sure, this was dirty work. Cochrane, for example, was the Tory party organizer in northern Ontario during the early 1900s, the back-room wheeler and dealer upon whom rested the responsibility for delivering the requisite finances and votes come election time. It also meant, however, that he was dogged by allegations that he achieved these ends only because he used his position as minister to threaten resource contractors in order to influence their voting behaviour. Ferguson was renowned for the same penchant. Peter Oliver, his biographer, notes that he had begun honing his skills in this area long before he arrived in the Ontario Legislature. For Hearst's part, he was capable of manipulating the levers of power for partisan benefit, but he was certainly in neither Cochrane's nor Ferguson's league in this regard.[1]

Despite their known allegiance to the patronage system, the three Tory ministers received sage advice about how to adjust the policies of the provincial state to the growing pulp and paper industry, which was now firmly rooted in northern Ontario. In fact, this process had begun while they sat in Opposition in the early 1900s, when Whitney – their own leader – laid out a clear roadmap for prudently developing the north's paper-making resources. The first step, he insisted, was to inventory the tracts of pulpwood so that everyone knew the basic facts regarding them, and then sell them using a transparent process to prevent abuses such as those he castigated the Liberals for committing. In terms of the latter, he was most concerned about the fact that, prior to 1905, the Grits had "contracted the habit of arrogating to themselves power to do things during the recess ... and when the House met forcing their supporters to swallow whatever they did. The result of this was that the Government held capitalists who were seeking concessions in the hollow of their hands, and could compel them to yield to improper demands."[2]

Some of the best insight into improving the system came from two professional foresters. The first was Dr Judson Clark, a former forestry professor at Cornell and a consultant whom the government had hired in 1904 as Ontario's first provincial forester. Like Whitney, he urged the government to cruise all pulpwood limits prior to tendering them, which would both confirm that the mills had perpetual timber supplies and foster informed debate about concession sales. Clark also emphasized that the government had much to gain from fostering a cooperative relationship with the paper mills. If the state recognized that they required secure, long-term tenure to their cutting limits and explicit renewals in their pulpwood leases, for example, it would assist them in financing their ventures (and thereby increase the industry's stability) and provide them with an incentive to invest in forestry practices on their concessions (which would greatly benefit the government through larger future stumpage returns). Clark stressed that the Liberals' pulpwood agreements had lacked this element of secure tenure, as these contracts had authorized cabinet to set cutting regulations arbitrarily. With only nominal information about the silvics of Ontario's forests, there was a danger that the government might establish harvesting rules that were based upon political – not forestry – considerations. Among others, Bernhard Fernow, dean of the new faculty of forestry at the University of Toronto, concurred with this view. He declared that the leases the Liberals had executed with the pioneering paper makers "must be considered ... entirely immoral contract[s], if the one contracting party, the government, reserves, as it does, the right at any time to change the conditions of the contract without timely warning. The lessee then is placing himself in the condition of being in the hands and good will of the lessor – a dangerous precedent!"[3]

In early 1906, the newly elected Tory government was presented with an opportunity to act on these sensible recommendations. At that time, several concessionaires who had signed pulpwood agreements with the Liberals applied to Frank Cochrane, the new minister, for short extensions of the deadlines by which they were to have completed their projects. The request from officials representing Rainy Lake Pulp and Paper Company was typical. Since signing their lease in 1903, they had spent significant time and money surveying their property before designing their mills and power station. They had paid a crew of forest rangers both to protect their pulpwood concession from fire and cruise it to satisfy financial backers that they controlled enough fibre to sustain their project. They had also negotiated with the Canadian Northern Railway for more favourable freight rates and the construction of a spur line. "We have *bona fide* and conscientiously carried out our contract as far as the exigencies of the situation would permit," the concessionaires asserted, and "impediments in our way were not of our making." Pointing out that they had now arranged financing, they requested that the government extend their pulpwood agreement for only one year to allow them to build their mill.[4]

Cochrane's reaction indicated that fostering a cooperative relationship with the pulp and paper industry was not his first concern. Shortly after he received the appeal from Rainy Lake and another firm in the same position, he summarily cancelled the leases of all concessionaires who had not fulfilled their contractual obligations. In the process, he openly chastised previous Liberal administrations for having made these "private bargain[s]."[5]

Cochrane's autocratic move sent an unmistakable message to owners of the province's existing mills, the financial markets, and parties contemplating pulp and paper projects in Ontario. The provincial government could be obstinate in insisting that lessees strictly adhere to the terms in their contracts even if there were seemingly understandable reasons preventing them from doing so. It was naturally in the public interest to abrogate pulpwood leases if they were being retained simply for speculative purposes, but the government tacitly recognized a short time later that this was not the case with regard to the contracts it cancelled in 1906.[6] Furthermore, the lumbermen were perpetually in arrears on their accounts with the department and repeatedly breached the provisions of their licences. Nevertheless, these transgressions had never spurred the government to react in such a peremptory manner. Cochrane's sweeping cancellation of concession leases also represented the pulp and paper makers' worst nightmare, whereby a change in government signalled a sudden and dramatic shift in the provincial state's attitude towards their industry.

Cochrane concomitantly announced a new policy for selling Crown pulpwood. The minister boasted that his government would discontinue the Liberals' practice of privately negotiating deals with mill developers. Instead, the Tories would begin tendering pulpwood limits because, in his words, "public competition should be given free play in the matter of the disposition of public property." This would theoretically make the process of determining who should be awarded a pulpwood concession more objective.[7]

Despite this promise, it was immediately apparent that "tendering" Crown pulpwood was simply another guise for brokering "private bargains"; Arthur R.M. Lower aptly comments that "for some reason or other the right company ... never failed to make the successful tender."[8] The reason was the government's decision to include an awkwardly worded clause in all pulpwood tenders which specified that "the highest or any tender not necessarily accepted." While this type of provision was often de rigueur in such instances to discourage absurd bids, it emasculated the very essence of a tendering process ostensibly designed to be a public competition and left selling Crown timber as susceptible as ever to back-room deals. The government could also only impartially assess tender bids if it had thorough cruises of the tracts it was selling, as this data served as the basis for calculating the relative values of the offers submitted. The Tories could also have increased the openness of the tendering process by publishing the cruise results. Between 1905 and 1919, however, the government rarely inventoried pulpwood concessions and fanatically guarded the results from the few timber cruises it carried out. In fact, the Tories accorded these data a level of protection which states usually reserve for matters of national security. The deputy minister – and then the minister's private secretary – kept these documents under lock and key in private files and apparently removed them when the Tories lost power in 1919. One deputy minister characteristically explained to a prospective tenderer that "these [timber] estimates and reports are entirely for Departmental purposes and are never divulged." As a result, the Conservatives' approach to tendering pulpwood rendered the process a sham.[9]

The Tories also misrepresented their actions in the spring of 1906 when they contended that their decision to reoffer for lease the cancelled pulpwood concessions was intended to facilitate the establishment of pulp and paper mills in Ontario. The Tories tendered these limits, but they did so in a manner that was hardly enticing to mill developers.[10]

Most notable in this regard was the government's policy of restricting concessionaires to harvesting only those spruce trees that were greater than eight inches in diameter. This was a bewildering cutting regulation considering that surveyors had always reported that most of the pulpwood along the waterways in northern Ontario – where black spruce flourished and which were the easiest areas to cut – ranged *between* four and eight inches. Moreover, most industry and government officials included spruce down to four inches – and sometimes three – in their estimates of merchantable pulpwood. It was true that white spruce, and black spruce on upland sites, grows to diameters much larger than eight inches. However, in an era when harvesting operations depended on river driving, the spruce that grew in valleys and lowlands was critical to a mill's wood supply. With regard to the inapplicability of this diameter limit to black spruce, E.J. Zavitz, a veteran forester with the Ontario government, commented that "this species often attains its maturity when six to eight inches in diameter and cutting operators should take everything of commercial value."[11]

Likewise, the eight-inch-diameter limit on spruce pulpwood was also surprising because there were no grounds for implementing it as a silvicultural tool. Had this diameter limit been intended as a forestry policy, it should have applied to all the timber limits – pulpwood *and* *sawlog* – which Cochrane sold at this time. In fact, there were far more compelling reasons for placing a relatively high diameter limit on pine instead of spruce. The province's pulpwood forests – except in a few areas – had yet to be tapped, whereas the lumbermen were gravely concerned over their dwindling supply of pine sawlogs. Throughout

Figure 6. Common Spruce Forest: The pulp and paper industry sought access to the huge swathes of pure black spruce that blanketed much of northern Ontario, especially in the boreal forest. This photograph illustrates the typically small diameter but densely packed stands on the northern Clay Belt. The Tories' decision to set diameter limits as wide as ten inches (at breast height) on this timber between 1905 and 1919, however, rendered much of it off-limits to the companies that leased these tracts of forest. The result was an increased demand for settlers' wood, much as the Conservatives had intended (University of Toronto Archives, A1972–0025_19P_1).

1906 and 1907, however, Cochrane tendered numerous large blocks of pine timber across the province without including any diameter limit in the terms of sale.[12]

While it remains a mystery how Cochrane had decided that this cutting restriction was appropriate for the few pulpwood limits he would tender in light of the fact that he had no timber cruise data for any of them, there is no doubt that he did so to benefit the government's colonization program. By significantly decreasing the quantity of timber a paper maker could potentially harvest from its pulpwood concession, the state had drastically increased the concessionaire's need for settlers' spruce.

What was to the benefit of the hinterland's pioneers, however, was to the grave detriment of its pulp and paper makers. On a practical level, the measure deprived prospective mill developers of much of their most accessible pulpwood and thereby greatly increased their operating costs. It also diminished the potential value of the leases to these concessions as collateral to finance the mills' capital costs. The few documents that survive from this period indicate the profound difficulties this curious provision caused pulp and paper makers, especially in raising funds for their ventures.[13]

Another aspect of Cochrane's retendering of the pulpwood concessions in 1906 was not conducive to establishing new mills in Ontario. Pulp and paper enterprises also required a guaranteed supply of cheap and plentiful water power. As the Crown's lawyer subsequently admitted before a royal commission, a "pulp area is no good unless you have water power."[14] All the parties to whom the Liberals had granted pulpwood concessions prior to 1905 already owned, leased, or were promised the privilege of developing cascades on rivers near or within their limits. But Cochrane's tender in 1906 mentioned nothing about either leasing power sites or a commitment by the government to arrange for them. The Opposition Liberals attacked the Tories for their policy and included in their platform for the 1908 provincial election a promise to correct this deficiency.[15]

In the end, little came of the Tories' sale of pulpwood concessions in 1906. They rejected bids from parties eager to build mills in Ontario for reasons they did not disclose, and this tender produced only two concession agreements. Neither of these led directly to even one ton being added to the capacity of Ontario's pulp and paper industry.[16]

These events set the tone for the Tories' fifteen years in office. During this time, they were oblivious to nearly all the advice they received regarding how to locate effectively the pulp and paper industry within a comprehensive development policy for the hinterland. Instead, the Conservatives, like the Liberals before them, made colonization their top priority in the north even though it was apparent that commercial wheat farming was a non-starter there. The Tories' strict adherence to the patronage system of dispensing Crown resources also drove them to show the province's lumbermen and pulpwood exporters remarkable favouritism, preferential treatment upon which a subsequent royal commission commented at length.[17]

In fact, new considerations drove the Conservatives to toe a much tougher line than the Liberals in dealing with the pulp and paper makers. Those involved in this industry during the Grits' reign had enjoyed close ties to the government and had been able to exploit these connections to their advantage. But after 1905, the industry became dominated by a new strain of entrepreneur who was generally disconnected from the government, which treated him accordingly. In addition, the Tories seemed intent upon demonstrating that they – not the pulp and paper makers – controlled the allocation of Crown resources, almost as if they had learned from the Liberals' mistakes in terms of being too closely identified with these modern industrialists. Finally, and perhaps most importantly, even though it will be seen that both the pulp and paper industry and the volume of pulpwood being exported from the province expanded dramatically during this era, concomitantly the hinterland's population – specifically those who were homesteading – grew exponentially; by the end of the Tories' decade and a half in office over 250,000 persons were living in northern Ontario. They produced an ever-greater supply of spruce, and being unresponsive to the industry's requests for self-sufficiency in terms of fibre supply was one of the critical means the state employed to generate a market for the settlers' timber. Although the pulp and paper makers were distressed by the Tories' lack of sympathy for and understanding of their enterprise, the Conservatives cared little. As Premier James P. Whitney stridently declared in response to one mill's pulpwood solicitation, "large tracts of land are not necessary for the business of any company."[18]

All the while, northern Ontario was becoming an increasingly attractive place in which to build a pulp and paper mill. The recession that lingered through the early part of the twentieth century and the failure of Clergue's enterprise in the Soo in 1903 undeniably undermined financiers' interest in investing in new ventures. But this cloud of bearishness soon lifted, and establishing or operating newsprint plants in the province soon came into favour again. In addition to the natural advantages accruing from establishing a mill in the province, northern Ontario's allure strengthened as a result of the continued rise in the demand for newsprint (especially in the Midwestern United States), growing concerns over the quantity of pulpwood available to American producers, and the elimination of American tariffs on newsprint over the course of 1911–13.

The upshot was an extraordinary paradox. The production of newsprint in Ontario literally exploded during the Conservatives' reign. The province had boasted roughly 100 tons of daily capacity in the wake of the 1905 provincial election. Fifteen years later Ontario was the newsprint capital of Canada. Its mills could produce more than 1,200 tons each day, or nearly half the Dominion's capacity. Practically all this growth had preceded the rampant inflation and newsprint scarcity that marked the 1917–20 period, indicating that Ontario's newsprint industry had not expanded in response to these exceptional circumstances. Rather, this phenomenon was a result of the competitive advantages accruing from operating a mill in the province, something to which the consistently large profit margins of the province's leading paper makers attested.

Nevertheless, the Conservatives played but a tangential role in this remarkable industrial expansion. They provided only a few mill developers with leases to either pulpwood concessions or power sites, and they often erected hurdles that impeded the progress of Ontario's newsprint makers. In fact, most of the growth in northern Ontario's newsprint capacity between 1905 and 1919 came either from mills which were already in existence when the Tories won power and grew during their stay in office, or operations whose expansion plans the Conservatives refused to assist in a significant way.[19] Of the six new mills constructed in the province during this period, the government saw fit to give only three of them Crown pulpwood concessions.[20]

The following two chapters tell the story of how the Conservatives handled the pulp and paper industry between 1905 and 1919, and illustrate the pattern of continuity and change in terms of the state's approach to it. Chapter 3 covers mill developments in northwestern Ontario and the "Spanish River" territory. There, the lumber industry had long dominated, and the Tories continued, just as the Liberals had before them, to favour its interests – and the interests of a few others – over the paper makers'. At the same time, the Conservatives broke new ground in dealing with both planned and existing pulp and paper enterprises by denying them the Crown pulpwood supplies they sought in an effort to stimulate the market for settlers' spruce. Chapter 4 reinforces this point in its analysis of mill projects between 1905 and 1919 in the Thunder Bay District and on the northern Clay Belt. The Tories proved especially adroit at taking this approach in the former region, whereby they were able to bob and weave their way around a series of prospective mill developers who persistently lobbied for the privilege of harvesting some of Canada's richest and most advantageously located stands of spruce. At the same time, the Tories assisted in both regions the pulpwood exporters, whose operations had long enjoyed tight patronage connections and been recognized as essential to sustaining the colonization effort. In fact, the Conservatives reached out to the exporters to such a degree during these years that it became difficult to tell if the government's actions were designed primarily to facilitate their business or settlement.

3 "We have been most lenient in allowing the company to run on"

Prior to 1905 the Liberals had awarded pulp and paper makers pulp-wood concessions and/or water powers in northwestern Ontario and the "Spanish River" territory (i.e., Sault Ste Marie, Espanola, and Sturgeon Falls), and industrialists had erected mills in the latter region and prepared to do so in the former. Nevertheless, the Grits had demonstrated that their priority in terms of northern development in these areas was to protect the lumbermen's interests against intrusion by the paper makers. This was only natural considering the sawmillers had represented the major manufacturing industry in these areas for some time and enjoyed tight connections to the government.

During the Conservatives' fifteen years in office, they adopted this approach but added their own twist to it, namely by playing what can only be described as "hard ball" with the pulp and paper makers. The Tory government denied practically every request they made of it, and dictated that they would gain access to only a few Crown resources and even then under very strict terms. In pursuing this course, the provincial state demonstrated a deeper commitment than ever before to aiding the lumbermen (and a few other groups interested in exploiting the north's bounty) and supporting the long-standing settlement agenda. The Tories did so even though bureaucrats within the department argued that the rapidly changing nature of the forest industry made it prudent to recognize the validity of the requests the pulp and paper makers were making of the government. These civil servants thus recommended, among other things, effecting a fundamental shift in policy, including reversing the state's priorities by subordinating the lumbermen's interests to the paper makers' in certain instances. But the Conservatives would have none of it, instead pursuing an approach to allocating Crown resources – particularly timber – that was crucial to the lumber industry's transformation in areas such as the Rainy River and Kenora Districts and the region above Georgian Bay.

The Tories' reluctance to assist the paper makers in northwestern Ontario and the Spanish River territory between 1905 and 1919 did not prevent the industrialists in these areas from contributing in a major way to the dramatic growth in Ontario's – and Canada's – newsprint capacity. This type of corporate industry also came with its seamier side, however. Entrepreneurs who believed in the efficacy of establishing and expanding paper mills in northern Ontario were not about to abandon their projects because the government did not fully support their plans; there was always the hope that the next election would bring to power a more sympathetic regime. Consequently, when the Tories denied them access to Crown timber, they found alternative supplies. Most often they bought spruce from settlers, just as the government had intended. The problem which arose, however, was that the paper firms' executives – usually at the insistence of the financial houses which backed their securities – worked to create the impression before the investing public that each mill controlled a cornucopia of pulpwood. Thus began the deception regarding pulp and paper operations in northern Ontario and the nature of their fibre supplies. While these were certainly not the ideal means of sustaining paper mills, until the government warmed to these enterprises the paper makers must have rationalized that they would have to suffice.

Soon after the Tories were sworn into office in 1905, E.W. Backus learned first-hand that the new regime was disinclined to facilitate his plans to develop northwestern Ontario's power and timber resources. Intent upon constructing pulp and paper mills in both Fort Frances and International Falls, Minnesota, he had secured a lease from the Liberals to the water power on the Canadian side of the Rainy River just before the election of 1905. The Grits had also promised to grant him the privilege of harvesting the pulpwood on the Rainy Lake watershed. Unfortunately for Backus, the Tories refused to honour their predecessors' pledge regarding the timber limit earmarked for him; it was conspicuously absent from the slate of pulpwood concessions that Frank Cochrane, the minister, tendered in 1906.

And so began the Tories' rough treatment of Backus. Soon thereafter, Cochrane was advised to sell another nearby tract in a manner that would facilitate the development of Backus's pulp and paper mill. In

Map 4. Timber Limits in Northwestern Ontario, 1905–1919

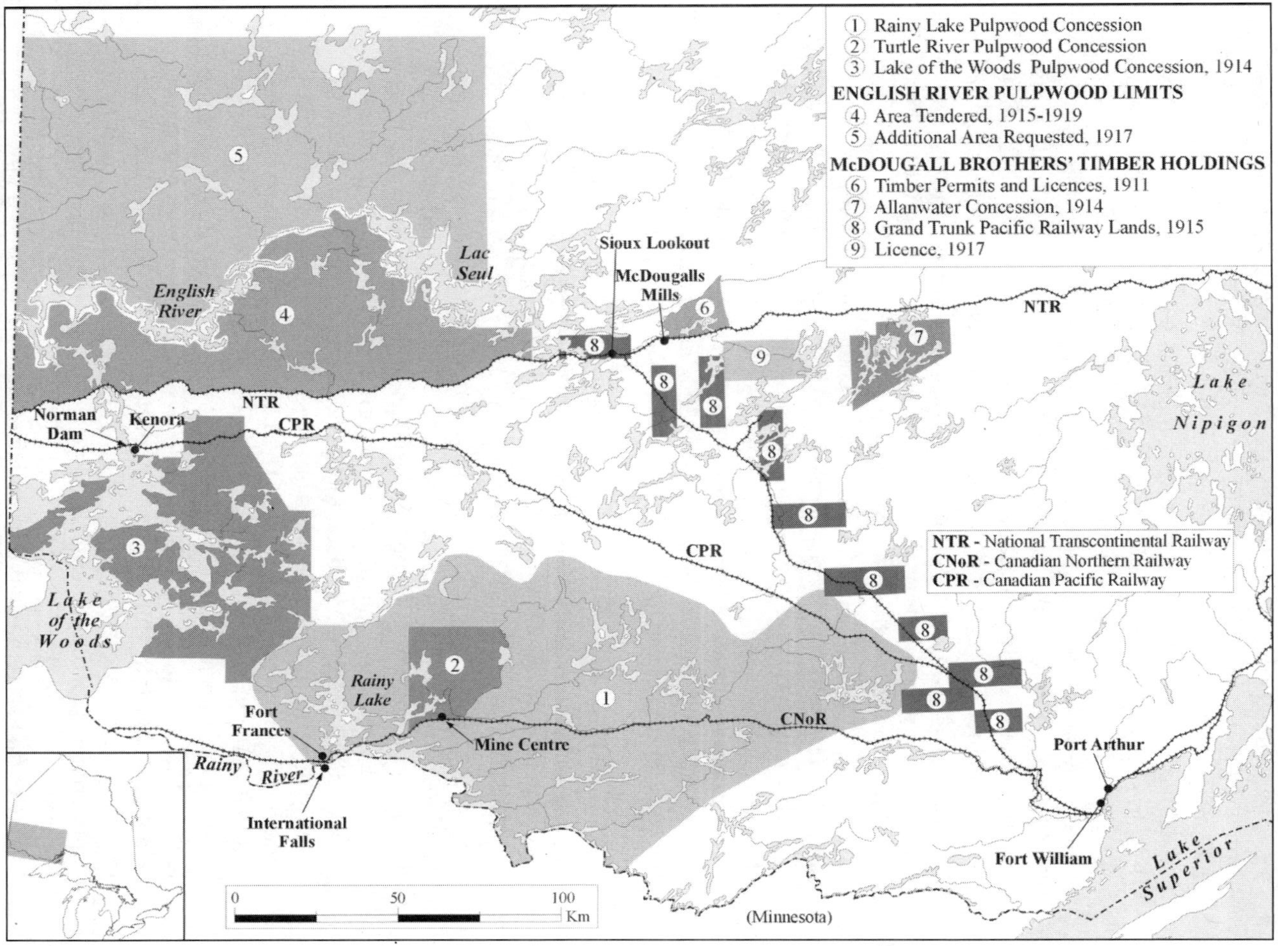

① Rainy Lake Pulpwood Concession
② Turtle River Pulpwood Concession
③ Lake of the Woods Pulpwood Concession, 1914

ENGLISH RIVER PULPWOOD LIMITS
④ Area Tendered, 1915–1919
⑤ Additional Area Requested, 1917

McDOUGALL BROTHERS' TIMBER HOLDINGS
⑥ Timber Permits and Licences, 1911
⑦ Allanwater Concession, 1914
⑧ Grand Trunk Pacific Railway Lands, 1915
⑨ Licence, 1917

NTR - National Transcontinental Railway
CNoR - Canadian Northern Railway
CPR - Canadian Pacific Railway

Lake Nipigon

Lake Superior

Port Arthur

Fort William

(Minnesota)

Sioux Lookout

McDougalls Mills

Lac Seul

English River

Norman Dam

Kenora

Lake of the Woods

Rainy River

Fort Frances

International Falls

Rainy Lake

Mine Centre

NTR

CNoR

CPR

Km

0   50   100

1906, the minister offered for tender the Turtle River pulpwood concession a short distance northeast of Fort Frances but provided no explanation for his decision to declare none of the bids "satisfactory" (Map 4).
Sustained pressure to sell this tract compelled Cochrane in the fall of
1907 to seek advice on the matter from Aubrey White, his deputy minister. The latter pointed out that valuable pine timber was scattered
among the pulpwood on the concession and that it would be best to
"cut [the pine] at the same time as the pulpwood so as to get full value
for the Province." But the danger inherent in such a scenario, he cau-
tioned Cochrane, was that it "would not be expedient to offer the pine
timber separate from the pulp timber, as it would be very inconvenient
and give rise to all kinds of trouble and misunderstanding if two owners were operating in the same territory for different timber at the same
time, or using the same roads, dumps and creeks and driving the same
streams." It would thus be best to have a pulp and paper maker harvest
both the pulpwood and sawlogs at the same time, and sell the latter to
the local lumbermen.[1]

But Cochrane ignored White's counsel when he retendered the Turtle
River pulpwood concession in October 1907 and instead ensured that
the tract landed in the hands of a local partisan lumberman. Cochrane
drew up terms of sale that included a nine-inch-diameter limit (which
was much larger than most of the tract's pulpwood),[2] demanded the
lodging of an unusually large deposit despite the period's recession,
and called for the construction of at least a 20-ton pulp and paper mill
costing $100,000. Although Backus had already taken steps to begin ex-
ploiting his water powers in Fort Frances and was seemingly ideally
positioned to win the bidding, Cochrane instead awarded the tract to
the lumber company in Mine Centre (Map 4). It was owned and operated by J.T. Horne, one of northwestern Ontario's most prominent
Conservatives. Horne had been lobbying Cochrane since mid-1907 for
a new timber limit to support his business, which consisted of turning
pine into railway ties and piling. The contract Cochrane gave Horne
stated that the firm could disregard the obligation to construct the new
paper plant with impunity, as this would only cause Mine Centre to
lose its right to cut the limit's pulpwood and not the pine. Moreover,
while licences to cut Crown pine timber had heretofore been limited to
relatively small tracts and terms of only a few years (always requiring
annual renewals), the Tories gave Mine Centre a twenty-one-year lease
to the sawlogs on the 450-square-mile Turtle River concession. Finally,
Mine Centre had requested that, if it ever decided to build a newsprint

mill, the government commit to providing it with enough pulpwood to sustain it for the duration of its agreement. The Tories agreed to do so, even though the Crown Timber Act prohibited the government from making such pledges and the Tories never provided such a guarantee to any of the province's bona fide newsprint makers.[3]

The upshot of this deal was a poignant example of the quid pro quo deals that were an integral part of the patronage system of dispensing Crown timber in Ontario. Not only did Mine Centre never construct a pulp and paper mill, in 1909 it "flipped" the Turtle River pulpwood concession to McKenzie, Mann and Company for $250,000 after paying the government a bonus of merely $32,000 for it two years earlier. Horne returned the favour just before the 1908 provincial election when he gerrymandered the boundaries of the ridings in northwestern Ontario, whose recent growth had required the number of local seats to be increased from two to four. Cochrane relied on Horne's political acumen in drawing these borders, and the latter proved his worth when all the new ridings returned Conservatives. In the end, neither Backus nor any other newsprint mill developer gained access to the pulpwood on the Turtle River concession for nearly two decades, even though lumbering operations there were suspended in 1915.[4]

Even without the Tories' help, Backus proceeded with his plan to develop the water powers and timber resources in northern Ontario and Minnesota. He incorporated a Canadian holding company, the Ontario and Minnesota Power Company, under which he organized the firms he created in the province. His main aim was to become a major newsprint producer for the Midwestern American market, and he realized the first stage in this plan in 1910 when his 200-ton newsprint mill in International Falls, Minnesota, began production. *Pulp and Paper Magazine of Canada* heralded this development, recognizing the natural market – "the middle states from Denver to Detroit" – it would serve.[5] Backus continued to lobby the Tories for access to the Rainy Lake pulpwood concession he had been denied as a result of the 1905 election, and he seemed to draw nearer his goal in 1911 when they agreed to tender the limit. They did so, however, with an eight-inch-diameter limit, a provision that *Pulp and Paper Magazine of Canada* described as "severe," and they rejected all the offers for the timber on the grounds that none of them was "satisfactory."[6] Nevertheless, Backus made history in 1914 when he completed his newsprint mill in Fort Frances, which was the first Canadian facility of its kind between Sault Ste Marie and the Rockies. It was also a noteworthy achievement because it was, as the Ontario government repeatedly reminded him, "not constructed as a result of receiving a ... Crown licence area." This compelled Backus's operation in Fort Frances to rely on pulpwood purchased from settlers in northwestern Ontario and Manitoba, cut from licences to the small, local "Indian reserves" and imported from his limits in Minnesota.[7]

While this was the reality, Backus presented a very different picture to the public, specifically to potential investors in his project. Whether it was his own idea or that of Peabody, Houghteling and Company, the firm which had agreed to underwrite the securities to pay for his industrial developments at Fort Frances-International Falls, the circular which publicized the sale of these instruments depicted his operations as being the locus of a luxuriant quantity of pulpwood, all of which conveniently drained to his paper mills (Map 5). The implication was clearly that this fibre was at his beck and call. Although Backus controlled a large volume of timberland in northern Minnesota, that which was found across the state's northern border was – as the Tories had continually reminded him – certainly not at his disposal.

Backus was also intent on erecting a newsprint mill in Kenora, but there, too, the local lumbermen threw a wrench into his plans. By 1913, he had purchased the Norman Dam at the outlet of Lake of the Woods, a site at which he would be able to generate hydroelectricity. He had also forged political alliances with Harold A.C. Machin, the Conservative MPP for Kenora-Rainy River, and the Kenora Town Council and Board of Trade. Supported by these backers, Backus met with William H. Hearst, the minister, in Toronto in May 1913 and convinced him to tender the timber Backus sought, namely the 1,860-square-mile Lake of the Woods concession (Map 4). But once the local lumbermen got wind of this news, they vehemently protested the sale on the grounds that they would lose access to the sawlogs that were scattered amid the pulpwood throughout the limit. At one point during their hastily called meeting with Hearst they presented such onerous demands that the minister was spurred to suggest to the gathering that the people of Kenora "do not want a pulp mill, as no mill could operate under the terms you propose."

When the dust finally settled, the Tories had appeased the lumbermen. After the tender closed, the Conservatives informed Backus that they were keeping his deposit and that he would lose it if he did not acquiesce to the terms they insisted be included in his lease. After over one year of negotiations, he finally caved. His contract for the concession obliged

Map 5. The Impression of Pulpwood Aplenty (Hagley Museum and Library, Item ID 08085043).

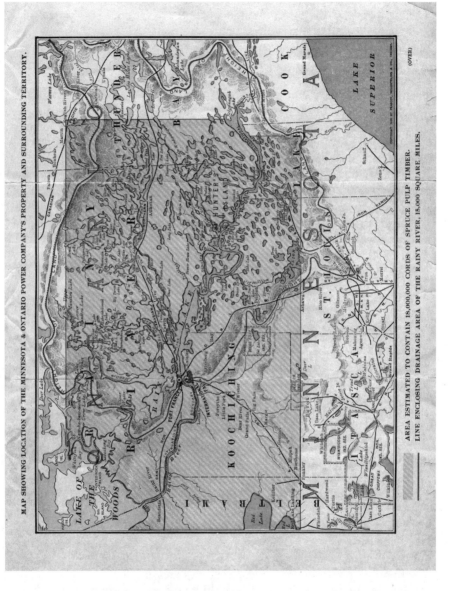

MAP SHOWING LOCATION OF THE MINNESOTA & ONTARIO POWER COMPANY'S PROPERTY AND SURROUNDING TERRITORY.

AREA ESTIMATED TO CONTAIN 18,000,000 CORDS OF SPRUCE PULP TIMBER.

LINE ENCLOSING DRAINAGE AREA OF THE RAINY RIVER, 15,000 SQUARE MILES.

(OVER)

him to construct a sizeable pulp and paper mill but provided the local lumbermen with unprecedented ease of access to his limit. His lease reserved all the pine on the concession for them and authorized them to cut any pulpwood they encountered in their operations. This clause had enormous ramifications because pine was scattered throughout the concession and the government was not obliged to compensate Backus for pulpwood he lost to the sawmillers as a result of this provision. Moreover, the contract reserved all the poplar on the limit for the local barrel-making firm and authorized it to cut this timber along with the pulpwood it encountered in the course of its operations. In no uncertain terms, the lumbermen enjoyed much greater privileges on the Lake of the Woods pulpwood concession than Backus, who was the concessionaire![8]

These aspects of Backus's agreement diminished its value as collateral, and so did his cruisers' latest reports. Even before the tender, his woodsmen had carried out cursory examinations that indicated that the Lake of the Woods limit was extremely poor in terms of spruce. Their thorough investigations during the First World War confirmed that it contained only about 600,000 cords of spruce (just over ½ cord per acre), enough to supply the mill called for under his new lease for just seven years.[9]

Backus was still determined to build a newsprint mill in Kenora, but he ran into problems generating sufficient power to supply this project. Kenora is situated at the foot of Lake of the Woods, which had two major outlets: the Norman Dam, which Backus already owned and which did not have a generating station, and the Town of Kenora's hydroelectric plant, which was too small to power Backus's proposed mill. In 1909 Canada and the United States had delegated adjudication of matters concerning boundary waters to the International Joint Commission (IJC). This included responsibility for regulating the level of the Lake of the Woods. In 1912, the IJC had begun an exhaustive study of this waterway to determine, among other things, the optimal level at which it should be maintained. The IJC had also informed Backus that it would likely use his Norman Dam to regulate the level of the Lake of the Woods and advised him to refrain from proceeding with his Kenora mill project, arguing that the IJC's plans could completely vitiate use of his dam for his purposes. With the Ontario government recognizing the validity of Backus's position in this instance, the issue remained in abeyance until the IJC had completed its five-year investigation (1912–17).[10]

Kenora's proximity to the Midwestern states and the presence of many other nearby power sites which could be developed continued to focus interest on this area's potential for newsprint production, but the Tories proved reluctant to facilitate such developments. Over the course of 1915–19, Frank Anson, president of a newsprint mill in northeastern Ontario (about which more will be said later), sought to establish a branch plant in Kenora. His initial interest lay in securing a lease to the pulp-wood on a 3,000-square-mile tract south of the English River, but when Howard Ferguson, the minister, tendered it in 1915, the government re-jected all the bids without explanation.[11] Anson then investigated the tract more closely and discovered that it averaged barely one cord of spruce per acre. As a result, when he knocked on Ferguson's door two years later with another proposal to build a mill in Kenora, he asked for the minister to tender a second tract consisting of 7,000 square miles north of the English River (Map 4). In response, Carroll C. Hele, Ferguson's private secretary, acknowledged that the government's own data indi-cated that the tract south of the English River was spruce deficient, but he insisted that the government could not tender the larger tract north of the river until it had been thoroughly cruised; this marked only the second time the Tories had insisted that such an inventory precede the sale of a pulpwood concession.[12] The Tories never carried out the cruise, and it took Ferguson nearly two years to reject Anson's proposal.[13]

The Tories' unwillingness to facilitate pulp and paper developments in northwestern Ontario between 1905 and 1919 contrasted sharply with their eagerness to meet the needs of the region's lumbermen. In addition to the examples already cited regarding the Mine Centre Lumber Company and the sawmillers in Kenora, the Conservatives im-mediately granted nearly every one of the local lumbermen's requests, often bending rules to do so. The legendary James A. Mathieu was par-ticularly adept at capitalizing on this preferential treatment. As *the* Tory patronage broker in the Rainy River area as well as its MPP for all but one term between 1911 and 1929, he openly admitted that his "political connections" were the secret to his successful lumber business.[14] On sev-eral occasions during the 1905–19 period, the government privately granted him (instead of publicly tendering) some of the finest pine stands in the province, transgressions of the law that enabled Mathieu to acquire vast quantities of timber at a fraction of their market value.[15]

The McDougall brothers – Alexander and Samuel – were equally adroit at drinking from this same patronage cup. Initially, they plied their pedigree to garner the timber limits they sought in dealing with the provincial government. As offspring of John Lorn McDougall (Junior), they benefited from the immensely important role their father had played in national politics during the late 1800s and early 1900s. He had served as a Liberal MP and MPP from the Ottawa Valley for roughly the first decade following Confederation, but it was after 1878 that he had etched his indelible mark on the country. In that year, Alexander Mackenzie – McDougall's dear friend and the prime minister – appointed him Canada's first independent auditor general, a title he would hold for the next twenty-seven years. Over this period, McDougall tenaciously endeavoured to bring "fiscal probity" to Ottawa's finances, reviewing practically every dollar in funds the national government disbursed. This brought him into conflict with Tories and Grits alike, but both parties saw fit to increase his salary and expand the size of his staff. This approach by the politicos no doubt reflected in large part their respect for McDougall's work, but also their realization that his position had given him unparalleled knowledge of each party's dirty laundry. At the time of his death in 1909, McDougall was a fixture in the country's inner circle of influence.[16]

Alexander, and Samuel to a lesser extent, learned early on how to exploit their father's connections to further their own business interests. To be sure, Alexander brought many skills and personal contacts of his own to the table. He had graduated from the University of Toronto in 1899 and had been awarded the gold medal for his standing in mathematics. During his time at the school, his classmates had included Arthur Meighen and George S. Henry, respectively the future prime minister and Ontario premier. After engaging in graduate work at Cornell, McDougall left to begin his career as an engineer, his first assignments including the bridge over the St Lawrence River at Quebec City and a stint with the Mexican Light and Power Company. He then returned to Canada, where he was employed for three years with the Public Works Department.[17]

Around 1906, Alexander McDougall left the civil service and embarked on what would end up being a two-decade involvement in contracting, primarily in the timber industry. His first forays entailed building railways. Initially, he and his brother Samuel laid a small section of the National Transcontinental Railway. Then the two of them joined forces with a number of associates, including C.J. Booth (the scion of J.R. Booth, Canada's lumbering patriarch), to form the Eastern Construction Company, and mining magnate M.J. O'Brien to form O'Brien, Fowler and McDougall Brothers. These firms built roughly one-third of the National Transcontinental–Grand Trunk Pacific Railway through northern Ontario in the early 1900s, and in the process, the

McDougalls rose to become lumber barons in the still-remote north-western section of the province. By 1910, they had established a town – and unabashedly named it McDougalls Mills – slightly east of Sioux Lookout, where they operated a sawmill and employed roughly 500 men in their woods operations in the years leading up to the First World War (Map 4).[18]

By this time, the McDougalls had demonstrated their ability to curry favour with the provincial government when it came to securing timber supplies. Although they always had more than ample wood to sustain their enterprise, it was never enough for them because of their constant financial difficulties. Beginning in 1907, for instance, the provincial Tories had given the McDougalls annual permits to harvest in the vicinity of the section of the railway they were building. Then in 1911, the Ontario government granted them timber licences covering an area that totalled 66 square miles, which was more than sufficient to provide them with trees for the foreseeable future.[19] A few years later, however, they asked for a 400-square-mile tract near Allanwater (just east of McDougalls Mills) and offered to build a tie-processing plant if the Tories granted their request even though they had yet to cut on their original timber licences (Map 4). Despite being in the midst of a bitter provincial election, and without insisting upon a cruise of the tract before tendering it (local Crown timber agents were shocked several years later to learn that the government had sold it and that they were responsible for supervising activities on it), the minister found the time to arrange the sale and accept the McDougalls' bid of five cents. He also gave them a remarkably favourable lease, one that included a twenty-one-year term and freedom not to build the tie-making plant until "market conditions justifie[d] erection of such plant."[20]

Even this largesse did not satisfy the McDougalls. In 1915, they used their contacts in Ottawa to secure a lease to cut the timber on the roughly 1,000 square miles between Fort William and Sioux Lookout that the Ontario government had granted the Grand Trunk Pacific Railway as a subsidy in 1904 (Map 4).[21] Although this represented a practically inexhaustible volume of wood for the McDougalls, in the fall of 1916 they applied to the Ontario government for another tract of Crown forest – nearly 155 square miles worth – just outside Sioux Lookout. They argued that they urgently needed it to ensure the continued operation of their small sawmill in McDougalls Mills because they had only a few years worth of timber remaining on their existing licences and concessions. Both the department's most senior official in Toronto and its best-informed field officer scoffed at the McDougalls' latest application. Albert Grigg, the deputy minister, was astounded by it in light of the large quantity of timber with which the Ontario government had already supplied the brothers (to say nothing of their enormous timber lease with Ottawa) and the minimal amount of cutting they had done. Likewise, William Magrach, the local Crown timber agent, had investigated the area for which the McDougalls had most recently applied and concluded that it was neither a railway tie nor sawlog proposition, as there was spruce there "sufficient to make a good Pulp Concession." Departmental officials thus resoundingly rejected the McDougalls' request to sell this tract. But Ferguson, the minister, intervened in the matter after Samuel McDougall paid him a visit and insisted that the department advertise the tract for sale without first cruising it (Map 4). Not only were the McDougalls again the sole tenderers for the timber, they would not cut one stick from either it or the Allanwater concession they had secured in 1914 for the better part of the next decade.[22]

It was not as if Ferguson should have felt obliged to reward the McDougalls. For years, they had been obdurate in their dealings with the department, repeatedly refusing to pay their annual licensing fees and the dues they owed for the small quantity of timber they cut from their original licences. Despite a deplorable record, the Ontario government had literally given them over 600 square miles of Crown limits – most of which contained large quantities of pulpwood that the McDougalls were not harvesting at this time – without compelling them to develop any industry.[23]

The upshot was an anomalous situation. The same provincial government had denied Backus's newsprint mill in Fort Frances the privilege of cutting even one square inch of Crown woodlands despite the fact that he had invested several million dollars in the enterprise. Likewise, the Tories had refused to lease the English River pulpwood concession to genuine paper makers who had sought to use it to support a new paper mill in Kenora.

The Conservatives' victory in 1905 signalled the beginning of a difficult period for the three pulp and paper mills – at Sault Ste Marie, Sturgeon Falls, and Espanola – which had been built in Ontario under the Liberals. Over the next five years, these enterprises floundered, as they were hindered by weak management and by the recession of 1907. Clergue's Sault Ste Marie Pulp and Paper Company, for example, only operated its groundwood mill and did not rebuild its paper-making facility that had burned down in the early 1900s.

This triad of mills was set on the road to recovery between 1910 and 1913 largely through the efforts of George H. Mead. A native of Dayton, Ohio, Mead had graduated in chemical engineering from the Massachusetts Institute of Technology in 1900. Five years later he had gone to work for the company that bore his family name and whose mills in Chillicothe, Ohio, manufactured fine paper. While the firm had been insolvent when Mead had arrived, by 1910 his leadership had turned it into one of the dominant producers in its field in the United States. Mead's uncle, Harry Talbott, was the company's president, and it was through Talbott that the Ohio-based paper maker became involved in Canada. Talbott's contract-engineering firm had built Clergue's steel plant at the Soo in the late 1890s as well as 150 miles of Clergue's Algoma Central and Hudson Bay Railway (ACR) shortly thereafter. Roughly one decade later, the interests who gained control over Clergue's pulp mill after his industrial empire in the Soo had gone under had asked Talbott for advice regarding the plant, and Talbott had directed Mead to investigate.[24]

This set Mead on the path to building what would soon become Canada's largest newsprint manufacturer. Over the course of 1910–11, he was instrumental in reorganizing Clergue's pulp mill in Sault Ste Marie, acting as its vice-president with Talbott as its president. Together, they revived the enterprise, which they renamed Lake Superior Paper Company. Around the same time, Dominion Bond Company acquired Spanish River Pulp and Paper Company in Espanola and completed its 200-ton newsprint mill, and purchased the assets of the plant in Sturgeon Falls. In 1913, these three enterprises were consolidated when Spanish River acquired control over Mead's mill in the Soo, and Mead was appointed head of the amalgamated concern.[25]

Under the new banner of Spanish River Pulp and Paper Mills, Mead drove to strengthen the company's position in the North American newsprint industry. The potential was tremendous, for the mills Mead now controlled had been stagnating for years, and nearby there were large additional stores of pulpwood and water powers that were available for lease. And like most of Ontario's paper makers, Mead's mills, compared with most of North America's newsprint producers, were ideally situated to sell in the Midwestern states. They enjoyed lower shipping costs because they were close to the market and were located either very near or on the Great Lakes. This allowed them to ship by boat instead of rail, further lowering the expense involved in delivering their product to customers. As *Pulp and Paper Magazine of Canada* acknowledged, Spanish River had been in the vanguard of "the invasion of the Chicago newsprint market" for this reason.[26]

Mead's plans for fortifying his company involved gaining the Ontario government's cooperation, but the Tories showed little interest in realizing this aim. His mills in the Soo, Sturgeon Falls, and Espanola had already mortgaged their leases to their pulpwood concessions and water powers to finance their operations, and because these contracts were considered poor collateral or had been pledged to raise additional funds, all three plants had also mortgaged their mill properties (at the same time as their Crown leases). This left them with no assets to offer as security against which they could raise further funds. All three mills also faced challenges with regard to either their supply of pulpwood or power, and in some instances both, and the provincial government controlled the means by which these issues could be addressed.

Mead initially turned to the timber issues facing the mill in Sault Ste Marie, but circumstances dictated that he first deal with a private interest, one that respected the pre-eminence pulp and paper makers placed on secure tenure to their raw materials. Clergue's plan for overcoming the pulpwood-deficient nature of the Crown pulpwood concession he had been granted in 1894 was to build a railway from the Soo over the height of land to tap the spruce-rich boreal forest. The Ontario government had agreed to subsidize the project with 1,500,000 acres in land grants, tracts that would be especially valuable because the mill would own them outright. The Tories had already begun allotting the ACR blocks of townships below the height of land, and all of them formed integral parts of the mill's original Crown pulpwood concession (Map 6). Just before Mead purchased the plant in 1911, however, the railway had been severed from Clergue's other industries, and it – as a separate corporate entity – thereby controlled the land grants. The mill had now lost both its cutting privileges on the land grants the government had already given the ACR and the territory that the government still owed the ACR in spruce-rich territory north of the height of land. Mead immediately opened negotiations with the railway to rectify this situation and quickly sealed a favourable deal. While the government limited Crown pulpwood leases to twenty-one years, Mead's contract with the ACR granted his firm cutting privileges for ninety-nine years on the lands the railway had already been granted and set stumpage rates for periods of ten years. Because the government still owed the railway significant additional areas, Mead presciently insisted that when the ACR received this territory it give the mill in the Soo "the first right of refusal to cut the pulpwood on the said lands on as favorable terms as it is prepared to accept from any other person, firm or corporation."[27]

Map 6. Significant Timber and Water Powers in the Spanish River Territory, 1905–1919

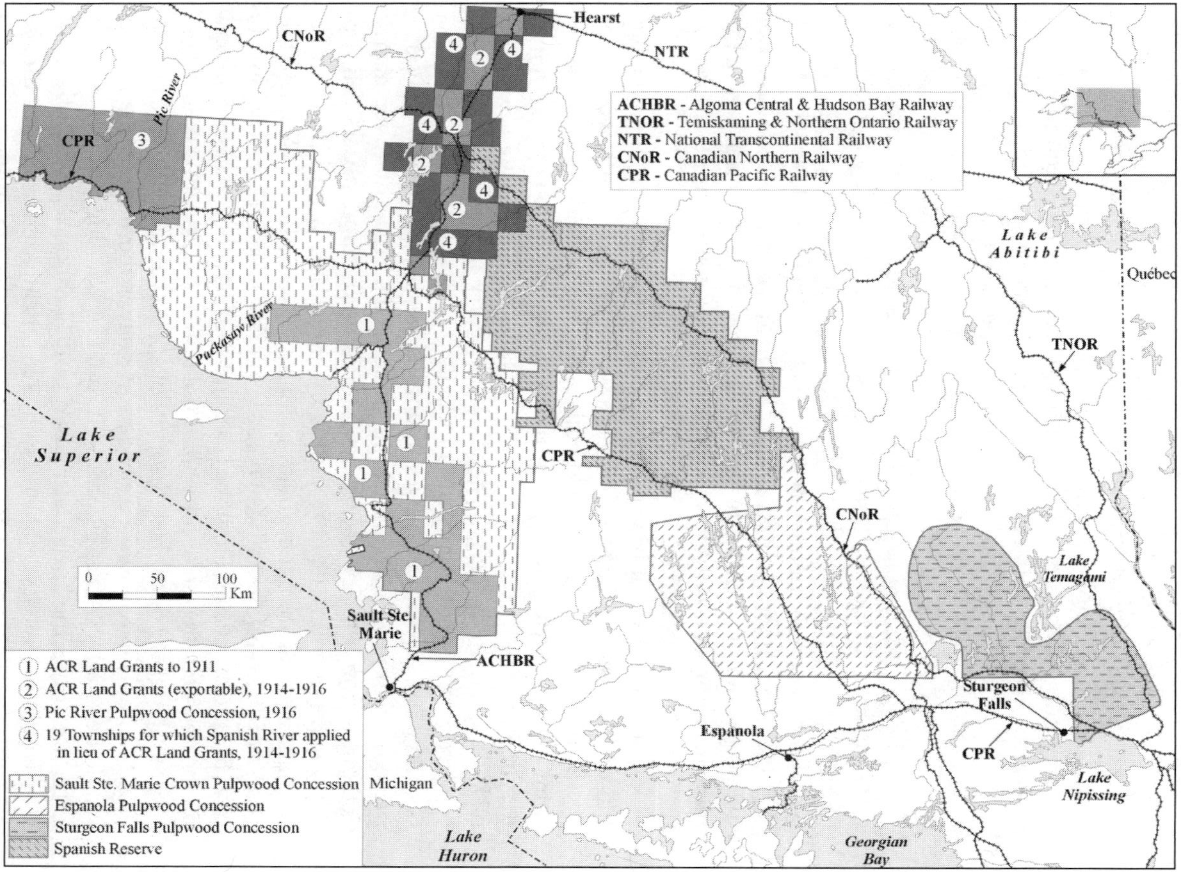
Hearst
CNoR
NTR
Pic River
CPR
ACHBR - Algoma Central & Hudson Bay Railway
TNOR - Temiskaming & Northern Ontario Railway
NTR - National Transcontinental Railway
CNoR - Canadian Northern Railway
CPR - Canadian Pacific Railway
Lake Abitibi
Québec
TNOR
Packasaw River
Lake Superior
CPR
CNoR
Lake Temagami
0 50 100 Km
Sault Ste Marie
ACHBR
Sturgeon Falls
Espanola
CPR
Lake Nipissing
1 ACR Land Grants to 1911
2 ACR Land Grants (exportable), 1914-1916
3 Pic River Pulpwood Concession, 1916
4 19 Townships for which Spanish River applied in lieu of ACR Land Grants, 1914-1916
Sault Ste. Marie Crown Pulpwood Concession
Espanola Pulpwood Concession
Sturgeon Falls Pulpwood Concession
Spanish Reserve
Michigan
Lake Huron
Georgian Bay

In marked contrast, Mead suffered a string of defeats when he sought the Ontario government's assistance in both confirming and supplementing the existing supply of pulpwood available to Spanish River in the Soo. Shortly after signing the agreement with the ACR, for example, Mead informed Frank Cochrane, the minister, about his plan to revitalize the operation by investing over $1,000,000 within fifteen months to restart the sulphite mill, upgrade the groundwood mill, and construct a large newsprint mill. In light of these expenditures, Mead was concerned about the wood supply available to the expanded plant. His representative thus emphasized to Cochrane that, above all else, he "would expect that no pulpwood would be sold or disposed of by the Government on lands that may be fairly deemed tributary to the Town of Sault Ste. Marie, and that might be required for a supply of pulpwood for our mills." Nevertheless, Cochrane refused to assure Mead that the government would protect his firm's interests in this regard, decisively demonstrating his position a few months later when the minister approved only three of the mill's six permit applications for that winter's harvesting privileges.[28]

Talbott and Mead still went ahead with their project in the Soo, but this only exacerbated Spanish River's worries about its pulpwood supply. By the end of 1912, they had built one of the country's largest newsprint manufacturing facilities. It produced over 270 tons per day, and they planned to increase it to 500 tons as soon as conditions warranted.[29] The plant in the Soo now consumed nearly 100,000 cords per year, however, and its cutting operations in the spruce-poor pulpwood concession it leased from the government were expensive and widely dispersed; it was now harvesting as far away as the Pukasaw River, nearly 200 miles from the Soo (Map 6). The mill understandably looked forward to augmenting its fibre supply by harvesting the pulpwood from the land grants that the government still owed the ACR. Over the course of 1913–14, the railway became eligible to select blocks along its new line north of the height of land and the Canadian Pacific Railway on the spruce-rich boreal forest. For the mill in the Soo, this would be a large and highly concentrated source of spruce, and despite the expensive rail haul that would be needed to deliver the fibre to the mill, it would be relatively cheap because it could be "hot logged."[30]

But the terms the Tories laid down in 1914–16 under which the railway would receive its final land grants practically rendered this timber supply unavailable to the newsprint maker in the Soo. Indeed, the eleven townships the government conveyed to the ACR were in the boreal forest and adjacent to the railway that ran directly to the mill's wood pile (Map 6). But for the only time in Ontario's history the government suspended the manufacturing condition on the pulpwood that grew on a railway's land grant, a move which greatly assisted the cash-strapped ACR. It would benefit handsomely from the willingness of American mills to pay over $1.00 per cord upfront for the timber on this land, a princely sum compared to the 40¢ per cord stumpage the mill in the Soo would have paid to harvest the timber under its cutting agreement with the ACR. Talbott and Mead had first right of refusal on this fibre, but they could exercise this option only if they matched any competing offers the railway received for this pulpwood. The government's decision in this case to render this pulpwood exportable had placed it beyond their economic reach. The ACR immediately sold almost all its latest land grants to two Wisconsin interests, Consolidated Water Power and Paper (one of the state's largest newsprint mills) and Northern Paper Mills (a pulpwood-procuring firm for four paper makers in the Port Edwards area); they owned about 550 square miles of these spruce-rich lands by 1917.[31]

This unexpected turn of events heightened the mill's concerns over its fibre supply, but again the Tories were unmoved. This worrisome situation prompted L.R. Wilson, Spanish River's vice-president, to send a lengthy entreaty to Howard Ferguson, the minister, in June 1916. Wilson reminded the government that it had traditionally depicted itself as a firm ally of Ontario's pulp and paper makers, and that the Sault Ste Marie mill, which was the province's largest, sought "more definite rights, making for permanence and stability." Wilson thus made several requests of Ferguson. Wilson reminded the minister that the plant's original 1894 agreement authorized it to cut pulpwood in "all territory on either side of all rivers flowing into Lake Superior west of Sault Ste. Marie." Openly admitting that a literal interpretation of this clause was illogical – it would allow Spanish River to claim cutting privileges on every watershed between the Soo and Ontario's border with Minnesota – Wilson asked only that the government confirm that his mill's pulpwood concession stretched from the Soo "westerly to where the Pic River empties into Lake Superior," an area in which the firm was about to begin harvesting. Similarly, Wilson requested that the government confirm the mill's cutting privileges on a tract on which it had traditionally operated, namely the Garden River watershed, which emptied into Lake Huron only a few miles east of Sault Ste Marie. Finally, Wilson requested that the government grant his mill licences to cut on nineteen townships along the ACR north of the CPR, presumably to compensate for the mill having lost access to the pulpwood on the railway's most recent land grants (Map 6). In conclusion, Wilson admitted that he had made this application because "from the financial view-point of the Company, and their capital requirements from time to time, they desire definiteness as to [pulpwood] supply so that their credit may not be impaired." For this reason, and aware that the company's existing concession lease would expire in only sixteen years, he asked the government to guarantee that it would renew the contract.[32]

Ferguson showed little sympathy for Spanish River's application and replied to it in a manner that drew a vehement protest from the company. Instead of immediately responding to Wilson's letter, the department dispatched James A. Oliver, the Crown timber agent in Port Arthur, to investigate the nature of the pulpwood on a 1,400-square-mile tract of Crown forest centred on the Pic River watershed, one of the areas that Spanish River believed was within its existing concession and had asked the government to confirm as such. Oliver had already informed officials in Toronto that existing data indicated that there was insufficient pulpwood on the Pic River concession to support a new mill project. Nevertheless, only twelve days after he had conveyed this information to Toronto, Ferguson hastily tendered the Pic River pulpwood concession under terms of sale which obligated the winning bidder to construct a new mill. Ferguson did not reveal how he intended to evaluate the offers he would receive for the tract, for no thorough cruise of the limit would be carried out before the bidding was set to close. L.R. Wilson, Spanish River's vice-president, was incensed by the minister's actions, arguing that it was "a violation of its rights." Then on 30 November, the day before the tender's deadline, he wrote Ferguson again to express his frustration at the minister's refusal to acknowledge his June 1916 letter for nearly six months. Wilson pointed out that the situation was exigent because his mill in the Soo had placed options to buy additional electricity from the local power company and machinery for the expansion of its mill, and it had only two weeks to make up its mind regarding these matters. Wilson confided to the minister that he was reluctant to proceed with these capital improvements "without definitely knowing that we will be assured of a wood supply to warrant such new work and to maintain the requirements of our present plant."[33]

Ferguson first ignored Wilson's latest appeal and then Spanish River's interests in the tender for the Pic River pulpwood. Opening the only two bids revealed that the mill in the Soo had submitted a record bonus of 60¢ per cord for the spruce, an offer that was one dime higher than that made by the other tenderer, James J. Carrick. The government openly admitted that Spanish River's offer was the highest, but it rejected the firm's bid because the company did "not undertake to comply with the condition of sale," which entailed "building a new mill." Not only did Ferguson's decision disregard timber agent Oliver's advice, but Albert Grigg, the deputy minister, confirmed a few years later that "at the time the Pic area was offered for sale, the Department had no estimate of the timber before it … The reports as to the amount of timber thereon were somewhat disappointing, and unfortunately revealed the fact that there was not sufficient pulp timber on this area to warrant the expenditure that had been provided in the general conditions of the sale." In no uncertain terms, Ferguson's insistence that a new mill be built had cost Spanish River the Pic River pulpwood.[34]

Only after Ferguson had awarded this timber to another party did he formally consider Spanish River's June 1916 application for confirmation and augmentation of its cutting privileges. A lengthy and curious departmental memorandum assessed the subject.[35] The document identified that the nub of the matter was to balance the need to place a "reasonable limit" upon the company's cutting privileges and "guarantee that its future should not be endangered by lack of raw material." In weighing these factors, the memo recognized that the mill's concession lacked spruce, "and on this account if the industry is to be maintained a large area should be set apart in order to insure a future supply of wood." By the same token, the government contended that it had carried out a "sample" timber cruise of Spanish River's pulpwood concession (despite a lack of evidence that it had ever done so) and that its data indicated that the area contained enough pulpwood to supply the mill for the twenty-one-year term of its lease. On this basis, the government rejected all the company's requests as laid out in Wilson's June 1916 letter. Parenthetically, over the next few decades the government sold to exporters most of the pulpwood on the townships along the ACR line for which the mill in the Soo had applied at this time.[36]

While Spanish River's officials were expressing their utter dismay with the government's handling of the situation, the Tories revealed the animus that had been driving their actions. "Your views on the matter constitute a considerable modification of what we believe is our position," Wilson bluntly declared to Ferguson, explaining that it was "a matter of regret to us, operating as we do, this immense plant at the Soo, that on the areas which you intimate we shall be confined to, woods suitable for pulp are generally scattered." When the government broadcast a short time later that the newsprint maker in the Soo was expanding and was "prepared to purchase [spruce] from settlers in order to insure sufficient pulpwood for their [sic] mill," it failed to mention that Spanish River had not chosen this path of its own volition. Incidentally, Charles McCrea, the Conservative MPP for Sudbury, admitted a short time later that Spanish River had every right to expect that it would receive the timberlands for which it had applied at this time along the ACR and on the Pic River watershed.[37]

Spanish River's newsprint plant in Sturgeon Falls encountered different but equally grave challenges in dealing with the Tories. Like the mill in the Soo, it leased a concession that lacked spruce, a deficiency that was exacerbated by the existence of the "pine priority clause" in its contract with the government. This provision gave the lumbermen's interests priority over the newsprint makers' by prohibiting the latter from cutting in the general area of pine timber. Because pine was scattered throughout its pulpwood concession, the mill in Sturgeon Falls was, by the early years of the First World War, able to operate in only a few small sections of its timber holdings. In an attempt to ameliorate its plight, beginning in October 1916 Spanish River requested that Ferguson add a few spruce-rich townships of unlicensed Crown land lying between its Sturgeon Falls and Espanola concessions to the mill's lease, but the minister turned down the company's repeated applications for these tracts (Map 6). Pushed to the wall, G.R. Gray, Spanish River's woods manager, took up the cudgels in March 1918 and pleaded his case to Ferguson. "Up to the present time," Gray began, "practically all the area upon which cutting may take place, without interfering with the pine … has been cut over and we are now faced with a situation where, if we are to have pulp[wood] for the operation of the Sturgeon Falls Mill, it will have to be obtained from lands on which there are also stands of merchantable green pine." Gray reminded the minister that a "perusal of the agreement entered into in respect of this Pulp Concession … will show that we are to receive a continuous supply of wood sufficient to keep the mills in operation." With Ferguson unswayed, Gray tenaciously wrote missive after missive that hammered home his case, yet the minister just as obstinately refused to budge. Unable to harvest from its own timber limit, the mill in Sturgeon Falls was forced to buy large volumes of pulpwood on the open market, even though doing so greatly increased its wood costs (there was a high demand for pulpwood in this area during this period).[38]

A solution to the problem created by the "pine priority clause" originated within the department and was supported by both the bureaucracy and Spanish River. In July 1918 Albert Grigg, the deputy minister, suggested to Gray that Spanish River harvest all the timber – both spruce and pine – from the townships in its pulpwood concession and then make the sawlogs available to the local lumber companies. Gray eagerly agreed with this proposal, prompting Grigg to ask a few of his forest rangers to comment on its merits. After spending several months carrying out field investigations, they reported back to Grigg in mid-October that they resoundingly endorsed the suggestion that Spanish River harvest all classes of timber, as their experience had proven that authorizing two parties to operate in one area was a recipe for disaster. Grigg's approach, they concluded, "would be in the best interests of the Department."[39]

Grigg went forth and composed a momentous memorandum to his minister – Bruce W. Hodgins and Jamie Benidickson describe how it supported "a reversal of policy with respect to the superiority of pine over pulp[wood]" that was inherent in the "pine priority clause" – but Ferguson was unmoved.[40] Grigg stressed that the government had leased pulpwood concessions to newsprint mills and that it was becoming increasingly difficult to carry out the spirit of these agreements because of the pine stipulation. Herein lay the problem, Grigg underscored, for it "would appear to be self-evident that where areas are specifically set aside for the exclusive operation for pulpwood by any particular company, it is somewhat contradictory to provide that certain areas within the concession are not to be operated in common with the rest of the area. It will be easily seen that if the Department did not dispose of the pine timber upon these areas, and continued to refuse the pulp companies the right to cut their pulp that we would in the near future reach the place where there would possibly be no wood available [to the newsprint mills]." Grigg also reminded Ferguson that the department opposed the idea of having two parties "whose interests are not identical, operating on the same area for different classes of timber," and that the solution lay in having the newsprint firms harvest all the wood from their concessions and sell the sawlogs to the lumbermen. Despite Grigg's seemingly impeccable logic, Ferguson preserved the status quo.[41]

The mill in Sturgeon Falls was also grappling with a shortage of hydro during this period, and in refusing to resolve this problem the Tories took the opportunity to flex their muscles vis-à-vis the paper maker. Its ability to generate power from its station near the mouth of the Sturgeon River depended on maintaining the water level in the up-stream reservoir – Lake Temagami – at the river's head. During a tem-porary shutdown of the paper mill in 1910, however, Minister Frank Cochrane had authorized the Northern Ontario Power Company (NOPC) to reverse from south to north the direction in which Lake Temagami drained; this increased the flow at NOPC's generating sta-tions in the Cobalt area. When the paper mill's officials expressed alarm over this move, Cochrane assured them that the government would revoke the permit to divert Lake Temagami when Sturgeon Falls need-ed the water. Leery of this promise, the town's concerned residents as well as senior officials from the paper mill sustained their protest of the government's actions. Water shortages had already led to the partial or complete shutdown of the mill's grinders even before the government had granted the power company this favour, and this had prevented the mill from producing annually the amount of paper required by the terms of its Crown pulpwood lease. In addition, the lack of water flow-ing down the Sturgeon River had also diminished its ability to drive pulpwood from the bush to its plant each year, thereby worsening its wood shortage. Irritated by the griping over this matter, Cochrane re-minded all concerned of the mill's breach of contract. "I have been more than surprised at this," the minister chastised the company when it ex-pressed yet again its anxieties over its power supply, "in view of the fact that we have been most lenient in allowing the Company to run on, though practically in default [of the terms of its concession agreement]. If these groundless and needless complaints ... continue, it may be nec-essary to return the compliment by taking up the question of cancelling the concession."[42] Despite Spanish River's vociferous campaign over the next half-dozen years to convince the department to cancel the power company's permit, and Cochrane's earlier pledge to do so, the government refused to take action. It also rejected Spanish River's con-tinual applications for a lease to develop Smokey Falls (twelve miles upstream from Sturgeon Falls) as a means of generating more hydro. This left the paper mill suffering from power shortages which limited it to operating at barely 60 per cent capacity between 1914 and 1919.[43]

Finally, Spanish River's third mill, the one in Espanola, faced the most serious challenge with regard to its fibre supply, and this time the Tories chose to temporize instead of resolve the issue. This pulpwood shortage was attributable to the presence of the pine priority clause in the company's concession lease, a preponderance of jack pine not spruce on its limit, and nearly two decades of cutting. By 1916, both its own woodsmen and an outside consultant had concluded that the spruce on its concession would last, at most, another five or six years. As a result, the latter recommended that Spanish River apply for another block of pulpwood north of its existing concession, a subject the company had already taken up with the government.[44]

On 19 September 1919, George R. Gray, Spanish River's woods manager, submitted an eight-page letter to Ferguson explaining Espanola's plight. As Gray's cohorts had done previously, he reminded the government of its repeated pledges to supply Ontario's newsprint mills with enough pulpwood to ensure their present operation and future expansion. In assessing the Espanola mill's fibre supply, Gray pointed out that its concession contained enough wood to support only a half-dozen more seasons of cutting, whereas its concession agreement "contemplates a supply for at least a period of twenty-one years expiring October 1, 1930." He added that his existing newsprint mill produced 53,000 tons annually, and that after the upgrade the company had already initiated, its capacity would rise to over 80,000 tons. To provide for the operation's timber needs, and because the mill needed "definiteness as to supply so that its credit may not be impaired," Gray asked for another concession within which his firm would be given the "exclusive right" to the spruce. This was a roughly 4,000-square-mile area lying north of the plant's concession, a tract which would become known as the "Spanish Reserve" (Map 6).[45]

Ferguson's reply was sympathetic in spirit but weak in action. He agreed that his government had publicly pledged to give the industry "stability by insuring it as nearly as possible an ample supply of raw material," and that from the "information there is available to me there would seem to be no doubt that your present supply of wood is sufficient to meet your requirements only for a very few years." And although he concluded that it was "in the best interests" of the province to provide the mill with additional fibre, he did not grant or even tender the limit for which the company had applied. He only promised to "reserve" it for Spanish River and work out the details later.[46]

Ferguson's refusal to take definitive action on behalf of this newsprint company in this instance was most extraordinary. He had made it a habit to respond immediately to the string of requests from the local lumbermen for private grants to prime timber tracts, in the process making a mockery of the law that required the government to tender all Crown wood. In 1919 alone, he had doled out 1,067 square miles of limits to sawlog contractors in this furtive manner, the vast majority of these in September and October, coincidentally on the eve of the election and at the very time of the Espanola mill's application. By the same illegal method he had dispensed hundreds of square miles of limits over the previous few years, and given many of them to parties which operated in the same woodlands as Spanish River. Nevertheless, Ferguson would do nothing more than reserve for the mill in Espanola the tract for which it had applied.[47]

It was at this point that George H. Mead, Spanish River's president, made a fatal error, the ramifications of which would not be felt for some time. Unprepared to have his industrial plans delayed by Ferguson's dawdling, Mead obstinately pushed ahead. He already knew that Alexander Smith, representing Peabody, Houghteling and Company, had agreed to finance Spanish River's project, but with one important caveat. Alexander had insisted that Mead first "furnish us [Peabody] with an official letter signed by you as President [of Spanish River], setting forth such facts as may be necessary for our presentation of the issue to the public." In other words, Smith demanded that Mead formally declare that the Espanola mill controlled a timber supply that was sufficient to sustain its operations in perpetuity, thereby indemnifying Smith against any liability in marketing Spanish River's securities and rendering Mead culpable if anyone chose to investigate the matter. Even though Mead knew he did not control the supplemental pulpwood concession, in October 1919 he provided Smith with a letter which confirmed that the Ontario government had recently conferred to Spanish River the "timber grant." Contemporaneously, Mead audaciously declared in the circular advertising the sale of the company's $3,500,000 worth of securities that his firm had forty years of wood at its disposal, another claim he, perhaps more than anyone, knew was untrue. This was hardly the first time he and Spanish River had misrepresented the truth about the firm's fibre supply to allay investors' concerns, and on this occasion his actions would come back to haunt him.[48]

Nevertheless, even without the government's support, Spanish River had pushed ahead with its ambitious expansion program. In the Soo, it had transformed what had been a derelict enterprise into a first-class mill that produced 270 tons of newsprint and 45 tons of wrapper paper. In Espanola, it had upgraded a facility that had produced only pulp for the first decade of its existence into a 200-ton newsprint plant by 1919, one that was on the verge of an enlargement to 323 tons. Finally, it had expanded the plant in Sturgeon Falls from a 60-ton newsprint operation to one more than double that size. This mill, and the one in the Soo, also manufactured excess quantities of sulphite pulp to supply the mill in Espanola, which did not make this product. As a result, by 1920 Spanish River was the Dominion's largest newsprint producer, representing over 20 per cent of Canada's and nearly 7 per cent of North America's total capacity. Its dynamic growth between 1911 and 1919 had occurred, however, with practically no assistance from the provincial government, whose attitude towards Spanish River during this period had been, by and large, an impediment to its success.[49]

4 "The jack-ass methods of that Department"

The victory of the Conservatives in 1905 signalled both continuity and change in terms of the Ontario government's handling of the pulp and paper industry in the Thunder Bay District and on the northern Clay Belt. Certainly filling these areas with settlers remained the provincial state's primary goal during the Tories' fifteen years in office, but they pursued this agenda with unprecedented vigour. There was a particularly pressing reason for them to have done so. The millions of homesteaders who flocked to Canada's prairies in the early 1900s represented living, breathing proof of that region's irresistible allure to aspiring farmers. The need to compete with the destination of choice for settlers prompted the Ontario government to invest more resources than ever in promoting the notion that commercial wheat farming was a viable option for those willing to take up a quarter section in the province's hinterland. While publicly this was the Conservatives' line, and they excoriated any and all experts who challenged their dogma, occasionally they admitted the truth that no one dared utter: homesteaders in places like Kamistiquia in the northwest and Kapuskasing in the northeast would depend for their existence on cutting spruce trees each year.[1]

This impetus drove the Tories to implement measures which aggressively stimulated the market for settlers' pulpwood. The most important means of doing so was to deprive bona fide pulp and paper ventures of the specific supplies of Crown fibre they hoped to obtain from the government. The Conservatives manifested their approach in a variety of creative ways, including refusing to sell particular pulpwood concessions, placing highly restrictive conditions upon the sale of others, and agreeing to provide a Crown spruce tract to a prospective mill developer but not the one he sought. For the Conservatives, mill projects were only ever means to achieving their settlement ends, and not industrial developments unto themselves. Remarkably, it will be seen that the fillip which prodded the Tories to tender a tract of pulpwood to what would become Ontario's most important newsprint producer was not the provincial state's view of the business as a worthy suitor for resources, but rather the government's need to respond to the strenuous lobby of local residents who wished to strengthen the demand for their most valuable crop.

Likewise, the Conservatives deepened the government's commitment to the export trade in spruce in an effort to foster support for the hinterland colonization effort, but there was one problem inherent in this policy. Just like the Liberals before them, the Tories were acutely aware that it was politic to present the facade that the government was strictly adhering to the manufacturing condition on Crown pulpwood and thereby doing all it could to facilitate the establishment and growth of the domestic pulp and paper industry. This was especially true during the Tories' reign, which was marked by an increasingly intense campaign to end the export of pulpwood from Canada. By the eve of the First World War, every government in the Dominion with jurisdiction over significant quantities of timber had enacted some type of embargo on pulpwood.[2] Typical of the Conservatives' public stance on the issue was the response Premier James Whitney delivered to iconic "Canadian" businessman Sir William Van Horne when the latter expressed his concerns in 1910 about the volume of spruce being shipped to the United States from the Thunder Bay District. "In every way possible," Whitney's soothing words to Van Horne read, "we will prevent the exportation of pulpwood."[3]

Whitney could deliver such empty pledges because his Conservatives devised better means than ever to deal with this potentially thorny issue. They followed in their predecessors' footsteps by making a mockery of Ontario's colonization and mining laws to assist those interested in exporting spruce; they ensured that all the most accessible townships in the Thunder Bay District were opened to settlement regardless of their suitability for farming (Map 7). The Tories went one step further when they passed legislation in 1914 to suspend the manufacturing condition as a "temporary" forestry measure, and thereafter gave new meaning to *pro tempore* by extending the provisions of the act for four years. Steps such as these drew more buyers from the Great Lakes states into the Ontario pulpwood market, as did the fact that the value of spruce doubled during the Tories' reign; this greatly expanded the range within which it was cost-effective for mills in the United States to acquire fibre. While companies in Wisconsin and Michigan were the principal American beneficiaries of these actions, patronage consider-ations dictated who in Ontario would be given the chance to profit from being the local entrepreneurs in this business. MPPs H.C. Scholfield and J.H. Hart, for example, were able to ply their Conservative connec-tions to acquire by the First World War, through their jointly owned Driftwood Lands and Timber Company, nearly 30,000 acres of veter-ans' land grants consisting of prime, exportable spruce on the northern Clay Belt.[4] The upshot was a significant rise in both the volume of pulp-wood leaving Ontario each year and the size and number of exporting firms operating in the province. Moreover, considering the clandestine nature of the exporters' activities, the evidence strongly suggests that at least as much fibre was exported as was used by the province's own pulp and paper mills during the Conservatives' years in office.[5]

  Some may argue that the Conservatives were merely creating compe-tition (and thus higher prices) for settlers' pulpwood by permitting ex-porters to expand their operations in Ontario, but the evidence suggests otherwise. The Tories could have achieved this end by facilitating the erection of mills in the sections of the province where the exporters flourished, but it will be seen that the government chose not to do so and only agreed to assist to limited degrees a few industrialists in carrying out their ventures in these areas. The evidence indicates that the Conser-vatives' approach of making exporting and not processing pulpwood the major economic activity in the Thunder Bay District and, to a lesser extent, the northern Clay Belt, was a function of choice not necessity.

  Finally, woven throughout this chapter is further evidence of the Ontario government's consistent inclination to remind pulp and paper makers who endeavoured to develop Crown resources that a handful of politicians were the gatekeepers – always – on these timber tracts and water powers. For the mills which wished to utilize the public's natural resources, the cost of accessing them was usually an acceptance that the provincial state – not industry – would dictate the rules of en-gagement. While the industry probably saw this as an absurd case of the tail wagging the dog, it would not be the last time that the Ontario government – particularly the Tories – would behave in this way.

The Thunder Bay District was an ideal location in which to construct pulp and paper mills during this period, but the Tories proved remarkably un-interested in providing Crown timber to facilitate their development.

Map 7. Land and Timber Situation in the Thunder Bay District, 1905–1919

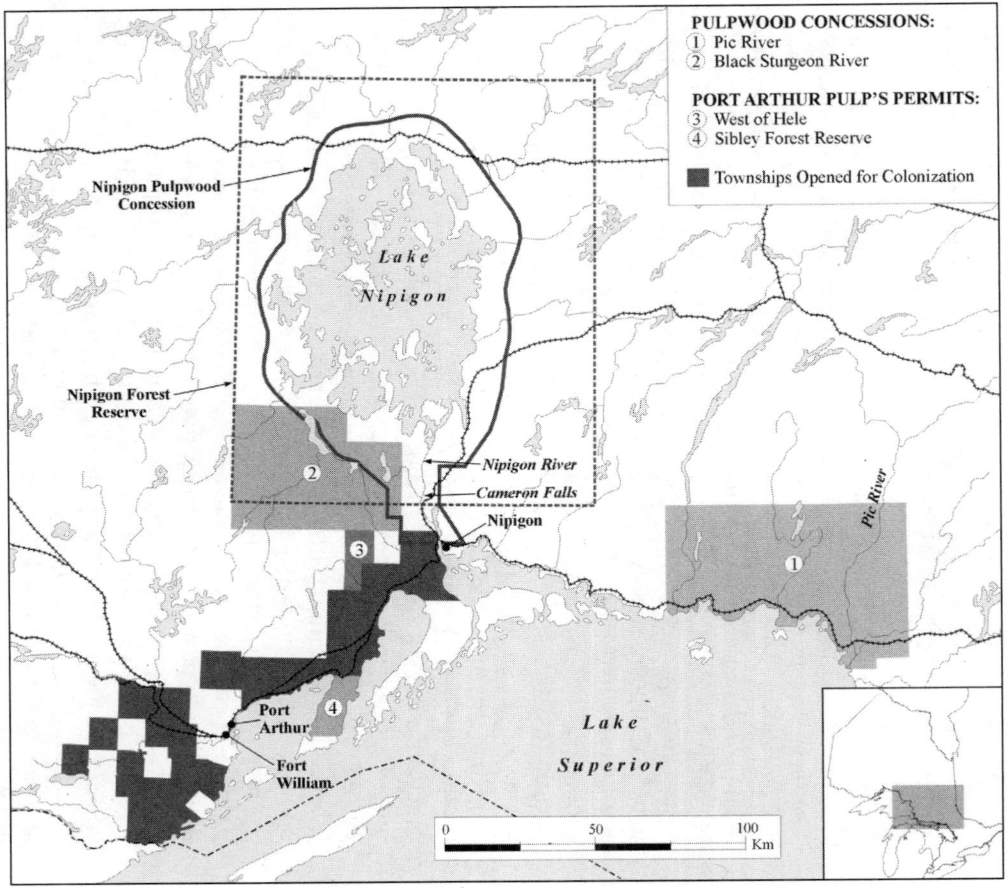

PULPWOOD CONCESSIONS:
① Pic River
② Black Sturgeon River

PORT ARTHUR PULP'S PERMITS:
③ West of Hele
④ Sibley Forest Reserve

■ Townships Opened for Colonization

Pic River

Nipigon River
Cameron Falls
Nipigon

Lake
Nipigon

Lake
Superior

Nipigon Pulpwood
Concession

Nipigon Forest
Reserve

Port
Arthur
Fort
William

0   50   100
Km

For reasons that were described in chapter 2, the Nipigon basin was particularly attractive in this regard. As a contemporary report about this area put it, "Nipigon has the three essentials" that a paper maker needed: a large quantity of pulpwood around the lake that was easily driveable to a mill along the Nipigon River; "an unlimited supply of cheap power that one [newsprint] mill could not possibly exhaust in any low water season"; and "[a] location on the Great Lakes affording a freight rate, on both exports and imports, lower than the other mills can possibly obtain."[6]

The Liberals had leased – several times – the pulpwood on this watershed to support the establishment of a newsprint mill, but the Conservatives took extreme steps to keep this prime fibre out of a mill developer's hands (Map 7). Almost immediately after the Tories had won power in 1905 they had executed an Order in Council to create a legislative obstacle to anyone ever leasing the Nipigon pulpwood. The Forest Reserve Act of 1898 had been enacted out of concern for the province's future supply of pine timber, and every protected "reserve" the Liberals had created thereunder was composed of white and red pine (e.g., the Temagami watershed). Moreover, the government openly admitted that there was practically no pine timber in the Nipigon basin, and the supply of pulpwood in northern Ontario had barely been tapped at this time. Nevertheless, the Tories established in mid-1905 the "Nepigon Forest Reserve." This 7,300-square-mile area encompassed practically the entire watershed and rendered all its spruce subject to more stringent regulations than other Crown timber.[7] Then, in early 1906, Frank Cochrane cancelled the pulpwood concession which the Liberals had executed with a group that had been on the cusp of developing the Nipigon basin's timber and power resources.[8]

Thereafter, the Tories agreed only to tender intermittently the Nipigon pulpwood concession and never lease it. For the first few years after their ascent to power, the Conservatives rejected successive bids for this timber on specious grounds considering they had no cruise data on which to base their assessment of the offers; they confoundingly rejected a few requests to sell this pulpwood because it was "virgin timber." Their handling of this coveted tract even raised the ire of J.T. Horne, the faithful Tory to whom Cochrane had literally given the Turtle River pulpwood concession in 1907.[9] A few years later, a high-profile group began lobbying for the government to sell the Nipigon basin's spruce to support a newsprint plant they wished to construct either along the Nipigon River or in Port Arthur, some sixty miles to the west. The consortium was led by William Mackenzie and Sir William Van Horne, two of Canada's leading entrepreneurs who also headed the management team of the Laurentide Paper Company, arguably the country's most successful newsprint maker. They were allied with S.A. Marks and James Carrick, both of whom were prominent Lakehead businessmen, the latter being the local Member of Parliament. In 1911, the enterprise appeared to take its first steps towards realizing its project when Marks secured a lease to develop the cascades at Cameron Falls on the Nipigon River, which would provide more than enough power to sustain a large mill (Map 7). But the Tories refused to sell the Nipigon pulpwood limit to Marks and company – or any other mill developers – at this or any other time during their fifteen years in office.[10]

Marks and Carrick eventually acquired a concession to support their proposed pulp and paper venture, but they did so in a way that would prove practically useless to the mill they hoped to build at the Lakehead. It will be recalled that Minister Ferguson had suddenly decided in the fall of 1916 to tender the Pic River pulpwood limit after Spanish River had applied to have it officially recognized as part of its Sault Ste Marie concession. Although the department's local timber agent had argued that the Pic River lacked sufficient fibre to support a new mill, Ferguson had insisted that the terms of sale require that one be constructed. He then rejected Spanish River's apparently winning offer for the Pic River limit on the grounds that the firm had not abided by the tender's terms and awarded it instead to Carrick, the only other bidder. Carrick, and his associate Marks, bid on this tract not because it was desirable for their purposes – the Pic's mouth was located roughly 100 miles from Nipigon and even farther from Port Arthur, the two possible locations in which they proposed building their mill; this would be very expensive wood for them (Map 7). Rather, Marks later revealed to a royal commission that Ferguson and William Hearst, the premier, had given him and Carrick an ultimatum. Ferguson and Hearst were enmeshed in a complicated and bitter battle with Sir Adam Beck and Ontario Hydro over control of the public utility's activities at the Lakehead, and they had set their sights on gaining the upper hand. They had threatened to cancel Marks's and Carrick's lease to the Cameron Falls power site on the Nipigon River if the two developers did not win the Pic River pulpwood concession. While Carrick had dutifully submitted a generous bid and been awarded the limit, he must have wondered why the government had literally demanded that he win a lease to this remote tract at the same time as the Tories refused to sell him one for the pulpwood in the nearby Nipigon basin.[11]

Also in the fall of 1916, the government tendered another pulpwood limit in the Thunder Bay District, and again the Tories determined it would not end up in the hands of those who had presented a shovel-ready paper-making project. A group of American and Canadian fine-paper makers, who controlled the Bryant Paper Company in Michigan and mills in southern Ontario under the name of Provincial Paper Mills Company, had begun lobbying Ferguson in mid-September to sell the timber on the 940-square-mile Black Sturgeon River pulpwood concession south of Lake Nipigon (Map 7). Provincial Paper agreed that if the government awarded it this tract, it would immediately construct a 50-ton sulphite pulp mill in Port Arthur and enlarge it to 150 tons or more "as soon as market conditions in Canada justify same." The company was prepared to pay a rich premium for this pulpwood, and its representatives pleaded with the minister for prompt action because they were presently unable to procure enough sulphite pulp to meet their needs. The government responded by tendering the Black Sturgeon limit in October 1916.[12]

The circumstances surrounding this sale were significant. As with the tender for the Pic River limit, the government discussed it in advance with Carrick and Marks and persuaded them to agree to develop Cameron Falls (which Marks leased) on the Nipigon River and supply their own project as well as the winning tenderer for the Black Sturgeon concession with power. In addition, this limit contained a rich storehouse of pulpwood, much of which could be driven directly to Lake Superior and towed a short distance to either the Lakehead or Nipigon for processing. Because there was pent-up demand for a pulpwood concession in the Thunder Bay District, inquiries about this tender poured in to the department from across Canada and the northeastern United States.[13]

While many parties submitted bids for the concession, Minister Ferguson dictated who won it. Aware that an accurate cruise of the tract was a prerequisite to objectively evaluating the offers that would be submitted, the Crown timber agent in Nipigon assured the minister that his office could carry one out shortly after the tender first appeared in the newspapers. But Albert Grigg, the deputy minister, informed him that the Conservatives had decided that they desired only "a general idea of the pulpwood." How the government transformed this cursory survey into precise data remains a mystery, but it used this information to determine that Marks was the winning bidder.[14]

The Tories then began placing a series of obstacles in the way of Marks and his partner Carrick developing the resources they controlled – the Pic River and Black Sturgeon pulpwood concessions and one of the waterfalls on the Nipigon River – to support a new mill. Marks was deeply distraught over the government's decision to draw up a lease to his Black Sturgeon pulpwood concession that lacked a renewal for a second twenty-one-year term and did not embody his "understanding with the Minister … [for] a new lease of the Cameron Falls Power."[15] Marks also informed the government that he and Carrick would combine their Pic and Black Sturgeon concessions to support a single mill, an arrangement to which the Tories formally agreed a short while later. But Hearst and Ferguson soon informed Marks that they had cancelled the latter's existing lease to Cameron Falls, and that Ontario Hydro would now supply the mill's power. Exasperated by the government's summary actions, in early May 1917 Marks sold his interest in the Black Sturgeon concession to Carrick. Marks was so disgusted with the Tories' handling of this matter that he later disparagingly remarked before a royal commission that "we were absolutely put out of business by the jack-ass methods of that Department."[16]

The Tories ensured that Carrick, who was now flying a solo mission to establish a mill at the Lakehead, fared no better. Holding both the Pic and Black Sturgeon concessions but no power lease, he began a protracted struggle with the provincial government and Ontario Hydro over the conditions under which the latter would supply his mill with electricity. By the spring of 1919, Carrick was enervated. Chastising the Tories a short time later for having "retarded for years the development of this whole northern country," Carrick sold his interest in the Pic and Black Sturgeon pulpwood limits to Americans George Seaman and Lewis L. Alsted. Through Seaman's eponymous firm in Chicago, he had built what was arguably the world's largest paper marketer. During the latter part of the First World War, he had been horizontally integrating his firm by deepening its control over paper producers such as Combined Locks Paper Company in Wisconsin, of which Alsted was president. In mid-1919, Seaman and Alsted incorporated Great Lakes Paper Company, through which they hoped to carry out their plan to build a newsprint mill in the Thunder Bay District.[17]

The arrival on the scene of two major players from the American paper industry like Seaman and Alsted mysteriously effected a fundamental shift in the Tories' attitude towards the holders of the Pic River and Black Sturgeon pulpwood concessions. Ferguson and Hearst recognized that Great Lakes Paper still lacked a power supply, and two weeks after the Tories had lost the October 1919 election they provided one in a highly unusual manner. Without informing Ontario Hydro's chairman of their actions, Hearst, as acting attorney general and in front of only Ferguson and two other now-defeated cabinet members, executed an extraordinary Order in Council. It authorized Ontario Hydro to supply electricity to the holders of these pulpwood leases even though the attached power contract was merely a draft and included rates that were known to be below cost (rendering the contract illegal under the Power Commission Act). Not surprisingly, the issue would be reopened by the new government immediately upon its accession to office.[18]

These events left Provincial Paper, at whose insistence the government had initially tendered the Black Sturgeon concession, in a bind which the government was disinclined to resolve. Wrongfully presuming that it would win the contest for this limit in February 1917, its owners had gone ahead and incorporated Port Arthur Pulp and Paper Company to carry out the venture and started building its mill. Ferguson ignored their vehement protests about how he had handled this affair, leaving the firm gearing up to begin production in late 1917 without enough pulpwood to process; it had been unable to procure a sufficient supply of spruce from local settlers. The company's mill manager and solicitor both pleaded with Ferguson to grant it a small licence south of Lake Nipigon and due west of Hele Township, entreaties the minister rejected (Map 7). Ferguson was also unmoved by appeals that came from within his own department. Deputy Minister Grigg indicated that he had "looked carefully into this situation and I am convinced that unless cutting rights ... are given to the pulp company, they will not be able to operate during the coming season." More adamant was James Oliver, the Crown timber agent in Port Arthur and that city's former mayor and president of its Board of Trade. Having for years toiled to facilitate the erection of a pulp and paper mill in his home town, he and his local fellow forest rangers had cruised parts of the Thunder Bay region's prime pulpwood stands, reported their findings to Toronto, and implored their superiors to sell these tracts to genuine mill developers, only to be directed by the Tories "not to do anything." Oliver's frustration boiled over upon learning of Port Arthur Pulp's difficulties in the fall of 1917. He reminded Ferguson that the townships from the Nipigon River west to Port Arthur had almost all been opened to settlement, thereby shutting out a large area from which the government could tender pulpwood limits. Oliver also emphasized that locals at the Lakehead were upset at the government's inertia and urged the minister to make timber available to the firm.[19]

Ferguson would provide only what was at best a stopgap solution to the mill's fibre supply problem. He granted Port Arthur Pulp a one-year permit (not a licence, which was renewable) to harvest a small quantity of timber in the area for which it had applied. In late 1917, he also tendered a licence for the Sibley Forest Reserve, which Port Arthur Pulp won (Map 7). This provided short-term relief to the company, but it was still without a pulpwood concession.[20]

The Tories' fifteen-year record of handling the Thunder Bay District's timber resources was revealing. They had implemented a variety of measures which had rendered a steadily increasing volume of prime spruce available to American mills in the Great Lakes states. It came in the form of wood cut by settlers, freehold tracts of pulpwood, and a half-decade suspension of the prohibition on exporting Crown spruce, and it often benefited the government's closest friends. During the same period, the Conservatives had shown little interest in providing industrialists who wished to erect pulp and paper plants at the Lakehead with the supplies of Crown pulpwood they sought. In addition, they rejected applications from numerous bona fide mill developers who had asked the government to tender relatively small pulpwood concessions to support their projects.[21] While dealing with the Conservatives during these years had proved immensely frustrating for the pulp and paper executives interested in exploiting Thunder Bay's industrial potential, the government's approach succeeded brilliantly in realizing its primary aim, namely bolstering the market for settlers' spruce. The Conservatives were even more effective at realizing this goal in northeastern Ontario, a subject to which we now turn.

The Tories were deeply committed to peopling the northern Clay Belt, and they believed that fostering a flourishing market for pulpwood was the best – and many would argue only – means of doing so. Ensuring that a large part of Ontario's spruce was available for sale in the United States was a prominent element in this plan. Not only would the Conservatives and their closest allies profit in the process, but they were even prepared – on at least one occasion – to help the exporters at the expense of furthering the colonization agenda. Another aspect of this strategy was to respond cautiously to overtures from entrepreneurs who were keen to build mills in this previously uncharted wilderness. In areas where the government believed there was little hope of establishing communities in the near future, for example, such as the relatively isolated western end of the northern Clay Belt, it refused outright to sell Crown resources to mill developers.[22] Closer to the southern Clay Belt, where agricultural communities had already taken root, the government agreed to provide access to the timber and water powers it controlled for only a few industrialists, and even then only under very restrictive terms.

Numerous entrepreneurs realized that the completion of the National Transcontinental Railway through the northern Clay Belt in the early 1910s created a string of ideal locations for constructing newsprint mills, one of which was located where it crossed the Mattagami River. This watershed was covered with black spruce and boasted several harnessable cascades. One of these, Smooth Rock Falls, was located just north of the intersection of the railway and river. It was a site to which pulpwood could be driven, at which power could be generated, and from which newsprint could be shipped. Duncan Chisholm, a Canadian businessman who was associated with the Traders Bank of Toronto, had investigated this potential and then pressured the government for an opportunity to exploit it. In asking that the Tories tender the 846-square-mile Mattagami River pulpwood concession in 1913 and provide a lease that ran far longer than the standard twenty-one-year term, he offered in exchange to build a 100-ton newsprint mill (Map 8).[23]

Chisholm won the bidding, but the Tories insisted that the leases he signed for the pulpwood concession and water powers in May 1914 include terms which were not to his liking. He was certainly amenable to the obligation in his timber contract to construct the paper mill within three years, for example, and he was thankful that the agreement was to run for an initial term of twenty years and two additional ones of sixteen years each. The government had restricted Chisholm, however, to cutting trees above seven inches in diameter even though the spruce on the concession averaged far less than this size. Chisholm's water power lease was much more straightforward, granting him the privilege of developing three cascades on the Mattagami River. On the same day he signed these leases, he assigned them to the Mattagami Pulp and Paper Company, which he and several American partners had incorporated to carry out the venture.[24]

By this time, Chisholm knew that the Ontario government had already encouraged competing interests to establish a claim to the pulpwood

Map 8. Pulpwood and Water Powers on the Northern Clay Belt, 1905–1919

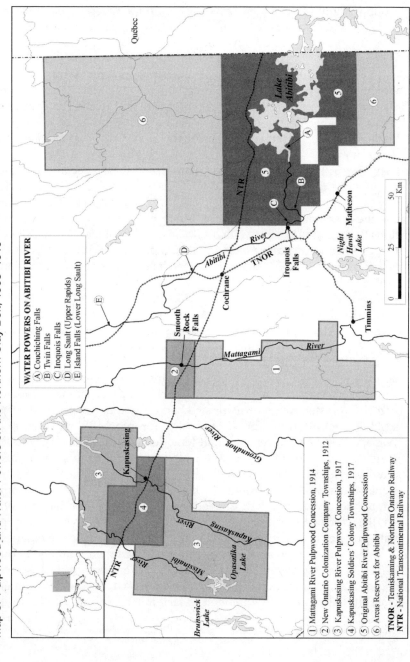

WATER POWERS ON ABITIBI RIVER
Ⓐ Couchiching Falls
Ⓑ Twin Falls
Ⓒ Iroquois Falls
Ⓓ Long Sault (Upper Rapids)
Ⓔ Island Falls (Lower Long Sault)

① Mattagami River Pulpwood Concession, 1914
② New Ontario Colonization Company Townships, 1912
③ Kapuskasing River Pulpwood Concession, 1917
④ Kapuskasing Soldiers' Colony Townships, 1917
⑤ Original Abitibi River Pulpwood Concession
⑥ Areas Reserved for Abitibi

TNOR - Temiskaming & Northern Ontario Railway
NTR - National Transcontinental Railway

around Smooth Rock Falls. The Tories – and the Liberals before them – had set aside many of the townships on the Mattagami River watershed – mostly on its east side – for their veterans' land-granting program. When Chisholm arrived on the scene, pulpwood contracting interests had already acquired hundreds of thousands of acres of this territory, which created potentially huge problems for his mill project. It made far less pulpwood available to his enterprise and raised the spectre of settlers moving en masse into the area and beginning to clear their lands using fire, thereby endangering the timber on his concession; this series of events had derailed numerous mill projects near the southern Clay Belt in the early 1900s. This latter issue was especially pressing because one township that was open to the veterans – Kingsmill – actually formed part of Chisholm's new limit. Moreover, the settlers would use the Mattagami River to deliver their wood to the railway, operations that would interfere with his. In an effort to obviate these difficulties, he began purchasing as many lots as possible. Within a few years, he controlled over 80,000 acres, transactions that netted the local land brokers a hefty profit.[25]

Of greater concern to Chisholm was the local pulpwood exporting enterprise the Tories had quietly established in his area through two of their supporters. On the eve of tendering the Mattagami River limit in 1913, the Conservatives had illegally executed a private agreement with William Rushworth and Ernest S. Wigle. The former was a lumberman who, after finding Premier Whitney unreceptive to his plans, had moved on to a more tractable member of the Conservative cabinet, namely Minister Hearst. Rushworth had only done so, however, after seeking support from E.W.J. Owens, a Toronto MPP, and Ernest S. Wigle, a Windsor lawyer who had long demonstrated his fealty to the Tories and was thus considered – as the transcript from a subsequent inquiry put it – someone with "close personal connections to the Department and ... a 'friend of the government.'" Rushworth and Wigle had acted on behalf of the American timber firm Jackson and Tindle, which had formed the New Ontario Colonization Company. As with practically all firms engaged in the pulpwood exporting business, it endeavoured to present the appearance of being an indigenous timber operator and agent of local settlement even though its base was south of the international border.[26] Its contract with the government was, after all, ostensibly intended to facilitate colonization. The Tories had sold it two entire townships – Kendrey and Haggart (a total area of just under 100,000 acres) – for the nominal price of $1 per acre, in return for which the company was obliged to clear 2,400 acres and settle six-teen families annually for twenty-one years. Failure to do so would nul-lify the agreement (Map 8). But New Ontario's sole interest in the land it had purchased was to clear the area of timber, specifically spruce pulpwood, which it could export with the minister's permission, con-sent which the Tories freely conferred throughout their time in office.[27]

Although there were many townships along the new Transcontinen-tal that the government could have allocated to alleged settlement com-panies, the Tories' decision to sell Kendrey and Haggart was immensely troublesome for Mattagami Pulp in Smooth Rock Falls. Mill builders assumed that they would be able to satisfy their needs for construction lumber by setting up a small sawmill and processing the timber that was closest to their building site. Pulp and paper entrepreneurs also banked on harvesting their nearest pulpwood stands to minimize their fibre costs during the first few years of their operation when they were incurring enormous capital expenses. In Mattagami Pulp's situation, however, New Ontario Company owned all the timber in the two town-ships which were closest to its proposed newsprint mill, and this pushed the cost of procuring both the lumber and pulpwood it needed to an unanticipated level. This was especially true of the spruce, which was exportable, freeing New Ontario Company to set high rates on this wood confident that American mills would probably be prepared to pay them.

Most remarkable about New Ontario Company were the extraordi-nary lengths to which the Tories – particularly Ferguson – went to pro-tect its existence. When members of the Opposition demanded in 1916 details of the extent to which New Ontario had fulfilled its colonization obligations, Carroll Hele, Ferguson's private secretary, assumed respon-sibility for providing the answer. Instead of directing the department to prepare a report as such circumstances demanded, Hele asked W.K. Jackson, New Ontario Company's president, for the information. Hele and Ferguson then told the deputy minister to accept the company's statement when preparing the Return for the House, even though it had not been vetted by government officials. Later, W.R. Plewman, an inves-tigative reporter for the *Toronto Daily Star*, inquired about the matter, and the deputy minister merely provided him with a copy of the 1916 Return. Plewman was also warned, with regard to the data he had re-ceived, "not to publicise them and that any criticism of a general charac-ter respecting the policy pursued in the case shall not be advanced until such time as you have the personal consent of the Minister."[28]

This aegis was needed because New Ontario Company did almost nothing to fulfil its "colonization" obligations and instead actually restricted and discouraged settlement. It only offered to sell prospective homesteaders tracts of its land-holdings at exorbitant prices, causing local settlers to complain vociferously to the government.[29] Predictably, this had led to the clearing of but a few hundred acres of land by 1919, instead of the more than 15,000 acres it ought to have readied for farming by this time under the terms of its contract with the government. It had, however, harvested at least 170,000 cords of pulpwood and lumber, and most of the former had been exported with the minister's blessing. Not only was this tally probably a gross underestimation (the company had operated completely unsupervised), but the exporters had paid the government a mere pittance for this wood. All the while, the Tories covered up New Ontario Company's activities instead of abrogating the agreement which it had flagrantly breached.[30]

In the meantime, Duncan Chisholm and Mattagami Pulp had pushed ahead with their project as best they could. Having begun construction in the fall of 1915 during an inflationary period, Chisholm was able to raise only enough money to finance part of his newsprint venture, namely a sulphite mill, which he had built by December 1916. Consequently, he renegotiated his pulpwood concession agreement with the provincial government to formally recognize this change in plans.[31]

The advantages that rendered Smooth Rock Falls an excellent site for constructing a newsprint mill were also available at a location forty miles west of it in Kapuskasing, named for the river on which it was situated. There, a remarkably similar series of events marked the early history of the mill project, but they highlight another critical element in the Tories' approach to the province's pulp and paper industry. They provide a cogent example of how, if given the option, the Conservatives would view such entrepreneurial endeavours strictly as vehicles for delivering settlers to the province's hinterland.

The story of the mill in "Kap" begins over the winter of 1916–17. At that time, a syndicate of American bankers and industrialists from Pennsylvania and New York backed a timber cruise of seventeen surveyed townships around Kapuskasing. This work was overseen by S.A. Mundy, who represented the Forest Supply Company of Bradford, Pennsylvania, and Elihu Stewart, a forester and former superintendent of the Dominion Forest Service. Their investigation confirmed that the forest on this watershed averaged about ten cords of spruce to the acre.[32]

Figure 7. The Benefits of Association: During the 1910s, the Conservative government erected obstacles in the way of the Mattagami Pulp and Paper Company to prevent it from realizing its plans to build a large newsprint mill in Smooth Rock Falls. But that did not stop the Tories from trying to capitalize on the publicity generated by the creation of another industrial enterprise in the province's hinterland. This illustration of the project appeared in the mid-1910s in a government report on its administration of northern resources. Ironically, the provincial state's actions at this time – and later – prevented the mill from ever reaching the scope portrayed in this drawing (*Report of the Minister of Lands, Forests, and Mines for the Province of Ontario for the year Ending 31st October 1916*, 134; Courtesy of the Queen's Printer of Ontario).

While Mundy and Stewart were enthused by their findings and anxious to proceed with their mill project, Ferguson had other priorities. In February 1917, Mundy and Stewart reminded the minister that they had begun discussing their project with him the previous autumn and that their timber cruise had focused on locating the best stands of pulpwood. In their words, the "principal work in looking over the tract was in order to ascertain what was timbered with a view of not including unforested areas such as burnt-over territory which would be the easiest to bring under cultivation." They asked Ferguson to tender the pulpwood on the Kapuskasing River watershed and lease them the falls found along it closest to the railway, and they urged him to take immediate action so that they could begin construction early in the spring and nearly complete it before the winter freeze (Map 8). Hearing nothing from the minister for nearly two months, they resubmitted their proposal, only to receive a disappointing response from the department in May. It explained that the government could not sell the Kapuskasing pulpwood limit before the tract had been cruised and that a new factor must be considered before any action was taken: a colonization scheme.[33]

Mundy and Stewart must have wondered why this last issue concerned them, but they soon learned the answer. They knew that Ferguson had announced plans in January 1917 to establish a soldiers' colony on the southern Clay Belt, but it was at least 150 miles from Kapuskasing. When Ferguson introduced the legislation to establish the "Kapuskasing Colony Scheme" in April, however, it was clear that he had fundamentally reoriented his plans. The minister reserved for his project five townships which formed the core of the timber limit for which Mundy and Stewart had applied (Map 8).

Ferguson had thereby created a set of problems for the mill developers which bore a striking resemblance to those which had been erected in the path of the newsprint venture in Smooth Rock Falls. The government had again set aside for a settlement scheme (i.e., it had rendered exportable the pulpwood on the supposed colonization areas) the townships that contained the timber that was most accessible to the proposed mill, making it much more expensive for the entrepreneurs to obtain the wood upon which they would initially rely for construction and processing purposes.[34] This was an especially serious issue at a time when the demands of the Great War had driven up labour costs.

Not only did this turn of events greatly hinder Mundy and Stewart's ability to interest financial backers in their venture, but potential investors' concerns would have been heightened by the news that the government intended to import thousands of settlers to the area who would be clearing forest and burning slash to make farms on their properties. Similar actions on the southern Clay Belt the previous summer had ignited a conflagration that consumed over 1,300 square miles of prime pulpwood forest and claimed over 200 lives. Finally, many adjudged the timing and nature of this settlement strategy to have been foolhardy, doomed to fail, and based on illogical thinking.[35]

But in the government's eyes, these issues were of slight consequence. Of greater importance was the fact that a group of industrialists was eager to erect a paper plant in a remote section of the province, and their project would draw settlers north and lead to the establishment of a new community there. As a result, before the government had given this enterprise the green light, it seized a golden opportunity to dictate that the shape of this new community would follow the state's – and not the mill's – plan, namely to establish as many new families as possible on the northern Clay Belt.[36]

The Tories provided more evidence that this was their driving motivation when they finally tendered the 1,740-square-mile Kapuskasing River pulpwood concession in September 1917. Although the spruce on the tract averaged well under seven inches in diameter, the government set this measurement as the minimum size of tree that could be cut in the original conditions of sale, and then one month later abruptly raised it to ten inches. As much as this adjustment in the tender's terms greatly diminished the value of the concession to a newsprint mill, it decidedly increased the mill's future need to purchase settlers' timber. It also understandably had a significant impact on prospective tenderers. The numerous inquiries about this pulpwood concession when the government had first advertised it resulted in only one party – Mundy and Stewart – submitting an offer.[37]

By this time, conditions in the Kapuskasing area had changed dramatically, and in Mundy and Stewart's favour. Ferguson's campaign to draw returned soldiers to the region had attracted an influx of settlers for whom the government was now desperate to find employment. This stimulus softened Ferguson's attitude towards Mundy and Stewart, making him amenable to providing them with access to the pulpwood under reasonable terms. These included permission to cut pulpwood "of all sizes," a privilege the Tories had never given any mill in the province, and a twenty-one-year renewal after the initial term had expired if the concessionaires fulfilled their obligations. In addition, the government required the lessees to build only a 100-ton pulp mill within three years and a paper mill only when and where cabinet decided. Less than one month after signing the agreement, Mundy and Stewart transferred it to the syndicate for which they had been acting, which had already incorporated the Spruce Falls Pulp and Paper Company to carry out the project.[38]

When it came to Spruce Falls Pulp's power lease, however, Ferguson was not nearly as generous. The Tories granted it the privilege of developing the minor water powers near Kapuskasing, and its lease understandably reserved to the Crown a portion of the electricity the company would generate in an effort to provide for the local community's needs. But the Tories had reserved so much power for this purpose that it left too little energy available to run the size of facility Spruce Falls Pulp was obliged to erect under its pulpwood agreement. H.G. Acres, Ontario Hydro's chief hydraulic engineer, identified this problem soon after the deal was signed. He reported to the government that the lessees were required to "build and operate a pulp mill of not less than one hundred tons daily capacity. With the Crown reserve of 2000 H.P. taken out, the residual capacity ... would only be sufficient for the operation of about fifty tons daily capacity."[39]

This provision derailed Spruce Falls Pulp's financing efforts. Its backers insisted that the "reservation clause" in the company's water power lease be amended as a precondition for their support of the project, an issue the firm repeatedly raised with Ferguson in the spring of 1919. Although the minister's successor would quickly resolve this difficulty in a manner that still protected the town's interests, Ferguson refused to alter the objectionable clause. He then exacerbated matters when he insisted in mid-1919 that Spruce Falls Pulp immediately build its mill. This was the situation when the Conservatives fell in the election of 1919.[40]

Like the Mattagami and Kapuskasing watersheds, the one that drained into the Abitibi River was well endowed with the natural resources needed to support a newsprint mill. Much of it was covered with dense stands of spruce pulpwood, and the Abitibi River held immense potential for generating power. Lake Abitibi was a large natural reservoir, and erecting a dam at its outlet could maintain its high-water level throughout the year and provide a continuous heavy flow of water. This was thus an ideal site for constructing a large, low-cost newsprint mill.

Whereas the government had conceived the mill projects in Smooth Rock Falls and Kapuskasing primarily as a means of facilitating colonization, the Tories were practically ordered by pioneers in the Abitibi district to do the same there. In the fall of 1910 homesteaders on the southern fringe of the northern Clay Belt had begun clamouring for the provincial government to take steps to assist them in the best way possible. Theirs was not a plea for better farm implements or seed, but rather something far more valuable. "Government Seeks to Make Home Pulpwood Market," *The Globe*'s front-page headline read, because "Settlers Dissatisfied." As the story went on to say: "With a view to supplying the settlers in an extensive area of Northern Ontario with what they have most desired since the country was opened up – a convenient market for their pulpwood," the Tories were set to tender the Abitibi River pulpwood limit in early 1911 and in a manner that greatly favoured the local pioneers. The government set a ridiculously high nine-inch-diameter limit on the concession's pulpwood, thereby rendering much of it off-limits and dramatically increasing the mill's future demand for settlers' timber.[41] While the Tories' tender of the Abitibi limit also made no provision for granting a water power lease, numerous parties still submitted offers hoping that they could negotiate better terms. After the minister deemed none of the bids "acceptable," the government was harshly criticized by the Toronto Board of Trade as well as the domestic pulp and paper producers for its handling of this matter.[42] In response to these attacks, the government included much more reasonable terms when it retendered the 1,560-square-mile Abitibi pulpwood concession in mid-1912 (Map 8). It reduced the diameter limit to seven inches, entitled the winning bidder to obtain a water power lease to several nearby cascades, and called for the construction of only a $500,000 mill capable of producing at least 100 tons of pulp within three years.[43]

Montreal businessman Frank Harris Anson was familiar with the Abitibi basin's immense potential for the production of newsprint and was bound and determined to exploit it. He had financed cursory surveys in this area that had confirmed its abundant pulpwood (at least in the river valleys) and water power resources. In partnership with Shirley Ogilvie, a prominent Canadian industrialist, Anson envisioned constructing a 500-ton newsprint mill in the soon-to-be-named town of Iroquois Falls amid this heretofore undeveloped hinterland. He was also acutely aware of the marketing advantages the location offered, as he would sell paper in "the middle and western United States, to which territory … [it would] … enjoy competitive freight rates [over] its chief eastern competitors."[44] Despite taunts from rivals who sardonically christened his venture "Anson's Folly," he and Ogilvie submitted the only bid and won the tender, and then Anson created the firm that soon became known as Abitibi Power and Paper Company.[45]

The Ontario government emphasized that its pre-eminent concern in this area remained facilitating settlement. When the minister announced news of this deal, he reminded the province's citizens that the "lands covered by this pulp concession are not withdrawn from sale or settlement, so that there is no monopoly or tying up of land." He also boasted that the new industry would "enable the settlers to dispose of their spruce timber removed in clearing their land, at prices which will afford them some profit." Within a few years settlers had claimed thousands of acres closest to Anson's mill, mostly on creeks and rivers that would make it easy for them to drive their pulpwood to the new plant.[46]

Abitibi had much bigger problems with regard to its hydro privileges because of the Tories' insistence that the government – and not the company – would set the terms under which Abitibi would access its energy supply. The Ontario government had been interested in determining the best means by which the new mill in Iroquois Falls could develop the local water powers, and so it had asked Ontario Hydro's engineers for a report. Their document recommended allowing Abitibi to maximize the development of the area's two best power sites and reserve to the Crown authority to regulate the level of Lake Abitibi by controlling a dam that the government ought to build at its outlet. In drawing up Abitibi's water power lease, however, the government almost completely disregarded Hydro's advice, most notably by restricting the company to developing only one power source, namely at Iroquois Falls.[47] Ferguson also created serious problems for Abitibi with regard to its *licence of occupation*, which granted the company permission to flood the river banks upstream from its power stations and dams. The document stated that Abitibi was obliged to develop and deliver 10,000 horsepower to the Temiskaming and Northern Ontario Railway (TNOR) "without regard to its own [Abitibi's] requirements." In contrast, Abitibi's *water power lease* stipulated that it had to make the 10,000 horsepower available to the TNOR only if it did not require this energy for its own use. Although there was much debate as to which document was paramount, the Tories made it clear that they believed it to be the former. The government also insisted that Abitibi's licence of occupation limit the company to raising the head at Iroquois Falls to a point far below the optimal level Ontario Hydro had recommended. This cast great uncertainty over the legality of Abitibi's hydro projects.[48]

Nevertheless, Anson was determined to disprove his detractors, and he pushed Abitibi to the forefront of the country's newsprint makers. By the end of 1914 his mill was producing 150 tons of groundwood per day, and one year later it was turning out 225 tons of newsprint daily, which was as much paper as its power supply would permit it to produce. Although this represented an enterprise far smaller than Anson desired, it was over twice as large and employed twice as many workers as the one called for under his 1912 pulpwood lease, and he had fulfilled his obligations more than one year earlier than required.[49]

Anson faced lingering problems with his power and pulpwood supplies, however. For example, the government had forced the company to build a dam at Couchiching Falls to regulate the level of Lake Abitibi. All parties recognized that it would be merely a temporary structure until a power station and permanent dam could be constructed farther downstream at Twin Falls, a site the government had not yet permitted Abitibi to develop. No one, therefore, was shocked when the makeshift dam at Couchiching Falls proved unable to lower Lake Abitibi quickly and far enough to suit authorities in Quebec, who complained that the height at which the level of the lake had been maintained had flooded land on their side of the border. Although an agreement was reached in early 1916 to resolve this issue, the dam at Couchiching Falls was in dire need of replacement.[50] In addition, Anson was deeply concerned about his mill's timber supply. The seven-inch-diameter limit in his lease with the Crown had eliminated a good part of the spruce from the company's potential fibre basket, and by the mid-1910s he realized that the initial estimate of his concession yielding ten cords of pulpwood per acre was inflated. Local settlers and prospectors were notoriously careless in using fire to clear the land, behaviour that Abitibi lobbied – unsuccessfully – for the government to curb.[51] Major swathes of Abitibi's timber limit had been burned as a result; the legendary Matheson fire of 1916 torched part of the company's mill, its wood pile, and over 300 square miles of its concession. This left Abitibi with a total of roughly 4,500,000 cords of pulpwood (an average of about 4½ cords per acre), a volume barely adequate to supply its existing mill in perpetuity and much less than was needed for the 500-ton newsprint mill it intended to build in Iroquois Falls.[52]

Anson thus appealed to the government in mid-1916 for assistance in resolving these resource issues, but his efforts would be for naught. Rightly predicting that officials in Quebec would soon insist that Abitibi lower the level of Lake Abitibi and realizing that the Couchiching dam could not accommodate this request, and worried about his firm's contractual commitment to supply the TNOR with power, Anson offered to double the capacity of his 225-ton newsprint mill in Iroquois Falls. In exchange he asked for a lease to construct a permanent storage dam and power plant at Twin Falls; either a release from the obligation to provide the TNOR with energy or a lease to the Long Sault rapids farther downstream from Iroquois Falls; and a tract of Crown timber that contained roughly 4,500,000 cords of pulpwood that was within the watershed of Lake Abitibi or south of the Transcontinental Railway (Map 8). Anxious to capitalize on the warm-weather construction season, Anson urged the government to consider his proposal and report back to him as soon as possible.[53]

The Ontario government reacted enthusiastically to Anson's proposition, news that Anson relayed to his financial backers, namely Alexander Smith of Peabody, Houghteling and Company in Chicago. Reporting on his negotiations with the government in May and June 1916, Anson explained that the department's director of surveys and Ontario Hydro had wholeheartedly endorsed Abitibi's plan. Ferguson had been particularly supportive of the firm's proposal, deeming it "reasonable and right" and committing to take it up at the next cabinet meeting. At that time, the minister promised to see to it that the government waived the TNOR's power reservation and allocate all the potential hydroelectricity on the Abitibi River to the company. Even when the minister insisted that the government would have to tender the new concession because of public criticism of the government's private deals, he assured Anson that it "would not be sold or granted to anyone but Abitibi." Ferguson had forthrightly told Anson that Abitibi's large investment meant that it "was entitled to get and would have all the protection which the Government of Ontario could give [it] and that nothing would be put in our way or remain undone on their part to see that [it] had both power and wood sufficient to keep the plant operating at maximum capacity and he [Ferguson] considered the Government of Ontario ... were bound to ... protect us in every way possible and that we could rely upon their doing so." The only catch, Anson reported to Smith in June 1916, was that he and Smith would have to take Ferguson's "word for it that we would be given them [i.e., the pulpwood and water powers], and he would not put this in writing, and his promise was to be considered entirely a personal matter as between himself, yourself and myself."[54]

Ferguson would not budge on a critical issue, however. During his ne-gotiations with the minister, Anson had stressed that one aspect of Abitibi's lease to its new pulpwood concession was crucial to financing the company's expansion. He advised Ferguson that Abitibi's investors were loath to back "the new proposition so long as the price to be paid for the extended limits was undetermined; that the security behind the new issue of bonds with this feature open was questionable and their value would be open to immediately [sic] criticism." Although Anson "em-ployed every argument" he could with Ferguson and offered to pay a premium for the privilege of harvesting this fibre, the minister adamant-ly refused to set the rate of dues Abitibi would pay for the spruce it cut from its supplemental limit if and when it secured a lease to this tract.[55]

Anson accepted the minister's word and, eager to take advantage of the summer weather, proceeded with his expansion program. After Ontario Hydro approved Abitibi's plans for the Twin Falls dam and generating station, the company began building it, and Peter White, the government's counsel, began drawing up the company's contract for this site.[56]

But Ferguson was keen to retain complete control over the situation and demonstrated his resolve by refusing to hand over the lease to Twin Falls even though he knew full well that the issue was particu-larly pressing for Abitibi. Heavy snows and rains in the early part of the year had exacerbated the problem of lowering Lake Abitibi using the inadequate makeshift dam at Couchiching Falls, causing Quebec's gov-ernment to demand that the water body be lowered to a level below that to which it, the Ontario government, and Abitibi had previously agreed. Anson vehemently protested this latest directive, arguing that it would limit Abitibi to operating at only 75 per cent capacity during the winter and that he had already remitted compensatory payments for flooding damages to the neighbouring provincial government. Still, he paid for the blasting of a new channel beside the temporary dam at Couchiching Falls to expedite lowering the lake's level even though he knew that doing so would seriously undermine the structure's integri-ty. Thereafter, a senior official from the department's Surveys Branch visited the site and reported that the problem was clearly the deficien-cies of the makeshift dam at Couchiching Falls and that the solution would come when Abitibi completed construction of its "new dam at Twin Rapids." Even though Ferguson echoed these views, responding to a harshly worded missive from the Quebec government by under-scoring his belief "that when the new dam is complete at Twin Falls ...

the present difficulties will be removed," he would not grant the company a lease to this site.[57]

The same animus also drove Ferguson to take the same dilatory approach to the supplemental pulpwood concession he had promised but not yet delivered to Abitibi, and this caused the company much more serious problems. Over the course of 1917–18, Anson continually reminded the minister that Abitibi had nearly completed its expansion project, which would see its operation consume over 200,000 cords of pulpwood per year. At this rate, the firm would exhaust the 4,500,000 cords of spruce on its existing concession in roughly twenty years. Anson emphasized to Ferguson that this volume of fibre was "wholly inadequate, and in fact this point has been forced most noticeably to our attention by the bankers through whom we expect to obtain the financial assistance necessary to complete our plant. In fact," Anson continued, "I may say that it would probably be impossible for us to secure the further funds necessary for the completion of our extension unless we can obtain sufficient additional limits to restore our reserves to approximately the basis they were with the plant at its original capacity." Anson added that problems had arisen in marketing Abitibi's securities because doubts existed about the expanded mill's fibre supply. Although Anson's spirits were temporarily buoyed in August by word from G.H. Kilmer, Abitibi's lawyer, that, during a meeting with Ferguson, the minister had promised to press the premier for the "advertising [of the limit] … at once," the government took no action on the matter.[58]

Ferguson waited until April 1919 to respond to Abitibi's applications for more fibre, and the news he delivered left the matter in abeyance. The minister agreed with Anson that Abitibi's present supply of pulpwood was insufficient, especially in light of its recent expansion, and that it was clearly the government's responsibility and "in the public interest" to assure that the company had "as nearly as possible an ample supply of raw material." Although Ferguson repeated his earlier pledge to assist Abitibi, he refused to grant it – let alone publicly tender, as the company had asked – the pulpwood concession for which it had applied. Ferguson agreed merely to reserve a limit for Abitibi's future use, and it bore little resemblance to the one for which Abitibi had initially asked. Much of it was a great distance from Iroquois Falls and on a watershed that flowed away from the company's mill. Harvesting this spruce would be very expensive (Map 8).[59]

The Tories proved even less inclined to assist Abitibi in resolving its power problems over the course of 1919, and this seriously undermined the firm's viability. The company had nearly completed its generating station and dam at Twin Falls, but without a lease to the site, it could not legally use the power it had harnessed there. This was a critical consideration for Abitibi because it was thus prevented from implementing its plan of transmitting the energy it tapped at Twin Falls to drive its expanded production of newsprint and sulphite pulp. Without this additional source of electricity, Abitibi was forced to sell the surplus groundwood pulp it was now producing at fire-sale prices, because the market for this product was flooded, instead of being able to convert it into newsprint, which would have been much more remunerative. Thus, it was the Tories' refusal to lease Abitibi additional power – and pulpwood – supplies, and not the war, which had caused the company its greatest financial difficulties during this tumultuous period.[60]

The Tories rubbed a few grains of salt into Abitibi's wound before they left office. The firm had fallen behind in paying the stumpage dues it owed for the wood it was cutting from its pulpwood concession, a debt that Abitibi explained to the department was the result of its low cash flow during its massive expansion program. Ferguson was not buying the company's excuse and demanded in mid-1918 that Abitibi remit at least a portion of what it owed. In addressing the issue, the government threatened that, although it had "no desire to embarrass [Abitibi]," non-payment might leave it no choice because "during these strenuous times [the department] was called upon for very large expenditures, and it is difficult to keep the revenues of the Province where we would like to keep them ... There is absolutely no source from which this money can be obtained other than that from people like yourself who have dealings with the Province, and upon whom we are depending for our revenues."[61] No doubt Abitibi was dumbfounded by Ferguson's unbending and hypocritical attitude in this instance. The minister had, after all, done nothing to punish the province's lumbermen, who were perpetually indebted to the department for hundreds of thousands of dollars during the Tories' reign. Instead, the Conservatives explained that, in these instances, they had "never failed to take into consideration the state of financial matters and to assist in preventing a crisis in the lumber trade by extending leniency to those indebted to it for timber dues."[62]

In the end, the northern Clay Belt had seen the construction of three new pulp and paper mills during the Conservatives' time in office, but these plants were not the product of a public policy committed primarily to fostering their strong growth and development. Rather, the provincial state had continued to push as its top priority in this region its settlement agenda; helping the pulpwood exporters was a close second. The result was that the new mills received uneven treatment from the Tories, who all the while insisted that they retain tight control over the industry's development. For companies like Abitibi, the government's approach meant that it had initiated and nearly completed its dramatic expansion program between 1916 and 1919 with little assistance from and, in some cases, despite the efforts of, the provincial government.

SECTION III

"In order to keep in office, they must play politics": The United Farmers of Ontario, 1919–1923

The election of the upstart United Farmers of Ontario (UFO) in 1919 held the potential to effect a dramatic shift in focus as far as northern development in general and forest administration in particular were concerned. The premier, E.C. Drury, demonstrated a keen interest in issues involving the province's trees, and his campaign platform had explicitly identified the need to end the government's penchant for allowing patronage to dictate how it handled Crown timber. In addition, Drury selected Beniah Bowman to be his minister of lands and forests. A farmer from Manitoulin Island, Bowman was also involved in the local lumber industry, and it was hoped that this association would provide him with insight into how to improve the sale and management of the province's timber. Moreover, Drury sought and received sound advice from some of the leading forestry experts in Canada regarding these matters. They all agreed that the premier's only option in this regard was to modernize the department by wresting control over the woodlands from the hands of elected officials and placing it instead into the lap of an independent "Commissioner of Forests" under whom a team of professional foresters would work.[1]

While the pulp and paper industry supported this initiative to end patronage as the governing dynamic in the department, the lumbermen succeeded in defending the status quo. Word leaked out about Drury's commitment to overhauling the administration of Crown timber by appointing the new forest commissioner, and it set off a pitched battle among all concerned. While the premier sought a shortlist of potential candidates from C.D. Howe, the dean of the forestry school in Toronto, a number of Drury's cabinet ministers tersely told Howe that they resented him "butting in" because, as Howe described it, they were "quarrelling among themselves" to see who could succeed in having one of their cronies – however unqualified – appointed to the post. Then, at a special meeting of the Canadian Lumbermen's Association held at the Ontario Legislature in late 1922 before Drury and his cabinet, the sawmillers insisted that the provincial government keep the department under the control of the minister, not an independent forester. When the Farmers fell in the election a short while later, little had changed in how the government handled Crown timber. As Howe put it, "the old secret understandings between [lumber] operators and [the department's] office are apparently being restored ... However highmindedly the Drury government started out, I think they ... learn[ed] that, in order to keep in office, they must play politics."[2]

By adhering to the patronage system in dispensing northern Ontario's Crown timber and water powers, the Farmers continued pushing the provincial government's traditional priorities. While the lumbermen benefited in the process, the Farmers made hinterland colonization their highest concern.[3] The natural corollary to this plan entailed offering the pulpwood exporters the state's wholehearted support not only because it was crucial to sustaining the settlement effort but also because it was a worthy cause per se. Facilitating the export of spruce involved allowing American pulp and paper mills and their Ontario subsidiaries to continue abusing the province's land grant and mining legislation, and protecting these operators from snoopy departmental officials who wished to uncover their transgressions of the law for all to see. The Farmers also began classifying "rossed" (i.e., debarked) pulpwood as "processed," thereby rendering it exportable. They even officially suspended the manufacturing condition on pulpwood in 1920, and when the Opposition railed against doing so because it would set "a bad precedent," Drury reassured everyone that his government would not permit "pulpwood to be exported in ... great quantity." The reality, however, was that the amount of unprocessed spruce leaving the province annually during the Farmers' four-year reign rose from under 200,000 cords to over 400,000, and these figures only represented pulpwood shipped from private not Crown lands.[4]

For those interested in Ontario's pulp and paper industry, the government's export policy was troubling. The spruce that was leaving the province during the 1919–23 period represented, as it always had, Ontario's most accessible fibre. This was a growing concern because the Farmers had begun cruising sections of the province's Crown forests using airplanes and ground crews, and the resultant data showed that

·there was far less pulpwood available in the province than the government had previously indicated.[5] The newsprint companies had drawn the same conclusions when they investigated the state of their concessions during the 1910s, disappointing news that had driven them to request supplemental supplies of pulpwood. While these developments pointed to an unprecedented need to protect Ontario's most readily harvestable spruce for the province's own pulp and paper industry, the government was instead facilitating its export.

At the same time, however, there was still enormous potential for growth in northern Ontario's pulp and paper industry. The Tories had repeatedly rejected offers from newsprint makers who had sought to lease pulpwood concessions either to support mills they hoped to construct in the province or expand their existing ones. Many interests were thus still eager to invest in Ontario's pulp and paper industry once a more receptive government came to power, and the change in newsprint pricing instituted in 1917 made it especially enticing to do so. Previously, the standard market price quoted for newsprint included the cost of delivering the paper to the purchaser (this was known as free on board, or f.o.b., mill), which could be quite substantial considering the bulky nature of the product. It discouraged newspapers in places like St Louis and Chicago from buying their paper from mills in Ontario because the publishers paid the same price for newsprint regardless of where it was made. After 1917, however, the price of newsprint was quoted f.o.b. purchaser; with the publishers now paying to ship their paper, they had a compelling reason to buy it from nearby producers. Considering the growing demand for newsprint in the rapidly expanding cities of the American Midwest and the fact that mills located on the shores of the Great Lakes could ship their paper by water, prudent newsprint makers recognized that establishing new or expanding existing mills in northern Ontario would give them a significant competitive advantage when they went to sell their product in their "natural market."[6]

The Farmers confronted these circumstances when they went to administer the hinterland's Crown resources, and their own political situation also weighed heavily on their minds. Not only were they neophytes at Queen's Park, but they had won merely a minority government, meaning their survival rested on the continued support of a handful of Labour members whose interests were often antithetical to their own. Moreover, on the campaign trail the Farmers had been outspoken critics of their predecessors' timber policy. Now that they were in power and many members of the previous government sat across from them in the Legislature, it was inevitable that their dealings with Ontario's forest industry would be subject to unforgiving scrutiny.[7]

In determining how to deal with the pulp and paper industry between 1919 and 1923, the Farmers charted an ambivalent course, and for good reason. The industry was now in its adolescence and thus an increasingly dominant economic force in the province's northern reaches, and the UFO had no experience in dealing with it. These factors drove Drury's government initially to be receptive to acting on the bureaucrats' advice and demonstrating an unprecedented sympathy for meeting the industry's needs. Shortly after taking office, for example, the Farmers committed to providing all "established" mills and those yet to be built under existing leases with perpetual supplies of spruce. A handful of savvy paper makers also realized that the patronage system of allocating Crown resources still prevailed; they thus did all they could to forge that special link with the provincial state. Their cause was furthered by the Farmers' realization that, at times, reaching out to certain players in the industry could deliver significant political benefits. By the same token, the UFO learned the hard way that befriending the paper makers – or even appearing to do so – could render it vulnerable to torrid political attacks the likes of which it could hardly have imagined. The Farmers were burned a few times on this account, and thereafter took a prophylactic approach to dealing with the pulp and paper industry by turning a deaf ear to its concerns. As a result, the industry grew enormously during these years, but largely through its own efforts and not because of government assistance.

The reasons for the increase in its size under the Drury government warrant particular attention. The entrepreneurs who erected or augmented mills in Ontario in the immediate postwar period, particularly in the Thunder Bay District, were not simply fly-by-night operators hoping to capitalize on rapidly escalating newsprint prices and the exceptional conditions that marked the end of the Great War. Industry had been trying for years to establish plants in the province (especially at the Lakehead) but had been rebuffed by the Tories, and it had interpreted the Farmers' victory as an opportunity to realize this aim. These paper makers recognized that operating a newsprint mill in the province could be a highly lucrative business, and the data explain the reasons for their confidence. During the pulp and paper industry's roller-coaster ride during the early 1920s, Ontario's newsprint makers remained arguably the strongest on the continent. The province's and the country's largest producer – Spanish River – and Canada's biggest mill – Abitibi – were very profitable and continued to pay dividends on all their securities, even though they faced rapidly declining prices in 1922 after having incurred inflated production costs over 1920–1.

The next two chapters detail how the Farmers dealt with Ontario's pulp and paper industry during their four years in office. Chapter 5 returns the focus to northwestern Ontario and the Spanish River territory, where the lumbermen had long been the primary object of the provincial government's affection. Although the UFO did not abandon this agenda in these regions, it took unprecedented steps to help a select few pulp and paper interests there. In these instances, the government was motivated by the remarkable bonds these industrialists had forged with it as well as by political expediency. Political considerations also explain why the Farmers largely shunned the province's largest newsprint maker during their reign. Chapter 6 examines developments in the Thunder Bay District and on the northern Clay Belt. Again in these areas, the Farmers recognized the political hay they could make by accommodating specific players in the pulp and paper industry. Others were not so fortunate, however, and the UFO snubbed them as a result.

5 "This Government should ... exercise responsibility of dealing with tenders"

The Farmers' approach to dealing with the pulp and paper industry in both northwestern Ontario and the Spanish River territory revealed how quickly and tectonically relations between the provincial state and this business could change. Since at least the turn of the twentieth century, and much to the dismay of pulp and paper entrepreneurs, the provincial state had given its highest priority to assisting the local sawmillers in both regions; the Tories had gone one step further during their decade and a half in office by actively hindering the establishment and development of pulp and paper mills in these areas. While certain rules and regulations, most notably "the pine priority" clause, continued to protect this agenda during the reign of the United Farmers of Ontario (UFO), the new regime seemed inclined – at least initially and then later selectively – to reach out to the paper makers like no other before it. But when the ground suddenly shifted under the Farmers' feet, naturally so too did their position on such matters. By then, however, E.W. Backus had already been able to convince the new government that facilitating his drive to build a pulp and paper empire in the northwest ought to be its pre-eminent concern. In sharp contrast, the UFO generally turned a cold shoulder to Spanish River Pulp and Paper Mills, which operated three newsprint plants north of Lake Huron.

It is relatively easy to account for the government's disparate actions in these instances. In the northwest, Backus availed himself of the opportunity created when the lumbermen's local point man, veteran Conservative MPP J.A. Mathieu, sat in Opposition for the first time. To Backus's credit, he also plugged his enterprise into the patronage network that dispensed Crown resources in Ontario, and made it politically expedient if not imperative for the elected officials to respond to his requests for help. As a result he was able to gain control over a string of pulpwood and water power assets across the western half of northern Ontario by the time the Farmers left office in 1923. Near the other end of the spectrum stood Spanish River. After an initial honeymoon period, during which the Farmers helped the company, changing political circumstances rendered it "company non grata" among Drury and his caucus members. This was especially true for Beniah Bowman, the minister of lands and forests, who seemed intent upon unilaterally formulating a strategy for the province's timber resources that ignored bureaucratic advice to respect the paper makers' rights and understand their needs. Spanish River's cause was also hurt by the appearance in its environs of the heavyweight in the American pulp and paper industry, International Paper Company (IP). The Ontario government was undoubtedly enchanted by the thought of this mighty corporation establishing a manufacturing base in the province and almost instantly embraced it as a result, but there was much more at work here than simply a powerful business interest preying on star-struck politicians. The Farmers extended the welcome mat to IP because the company was adept at tapping into the province's patronage network to achieve its ends, even if it meant damaging the interests of the province's existing pulp and paper mills.

Perhaps more than anyone in Ontario, Edward W. Backus recognized the favourable opportunity presented by the Tories' defeat in the 1919 provincial election, and he immediately capitalized on it. Having suffered during their fifteen-year reign from his inability to develop the special connection with the provincial government's key personnel like the one he had enjoyed during the Liberals' term in office prior to 1905, he was determined to rebuild it with the UFO.[1]

The most important tie led directly to Peter Heenan. Born in Ireland in 1871, Heenan had emigrated to Kenora just after the turn of the century and worked for years as a master mechanic for the Canadian Pacific Railway. He rose to be northwestern Ontario's most prominent union leader by the eve of the First World War, served as a five-term alderman in Kenora, and ran successfully as the Labour candidate in the riding in the provincial election of 1919. During his campaign, Heenan had wedded his political fortunes to bringing industrial development to northwestern Ontario in general and Backus's newsprint mill to Kenora in particular, and he pushed Drury to facilitate this agenda once the UFO won office. Adding irresistible weight to his lobby was the fact that he had rallied the eleven Labour MPPs into supporting the minority Farmers government. Facilitating the erection of Backus's mill plans in Kenora and elsewhere would be Drury's quid pro quo for keeping the Labourites onside and the Farmers in power.[2]

Backus further cemented crucial alliances with the Farmers by retaining two of their closest friends, Robert T. Harding and Gordon Waldron, to act on his behalf in negotiating for Crown resources. Harding was a close friend of several prominent Farmers, including their provincial treasurer, Peter Smith, and Drury had also appointed Harding to act as Crown counsel to the royal commission it established to investigate the Conservatives' allegedly corrupt administration of timber. This placed Harding in an extraordinarily powerful position, especially after Backus had conveniently guaranteed the Timber Commission's early success when he had passed along to Harding details of Ferguson's illegal timber dealings with Backus's foe in Fort Frances, J.A. Mathieu. With Drury eager to use the commission to eradicate Ferguson permanently from politics, and with this inquiry holding the headlines during the first part of the Farmers' reign, Harding became a de facto member of the government's inner sanctum. Like Harding, Waldron was on intimate terms with the Farmers. He was both their long-time solicitor and runner-up candidate to act as their attorney general, and the Farmers hired him to represent them during the final stages of the Timber Commission's hearings.

While Backus could count on the likes of Harding and Waldron to push his cause with the Farmers, there were a number of other parties who supported him in achieving his first goal: building a newsprint mill in Kenora. It will be recalled that Backus had won a lease to the Lake of the Woods pulpwood concession in 1914 (and already owned the Norman Dam at one of the lake's two outlets), but he had delayed beginning his project after learning that both the fibre supply and the power available to the enterprise were insufficient. The Dominion government, for one, was eager to rectify this situation. It was under intense pressure to find a nearby supplier for prairie newspapers that were on the verge of ceasing publication for lack of paper, and it hoped a mill in Kenora would ease this crisis. The town's residents also believed this new industry would be the panacea for their problems. Their municipality was drowning in a sea of debt, some $330,000 by 1919, which it had accumulated as a result of two factors. It had fought a protracted legal battle to protect its right to the generating station it had constructed in 1905 at one of the two outlets to Lake of the Woods, and it had been unable to sell the electricity it had been producing there because the pulp and paper mill it had believed would be forthcoming to consume this power had never materialized.

These forces – particularly Backus's tie to Heenan – coalesced to produce nearly all the resources Backus had been seeking to support his mill project in Kenora. First, he entered into a contract with the town of Kenora to purchase its power plant, relieve it of its debt, and build a large paper plant. Then, backed by the town council and the Canadian Daily Newspaper Association, he formally applied to the Ontario government for a lease to both the English River pulpwood concession and the White Dog rapids near the confluence of the Winnipeg and English rivers. He would tap this energy source, and exploit the spruce on both his existing Lake of the Woods concession and the one for which he had applied along the English River to support his new mill. Recognizing that both of the aforementioned pulpwood tracts were poor in terms of spruce, he also made it clear that his hope was to secure a supplemental concession if and when there was concrete evidence that he would need one.

Drury responded by ensuring that Backus's proposal was properly vetted and that the government acted in a manner that assisted its realization. The premier presented Backus's plan to cabinet in mid-September 1920 along with crucial data regarding the timber tracts under consideration. Numerous investigations by the government's own forest rangers had confirmed that both the English River and Lake of the Woods pulpwood concessions, although relatively large in size (respectively 3,046 and 1,860 square miles), were poor in terms of spruce. As a result, Ontario's provincial forester had recommended that the new mill in Kenora would require "a comparatively large area" containing "at least 4,500 square miles," and that constructing the new industry would "involve eventually the necessity of looking elsewhere for a further supply of timber."[3]

This news fundamentally shaped how the Drury administration proceeded. It decided to tender the English River limit and concomitantly enter into an agreement with Backus. The contract promised Backus a lease to White Dog Falls on the English River, reserved to the Crown the right to regulate the level of Lake of the Woods using Backus's Norman Dam, restarted his 1914 Lake of the Woods agreement, and doubled the stumpage dues he paid for the wood he cut from it. In addition, the deal obliged Backus to build a small mill immediately and tender for the English River concession; if he won the latter he would be obliged to expand the size of his mill as per his agreement with the Town of Kenora. Lastly, the contract recognized the deficient nature of the spruce available on the two concessions in question by giving the minister three years to investigate the matter thoroughly. If the new reports verified that the tracts contained a volume of fibre that was insufficient to support the newsprint mill Backus was legally bound to build in Kenora, the agreement required the minister to tender an additional concession "to the north of the English River ... [to] ... provide the necessary timber and pulpwood for the said purpose." Drury's decision to include this latter provision seemed all the more justified after he received confidential confirmation from both industry and government sources that the English River concession averaged merely ½ cord of pulpwood per acre that could only be harvested at considerable expense.[4]

The rest of the activities surrounding this transaction were simply part of a predictable denouement that appeared to produce a slew of benefits for all concerned. Three days before Christmas, the Farmers announced that Backus had won the tender. After verifying his financial standing, the government entered into an agreement with him for the English River pulpwood concession that obliged him to complete a 200-ton newsprint mill in Kenora within two years. In exchange, he was privileged to cut "all merchantable timber" on the tract; no diameter limit was mentioned. The minister also gave Backus a personal pledge that, although the contract ran for only one twenty-one-year term, "there can be no question that the grantees shall be entitled to a renewal or renewals."[5] Thus, after nearly two decades, Kenora would finally get its newsprint mill and the economic advantages which accrued from it, and be relieved of its debt. Backus would gain a well-placed facility and add another piece to the industrial empire he was building. Finally, these events would obviously redound to Heenan's benefit. As James Little, a veteran Tory observer at the Lakehead, dejectedly commented after hearing of the deal between Backus and the government, "Of course Peter [Heenan]'s connection with the transaction has made him solid in the town of Kenora and he is going to be a mighty hard man to beat up there."[6]

What should also have been a coup for the Drury government, however, quickly turned into its worst nightmare. After news of the various agreements with Backus became public, Howard Ferguson, now leader of the Opposition Tories, mercilessly attacked them and brilliantly recast them as venal deals in an effort to resurrect his moribund political career. Among other tactics, he publicized some of the data from the original timber cruises of the areas in question, figures which had long ago been discredited, to argue that the Farmers had sold Backus a veritable mountain of timber for a measly sum. He similarly accused the Farmers of having granted Backus control over the entire Lake of the Woods–English River watershed, a charge that Ferguson knew was untrue. He also ensured that the partisan *Toronto Telegram* published verbatim his outlandish charges, along with a series of political cartoons depicting Backus as the detestable robber baron who had employed chicanery to mulct the hapless Drury – and citizens of Ontario – of their precious natural resources (Figure 8). Backus's libel suit against the *Telegram* was too little, too late, in the face of this onslaught. Even Drury's biographer concedes that "in spite of the cabinet's efforts, the Backus deal would continue in many circles to be regarded as a flawed and dubious transaction."[7] More importantly, Ferguson's masterful performance indelibly marked Backus in the province's collective consciousness as the villainous capitalist. It also signalled the beginning of the former's remarkable renaissance that would see him ascend to the premier's office.[8]

Nevertheless, Backus felt that he had signed leases to enough resources to propel his mill project in Kenora forward, and although it still ran into a strong headwind, he pushed ahead. The furore Ferguson had stirred up around the Farmers' dealings with Backus had caused Drury to reconsider granting the lease the premier had promised to Backus for White Dog Falls. This left Backus dependent upon the energy he could generate at the power station at the outlet of Lake of the Woods, which he had purchased from the Town of Kenora. To increase the electricity it could produce, he sought to regulate the level of Lake of the Woods. But this plan encountered fervent opposition from the Dominion government, which sought to protect its power interests downstream on the Winnipeg River in Manitoba. Just as it appeared Drury would side with Ottawa in the dispute, Heenan intervened to convince the premier to defend Backus's interests; the matter would remain unresolved until 1928. In the meantime, Backus proceeded to build his newsprint mill in Kenora, which officially opened in 1924.[9]

Backus was also successful in obtaining resources from Drury's government for his other projects, although his record at Fort Frances–International Falls was decidedly mixed. Between 1910 and 1914, he had built a newsprint mill in each of these towns that straddled the Rainy River, and he had constructed the one in Fort Frances without the benefit of a pulpwood concession because the Tories had refused to grant him the tract the Liberals had promised him in 1905. Backus tried – and failed – to resolve this issue with the Farmers before they left office in

BACKUS IS WILLIN'

HON. E. C. DRURY.—"I'm handin' over the only animile in the hull district to you, but if anyone else wants the stack, of course ye'll have to bid agin' 'em fer it."

Figure 8. Backus as Yankee Robber Baron (*Toronto Telegram*, 15 November 1920).

1923. He did, however, supplement the mill's power supply by securing in November 1922 a lease to develop the rapids on the Seine River, which drained Lac des Mille Lacs and emptied into the northern part of Rainy Lake. Backus's contract with the government also authorized him to transmit to his mill in International Falls any surplus power he developed in Ontario, an export privilege he had enjoyed since 1905.[10]

During the Farmers' time in office Backus also succeeded in laying the foundation for building additional newsprint mills in other sections of northern Ontario. The Conservatives had refused, for example, to sell the Nagagami River pulpwood concession on the northern Clay Belt despite a series of applications for it, but the Farmers responded favourably to these inquiries (Map 10 in next chapter). After cruising the 2,300-square-mile tract, the government tendered it in mid-1921 without stipulating any diameter limit on the timber, promising a water power lease to the successful bidder, and requiring a 100-ton pulp mill to be built. Mindful of the brouhaha that had surrounded his tender for the English River timber, Backus had directed his lawyers to incorporate discreetly the Transcontinental Development Company just prior to the tender, which allowed him to keep his acquisition of this rich fibre supply a secret, at least for the time being.[11] Because the North American pulp and paper industry was plagued by overcapacity at this time, particularly in terms of pulp (many pulp mills fell into receivership in 1921), Backus applied to the Farmers for permission to delay breaking ground on the project. His request also reflected the difficulties his survey team had encountered in locating a local waterfall capable of generating enough power for a mill. The government recognized the legitimate reasons for this appeal, and granted it.[12]

Backus also acquired a lease to the 3,400-square-mile Long Lac pulpwood concession, but in a most circuitous way (see Map 10 in the next chapter). The Farmers first cruised the limit and then tendered it at the same time and under almost identical terms to those which applied to the sale of the Nagagami concession. John Homer Black, a prominent Toronto businessman and president of Great Lakes Paper Company, was the winning bidder. Black's lease gave him roughly two years to build a million-dollar, 100-ton pulp mill and set no diameter limit on the pulpwood he could cut. Citing the same difficulties as Transcontinental (the overcapacity in and uncertain state of the pulp and paper industry and lack of sufficient nearby water powers), Black asked for an extension of the deadline by which he was to fulfil his contractual obligations. The Farmers agreed and merely obliged Black to erect his mill "with all convenient dispatch." In April 1923, Black assigned his interest in the Long Lac limit to Lewis L. Alsted, who, with fellow American George Seaman, was associated with Black in the Great Lakes Paper undertaking. Alsted and Seaman already owned leases to the Black Sturgeon and Pic River concessions. This meant that Great Lakes Paper now controlled three pulpwood tracts comprising a total of over 5,000 square miles and holding at least 11,000,000 cords of spruce, enough to support a large newsprint mill the firm planned to build at the Lakehead.[13]

Prior to acquiring the Long Lac limit, Alsted and Seaman had been steering Great Lakes Paper through troubled waters which the Farmers initially refused to calm. A few weeks after the Tories' defeat in 1919, they had executed an Order in Council authorizing Ontario Hydro to enter into a contract to supply power to the company. This agreement was illegal (because the price set for power was below cost) and Alsted and Seaman refused to sign it (because the contract was legally unenforceable). Upon his accession to power, Drury faced the formidable task of resolving this complicated situation that involved Ontario Hydro, the local ratepayers, and the municipalities of Port Arthur and Fort William, both of which were vying for Great Lakes Paper to construct its mill in their bailiwicks.[14] Moreover, the issue of its power supply was critical for the company, a point the firm constantly pushed with the Farmers. Not only was the price of power a crucial determinant of a mill's profitability, but a newsprint producer needed an energy contract that provided it with a "continuous supply" of power, a clause that was absent from the agreement Ontario Hydro had offered Great Lakes Paper. The firm's lawyers thus underscored to the government that it would lack "the right to enforce [its] contract in the Canadian Courts," thereby making it "[im]possible for them [i.e., Great Lakes Paper] to use ... [the power contract] with their bankers for financing purposes." Ontario Hydro's contract also prevented the company from promising its customers that their supply of paper would be uninterrupted, a pledge upon which newspaper publishers insisted. With the solicitors for Great Lakes Paper pointing out that private power companies would agree to provide a "continuous supply" of energy as a matter of course, they asked the government for "either ... control of a power development or ... a power contract which w[i]ll ensure the delivery of commercial [i.e., continuous] power to us." Despite the intense pressure to resolve this issue, including several royal commissions that touched upon it, the matter still lay undecided in early 1923.[15]

But as the June provincial election approached and several noteworthy facts regarding Great Lakes Paper came to light, the Farmers reached out to the firm. The first was Backus's involvement with the company, as his name suddenly appeared on its board of directors. It is unclear exactly when he became a partner in this firm, but experience had taught him that it was wise to conceal his involvement in Ontario's newsprint industry.[16] Then in April 1923, the government authorized Ontario Hydro to enter into a contract to provide power to Great Lakes Paper, and the agreement embodied most of the terms for which the company had been fighting, including a guarantee of "continuous electrical power." Finally, nearly three weeks after the Farmers had gone down to defeat in the election, Drury hastily organized a cabinet meeting during which he oversaw the execution of an Order in Council. It acceded to Great Lakes Paper's wish to establish its enterprise in Fort William instead of Port Arthur and to use all three pulpwood concessions – the Pic, Black Sturgeon and Long Lac – to support one mill. Not surprisingly, Ferguson's new Tory government would immediately reopen the matter when the Legislature resumed sitting later that summer.[17]

Of all the entrepreneurs conducting business in Ontario, Backus must have most regretted the Farmers' defeat in the 1923 election. During their four years in office, he had amassed a string of pulpwood concessions and water powers that would serve as the foundation upon which he would continue building a forest products and hydroelectric empire in northern Ontario. While the many factors that explained the Farmers' favourable treatment towards him have already been described, a short article in the 19 December 1922 edition of the *Fort William Times-Journal* captured the nub of the matter. The headline exclaimed "Backus Gives Credit to Heenan as the Man Who Put Kenora on the Map," and the piece described how Heenan had fought the battle for both Kenora and Backus "against interests that were determined to keep Backus out."[18]

Spanish River had emerged as Canada's largest and one of its most successful newsprint producers by the end of the Great War. Upon the Farmers' accession to office, George H. Mead, Spanish River's president, immediately took steps to strengthen his firm's position. He established a western branch plant (discussed in the next chapter), sought out other potential locations, and announced his intention to expand significantly his three flagship mills in Sturgeon Falls, Espanola, and Sault Ste Marie. To support this latter effort, Mead looked for the

Ontario government's assistance in terms of acquiring pulpwood and water powers, something which had not been forthcoming from the Tories.[19]

With regard to its power supply, Spanish River scored an immediate, albeit limited, success. In mid-1920 the Farmers agreed to redress the energy deficiency with which the company's mill in Sturgeon Falls had been grappling by granting Spanish River a hydro lease to Smokey Falls. Within a few years, Spanish River had built a power station capable of generating nearly 12,000 horsepower at this location. This new plant, like the mill's turbines, depended for its water flow upon Lake Temagami upstream. Because the government continued to restrict the quantity of water the company could store in this reservoir to protect local water power and recreational interests, its new generating station operated far below its potential. As a result, the Sturgeon Falls mill continued to endure intermittent shutdowns and was still unable to produce to its capacity.[20]

That was the end of Spanish River's success in dealing with the Farmers, and it – specifically Mead, its president – shared responsibility for this reversal of fortunes. The company suffered its worst defeat in Espanola, where it had begun dramatically increasing the size of its newsprint mill in 1919 after then-minister Ferguson had promised to "reserve" – instead of grant – for its use an additional pulpwood concession. Nevertheless, Mead had misrepresented the truth when he assured Spanish River's financiers – and its investors – that the Espanola project had secured its supplemental timber supply. Anxious to sign a contract for this fibre to rectify the situation, Spanish River presented its case to the Farmers shortly after they attained office.

The Farmers were initially amenable to executing a lease to the tract, but their support for doing so dissipated. Ferguson capitalized on the fallout from the tumult he had instigated over the Farmers' relationship with Backus to see that they had been hoisted by their own petard. Ferguson's consummate ability to turn the tables on the Farmers during the latter part of the Timber Commission's hearings in early 1921 included completely recasting – and miscasting – this issue. He craftily painted his reservation of the "Spanish Reserve" as a prodigious gift to the company and another example of how a timber company executive – this time Mead – had exploited his cosy relations with the government. The crucial aspect of his dazzling performance was that *The Farmers' Sun* bought it unquestioningly. The commission's de facto purpose had been to obliterate Ferguson's political presence in Ontario by

Map 9. Timber Situation around the Espanola Mill, 1919–1923

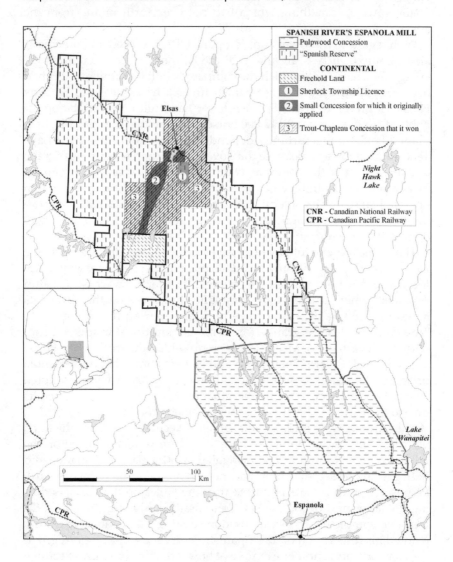

SPANISH RIVER'S ESPANOLA MILL
- - - Pulpwood Concession
"Spanish Reserve"

CONTINENTAL
Freehold Land
① Sherlock Township Licence
② Small Concession for which it originally applied
③ Trout-Chapleau Concession that it won

CNR - Canadian National Railway
CPR - Canadian Pacific Railway

Elsas

Night
Hawk
Lake

Lake
Wanapitei

Espanola

0   50   100
                    Km

publicizing his sordid administration of Crown timber, and to achieve this aim *The Farmers' Sun* – as the UFO's official organ – had assiduously conveyed every aspect of his dealings to its readers. When reporting on Ferguson's reservation of the tract for which Spanish River's mill in Espanola had applied, *The Sun*'s front-page headline proclaimed that "Hon. H.G. Ferguson Gives Away over 5000 Square Miles by Letter." Although this was not an accurate description of what had happened, the damage had been inflicted. The Farmers could now hardly turn around and grant the pulpwood concession to Spanish River when they were criticizing the former Tory minister for having allegedly done exactly the same thing!

Ferguson then took steps which practically prevented the Farmers from assisting Spanish River any time soon. While he indignantly defended himself against *The Sun*'s charges that he had granted the Espanola mill its "reserve," he began pushing the commission to probe Mead's dubious dealings with Spanish River's financial backers, Peabody, Houghteling and Company. In doing so, he outlined Mead's own role in this affair and thereby pushed Spanish River to the brink. The situation was primed for triggering a bear run on its shares, which were already on a downward trajectory due to the recession and to turmoil in the industry. Forced to take decisive action, the company hastily filed an injunction to limit the scope of the inquiry's investigation, but this simply validated in the public's mind Spanish River's duplicity. This impression was only reinforced when the Farmers took the advice of their legal counsel on this file. He recommended that the commission refrain from probing deeper into this mess because, as he put it, doing so "may involve an enquiry into the Stock Exchange dealings of the officials of the company and others and the stock market situation just now is and has been so serious for some four months past that I do not want the commissioners to be blamed for any serious fall in the stock." The upshot was an unmitigated public relations disaster for Spanish River. Hereafter anyone seen to be assisting the company would be deemed guilty by association. The ensuing uproar compelled the company to suspend its plans for expansion in Espanola pending the Farmers' final ruling on the issue.[21]

Even still, once the Timber Commission wrapped up its investigations, Bowman took steps that strongly suggested that he would lease Spanish River its pulpwood reserve. During the summer of 1922, he asked for and received the company's cooperation in cruising the timber on this concession. Spanish River probably viewed the fact that the department charged the company half the project's cost as the government's tacit recognition of its claim to this fibre. On 26 March 1923, after the results from the inventory had been tallied, Spanish River's lawyers officially reapplied for the tract that Ferguson had reserved for it nearly four years earlier. Despite the wholehearted support of the local community and its Liberal MPP, it was apparent that a new factor had entered the equation.[22]

International Paper Company (IP) was the world's largest newsprint firm, and was about to scuttle Spanish River's plans. Based in upper New York State and New England, it was Spanish River's major rival. IP's growing concerns over its diminishing spruce supply in the northeastern United States had prompted it, beginning in the 1890s, to purchase vast tracts of Canadian pulpwood lands and establish subsidiaries in the Dominion to procure fibre for its American mills. This included establishing a beachhead in Ontario, but these holdings were nearing exhaustion by the end of the First World War. IP had then purchased from a pulpwood exporting firm roughly 45,000 acres worth of veterans' land grants near Chapleau and incorporated in the province the Continental Wood Products Company (its name was derived from Continental Paper and Bag Mills Company, one of IP's American subsidiaries and the world's largest kraft paper manufacturer). To process its newly acquired timber for export, Continental erected a rossing plant (and small sawmill) about 180 miles northwest of Sudbury on the Canadian National Railway at a site rechristened Elsas in honour of Continental Paper's president (Map 9). Almost immediately upon commencing operations, Continental began complaining that its freehold timberlands contained far less pulpwood than it had been promised, prompting it to turn to the Ontario government for help.[23]

In doing so, Continental took a fundamentally different – and far more successful – tack than Spanish River. The latter firm had consistently presented the minister of lands and forests with thoughtful and well-researched applications for timber and water powers, but to no avail. In contrast, Continental presented no such plans and instead endeavoured to forge crucial links to the government by dealing through intermediaries whom the provincial state trusted and who understood what was required to ensure success in negotiating for pulpwood and hydroelectric leases. Continental retained Gordon Waldron, for example, one of the Farmers' closest friends and a linchpin in Backus's successful efforts to win over the Drury government. The firm also hired L.E. Bliss to act as its vice-president and manage its operation in Elsas.

As a twelve-year veteran of the department, Bliss knew which of its most restricted corridors of power led to victory in terms of securing control over Crown resources and had gained access to them. In fact, Bliss's connections and influence became so well known that other parties sought to use him to advocate for their causes.[24]

Furthermore, Lady Luck smiled on Continental. The imbroglio that had erupted around Spanish River and its reserve had landed Minister Bowman in a delicate situation. Overseeing the portfolio of lands and forests naturally made him interested in fostering development in the Spanish River territory, yet at the same time he must have felt slighted by Mead's firm for having embroiled him in such a predicament and loath to assist it as a result. Casting about for a means of presenting at least the facade of industrial progress in this region, Continental was only too happy to oblige him.

It was thus not surprising that Bowman proved remarkably sympathetic to that company's appeals for Crown resources despite the myriad reasons not to be. After the minister initially rejected Continental's request to tender the timber in Sherlock Township, which was spruce rich and in the heart of the Spanish Reserve and just south of Elsas, for example, its officials convinced him to relent and it won the licence uncontested. While this transaction was hardly out of the ordinary, Continental's request for a 200-square-mile pulpwood concession upriver from Elsas was. For starters, the tract it sought formed the heart of the Spanish Reserve (Map 9). Moreover, although Continental's application made the obligatory gesture towards developing the province's own pulp and paper industry by proposing to build a small kraft paper mill under "reasonable conditions ... within a reasonable time," it underscored that the primary impetus behind seeking this timber was to sustain the firm's existing pulpwood exporting business.[25]

Bowman's initial reaction to Continental's application reflected the influence Waldron and Bliss were wielding and the mindset of a minister rapt at the thought of IP, the continent's major pulp and paper maker, setting up shop in the province. Undeniably, it would be a boon to northern Ontario's development to have IP establish a kraft (not newsprint) mill that would both diversify the province's pulp and paper industry and utilize small-diameter jack pine, an underused tree, and not spruce, for which the demand was very high. These considerations caused the minister, in his correspondence with Continental, to mention neither the government's commitment to reserve for Spanish River the timber for which Continental had applied nor the department's policy of setting aside pulpwood for "established" mills before considering requests from new ventures. Bowman did not even query Continental about its plans to export much of the pulpwood it was seeking, and he expedited matters in late December 1922 when he instructed Continental in the art of preparing an application for a pulpwood concession in a manner which he believed would be palatable to the government, a courtesy the minister provided to no other party during his term in office.

Thereafter, Bowman single-mindedly pushed Contintental's cause at the expense of Spanish River's. Along the way he ignored the concerns raised by Walter Cain, the deputy minister, about how the size of the pulpwood concession for which Continental had applied had grown from its original scope of roughly 200 square miles in mid-1922 to over five times that size six months later. Although besieged for some time by Spanish River's officials, who had been pressing for a lease to their long-promised reserve, Bowman instead responded favourably to Continental's request to sell immediately the timber for which it had applied, which was named the Trout-Chapleau concession and covered the entire middle portion of the Spanish Reserve (Map 9). He ushered the tender for the tract through Cabinet in March 1923 without mentioning that he had allowed Continental to draw up its terms, a golden opportunity on which the company's lawyers had fully capitalized. The operative condition they set was the requirement to construct by mid-1925 a 75-ton kraft pulp mill near Elsas, a term which essentially precluded Spanish River from bidding for the pulpwood it needed and had long been promised. It simply made no sense for Spanish River to construct another mill – this one for kraft – so close to its existing newsprint facilities when it could transport the pulpwood from the Trout-Chapleau concession by rail to its mill in Espanola. Even *Pulp and Paper Magazine of Canada* noted how the terms of sale for this "tender" made it nothing more than a private sale.

Bowman continued to indulge Continental. To further its interests, the minister allowed a mere two months for prospective bidders to investigate the 1,049-square-mile concession. Although the department had jointly cruised with Spanish River the Spanish Reserve in 1922, and had a report on the Trout-Chapleau block it was selling at this time, Bowman refused to permit other parties who requested access to this data to view them. Then, when Drury questioned Bowman about the desirability of allowing such a short period to investigate the limit, the minister bore false witness against his premier by replying that he "considered that between two and three months should be ample time for anyone interested in the area to cruise same, having regard to the information the Department has on record, which is available if and when sought." Finally, Bowman was adamant that the government should ignore Spanish River's protests against the sale of the Trout-Chapleau limit. The minister conceded that "the Spanish River Pulp and Paper Mills, for whom the area had been set aside, strenuously resented the Crown taking any part of it, and insistently represented to the Crown that it would be unfair to do so." But Bowman asserted that cabinet had approved the plan to tender the Trout-Chapleau limit, and that it should proceed.[26]

And he made certain that it did proceed along what can only be considered a preordained path. Bowman would argue on several occasions in the spring of 1923 that he was unable to resolve issues involving Crown resources because of the impending provincial election that was set for June.[27] In addressing the tender for the Trout-Chapleau limit for Continental, however, Bowman insisted to Drury in early June that "this Government should assume and exercise responsibility of dealing with tenders, and it was felt that the opening of them should be prior to the Election." Then, undeterred by his party's resounding defeat in the 25 June election, the minister moved quickly to close the deal. Continental was expectedly the sole bidder for the Trout-Chapleau limit, and the department's solicitors hastily drew up a concession agreement that required only Bowman's signature and not cabinet approval to become binding. By 10 July, over two weeks after the election, Continental had its lease, which contained no surprises. It required the company to build only a 75-ton kraft pulp mill by 1 June 1925.[28]

International Paper's subsidiary had thus garnered a strategic and rich tract of spruce pulpwood that had been specifically set aside for its competitor's "established industry" in Espanola. Continental's neat 1,049-square-mile limit contained what was estimated to be roughly 1,500,000 cords of spruce. It thus represented nearly one-third of the total volume of this species found on the entire Spanish Reserve, and it was also the largest block of high-density pulpwood in the area; it would be relatively cheap to operate. What made Continental's acquisition of this limit most extraordinary was the fact that the government had obliged the company to build a mill that produced kraft, which was made from jack pine. There had been no reason, in other words, for the government to give Continental the privilege of harvesting any spruce, let alone this vital section of it. Spanish River could hardly be faulted for pondering the notion that IP had acquired this concession simply as a ploy to deny its rival this timber.

Nevertheless, Spanish River had no time to sulk. On 16 April 1923 Bowman informed the company that its lease to what remained of the Spanish Reserve was ready to be signed. The minister added, however, that this contract would have to be submitted to cabinet for approval, a condition he had not attached to Continental's lease. After Bowman signed Spanish River's agreement on 15 May, he never found the time to present it to cabinet. When he left office shortly thereafter, the Espanola mill still had no lease to any part of the reserve that the provincial state had promised it back in 1919. This was a strange policy indeed for a government committed to providing wood to "established" mills.[29]

6 "Established industries which ... have but scant supply"

In the Thunder Bay District and on the northern Clay Belt, the Farmers dealt with the pulp and paper industry while considering a host of factors both old and new. The former included the state's traditional drive to realize its pre-eminent goal in both regions, namely to populate them, by creating for the settlers the most dynamic market possible for their spruce. The UFO was committed to furthering this agenda and did so both by denying most existing mills' requests for fibre resources and by facilitating the work of the pulpwood exporters, a group whose close association with the government often spurred the elected officials to assist it as an end unto itself. At the same time, the maturation of the pulp and paper industry in these areas of the province confronted the Farmers with a double-edged sword. The UFO realized that befriending certain mills was a pragmatic means for realizing tangible benefits, but fatal pitfalls could await a government which was seen currying favour with a pulp and paper maker.

These determinants caused the Farmers to treat the pulp and paper industry in the Thunder Bay District and on the northern Clay Belt in a manner that was relatively straightforward and easy to explain. The former region's numerous strengths as a location in which to manufacture newsprint attracted three new mill projects within one year of the Farmers' taking office. This hive of activity prompted *Pulp and Paper Magazine of Canada* to predict that the region would "shortly become the leading pulp and paper centre of the Dominion." The trio of new enterprises, however, and the original mill that had been established at the Lakehead in 1917, were built without the benefit of Crown pulpwood concessions. The Drury government promised to provide timber to several of these operations but refused to do so because it stimulated demand for homesteaders' pulpwood and these interests lacked that special connection to the government to realize their ends. Moreover, the UFO had been severely burned by Ferguson's manipulation of the facts regarding both its relationship with Backus and the Ontario government's dealings with Spanish River, and the aforementioned mills at the Lakehead were all contaminated by the fallout from those affairs. In contrast, the Farmers took extreme steps to favour the Thunder Bay District's original mill simply because it was expedient to do so.

Similar factors played out – but in different ways – on the northern Clay Belt. There, three pulp and paper interests had established themselves during the 1910s, and the Farmers showed two of them little sympathy. They took this approach to the first, Abitibi, because it was struck by the same political malaise which had afflicted both Backus and Spanish River, and because Bowman was determined to demonstrate that he was in no way captive to this pulp and paper firm. The UFO subjugated the interests of the second, Mattagami Pulp, because the government sought to realize other aims in the area. By the same token, the Farmers took a remarkable shining to the mill project in Kapuskasing, which was taken over by Kimberly-Clark during their reign, after the company recognized that the government needed it more than it needed the government. The firm was thus able to compel the Farmers into marrying the provincial state's interests – although it was really a "shotgun" wedding considering the lack of viable options – to its pulp and paper operation and reap a bountiful dowry as a result. As unusual as this behaviour was, it was a sign of things to come.[1]

George H. Mead was one industrialist who believed in northern Ontario's potential as a site to manufacture newsprint. As president of Spanish River Pulp and Paper Mills, he had committed to enhancing its newsprint plants in northeastern Ontario (in Sturgeon Falls, Espanola, and Sault Ste Marie) during the late 1910s and early 1920s. At the same time, he was anxious to establish a foothold in the province's northwest, and an opportunity to do so presented itself shortly after the end of the First World War. In August 1920, the Mead Investment Company (MIC), the financing arm for his pulp and paper ventures, signed a lease with the Dominion government for the privilege of harvesting the pulpwood on the land grants which had been given to the Grand Trunk Pacific Railway (GTPR) northwest of Fort William. The agreement ran for twenty-five years (with a provision for renewals), and obliged MIC first to construct a pulp and then a 100-ton newsprint mill and supply

Canadian dailies and weeklies with paper in the event of another short-age like the one that had followed the war. MIC also secured a fifty-year agreement with a local private utility to provide for its project's energy needs and incorporated the Fort William Paper Company to carry out the venture.[2] By May 1921, its groundwood mill was producing 100 tons per day, but MIC was under the gun to construct an accompanying newsprint line. Not only did the firm's lease with Ottawa for the timber on the railway lands require it, but the low price of groundwood pulp at this time was bankrupting mills that only manufactured this product.[3]

The problem was that the project required a supplemental fibre sup-ply to support its operation, an issue that Fort William Paper had al-ready raised with the Ontario government. The company's investigations had revealed that the railway lands it leased held only 500,000 cords of spruce, which a 100-ton newsprint mill would exhaust in fourteen years. This dim estimation was corroborated in early 1921 by B.M. Wylie, the department's local timber agent, who confirmed that most of the timber on the GTPR's tracts was unsuited to making newsprint because it was jack pine. He thus recommended that the Ontario government effect a "re-adjustment of the ... holdings of the Company, because from the enormous out-lay in money they are making to provide means for man-ufacturing paper, they will have to be supplied with a Spruce area." Fort William Paper had first requested just such an area before it had even broken ground on its project, and in mid-1922 it submitted an official proposal to the Farmers. After explaining its fibre shortage, and recog-nizing the need to put forth a quid pro quo to the provincial govern-ment, the company offered to construct a 150-ton newsprint mill within one year conditional upon receiving a pulpwood concession containing roughly 4,000,000 cords of spruce located due north of Fort William (Map 10). To buttress its case, the firm reminded the Farmers of their guarantee to supply all "established" pulp and paper mills with "per-petual" supplies of timber. For Spanish River, this pledge embodied the concept of operating its pulpwood limits on a sustained yield basis, a principle that it had already adopted for its forest management program in northeastern Ontario. Fort William Paper had asked for 4,000,000 cords of pulpwood because it would supply a 150-ton newsprint mill for sixty to seventy years, equivalent to roughly one rotation of the spruce in the local woodlands.[4]

In responding to the application, Beniah Bowman, the minister, played coy, behaviour which the company clearly misread. On the one hand, his actions suggested that he had earmarked for the firm the

Map 10. Pulpwood Situation in Northwestern Ontario, 1919–1923

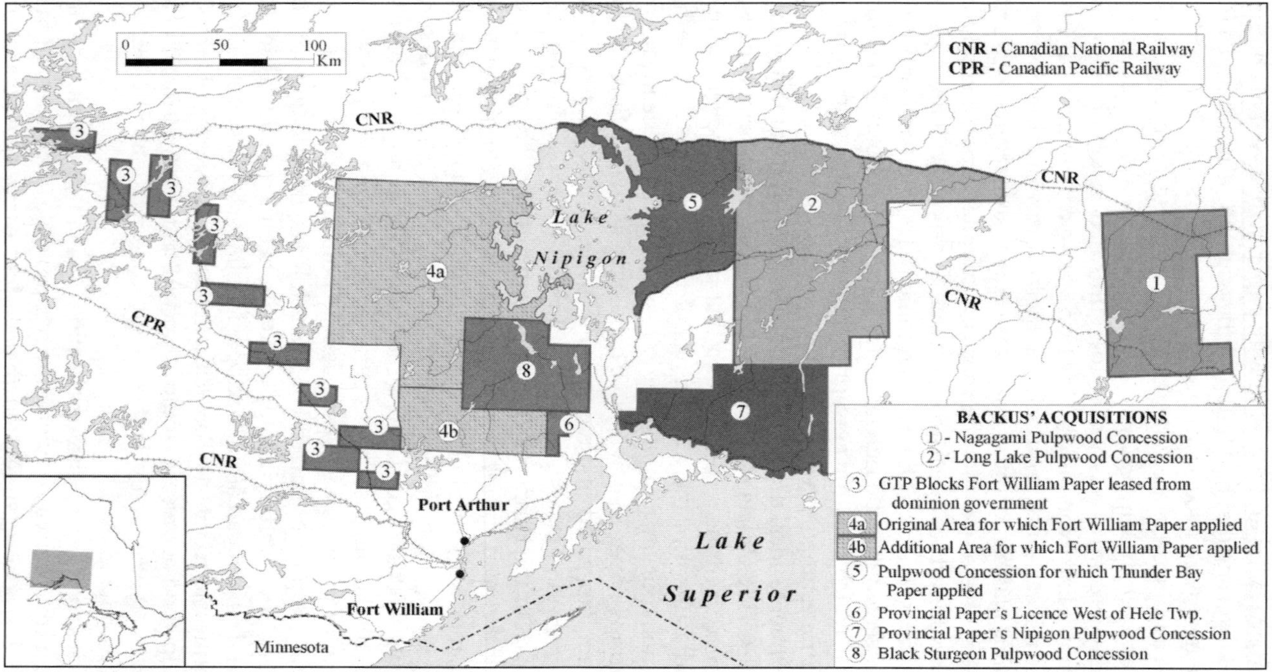
0
50
100
Km
CNR - Canadian National Railway
CPR - Canadian Pacific Railway
CNR
CNR
CNR
CNR
CPR
Lake
Nipigon
Lake
Superior
Port Arthur
Fort William
Minnesota
4a
4b
BACKUS' ACQUISITIONS
1 - Nagagami Pulpwood Concession
2 - Long Lake Pulpwood Concession
3 GTP Blocks Fort William Paper leased from dominion government
4a Original Area for which Fort William Paper applied
4b Additional Area for which Fort William Paper applied
5 Pulpwood Concession for which Thunder Bay Paper applied
6 Provincial Paper's Licence West of Hele Twp.
7 Provincial Paper's Nipigon Pulpwood Concession
8 Black Sturgeon Pulpwood Concession

pulpwood concession it sought. Over the course of 1920–3, for example, Pigeon River Lumber Company, a large Wisconsin-backed pulpwood exporting enterprise at the Lakehead, continually asked for the Farmers to grant it a pulpwood limit within the area covered by Fort William Paper's application. Even though Pigeon River offered to construct a new pulp and paper mill in the area, and despite the accompanying letters from local politicians in support of its cause, Bowman rejected Pigeon River's entreaties on the grounds that Fort William Paper had already requested this tract, and that it had priority because it was an "established" mill. Interpreting the Farmers' attitude as an indication that they would soon grant the company its concession, Fort William Paper proceeded with its proposed project; its 150-ton newsprint mill was fully operational by January 1923. Apparently this commitment was still not enough for Bowman, however. In December 1922, he informed the company that it would only receive its fibre supply if it committed both to doubling the capacity of its facility and to purchasing a large block of electricity from Hydro's Nipigon development. Fort William Paper was shocked by this unexpected condition. Its solicitor reminded Bowman that "the evidence of [his company's] good faith" was already manifest in its new newsprint mill. Nevertheless, the company was acutely aware that the only source from which a pulpwood limit could come was the provincial government, and so it agreed to Bowman's demands. But the minister still did not act on the matter.[5]

Fort William Paper was not the only mill in the Thunder Bay District waiting for a pulpwood concession. Kaministiquia Pulp and Paper Company had built a mill in 1920 without one and had thus initially depended on local settlers for its fibre supply. Unfortunately for the firm, it had undertaken its venture at a time of hyper-inflation and had been forced to pay rapidly escalating prices for building materials and pulpwood during its first season of production. The next year's severe recession then hammered down the demand for and price of the groundwood pulp the mill manufactured from its partially completed facility. Unable to bear this burden, Kam Pulp went into receivership in 1921. At this point, George W. Mead (no relation to George H. Mead, Spanish River's president), a veteran American paper maker, became interested in the property. President of Consolidated Water Power and Paper Company in Wisconsin, which had been exporting pulpwood from the province since the early 1900s, he recognized the value of the defunct mill and the extraordinary factors which had been its undoing. When C.D. Howe, the soon-to-be-federal-politician who stood behind

Kaministiquia Pulp, offered to sell Mead the plant's assets at a favourable price, Mead jumped at the chance. He purchased them in February 1922 and renamed the project Thunder Bay Paper Company. By the spring, the mill was producing 60 tons of groundwood per day, which Mead shipped to his mills in Wisconsin for conversion into newsprint.[6]

Mead had purchased the mill only after Drury and Bowman had personally promised to grant it a sufficient supply of pulpwood. Mead had explained in a letter to the Farmers prior to acquiring Kam Pulp that he was prepared to buy and significantly expand the bankrupt plant. At the same time, he emphasized that, if he did so, "we shall be in a precarious position regarding pulp wood and we shall have to come to you for your support in finding a means for us to operate the plant and to increase its capacity, eventually expanding it to a paper mill of fair proportion." Drury and Bowman had then verbally committed the government to providing for his fibre requirements, reassurances that had prompted Mead to spend nearly $700,000 on buying the property and building a 60-ton sulphite pulp line alongside the existing groundwood one.[7]

But, just as with Fort William Paper, the Farmers refused to convert their promises into action. Throughout the summer and fall of 1922, Thunder Bay Paper's executives repeatedly met with Drury and Bowman and offered to expand their operation into a fully integrated newsprint mill just as soon as the government provided them with an opportunity to acquire a timber limit, specifically one on the east side of Lake Nipigon (Map 10). "The Company would not feel justified," they explained, "in expending the large amount involved in the enlargement above mentioned, unless the pulpwood was available. The Government has recognized that this is a legitimate precaution, as it has been stated several times by members of the Cabinet that existing mills must be looked after, as regards wood, before the erection of any new mills is encouraged." They added that Thunder Bay Paper's expanded operations would require another 7,500 horsepower from Ontario Hydro's Nipigon development, a sale that would reduce the enormous deficit the public utility was running in the district. In response, Bowman would provide the company only with a written pledge which reiterated "that the Government is anxious to see that all existing pulp mills acquire adequate pulp limits to permit them not only to carry on, but to expand."[8]

By late 1922, the persistent lobby by both Fort William Paper and Thunder Bay Paper for pulpwood concessions pushed Drury to direct Bowman to take action. Realizing that the Gregory Commission into

Ontario Hydro would soon be reporting on the utility's Thunder Bay System, Drury urged his minister to formulate a policy for the pulp limits in the Lake Superior–Lake Nipigon watersheds which fell within the "N[i]pigon Power zone." In response, Bowman recognized that there were certain pulp and paper "industries established at Port Arthur and Fort William whose future depends upon their obtaining a supply of pulpwood from this region ... These concerns are desirous of expanding and increasing their capacity and have on several occasions personally expressed the hope that nothing would be done in connection with disposing of timber in the Nipigon Watershed without giving consideration to their necessities and future." Bowman assured Drury that the department had already begun cruising the timber sought as a precursor to selling it, and that this work would be wrapping up in early 1923, thus clearing the way for a tender.[9]

Fort William Paper then unexpectedly appeared to have secured its limit. After the department was deluged with a flurry of telegrams and letters from municipal leaders in support of the company's application, in February 1923 the government's solicitors drew up an agreement with the mill. In exchange for building another 160-ton groundwood unit as the first step in doubling its newsprint capacity and taking at least 7,500 horsepower from Ontario Hydro's Nipigon power plant, the Farmers would lease it a pulpwood concession west of Lake Nipigon. This limit was larger than the one for which Fort William Paper had been lobbying, an augmentation that reflected the fact that the company would now be obliged to construct and operate a newsprint mill of 300 not 150 tons (Map 10).[10]

Spurred by stories of this impending deal, Thunder Bay Paper made another presentation to the government in mid-March. With the firm's case buttressed by a telegram from the mayor of Port Arthur, its representatives re-emphasized that mills needed to be assured of sufficient pulpwood supplies in order to finance their operations, as "bonding houses w[ere] very chary in advancing money to mills whose timber supply, which is the heart of their business, must be obtained in ... an uncertain manner." With Bowman still non-committal, three of Thunder Bay Paper's directors – led by George P. Berkey – travelled from Wisconsin to Toronto to see Bowman. They reminded him that, prior to purchasing Thunder Bay Paper, they had "received great encouragement" from the mayor, minister, and premier, all of whom had provided "assurances that the Company would be taken care of in the line of timber limits in the event that it made a substantial and bona fide investment in such mill. On such assurances the purchase was made and a large additional expense was incurred by said Company in improvements and extension." Berkey tersely stated that the "time has now come when the Company must have assurances of something definite along this line" and agreed that it would meet all reasonable conditions for expansion if it were assured a "permanent timber supply." Before returning to the United States, Berkey and his entourage received word from Bowman that the government had considered their case and had "determined that an area on the east side of Lake Nipigon [for which they had applied] shall be offered [for tender]."[11]

But as the spring thaw began softening the snow pack in the Thunder Bay District, events unfolded in a manner that boded ill for both Fort William Paper and Thunder Bay Paper. Rumours of the former's private deal with the government aroused protests in the Legislature and press. Drury had been critically burned by the Opposition's attacks on his handling of Backus's pulpwood concessions and by revelations regarding the pulpwood reserve the government had set aside for Spanish River's mill in Espanola, and he was determined not to be grilled again. He thus refused to grant privately either mill a timber limit no matter how strong the reasons in favour of doing so. This meant that the Farmers would not execute the draft agreement with Fort William Paper, but that this company could still win the concession it desired in a public tender.[12]

But again, the Farmers' fear of political repercussions drove Bowman to refuse to push this file forward. On 13 April 1923, the government executed an Order in Council that made specific reference to both Fort William Paper and Thunder Bay Paper in explaining that these "established industries … which have but scant supply" of pulpwood were in need of "assurance of a reasonable continuance of business." The Order thus authorized Bowman to tender "forthwith" a tract of pulpwood on both the west and east sides of Lake Nipigon, and immediately thereafter department officials drew up the terms of sale. The matter died there, however. Despite the element of urgency which pervaded the Order, the government's repeated promises that the limits would be made available, and the fact that the department had cruised them and cabinet had repeatedly discussed this timber sale from mid- to late April, the minister did not press to have the Executive Council pass an Order authorizing this tender.[13]

Nor would Bowman reassure these two firms that the government would meet their pulpwood needs. On behalf of Thunder Bay Paper,

F.N. Youngman wrote the minister in May 1923 to express both his anxiety at not having seen the advertisement for the Nipigon limits in the newspapers and his fear that the recent announcement that the Legislature was to be dissolved might mean that his company's distressing situation would remain in abeyance until after the election. Having assumed that the tender was proceeding, his firm had gone ahead with its plans for expanding its plant, and Youngman stressed that "these extensions and expenditures are not warranted unless we are assured of an ample supply of timber by the Government." If the Farmers had, in fact, decided against tendering this pulpwood, Youngman asked "the Government [to] write and assure us that this area will be reserved until such time as the Government deems it in the interest of the Province to dispose of it in some manner. Such a statement will relieve our minds and let us know that the Government will carry out its obligations, protect our investment and allow us to plan confidently for the future." Even though Bowman had used the pending June election as the reason for hastily wrapping up the sale of a pulpwood concession to International Paper's subsidiary, in this instance he did not even reply to Thunder Bay Paper's inquiry. Moreover, Bowman refused to offer for lease another pulpwood concession for a mill developer in the Sioux Lookout area explicitly because of the imminent election.[14]

While the Farmers did not provide those interested in producing newsprint in the Thunder Bay District with pulpwood concessions, they had a compelling reason to permit the region's only non-newsprint maker to virtually write its own ticket in terms of acquiring Crown timber. Provincial Paper Mills, one of the country's largest fine-paper makers, had built a small sulphite mill in Port Arthur in 1916–17 without the benefit of a pulpwood concession, and had appropriately named the firm Port Arthur Pulp and Paper Company. Howard Ferguson, the minister, had permitted it to harvest only a small quantity of spruce for a limited time from two nearby tracts of Crown land. Upon the Farmers' accession to office, they agreed to tender one of the small limits on which Port Arthur Pulp had been operating. The period's rampant inflation and the Tories' long-standing refusal to sell pulpwood in the Thunder Bay District, however, pushed the bidding for this limit to dizzying heights. Port Arthur Pulp won the tender for the 72-square-mile limit west of Hele Township, but it had been compelled to bid a princely bonus of $5.25 per cord to best its rivals (Map 10). With stumpage pushing the Crown charges per cord of this spruce to over $6.00, Port

Arthur Pulp's victory was pyrrhic; the price of this fibre rendered it practically inoperable.[15]

In the meantime, Provincial had been pressuring the government to give its mill in Port Arthur a large Crown pulpwood concession, and Bowman ensured that it realized this aim. The company's lawyers' initial request for the Farmers to grant it privately a large tract of Crown forest south of Lake Nipigon was rejected by the department's officials, who explained that the government's policy was to cruise all tracts of timber before selling them (Map 10). Provincial's officials then leaned on Bowman. To improve their leverage, they threatened to shut off the paper supply to magazine publishers in Ontario if the government did not take immediate action, bluster that a nervous president of *Saturday Night* conveyed to the premier in September 1920. Bowman was clearly moved by these appeals, as he agreed both to tender the 1,240-square-mile Nipigon limit for which Provincial had applied, and to do so without first cruising it. He thus had no accurate inventory of the timber on this limit, making it impossible for him to calculate objectively the value of the bids he would receive.[16]

Two factors made this concession particularly valuable. This part of the province's boreal forest was believed to average upwards of five cords of spruce per acre. More importantly, as this was the only remaining large tract of unleased Crown woodlands in the district whose waters flowed directly to Lake Superior, it would be relatively cheap and easy to operate. Not surprisingly, the Thunder Bay District's pulp and paper makers expressed intense interest in this tender, which marked the last opportunity to secure a substantial, inexpensive source of high-quality spruce near Port Arthur, Fort William, and Nipigon.

Nevertheless, Bowman ensured that only Provincial would be able to bid on this timber by permitting the company's officials to write the terms of sale. They drew up a tender that included a provision obliging all bidders to operate pulp and *fine*-paper mills which produced "a quality of paper equivalent to that now in use in publication of school books by the Department of Education." It was widely known that no other mill in the district was geared towards manufacturing this product; they either already produced groundwood and/or newsprint or had committed to doing so. One disgruntled observer caustically noted after the department refused to accord him a similar privilege of setting the terms of his tender that it was clear "that the Nipigon Limit was put up at the request of the Provincial Paper Mills and the conditions were deliberately and properly framed … [for] the industry they wanted, namely, book paper." It was rather anticlimactic when only one offer was submitted and the government awarded the limit to Provincial.[17]

The firm's influence did not stop there. Bowman gave its lawyers carte blanche to dictate the provisions of the agreement it signed for the pulpwood concession. Whereas every other lease of this kind had called for the construction of new mills or the expansion of existing ones, Provincial's solicitors saw to it that their client's agreement simply required the company to "operate" pulp and paper mills valued at a minimum of $1,500,000 in the Thunder Bay District or "at the Grantee's option at some other place." Cognizant that the firm's existing facilities were worth at least this amount, Provincial's legal counsel had guaranteed that it would thus fulfil its contractual obligations simply by continuing to manufacture pulp at its small Port Arthur mill and paper at its three mills in southern Ontario. In addition, the company was not compelled to cut any wood from its prime new limit, and it would not for over one decade even though it had adamantly insisted that it had desperately required this fibre.[18]

Good fortune alone had not dictated Provincial Paper's remarkable success in dealing with the Farmers. The Ontario government undoubtedly valued newsprint mills for the jobs they created and their contribution to developing the hinterland, but the province had no real need for the type of paper they produced. The provincial government's constitutional responsibility for education, however, gave it a profound interest in fine paper, specifically that on which school texts were printed. Ontario's Department of Education had traditionally experienced great difficulties in procuring a sufficient supply of book paper at an affordable price, especially during the latter years of the First World War. A royal commission struck by Ottawa in 1917 failed to improve the situation, and the Farmers exacerbated the problem when they publicly committed to provide all schoolchildren in the province with free texts. The culprit at the centre of the crisis was readily identifiable, as Provincial produced 80 per cent of the book paper used by Canadian publishers at this time. Sensitive to the power it wielded as a result, the firm demonstrated uncanny timing and keen political savvy when, at the height of this quandary, it had offered the Ontario government a way out. A certain supply of book paper at a reasonable price in exchange for receiving its pulpwood concession was an offer the Farmers could not possibly have refused. Just as Backus had figured out a means of making it politic for the state to meet his needs, so too had Provincial Paper.[19]

It was a very different story for most of the pulp and paper enterprises on the northern Clay Belt, including Abitibi Power and Paper Company. Its president, Frank Anson, had constructed a large newsprint mill in Iroquois Falls in the mid-1910s after Ferguson and the Tories had promised to assist him in this endeavour. Because they did not honour their end of the deal, Anson viewed the Farmers' ascent to power as an auspicious omen for his enterprise.

And for a brief period, it was. Abitibi had been suffering from a power shortage because the Tories had committed to granting it a lease to develop the hydroelectric potential at Twin Falls but never delivered the contract. Surprised to learn of this situation, the Farmers immediately rectified it by granting Abitibi a lease to the site. This permitted the company to complete its hydro project, the energy from which powered the three new newsprint machines Abitibi installed at this time. This raised the mill's capacity to over 500 tons and established it as one of North America's lowest-cost and largest newsprint producers.[20]

But then the company's luck in dealing with the Farmers ran out, largely because of Ferguson. By mid-1921, the erstwhile minister had masterfully turned the tables on the Timber Commission by tarring the likes of Backus and Spanish River as renegade industrialists who had the Drury government at their beck and call, and Ferguson painted Abitibi with the same brush. He did so by practically forcing the investigation to address the decision he had made while minister in 1919 to set aside as a "reserve" for Abitibi a 2,200-square-mile pulpwood concession for which the firm had begun applying when it had initiated its expansion program during the latter part of the Great War. The commission learned that Anson had then misrepresented the "reserve" as a "grant" to his financiers – just as Mead and Spanish River had done – in order to assure them that his company had legal access to a sufficient fibre supply, which it clearly did not. When Abitibi began lobbying the Farmers to give it the timber Ferguson had promised it, Ferguson was able to depict the deal as a sell-out of the public interest, one that he had not stooped to make. Although Minister Bowman continually promised Abitibi that it would be "assured of an ample supply of wood convenient to its mill," he went to extreme lengths to avoid closing the deal for fear of the criticism it would unleash from Ferguson's corner. Even though Abitibi's contract for the limit was ready to be executed by the end of May 1923, Bowman waited until 12 July – nearly three weeks after his party had lost the 25 June election – to sign it. Whereas he had not required Continental's pulpwood concession agreement to be approved by cabinet, Bowman returned the executed copy of Abitibi's contract to the firm's lawyer on 12 July and informed him that "you will note that I have signed subject to the approval of the Lieutenant-Governor-in-Council." No cabinet meeting was held to ratify the agreement, leaving Abitibi without its promised supplemental limit when the Farmers were unseated.[21]

The company thus ratcheted up its efforts to conserve the fibre supply it controlled. Abitibi continued its policy of purchasing lots from homesteaders who had acquired property on the company's pulpwood concession, and maximized the volume of pulpwood it bought from settlers in Ontario and Quebec. Furthermore, Abitibi initiated a forestry program in an effort to develop the means by which it could manage with greatest efficiency the pulpwood concession it leased from the government.[22]

When it came to addressing Abitibi's requests for help with its power supply, Bowman seized this opportunity to champion his personal agenda. Ever mindful of the pall which Ferguson had cast over the company's operations, Bowman knew full well the political advantage that would accrue from distancing himself from the firm. To demonstrate his ministerial independence, Bowman pursued a capricious policy in dealing with Abitibi's power issues. Although some onlookers may have been unable to decipher the message he was delivering in the zigzags he left all over this file, his ultimate decision to refuse to help Abitibi – and even damage its interests in this regard – showed the electorate that his was an office that this paper maker had not bought.

The major bout on this card pitted Abitibi against a local mining firm. The former had applied for a lease to develop the Long Sault rapids on the Abitibi River just north of the National Transcontinental Railway (Transcontinental) in 1916 and again in early 1921 as part of a plan to tap all the area's water powers to enhance its newsprint production (Map 8). At the same time, mining magnate Noah Timmins, who was president of Hollinger Consolidated Gold Mines in the town that bore his name, let Bowman know that he, too, eyed the hydroelectric potential at Long Sault. Timmins applied to Bowman for a lease to develop these rapids as a means by which his operation could escape the grasp of the Northern Canada Power Company, from which Hollinger was obliged to purchase its electricity "for the life of its mine." Timmins protested the high rates his firm was charged relative to his local competitors and what he perceived as the inadequate service Northern Canada provided.[23]

In the battle that ensued between Timmins and Abitibi for the undeveloped water powers on the Abitibi River, Bowman made it clear that he would always side with the former, come what may. In seeking a lease to develop the Long Sault rapids, for example, Timmins stressed to the minister that he fully expected to reap the benefits from the regulatory dam Abitibi had constructed upstream to control the river's flow but that he had no intention of defraying any of the costs Abitibi incurred in operating it. Moreover, Timmins's plan envisaged no new development for northern Ontario and instead sought merely to improve his firm's profitability by securing its own energy source. Abitibi's proposal, in contrast, committed to expanding the capacity of its newsprint operation in exchange for receiving additional water powers. Although Bowman had drafted a lease by April 1921 to give Timmins the Long Sault rapids, Abitibi's howls of protest prevented him from executing it and compelled him to seek counsel on the issue from outside consultants, departmental officials, and Ontario Hydro's own experts. All of them sided with Abitibi in this dispute, particularly because the government had learned long ago that it was always best to restrict to one party the right to develop all the water powers on a river.[24]

But Bowman was determined to see Timmins and Hollinger prevail, and in the end, the minister realized this end. Timmins tried a new approach in July 1922 when he applied to develop another site farther down the Abitibi River, namely Island Falls (also known as the "lower Long Sault rapids"). Bowman eagerly approved Timmins's request, but then departmental officials let him know that Abitibi had already applied four months earlier for a lease to these cascades, those at the nearby Abitibi Canyon, and a proximal tract of pulpwood to support a new mill it proposed building north of the Transcontinental Railway. Moreover, the government's solicitors bowed to the minister's command to draft a lease for Hollinger to develop Island Falls, but it included a provision that respected Abitibi's interests in regulating the Abitibi River. When Hollinger protested the existence of this clause, Bowman struck it from the draft agreement. After several more months of wrangling, the minister took advantage of Drury's absence from a cabinet meeting in April 1923 to execute an Order in Council that granted Hollinger a lease to develop Long Sault without restriction. Only days later, and without explanation, Bowman reversed himself and substituted Island Falls for Long Sault in Hollinger's agreement, sending Abitibi into a rage. Not only had it sought to develop this site itself, but it had learned that Hollinger's contract obliged the government to regulate the Abitibi River to protect both Hollinger's and Abitibi's interests; this would prevent Abitibi from maximizing the energy it derived from its existing hydro developments at Twin Falls and Iroquois Falls. Bowman's capstone achievement for Hollinger occurred on 13 July, nearly three weeks after his party had been trounced in the 1923 election. On that day he found the time to assemble a quorum of cabinet ministers to amend Hollinger's lease to the firm's liking.[25]

Bowman paid Abitibi no such consideration. The newsprint maker had formally reapplied on 4 May 1923 (for the third time in seven years) for the privilege of developing Long Sault as part of its plan for adding 200 tons of capacity to its mill in Iroquois Falls. Although the document was ready for the minister's signature before the June election, he chose to leave it – unsigned – among the paperwork on his desk when he and his party were booted from office.[26]

Bowman determined that Abitibi's closest pulp and paper neighbour would also lose the battle for the local Crown resources during his time in office, but for different reasons. Duncan Chisholm, the power behind Mattagami Pulp and Paper Company in Smooth Rock Falls some 60 miles northwest of Iroquois Falls, had leased a pulpwood concession and water powers from the Tories on the eve of the First World War to support a newsprint mill he intended to build. Circumstances beyond his control had temporarily prevented him from completing the project, however, leaving him with a large sulphite mill instead. Just before Chisholm had undertaken his enterprise in Smooth Rock Falls, the Tories had privately sold New Ontario Colonization Company two townships – Haggart and Kendrey – for the nominal price of $1 per acre even though this land, specifically the timber on it, was integral to Chisholm's mill venture. New Ontario's deal with the government had obliged it to settle the area (Map 8). Although it did practically nothing in this regard, the former minister, Howard Ferguson, had not cancelled its contract but rather endeavoured to conceal its activities, which consisted of harvesting large quantities of timber, mostly pulpwood for export. The details of this deal were uncovered by the Timber Commission in 1920–1 and made headlines across the province. They also provided the Farmers with more than enough evidence to abrogate New Ontario's agreement because it had been breached.[27]

Mattagami Pulp had one compelling reason for wanting the Farmers to cancel New Ontario's contract. Recognizing the immense untapped hydroelectric potential in northern Ontario, early in the twentieth century the government had implemented a standard policy of reserving in its surveys a one-chain (66 feet) allowance along the banks of all major waterways to prevent any land from being alienated within a zone that would likely be flooded by future power developments. Even though this condition had been included in the deeds the Tories had given New Ontario when they sold Kendrey and Haggart Townships to the company back in 1912, the company had constructed its headquarters, rossing mill, and small sawmill partly within the exclusion zone a short distance upstream from Smooth Rock Falls. New Ontario had thus vehemently protested to the Tories in 1916 after the government approved Mattagami Pulp's plans to flood a portion of this reservation, but then-minister Ferguson had chastised it for its impertinence in this instance. "You are doubtless aware," began the minister's lecture in the regulations governing such matters, "that the Crown has vested in it a chain reserve along the banks of all rivers. The Crown may allow anybody to flood this chain reserve without reference to any third party." Two years later, L.V. Rorke, Ontario's director of surveys, similarly admonished New Ontario for trying to legitimize its actions retroactively by applying for a licence of occupation to the land within the reservation which it had foolhardily developed.[28]

After the Farmers won power, the fact that New Ontario had no legal grounds on which to stand (or build) did not stop it from launching a series of offensives, but Premier Drury demonstrated that he would not suffer the firm's antics and he moved to terminate its existence in the region. In mid-1920, for example, New Ontario filed an injunction to prohibit Mattagami Pulp from raising the river's level to the point it required in order to generate enough power to support the newsprint mill it wished to build in Smooth Rock Falls because doing so would flood New Ontario's buildings. Mattagami Pulp's lawyer immediately took the matter up with the government, which reassured him that New Ontario's case was baseless. Then in late 1921, after Drury gave New Ontario the requisite six months' notice for terminating its contract with the Crown for non-performance, New Ontario countered by filing another legal action that defended its woeful performance in fulfilling its obligation to settle the area by arguing that the war had prevented it from doing so. New Ontario won the court's support for preventing Mattagami Pulp from raising the river any farther until the matter could be investigated. This inflicted a critical blow on Mattagami Pulp, as it had raised the additional funds, which it could have spent on completing its newsprint mill, but it was now enjoined from realizing this aim. All the while, New Ontario disingenuously offered to resolve the matter by allowing Mattagami Pulp to buy it out for the inflated price of $800,000, or roughly eight times the amount it had initially paid for the property.[29]

Then, on the eve of the 1923 provincial election, Minister Bowman found time to negotiate an arrangement with New Ontario that did nothing to resolve the problems it had created and reflected the provincial government's traditional loyalty to Ontario's pulpwood exporters. He did this even though he was acutely aware of Mattagami Pulp's request that any deal the government made with New Ontario clear the path for Chisholm to complete his heretofore stalled newsprint mill project in Smooth Rock Falls. On 22 May 1923, Bowman initiated a "walking"[30] Order in Council that passed without Drury's approval. It released New Ontario from its settlement obligations and decreed that the government would retain the sum (under $100,000) the company had paid for its land. This was a paltry price to pay for the immense quantity of timber it had already cut, which was valued at over $1,000,000. New Ontario agreed to release a percentage of lots annually for settlement purposes, but in exchange the government extended the firm's cutting rights on its two townships for another eight years and required it to pay only simple dues for the wood it harvested during that period. This deal constituted a complete sell-out to New Ontario. The firm was now released from its colonization obligations, in which it had never had any interest, and was free to clear these townships of their remaining timber, which had always been its sole ambition. Meanwhile, Mattagami Pulp could still not proceed with its newsprint mill.[31]

Mattagami Pulp faced a number of other challenges. The dramatic plunge in pulp prices in 1921 spelled doom for many Canadian sulphite producers, including Mattagami Pulp, which slipped into receivership. It faced an even greater problem as far as its pulpwood supply was concerned. New Ontario's behaviour had prevented it from completing its newsprint plant and confined Mattagami Pulp to producing only sulphite pulp. This process required far less power because it relied on chemicals not friction to break down the wood fibre, but it used roughly twice as much pulpwood. Consequently, the mill would now consume the roughly 3,000,000 cords of spruce on its original concession, which would have lasted over eight decades had it been able to build the 100-ton newsprint mill it had initially intended, in just over thirty-three years.

To address this situation as well as its power shortage, Chisholm, the firm's founder and president, looked to Bowman for assistance. Throughout 1922 and into the early spring of 1923, Chisholm repeatedly explained his urgent desire to complete his newsprint mill and asked for a supplemental pulpwood limit and a lease to develop two water powers on the Mattagami River below Smooth Rock Falls to support the project. The most important of these was Smoky Falls, from which it was estimated that over 70,000 horsepower could be generated. Hearing a disquieting rumour that another suitor was now vying for the same sites, Chisholm pleaded with Bowman in early May not to take any action until Chisholm had personally presented his case. Unbeknown to Chisholm, his entreaty was already too late.[32]

Chisholm was unaware that the interests in Kapuskasing, some 40 miles west of Smooth Rock Falls, had already gained the inside track in the race to acquire these resources. S.A. Mundy and Elihu Stewart had secured leases to a pulpwood limit and water powers in the Kapuskasing River watershed in 1917. Their mill project, Spruce Falls Pulp and Paper, had faced numerous challenges, however. Then-minister Ferguson had set aside a large chunk of its timber concession for his ill-advised colony of returned soldiers, and investors had baulked at backing the paper plant project because the government had limited its hydroelectric resources (Map 8). Unable to resolve these issues, in 1919 Mundy and Stewart sold their leases to one of the leading American pulp and paper firms: Kimberly-Clark Company (KC), based in Neenah, Wisconsin.

KC looked to Ontario's hinterland resources to buttress its operations in the United States. Its founders had built a newsprint mill in Wisconsin in the 1870s to capitalize on the growing Midwestern American market, and the company had quickly become the region's leading producer. By the early 1900s, however, the decreasing price of newsprint, the rising cost of pulpwood, and the anticipated removal of the American tariff on newsprint had prompted KC's management team to shift gears and begin manufacturing a wide range of personal health and hygiene products made from "cellucotton" (a fluffy absorbent material derived from high-quality wood fibre). KC completed its reorientation in 1918 when it abandoned newsprint production, but like its fellow pulp and paper producers in the Great Lakes states, it suffered from a shortage of spruce pulpwood. This situation was especially troubling for KC because it converted its pulp into products other than newsprint (i.e., the same amount of pulpwood produced twice as much newsprint as it did sulphite pulp, from which cellucotton was made). KC partially resolved this issue by purchasing spruce woodlands in Wisconsin and Minnesota, but it still sought large quantities of pulpwood and high-quality sulphite pulp to feed its conversion mills in the United States, particularly the one in Niagara Falls, New York.[33]

KC was unquestionably interested in setting up shop in Ontario, and the Farmers were utterly desperate to achieve this end. They were under intense pressure to formulate a solution to the crisis that had developed in Kapuskasing. Repeated visits to Queen's Park by delegates from the Kapuskasing soldiers' settlement and a royal commission into the botched colony over the course of 1919–20 had elicited a public outpouring of sympathy for the locals' desperate plight. All agreed that the solution lay in expediting the erection of the pulp and paper mill that Ferguson had used to entice the veterans to this remote location in the first place. As the commission's report put it in March 1920, "the condition of the settlers in Kapuskasing is such that immediate action on the part of the Government is imperative."[34]

This "imperative" drove the actions of both the Farmers and KC in this matter, particularly the latter, which was acutely aware that the leverage this exigent situation had given it vis-à-vis the government would allow it, and not the politicians, to dictate how its project would proceed. L.V. Rorke, Ontario's director of surveys, hosted a tour for KC's representatives of the nascent town of Kapuskasing and the local timber limits and water powers. Rorke reported that the firm's principals were sufficiently impressed by what they had seen to proceed with a mill project, and he had thus urged the Drury government to accept "any reasonable concession ... that they may require in order to create the industry proposed and a market for settlers in the district." KC capitalized on the Farmers' vulnerability by presenting a long list of demands that aimed at fundamentally revising the pulpwood and water power leases Mundy and Stewart had signed in 1917. Among other things, KC asked that it be obliged to build only a small pulp mill immediately, no newsprint mill before 1928, and no paper plant at all if it constructed a large pulp mill, and that it be absolved from providing any electricity to the local community for the foreseeable future. Most importantly, KC pushed for the Ontario government to become partners in this enterprise. Whereas other nearby pulp and paper companies such as Abitibi and Mattagami Pulp had been forced to fund the development of their communities out of their own pockets, KC sought to tap the public purse to pay for this potentially onerous expense.[35]

With the Farmers solicitous to facilitate KC's involvement in the effort, and with KC pressing Drury for an immediate response to its offer, the premier had little choice in the matter. It took him only a few days to execute, as acting minister, new agreements that embodied nearly all

KC's wishes. As Drury confided to KC's lawyers, he had been forced "to make such reasonable concessions as will enable you to get the pulp mill into operation at the earliest possible date." KC had secured its cheap, high-quality source of bleached sulphite pulp.[36]

Two aspects of KC's project made it unlike every other mill in Ontario. The company's tight connections to Wisconsin's leading banks allowed it to finance this venture without selling one single bond. Having long been loath to borrow either to expand or upgrade its operations, KC and its directors provided the funds to finance Spruce Falls Company, the concern they incorporated to carry out their venture in Kapuskasing. None of Spruce Falls's $7,000,000 worth of securities – 20,000 preference shares and 50,000 common – were issued to the public.[37]

Its second distinguishing feature, which was far more important, was the Ontario government's decision to link itself inextricably to KC's pulp and paper mill at this time. By early 1921, the Farmers had passed legislation that formalized their commitment to spend roughly $500,000 on municipal infrastructure for Kapusaskasing as well as back the bonds the town issued to fund housing construction. This was an unprecedented joint public-private venture for the provincial state, and its vitality now depended practically entirely upon the health of the mill that KC was obliged to construct. No doubt this was part of KC's shrewd design, as it meant that this company was eternally ensconced in the hearts and minds of Ontario's elected officials. It would be difficult to imagine a better means by which the pulp and paper maker could inveigle from the government positive responses to its future requests for assistance.[38]

KC wasted no time in tapping into this goodwill, much to Mattagami Pulp's chagrin. First, KC asked the Ontario government to extend the deadline by which it was to build its pulp mill on the grounds that the market for sulphite was flooded and adding new capacity would only exacerbate the problem. Within days of receiving the request, the Farmers granted it. KC's next request was much more significant and deleterious to Mattagami Pulp's interests. On 26 April 1922, one week after Mattagami Pulp had applied to the government for a lease to develop Smoky Falls and the other nearby water powers, Frank Sensenbrenner, KC's president, applied for the same privilege. He argued that, even though his firm already leased three water powers on the Kapuskasing River, these were insufficient for the scope of the project the company was planning to undertake. Sensenbrenner explained that, although KC's contract with the government obliged it to construct merely a 50-ton newsprint mill by 1928, it desired to eventually build a 550-ton facility that would necessitate harnessing Smoky Falls. Moreover, because KC intended to wait nearly five years to develop these water powers, Sensenbrenner asked Bowman to deviate from departmental protocol that called for the water power lease to include a specific date by which the site was to be developed. When Bowman presented the matter to the premier, the minister said nothing about Mattagami Pulp's standing application for these same water powers. Furthermore, Bowman steadfastly refused to give Mattagami Pulp's lawyers the opportunity to present their case to the government. On 3 May, barely one week after Sensenbrenner had submitted his application for Smoky Falls, Bowman leased this site and the other nearby cascades to KC.[39]

KC's new power lease was a boon to the company for several reasons. It gave KC access to a potential energy supply – 70,000 horsepower at Smoky Falls alone – that was far in excess of its future power needs, and set no deadline by which it was obliged to develop these sites. Smoky Falls would lie undisturbed for nearly another half-decade even though Mattagami Pulp needed this untapped energy, and the other cascades – such as Devil Rapids – for much longer than that. KC was acutely aware of the strategic advantage that accrued from being granted these rights over these resources, namely precluding potential rival pulp and paper makers such as Mattagami Pulp from exploiting them. As a subsequent in-house report put it, KC's water power lease to develop Devil Rapids "argues against the right for its development being available for others and for the control of prices of adjoining pulp wood properties of the Crown."[40]

While Bowman considered the issue closed, Mattagami Pulp's representatives did not. Upon learning of the government's actions, W.J. Boland, the company's solicitor, fired off vehement protests to Bowman. Boland reminded the minister that, because Bowman had led Mattagami Pulp to believe that this matter would stand until the end of the present session of the Legislature, news of KC's lease to Smoky Falls "gave us a distinct shock." Adding that his clients, "in view of all that happened in the past" certainly deserved the privilege of developing these cascades, Boland pleaded for consideration. To buttress his case, he cited the department's own policy of religiously adhering to the principle of "one company, one river" in allocating water power leases to private interests in northern Ontario. Boland pointed out that when he had been acting for a different client who had been seeking a water power lease, the department had turned down his request on the grounds that another party had already acquired power privileges on the river in question. Boland thus reasoned that Mattagami Pulp had laid claim to the water powers on the Mattagami River near Smooth Rock Falls, and it should thus be given the opportunity to develop Smoky Falls on the same waterway.[41]

But Bowman obstinately refused to discuss the matter with Boland or any other official from Mattagami Pulp before he left office. As the Farmers government went down to defeat in June 1923, Mattagami Pulp could only sit back and acknowledge that Bowman's prompt and favourable treatment of the New Ontario Company and KC, and the minister's decision to ignore Mattagami Pulp's repeated requests for assistance, spoke volumes about the government's commitment to the pulpwood exporters and the degree to which it was willing to support the mill project in Kapuskasing now that it had a vested interest in seeing the undertaking flourish.[42]

SECTION IV

"The chief is the whole show": The Conservatives, 1923–1932

As with every newly elected administration in Ontario since the turn of the century, the Conservatives won power in 1923 under G. Howard Ferguson promising to modernize the government's administration of its hinterland Crown resources, particularly timber. One of the crucial challenges they faced was dealing with the province's newsprint industry, which had matured and now represented a major presence in the hinterland. By this time, converting spruce into newsprint had become Ontario's and the country's primary manufacturing activity, and it led the nation in terms of gross value of production and wages paid and was second in employment. It also formed the backbone of communities across the province's northern reaches.

While the Tories' reform pledge turned out to be disingenuous, the industry's raised stature introduced new dynamics which the Conservatives were forced to consider with the old when they dealt with the pulp and paper industry during their time in office (1923–34). To be sure, the provincial state's pre-eminent goal in the hinterland was still to populate it, and by extension this entailed making a mockery of the manufacturing condition on pulpwood by helping those who wished to export spruce. Ferguson was so successful in this regard that the "official" quantity of spruce annually shipped from the province to the United States rose to over 400,000 cords immediately upon his victory in 1923 and peaked at over 600,000 cords five years later; the actual figures were probably much higher. Likewise, the government's agenda in northern Ontario also involved assisting the lumbermen, particularly in adapting to changing forest conditions and markets. In the words of J.I. Hartt, a former Tory MPP and veteran sawmiller whom Ferguson appointed the province's Inspector of Timber Agencies in late 1923, "the whole policy of the Department is the conservation of the forests so that the lumbering industry can be maintained in the centuries to come."[1]

Ferguson was sympathetic to the province's traditional forest industries because they were so enmeshed in the patronage system of dispensing Crown resources, and he attached an unparalleled importance to this network in administering Crown resources even though doing so flew in the face of contemporary trends. From the perspective of his office in Queen's Park, dispensing public timber and water powers was largely an exercise in opportunism for him and his party; even his sympathetic biographer describes Ferguson as having been identified throughout his career with "patronage, the party fund and machine politics." His penchant in this regard put him out of step with Ontario's rapidly maturing Department of Lands and Forests. During Ferguson's tenure, it hired dozens of foresters and elevated their status within the bureaucracy by charging them with formulating long-range plans for the rational development of the province's Crown resources, an end most pulp and paper firms were eager to see realized. Paradoxically, however, this professionalization of the provincial bureaucracy occurred at a time when the elected officials were least interested in implementing its policies.[2]

Ferguson's preoccupation with administering Crown resources in a way that was politically expedient drove him to exercise imperious control over his government. Historians have long recognized the premier's dictatorial proclivity but they have not fully appreciated the extent to which Ferguson obsessively wrapped the reins of power tightly in his hands. This was particularly true when it came to administering the forest industry, for in this realm, "the chief," as he was known, was essentially a one-man government. He turned a deaf ear to the counsel offered by the department's new cadre of foresters, nearly all senior newsprint executives, and even his own colleagues, including his ministers of lands and forests, James Lyons (1923–26), a hardware dealer from the Soo, and William H. Finlayson (1926–34), a lawyer from Midland, about whom more will be said below.

Only with a select few would the premier share decision-making power during his reign. Foremost among them was Carroll C. Hele, whom Oliver charitably describes as Ferguson's "political fixer." While little is known about either Hele's background or his career in the shadows of Ontario's political economy, the Tories had first hired him in 1911 as the department's private secretary because, as the Order in Council put it, he was "a person of special attainment and employed as such." For most of the next two decades, Hele was one of Ontario's most powerful officials, a virtual kingmaker who often determined the fate of those who sought access to Crown resources. At one point he admitted to a royal commission that he was "an industrial trustee" for "private people in the United States," but refused to identify them on the grounds that his "usefulness to my employer would be over if I told." He also served as Ferguson's private secretary from 1914 to 1934, during which time he faithfully defended "the chief" every step of the way and was the sole person who could decipher Ferguson's coded messages. When the latter looked to be on the ropes during the Timber Commission's hearings in the early 1920s and the Beauharnois scandal some dozen years later, for instance, it was Hele who arrived in the nick of time to rescue Ferguson. Hele's activities – and those of Allan Ferguson, Howard Ferguson's nephew whom the latter appointed a deputy minister in the department during the mid-1920s – have made the historians' job of piecing the puzzle together exceedingly difficult, as they ensured that papers pertaining to the government's more unsavoury activities were either spirited out of the public purview or written in an idiom that only they understood.[3]

Ferguson's Machiavellian approach to administering Crown resources took different forms at different times. At its core was a clear understanding for those who sought access to Crown assets; the chances of Ferguson granting their wishes was directly related to the generosity of the offering they made to the Tories. He was so committed to this modus operandi that he was prepared to stick to it even if it meant that Ontario lost opportunities to develop new northern industries. Ben Alexander, a pulp and paper industrialist from Wisconsin who held the patent to "masonite," a state-of-the-art building material made from compressed wood, endeavoured to procure a timber limit in Ontario in the mid-1920s as the first step towards establishing a production facility north of the border. During his preliminary negotiations with the Conservatives, however, he learned of the "hidden costs" involved in gaining access to Crown resources. Alexander then told his liaison with the government in 1927 that if the Ferguson government "expect[s] commissions ... there is no use in pursuing this matter any further." It did, and Alexander did not.[4]

The "commissions" were usually delivered to a coterie of "lieutenants." Two of this period's best known "bagmen" were James Little and Donald Hogarth, seasoned and prominent businessmen at the Lakehead. Hogarth was the Conservative MPP for Port Arthur almost continuously between 1911 and 1934, while Little was his closest associate. These two played various roles in this arrangement. Sometimes it involved simply fixing a tender to ensure that a valuable timber limit ended up in the hands of a well-connected Tory.[5] At other times, Little and Hogarth orchestrated more involved deals that profited both them and the Conservatives' war chest. Perhaps the most extraordinary example of just such a transaction occurred in 1929–30, when they brokered the sale of a large block of prime pulpwood north of Sault Ste Marie to Consolidated Water Power and Paper in Wisconsin. Ferguson personally approved this bargain and undoubtedly had a hand in persuading certain members of the department to produce fabricated cruises to rationalize it. The upshot saw Little, Hogarth, and their associates net $500,000. They planned to launder their proceeds through the Corn Exchange in Chicago and were expected to contribute roughly one-tenth of their take towards the federal Conservatives' election campaign in northwestern Ontario in 1930.[6]

Ferguson shrewdly ensured, however, that profound uncertainty pervaded his lieutenants' dealings with him. While it has generally been believed that the likes of Little and Hogarth enjoyed untrammelled influence with "the chief" during this period, this was not the case. Ferguson deliberately refused to give his cronies this type of power to ensure that he kept them dependent and subservient.[7] Certainly, Little and Hogarth were likely to be successful agents when their clients were lumbermen or pulpwood exporters, the traditional forest industrialists to whom the government was favourably disposed. But it will become clear that, when Little and Hogarth were hired by interests outside these spheres, particularly the pulp and paper makers, it was an entirely different matter. Noah Timmins, the gold-mining magnate, learned this harsh lesson after paying $25,000 to engage Hogarth as his intermediary with the Tories in the mid-1920s thinking that this would gain him the local Crown resources he sought. When Hogarth failed to deliver the goods, Timmins was so angry he chopped Hogarth's retainer by 60 per cent.[8]

But it has already been mentioned that there was another, novel element to the way in which Ferguson administered the hinterland's Crown resources. He certainly did so in a manner that both furthered the provincial state's traditional priorities and clung to the patronage system, albeit more tenaciously than his predecessors. By the same token, the premier recognized that the rules governing conduct on the playing field of northern Ontario's industrial landscape had changed forever, and he was committed to learning them intimately in order to succeed. Regardless of his feelings about the pulp and paper industry, by 1923 it was entrenched as a major force in the province's hinter-land. What was thus needed in the face of this fait accompli, at least in Ferguson's eyes, was a plan for managing the paper makers in a way that enriched his and his closest associates' fortunes. He knew full well that coddling the new staples industry would generally not achieve this aim but that there would be occasional exceptions to this rule. As a result, he developed an ad hoc approach to handling it.

The departure point for achieving his goals in this realm involved making it patently clear to his caucus that he was prepared to be des-potic in handling the pulp and paper industry if it served his ends. Over the course of 1923–5, for example, his minister, James Lyons, out-lined a policy for dealing with Ontario's pulp and paper industry that responded to both its needs and circumstances. First, he declared that his government would closely monitor the demand for and supply of pulp and paper to prevent the overproduction of either one. This was a timely message because the industry's rapid growth after the First World War had created a serious glut in its market. Not only did a host of experts agree that the new capacity coming on line each year was only exacerbating this already distressing situation, but the data sup-ported their view. The Canadian newsprint industry operated at an average of just under 87 per cent during the first half of the 1920s, and Lyons repeated throughout 1924 and 1925 that this market was "very much depressed and will likely be for some time."[9] Second, the min-ister assured mill owners in his province that his government would take care of their fibre requirements. In his words, the Conservatives would provide "a continuous supply of raw material for the existing industries and for other industries that the province may approve of, not for twenty or thirty years, or for fifty years, but in perpetuity." To Ontario's newsprint makers, these two pledges must have seemed like pennies from heaven.[10]

But within short order, Ferguson undid them according to a plan whose logic apparently he alone saw. First, he announced shortly af-ter he had won office in 1923 a moratorium on providing the pulp and paper industry with timber unless the situation proved "urgent." Then two years later he agreed to give the newsprint makers leases to pulpwood concessions but only if they significantly expanded their operations even though this would only exacerbate their industry's overcapacity problem. While much more will be said in the pages that follow about this seemingly illogical approach, Ferguson compounded the industry's problems in 1925 when he practically doubled stumpage dues on Crown pulpwood. Not only did he do so at a time of falling prices for newsprint, but his government cited the overcapacity that afflicted the province's lumber industry as grounds for leaving the rates for pine sawlogs unchanged.[11]

Ferguson felt that this magisterial attitude was needed to exploit the industry's existence for his gain, including at times appearing to help it. Ferguson was willing to provide several newsprint makers with fibre in the mid-1920s, for example, but only after unilaterally setting the terms under which they would enlarge their operations; the timetable for this expansion just happened to set off a flurry of construction activity which coincided with the next time he faced the electorate.

But the degree to which Ferguson mastered the artifice of appearing to be the industry's dearest friend when he believed presenting this impression redounded to his advantage was best illustrated in the run-up to the 1926 election, and the setting was the town of Cochrane. Ferguson had served as acting minister of lands and forests for most of the year, and after appointing William Finlayson to succeed him in this post, he informed the new minister that Abitibi was planning to construct a new paper mill in Cochrane just north of its existing mill in Iroquois Falls. There was nothing to substantiate the premier's claim apart from a curious letter that Ferguson insisted he had received from the company, but the premier assured Finlayson nonetheless that it was the ideal time to announce this new development because this upbeat news would sway voters in northeastern Ontario to the Tory side.[12] Astute local observers, however, immediately recognized Ferguson's ploy as a sham. They grilled H.E. McGill, the riding's Conservative chieftain, about how Abitibi was going to supply the more than 20,000,000 gallons of fresh water that a paper plant required each day to a mill in Cochrane, which was ten miles from the nearest sizeable river. McGill was unable to provide the answers to satisfy resident critics, who dismissed the proposed project as "only political propaganda." Hele, Ferguson's private secretary, tried to assuage McGill's concerns by pointing out that the details regarding supplying the new mill with "hydro" would be worked out later. McGill replied that Hele had completely "missed the point," and explained in a telegram that "our opponents are killing value of announcement by creating impression this is only propaganda and not bonafide as newsprint mill could not be operated in Cochrane owing to lack of water." Although Hele still did not get it, and despite the illusory nature of the scheme, the ruse achieved its aim. The Tories wrested the riding from the Liberals.[13]

Like Drury before him, Ferguson also realized that although there was more to be gained by subordinating the interests of the pulp and paper industry to other priorities, reaching out to it selectively could be beneficial. Assisting a mill which produced a type of paper the government needed was just such an occasion. So, too, were situations involving two major pulp and paper firms from the United States, namely Kimberly-Clark Company (KC) and International Paper Company (IP). Although Ferguson's rhetoric remained ardently anti-American, his actions belied his words.[14] On the one hand, it was relatively simple to understand his affinity for KC. Premier Drury had, after all, essentially made the Ontario government a partner in the company's mill project in Kapuskasing.

On the other hand, it is much more difficult to decipher how IP, specifically Archibald R. Graustein, its dynamic president between 1924 and 1936, was able to win over Ferguson. Beginning in the mid-1920s and for roughly the next ten years, Graustein fervently strove to re-establish IP's hegemony in the newsprint industry by shutting down its scattered array of small mills in the US and building or acquiring a few monstrous, state-of-the art plants in Canada. He only realized this end because he, unlike so many of his rival pulp and paper executives in Canada, demonstrated an acute sensitivity to the pre-eminent role politics played in determining the winners and losers in the Dominion's resource-extraction industries.[15]

To ensure that he came out on top, he engaged in a comprehensive rebranding exercise of IP's image in Canada to distance it from its reputation; it had long suffered from its association with illegal efforts to monopolize the sale of newsprint and from the primary role it had played in exporting pulpwood from Canada. Graustein's first step involved enshrouding IP in a veil of "Canadianness." He incorporated a *Canadian International Paper*, created a public relations department to manage carefully how its activities were portrayed north of the border, and, most importantly, plugged the new CIP into the Canadian patronage networks at both the provincial and national levels. He did so by discussing his plans for his Canadian operations with the country's political and economic elite, and consulted with them and took their advice about whom to appoint to CIP's executive; R.B. Bennett, Canada's tenth prime minister (1930–5), not only sat on CIP's inaugural board of directors, but immediately after winning the Tory national leadership convention in

1927 he scurried to New York to visit with Graustein. Through moves such as these, Graustein achieved his goal, which was, as he later revealed to an American Congressional inquiry, "getting prominent men in whom Canada had confidence to sit on the Board of Directors of that Canadian Corporation and watch what we were doing and know what we were doing and know why we did it." By shrewdly tying the fortunes of these pre-eminent Canadians to CIP, he gave them a vested interest in rationalizing the firm's actions across the Dominion.[16]

And by the mid-1920s, Graustein had clearly won Ferguson over. While the pages that follow provide convincing evidence of the strength of the chief's affection for IP's president, one example from 1925 serves as crucial background to this story. At that time, Ferguson single-handedly awarded IP's subsidiary, Gatineau Power, a contract that made it the largest private provider of electricity to Ontario Hydro. Not only did the premier's move go against the wishes of Ontario Hydro's own engineers and Adam Beck, its veteran and recently deceased inaugural chairman, but the terms of the deal ensured that IP reaped truly scandalous profits over the next few decades, money that was crucial to subsidizing Graustein's campaign to win "the newsprint wars."

With this in mind, we turn to the details of Ferguson's administration of northern Ontario's timber and water powers in general and the province's pulp and paper makers in particular during the 1923–32 period. Due to the complex nature of this story, it will be told in five chapters. The first four deal with the previously described regions into which the province's mills have been grouped. Chapters 7 and 8 focus on the Thunder Bay District and highlight the old and new trends that were prevalent during this period. The former include the provincial state's traditional allegiance to the lumbermen, while the latter reveal how Ferguson set out to exploit the pulp and paper industry for political gain. Chapter 9 turns to the trio of mills on the northern Clay Belt. There, KC capitalized on the special bond it enjoyed with the Ontario government to garner all the local Crown resources it sought, thereby leaving its closest neighbour in Smooth Rock Falls vanquished. Ferguson also put Abitibi through the wringer after having painted it with a black brush during the Timber Commission's hearings a few years earlier. This theme is also a major part of chapter 10, which focuses on northwestern Ontario and the Spanish River territory. Ferguson made life difficult for both Backus and Spanish River because it was tactical, because they lacked a connection to his government, and because of the provincial state's continued allegiance to the lumbermen.

Finally, chapter 11 represents a fundamental break from the pattern of the previous chapters. It analyses not regional developments but rather the newsprint crisis of the late 1920s and early 1930s and the role the Ontario government played during this pivotal period. It reveals the paradoxical nature of Ferguson's behaviour during these years, whereby his approach was inimical to the interests of Ontario's newsprint makers but advantageous to their long-time rival, IP.

7 "For political purposes"

Nothing spoke more directly to Ferguson's preoccupation with political expediency in handling Ontario's pulp and paper industry than his dealings with the mills in the Thunder Bay District during the first few years of his premiership. This region was home to three newsprint interests that lacked pulpwood concessions, but by early 1925, each had hammered out an agreement to obtain one with the blessing of the minister, James Lyons, and senior departmental officials. In fact, these deals embodied some of the fundamental changes for which government bureaucrats had been lobbying for years. These included accepting that the industry's requests for perpetual supplies of timber were legitimate and that the government should grant them, and placing the interests of the pulp and paper makers ahead of the lumbermen and pulpwood exporters' in certain instances. The mills' draft contracts also recognized that the newsprint market was flooded, and owners were asked to expand their mills moderately and only when conditions warranted. Lyons was unable to implement his plan and grant the timber limits, however, because Ferguson refused to lift his moratorium on selling pulpwood. When the premier finally decided to take action in mid-1925, he dictatorially undid Lyons's arrangement, unilaterally determined how much wood the newsprint mills required, and ordered them to dramatically expand their enterprises, beginning immediately, even though their industry was plagued by overcapacity. At the same time, Ferguson demonstrated his unbridled affection for International Paper Company and could not do enough to assist it.

The chief's behaviour left many observers puzzled, but there was a method behind his actions. He created conditions that were conducive to calling Ontarians to the polls. He ensured that, during the months prior to the 1926 election, signs of prosperity occupied the minds of the voters in the Thunder Bay District, especially those who anticipated filling the promised new jobs. To Ferguson's mind, what was best for the newsprint industry was not necessarily best for him.

Ferguson's announcement in 1923 that he was placing a moratorium on selling pulpwood limits was especially shocking for two newsprint makers in the Thunder Bay District: Fort William Paper (owned by Spanish River) and Thunder Bay Paper (a subsidiary of Wisconsin-based Consolidated Water Power and Paper). The owners of these plants had established and expanded their enterprises between 1920 and 1923 only after the Drury government had promised to lease them pulpwood concessions around Lake Nipigon. The Farmers had announced their intention in April 1923 to tender the limits for which these two companies had applied, but did not do so prior to their defeat in June (Map 11). These mills expected the freshly elected Tories to carry out this sale immediately, and they – and their local supporters – pressed their case with the new government. Both agreed to expand their operations when conditions warranted if they acquired this timber, and asked that any deals they signed with the Conservatives be "approved by the Legislature" – and not merely executed by Order in Council – to improve the contracts' legal standing. But when Ferguson declared an end to tenders for pulpwood, these mills – and Ontario's entire pulp and paper industry – again realized their worst nightmare: a change in government had signalled a dramatic shift in the government's approach towards their enterprises.[1]

Veteran Tories Donald Hogarth and James Little were in the vanguard of the forces battling to convince the government to sell the Nipigon pulpwood to the newsprint mills. Hogarth had been a three-term MPP (1911–23) in Port Arthur and Little a local contractor and one of Hogarth's closest associates. While they were long-time boosters of industrial development in the district, they also had ulterior motives for pushing the mills' agenda. Hogarth and Little were involved in several schemes from which they, and apparently the Conservatives, would profit handsomely. One of their aims was to establish a near-monopoly over the region's production of railway ties. Not only had the demand for and price of ties risen drastically, but the railroads looked to the Thunder Bay District to meet their timber requirements in western Canada. Jack pine was the primary species from which ties were made at this time, and it was interspersed with spruce pulpwood

Map 11. Timber Situation in the Thunder Bay District, 1923–1926

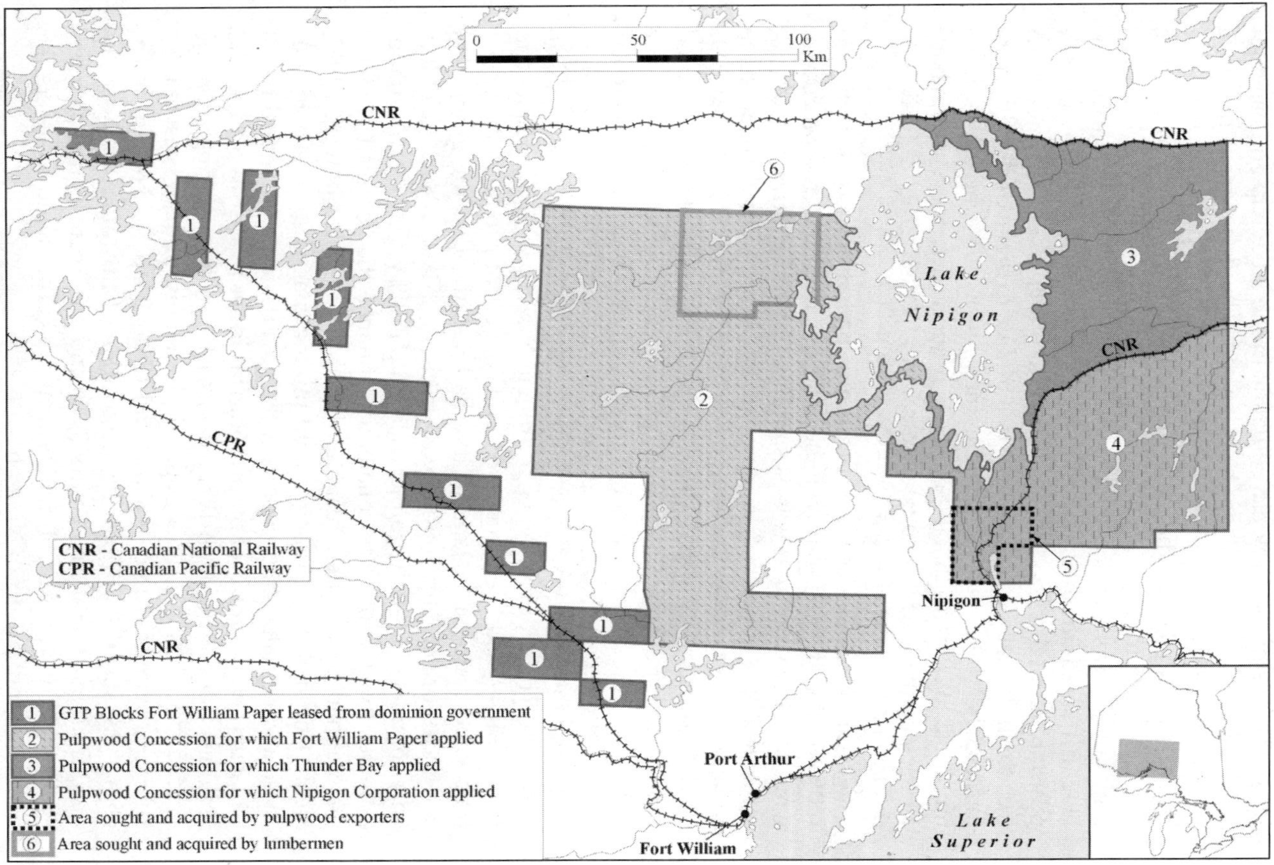
0
50
100
Km
CNR
CNR
CNR
CNR
CPR
CNR - Canadian National Railway
CPR - Canadian Pacific Railway
Lake
Nipigon
Nipigon
Port Arthur
Fort William
Lake
Superior
1 GTP Blocks Fort William Paper leased from dominion government
2 Pulpwood Concession for which Fort William Paper applied
3 Pulpwood Concession for which Thunder Bay applied
4 Pulpwood Concession for which Nipigon Corporation applied
5 Area sought and acquired by pulpwood exporters
6 Area sought and acquired by lumbermen

in some parts of the Crown woodlands in the Lake Nipigon basin for which the newsprint makers had applied. The department had long recognized that it was problematic to permit two operators with separate interests to harvest the same area and had thus advocated a plan to have the newsprint makers harvest both the spruce pulpwood and jack pine sawlogs from a tract, and then sell the latter to the local tie makers. Hogarth and Little had wholeheartedly supported the department's position, and with good reason. The two entrepreneurs intended, before the mills gained control over this timber, to make deals with them to act as their brokers for the pine on their pulpwood concessions. Little remarked to Hogarth that if their strategy succeeded, they "would have all the jackpine that would be necessary to furnish either railway with ties for the next twenty years."[2]

Several of the district's newsprint mills had also hired Hogarth and Little to act as their liaisons with the government, and their arrangement with Thunder Bay Paper was as simple as it was lucrative. It called for Little and "his associates" to represent this firm in "its negotiations to acquire timber lands in the Province of Ontario, and … render valuable services to said party in that behalf." In return, Thunder Bay Paper would pay Hogarth and Little $100,000 and promise to assist them in gaining title to the jack pine on the company's concession after it had been granted.[3]

Hogarth and Little agreed to perform the same service for another firm, but this deal was much more complicated. Like Fort William Paper and Thunder Bay Paper, the mill in Nipigon – Nipigon Fibre and Paper Mills – had been frustrated in its endeavour to obtain a Crown pulpwood concession. James Little had spearheaded the group that had incorporated Nipigon Fibre after the First World War, but it had only completed a small groundwood pulp mill by 1921 when, without a timber limit to offer as collateral to finance the completion of the plant, it had gone under.[4] Just after the Tories regained power in 1923, Noah Timmins, the Hollinger gold-mining magnate, agreed to purchase and revitalize the property if the government guaranteed to sell him a perpetual supply of pulpwood. The Tories made this pledge, and Timmins bought Nipigon Fibre. To assist him in acquiring what he needed from the government, specifically a limit south and east of Lake Nipigon, Timmins hired Hogarth and Little (Map 11). His agreement with them stated that upon the acquisition of this pulpwood concession, Timmins would pay them $50,000 and give them a one-half interest in the new company Timmins would incorporate to complete the newsprint mill project in Nipigon.[5]

Ferguson knew of Hogarth and Little's special association with this enterprise and tacitly approved of it, but the premier was acutely concerned about the political damage this connection could potentially cause him and his party if it became public knowledge. Hogarth and J.I. Rankin, Timmins's representative, had already taken one step to conceal it by carrying out the sale of Nipigon Fibre's assets to Timmins through a holding company, Guaranty Investment Corporation. They then vehemently denied rumours that this latter firm was connected to Timmins. But Hogarth and Little shared a 50 per cent interest in the future mill, and both they and Timmins were anxious to have themselves appointed directors of the holding company and then Nipigon Corporation, the new firm that Timmins incorporated to carry out the venture. Ferguson, however, was equally adamant that Hogarth and Little should remain hidden in the shadows. Hogarth relayed word to Little in early December 1923 that "G.H.F. thinks it would be indiscrete [sic] for us to go on the Board but says I should have some official status with the operating Coy. Thus I can approach the Government logically [for a timber limit], whereas now I'm simply an ex-politician + friend of members of the Government." Timmins relentlessly pushed throughout the first half of 1924 for Hogarth and Little to join his board, but the premier demonstrated his absolute control over such matters by vetoing their appointment.[6]

In mid-1924, with the government still unwilling to sell the mills any pulpwood, Hogarth tried a slightly different tack. He began pleading on behalf of the three newsprint makers that had applied for concessions in the Nipigon basin: Nipigon Corporation and Thunder Bay Paper (which had retained him as their conduit to the Tories) *and* Fort William Paper (which had not). Hogarth stood to gain personally if the first two of these three firms were granted the limits they sought, and he had been advised that Spanish River's Fort William Paper was "very strong with [minister] Lyons" and that it would be prudent to "cooperate with them to get best result."[7]

Hogarth presented a convincing case for the Tory government to take immediate action. He pointed out that the areas in question had already been cruised and were thus ready to tender. He also challenged Ferguson to practise what he preached and abide by his government's declared policy of allocating sufficient timber "to give security to existing enterprises and to enable such industries to expand to economic proportions." Furthermore, he underscored that these three newsprint mills did not lease Crown pulpwood concessions and were dependent on the open market for their fibre supply. This was causing them to "express uneasiness regarding the protection of present investments on account of the absences or inadequacy of timber reserves and indicate their intent to proceed immediately with definite extension programs when security by way of timber reserves has been arranged." In this regard, Hogarth recommended that the government could dramatically strengthen the mills' positions by making certain that any new concession leases were "binding only when ratified by the Legislature ... By this method, the Legislature and the Public are made fully aware of all the facts and circumstances, and whatever is to be said by way of criticism would be said at the time – not afterwards. The concessionaires would be placed in the best possible position for financing, by reason ... of the ratification by the Legislature their Agreements will be unassailable. No responsible member would oppose propositions worked out along these lines."[8]

Hogarth's efforts appeared to bear fruit. By the end of 1924, Lyons, the minister, had arrived at a basic understanding with Thunder Bay Paper, Nipigon Corporation, and Fort William Paper. He would give them the concessions for which they had been lobbying and they would undertake modest and gradual expansion programs. Thunder Bay Paper and Nipigon Corporation would establish 200-ton newsprint mills adjacent to their existing facilities within a reasonable time, perhaps as soon as four years. Likewise, Fort William Paper would add 200 tons to its existing 175-ton newsprint facility when market conditions warranted.[9]

The mill owners emphasized two crucial aspects to this arrangement. They unquestionably accepted that expanding their enterprises would be, as it always had been, the price for leasing Crown pulpwood concessions. But they asked that their contractual obligations be both logical and reasonable and that the government lease them enough fibre to supply their mills in perpetuity. F.N. Youngman, Thunder Bay Paper's mill manager, succinctly spelled out these matters. He asked that the government provide him with the standard 2,250,000 cords of pulpwood for every 100 tons of mill capacity and insisted that his mill expansion "be arranged to take place over a reasonable period of time so that the market could absorb it ... It would not be in the interests of the Province or to our own interest to be forced to contribute a further flood of news print on a badly over supplied market, as new machines are coming in faster than the demand is growing. The Government, of course are aware of this situation and I am sure will take this into consideration when fixing conditions." Ernest Rossiter, one of Nipigon Corporation's directors, echoed this position, as did Hogarth's partner, Little. "Having regard to either imposed or voluntary future expansion of plant," Little proclaimed, "nothing short of perpetual supply of wood would warrant anything very considerable."[10]

Lyons unequivocally supported selling this pulpwood forthwith to these companies on the basis outlined above, but the power to decide this matter rested with Ferguson, "the chief," who occupied the office in the Legislature directly above Lyons's. Hogarth spent countless evenings discussing the sale of the Nipigon pulpwood with Lyons, but the minister made it clear that his hands were tied. Hogarth confided to Little on numerous occasions that "the chief in the final analysis will be the doctor ... the chief is the whole show and ... Lyons and the other Ministers pretty well do as they are told."[11]

At this point this meant doing nothing, for "the doctor" was not prepared to approve the arrangements Lyons had made with the Thunder Bay District's mills. Ferguson's inertia was at first glance difficult to understand. The government's foresters had finished cruising the areas, and the department's *Annual Reports* continually reaffirmed the Tories' commitment to "afford going concerns opportunities to get additional supplies to secure investments, improve labour conditions and maintain community life." The *Reports* even recognized that "certain established concerns are in crying need of raw materials," and that these same industries were practically dependent on settlers' pulpwood because "no Provincial Crown areas hav[e] been acquired by them." Ferguson had repeatedly promised Hogarth since late 1923 that the Tories would sell the concessions, but the issue remained unaddressed in the spring of 1925.[12]

And then suddenly Ferguson relented. In June of that year, he announced the largest and most important tender of pulpwood concessions in provincial history, whereby he would sell the tracts in the Nipigon basin for which the three newsprint companies had applied and other concessions on the northern Clay Belt. The premier explained that he had also improved the tender system to ensure that this pulpwood sale would be carried out with an unprecedented degree of openness and probity.

Ferguson's boasts sounded impressive, but they bore little resemblance to his actions. Most importantly, the government asserted that "in fairness to both prospective bidders and the Crown, it was decided to provide the Crown's estimate of the various classes of timber ... Thus all tenders now contain estimates of the material." Nevertheless, Ferguson's government refused to publish the results of the Nipigon cruises, and the premier insisted that the data be locked in the deputy minister's desk amid Ferguson's "private official records." To the numerous inquiries the government received about the volume of fibre available on the Nipigon limits it returned a series of brusque replies in which it explained that the "Department is not furnishing intending purchasers with the estimated quantity of pulpwood on each area. This must be ascertained by personal exploration or otherwise."[13]

The government was equally secretive about announcing who had won the Nipigon pulpwood tender, which closed on 10 September. By that date, the three newsprint companies had submitted their proposals, which were practically identical to the ones that the minister had previously accepted. It should have been a relatively straightforward matter of evaluating the bids and allocating the pulpwood, but September drifted into October, and October into November, with no announcement. Under pressure from their constituents, northern Tory MPPs turned to their "chief" for an official statement. Ferguson assured them that the delay was the result of his officials "carefully checking up on the standing of the various tenderers" and that it was imperative that the government "ascertain the production in each case, and the cordage available to each plant, not only with their present capacity, but with the contemplated immediate expansions. It is found that none of these plants had sufficient raw material behind them to guarantee any considerable length of time. Of course they must have a future assured if they are to interest capital and if our forestry operations are to be carried on in a way that will secure reproduction and perpetuity. We are selling these plants sufficient cordage to provide for their needs ... They get the Government's guarantee that their needs will be met."[14]

Those close to the premier soon learned of the reasons behind the delay. Two groups had been fiercely opposing the sale of these pulpwood concessions, the most vocal of which was the Lakehead's coterie of pulpwood exporters led by Frank Keefer. He was the Tory MPP for Port Arthur, Ferguson's appointee as the province's first and only legislative secretary for northern Ontario, and a long-time business associate of W.H. Russell, arguably the Lakehead's most infamous pulpwood pirate.[15] Having already abused the province's settlement and mining laws to strip the pulpwood from much of the lakefront between Nipigon and Port Arthur, the exporters eyed Booth, Purdom, and Ledger Townships along the Nipigon River (Map 11). The Tories had previously allowed Russell and his allies to use veterans' scrip to acquire about 20 per cent of the land within these townships; the Crown still held the remaining lots, which supported nearly 500,000 cords of pulpwood that the exporters eagerly sought.[16]

That was the problem. Because the spruce in these townships represented a rich and easily accessible source of pulpwood, it represented an integral part of Nipigon Corporation's application for a pulpwood concession. This timber would be relatively cheap to cut compared with the rest of the company's limit, as the latter would require significant investments in river-driving equipment and waterway improvements. Harvesting in these three townships would balance the mill's wood costs, a point the company had stressed ever since it had begun discussing the matter with the government. Fortunately for Nipigon Corporation, since the early 1920s the department's senior officials had adamantly supported giving it this timber. Moreover, investigations had now proven that these townships were largely unfit for agriculture, leaving no logical excuse to throw them open to settlement.[17]

The battle thus pitted the pulpwood exporters, represented by Keefer, against Nipigon Corporation, Hogarth and Little's client, and the prize was the pulpwood in Booth, Ledger, and Purdom. Keefer had begun presenting the exporters' case immediately after the 1923 election, asking that the Tories make these townships available to settlers. Although Hogarth and Little were aware of the department's steadfast opposition to such a move, they were acutely concerned about the pirates' machinations and designs on this wood and consequently closely monitored the exporters' movements. After learning in early 1925 that Keefer had intensified his efforts on the exporters' behalf, Hogarth and Little took comfort in one crucial fact. Referring to the three townships, Hogarth and Little had learned that the "Department have not the slightest intention of throwing them open," a position that the minister, the deputy, and the government's senior ranking forester all supported. Nevertheless, Little insisted that Hogarth remain vigilant, urging him to "keep [his] eye very closely on this situation. While the Department has a right at any time to withdraw an area from a timber limit for bona fide settlers, I don't think it would do so once an area was allocated [to a newsprint mill] just to please a pulpwood farmer, but if they withdraw any of those townships prior to a sale or allocation, it would very much lessen the attractiveness of our area."[18]

Keefer's actions in defence of the interests of another group of timber operators at the Lakehead contributed further to the delay in finalizing

Figure 9. A Pulpwood Pirate Ship: Despite the Ontario government's ostensible ban on exporting pulpwood logs from the province, it facilitated the dramatic expansion of this activity between 1894 and 1932 in an effort to stimulate the domestic market for settlers' timber. Those who engaged in this practice by abusing Ontario's settlement legislation to obtain acres of virtually free spruce were derisively referred to as "pulpwood pirates," and Walter H. Russell was one of the most successful swashbucklers. In this shot from the mid-1920s, his haul is being loaded by a steam-powered jackladder near Nipigon, one of his most famous haunts and an area in which the provincial government favoured the exporters' interests over those of the domestic newsprint producers (Nipigon Historical Museum Archives, nmp 6899).

the sale of the Nipigon pulpwood concessions. Lumbermen, specifically tie contractors in the Thunder Bay District, had been aggressively pushing the Ontario government for several years to allow them to harvest the jack pine from a 400 square mile tract on the west side of the lake that formed a crucial part of the concession for which Fort William Paper had applied (Map 11).

As a matter of principle, Lyons adamantly rejected the tie makers' demands. He repeatedly pointed out to them that experience had proven that it was a recipe for disaster to permit two parties with distinct interests to operate the same tract of forest, and that there were still thick stands of prime jack pine outside the Nipigon pulpwood concessions for the tie contractors to harvest. The tie makers' penchant for disregarding the government's prohibition on manufacturing axe-hewn ties in the bush had also caused many fires, and permitting such practices to continue on a pulp and paper mill's limit would jeopardize its future fibre supply. Lyons thus supported an arrangement whereby the pulpwood concessionaires harvested all species on their limits and disposed of the jack pine logs to the lumbermen. The department's senior officials had advocated this approach for some time, and it was coincidentally a policy that would also facilitate Hogarth and Little's plan for gaining control of the district's supply of tie timber.

Lyons was determined to place the interests of the pulp and paper mills ahead of the pulpwood exporters and tie contractors', but Ferguson was not. In early November, Hogarth and Little heard that "for political purposes" the government was reversing the minister's priorities. A few weeks later, Hogarth learned from Lyons that Lyons had been told to go to Ferguson's office and "was advised by the Premier in the presence of Keefer et al. that he [Ferguson] had decided to withhold from the grant to the Fort William Company four hundred square miles ... on the West side of Lake Nip. + 3 Nipigon townships [Booth, Purdom, and Ledger], to be withheld" (Map 11). The upshot, Hogarth declared, was that Keefer, the exporters, and the lumbermen had "succeeded in ... interfering with the plan of both the Fort William Company and the Nipigon Corporation, and I have no doubt the other ... companies, because, naturally, there must be some readjustment of concession boundaries in order that all may be treated fairly ... From the standpoint of the public interest, the Government have not any justification for their action, and Lyons in his private conversations with me freely admits this, and I can assure you he is just as upset by what has happened as we ourselves ... From his conversation I gather that he feels the decision of the Premier very keenly, and it is evident that the decision was entirely the latter's."[19]

On 25 November Ferguson delivered more bad news to the newsprint firms when he informed Fort William Paper, Thunder Bay Paper, and Nipigon Corporation that he would accept their tender offers only under certain conditions. He insisted that they all raise their bids to $2.00 per cord, the sum Fort William Paper had tendered, which was the highest offer among the applicants. Ferguson also demanded that the government reserve the right to adjust the "area[s] you are to cut wood from" and include "such other conditions" in their leases that he deemed necessary. F.N. Youngman, representing Thunder Bay Paper, was incensed by these provisos. "We sincerely hope," his dispatch to the department read, "that it is not the intention of the Government to reduce the area in any way which we applied for. To do so would seriously handicap our development program, for we blocked out an area which we know contains the minimum amount of wood necessary for the large development which we have in mind, and we would appreciate your assurance on this."[20]

Shortly thereafter Ferguson changed his position again, demanding now that the newsprint mills dramatically revise the tender offers they had submitted back in September. Despite the glutted newsprint market, he ordered them to immediately begin expanding their mills to a minimum of 400 tons. The premier also ignored Lyons's pledge to provide them with perpetual supplies of pulpwood (i.e., roughly 2,250,000 cords of pulpwood for every 100 tons of newsprint capacity) when he announced that, for each 100 tons of capacity, the mills in the Thunder Bay District would require only 1,500,000 cords to sustain them in perpetuity. Ferguson's figure was based on a crop rotation of "forty years," which, he contended, "is estimated as the average period required to reproduce pulpwood of merchantable dimensions." In the history of Canadian forestry, no one had ever suggested that a pulpwood forest could be reproduced in a mere forty years, and many deemed the figure of sixty years to be overly optimistic.[21]

Abiding by Ferguson's executive orders was the only means of gaining access to pulpwood concessions, leaving the three newsprint makers little choice but to redraft their tenders. Nipigon Corporation, Thunder Bay Paper, and Fort William Paper offered to expand their mills to a minimum of 400 tons, but only when market conditions and other practical considerations warranted. At the same time, they naturally requested that doing so be dependent upon the government providing them with a perpetual supply of pulpwood as they, not Ferguson, defined it. More than anyone else, G.R. Gray, Fort William Paper's president, emphasized that wood supply was of paramount importance to a newsprint interest. "To maintain this industry," he asserted, "raw material is essential and stability of investment is predicated on a supply of wood made available for the purposes of the Company to assure permanence; this supply should be for not less than 60 years."[22]

Ferguson deemed even these revised proposals inadequate, as he presented the companies with pulpwood concession leases that were radically different from the firms' latest tender offers. The employment clauses in their new contracts convincingly demonstrated this dissonance. Concessionaires had consistently argued that it was impractical for a mill to guarantee that it would employ a large number of workers during each year of its lease because the newsprint industry was highly cyclical and underwent rapid changes in technologies which quickly resulted in marked improvements in mill efficiencies.[23] It was also practically impossible for a mill to determine how many men it employed in its woodlands because it purchased a significant part of its annual fibre requirements from subcontractors or jobbers (operating on the concession) and settlers who were not on the firm's payroll. Nevertheless, Ferguson handed each newsprint firm a lease that obliged it to employ annually a specific and hefty number of workers in the mill and woodlands, and stated that failure to do so would void the contract. Worst of all, the government included figures in the employment clauses that were completely arbitrary, something that former premier William Hearst, whom Ferguson entrusted with drafting the contracts, openly admitted. Nipigon Corporation's new lease, for example, required it to employ 1,500 men in its bush operations to harvest the wood needed by its 200-ton newsprint mill, whereas Thunder Bay Paper's obliged it to engage exactly twice as many – and presumably far less efficient – workers to carry out the same task.[24]

The mills were predictably irate over the Tories' inclusion of these whimsical and illogical terms in their Crown leases. A veteran financier of pulp and paper projects pointed out to one of the firms that these employment provisions were redundant, "objectionable and embarrassing," because the enormous investments in these ventures meant that "self-interest would prompt you to run the plants to the fullest extent possible." While the companies urged the government to temper these employment terms, Ferguson was obstinate.[25]

The newsprint mills found another aspect of their leases even more repugnant. Ferguson insisted that they expand their plants and spend specified amounts according to a rigid timetable, and he obliged them to begin augmenting their enterprises forthwith and complete 400-ton newsprint mills within five years. Although it had taken three decades for the one dozen mills in Ontario to establish 1,000 tons of newsprint capacity, Ferguson was now dictating that the three plants in the Thunder Bay District double this total in a fraction of the time and during a period in which the market was glutted. Even Peter Oliver, Ferguson's biographer, is at a loss to explain the premier's attitude. Oliver asserts that "somehow, in a way that is not clear, the government had decided that … a massive expansion was in order. … Clearly the administration was responding … only secondarily to the wishes of the operators."[26]

Finally, the newsprint firms railed at the government's decision to insert a short clause at the end of their agreements. It authorized the minister to determine the true intent and meaning of the contract and stated that his decision in this regard was "final and binding" upon the signatories. Even though the industry fought the granting of such discretionary powers, the Tories knew that the newsprint producers' remonstrations were futile. When Nipigon Corporation vehemently objected to this clause in early 1926, Hearst assured the minister, "I do not think … they will strongly press this object. It no doubt leaves very strong power in your hands, but the Company is practically in the power of the Government anyway."[27]

The Crown pulpwood concession agreements that the Tories executed at this time reflected this power imbalance. The lease Thunder Bay Paper signed in January 1926 required it to construct a 400-ton newsprint mill by the end of 1931 even though its new concession contained just over 4,000,000 cords of spruce, under one-half the amount it required to supply this enterprise in perpetuity. Thunder Bay Paper had no option other than to construct hurriedly its new sulphite mill and the first stage of its newsprint plant as per its lease, and at the end of 1926 the government asked for a sworn affidavit that the company had fulfilled these obligations. The firm avoided breaching its contract through to the end of 1928, but by the next year it was technically in default because it had not spent the requisite amount on its expansion.[28]

Nipigon Corporation had even greater difficulties because of its new agreement, which it also signed in January 1926. In addition to its obligation to construct a 400-ton newsprint mill by the end of 1931, the government had excluded from its pulpwood concession the three townships it considered crucial to its project (Booth, Purdom, and Ledger) and handed them instead to the exporters. This had created an enormous and multifaceted predicament for the company. It had wrongfully assumed that its pulpwood concession would include these townships and had thus already dispatched crews to harvest roughly 50,000 cords from them. Ernest Rossiter, Nipigon Corporation's vice-president, explained to the government that it had been "much to the surprise and chagrin of the company that the township of Ledger, along with the two other townships, were excluded from the area covered by the agreement made with the Crown." Compounding the company's problems, Rossiter explained, was the fact that it was "not ready at the moment to enter on the large area covered by the agreement and take out a supply to meet the requirements of a 400-ton mill, as called for by the agreement, because of the unnecessary over-head expenditures in connection therewith [i.e., driving equipment and river improvements]." These considerations compelled Rossiter to ask that his firm be allowed to take out roughly 70,000 cords of pulpwood from these townships to ensure that it had enough spruce to support its expanded mill during its inaugural stages of operation. In response, the government granted Nipigon Corporation permission to take out less than one-third of this total.[29]

Nipigon Corporation then decided to cut its losses, specifically because of the premier's monocratic actions. Timmins had had enough of dealing with Ferguson. Hogarth described how, even by early 1924, Timmins had "cursed the day he went into the Nipigon venture." The problem was that Timmins had sunk a significant sum – $400,000 – into the project. As Hogarth put it, this investment "ties his [Timmins's] hands + prevents action to assert his rights as he knows perfectly well that he cannot get timber if Ferguson or his Government is attacked." As a result, sometime over the winter of 1926–7 Timmins quietly sold his small mill and pulpwood concession lease to International Paper, a deal that netted Hogarth and Little nearly half a million dollars – apparently tax exempt – for their share in these assets.[30]

This transaction effected a sudden softening in Ferguson's attitude towards Nipigon Corporation, one that reflected the premier's fondness for IP. J.I. Rankin, who stayed on as Nipigon Corporation's treasurer, asked the government in February 1927 for a two-year extension to fulfil the company's obligation to construct a mill as outlined in its pulpwood lease. The impetus behind his request, he pointed out, was "the present overproduced condition in the newsprint paper manufacturing industry, and in our opinion this present overproduction will not be absorbed in the markets available to us for at least two years." If

Ferguson's track record was any indicator, he should have summarily rejected Rankin's request. After all, only a few months earlier he had forced the newsprint companies against their will to commit to expanding their enterprises according to an impractical, rigid, and rigorous schedule at a time when it was already clear that the market for their product was oversupplied. Moreover, IP was busily constructing massive new mills in Quebec and New Brunswick at this time of flooded newsprint markets, and the Tories had every right to demand that it do the same in Ontario. But Ferguson instead concurred with Nipigon Corporation's assessment that the newsprint industry was in an "overproduced condition" and thus permitted it to postpone its development for two years.[31]

The Tories continued to be sympathetic to IP's new subsidiary. The government never demanded that the firm post the $150,000 guarantee bond that it required all concessionaires to submit to protect the department against non-fulfilment of their contractual obligations. This was a remarkable exception considering Nipigon Corporation had done the least to carry out its expansion and was now going to delay its project for another two years. Then in June 1927 the government permitted the company to close its small mill in Nipigon without penalty. The Tories even defended this move to the local municipal officials and fully endorsed IP's view that this closure was warranted because "the condition of trade is very discouraging." The coup de grâce came a few months later when the government allowed Nipigon Corporation to begin exporting spruce pulpwood that it had cut from its Crown concession area because of the glutted newsprint market. Remarkably, what Ferguson had heralded only eighteen months earlier as a new 400-ton newsprint mill in Nipigon had, by the fall of 1927, closed its small facility with impunity, postponed carrying out its construction obligations for two years, and begun exporting some of the area's most accessible spruce pulpwood.[32]

In the end, Ferguson had carefully manipulated his administration of pulpwood resources for political purposes and to the detriment of the Thunder Bay District's newsprint makers. Forcing the mills to undertake monstrous expansion programs beginning in late 1925 created a flurry of activity in the Thunder Bay District, and it undoubtedly contributed to the Tories' electoral success the following year. They went from holding only half the seats in northern Ontario in 1923 to controlling nearly all of them in 1926.

Figure 10. Unrealized Potential: By the late 1800s the mouth of the Nipigon River was prized by newsprint makers as one of the best spots in Canada at which to build a mill, but the provincial government refused to allow a succession of business interests to lease the rich local fibre supply until the mid-1920s. By then, industrialists had erected the small groundwood plant pictured in this rare photograph of the enterprise, and it landed in the hands of the iconic gold-mining magnate Noah Timmins. He sold it, however, after Conservative Premier Howard Ferguson insisted he dramatically expand it according to an illogical timetable and refused to provide him with the fibre he needed to sustain it. After International Paper acquired the plant in 1927, Ferguson allowed the firm to close it with impunity, to delay building the large newsprint mill the government had insisted Timmins construct, and to export the spruce it was cutting from its Crown pulpwood concession (Nipigon Historical Museum Archives).

8 "Political connections ... of the strongest kind"

By the end of 1925, Ferguson had yet to address Fort William Paper's application for Crown pulpwood on the west side of Lake Nipigon, but when he finally did so, the firm may have wished he never had. The company had built its newsprint mill four years earlier on the promise that the Ontario government would provide it with a pulpwood concession. Soon after the Tories had won power in 1923, the company reached an agreement on an area with James Lyons, the Conservatives' Minister of Lands and Forests, and on this basis it tendered for one of the tracts the Tories had advertised in mid-1925. Just before the end of the year, however, Ferguson made it clear that Fort William Paper's decision to use Lyons as its conduit with the government meant that it had bet on the wrong horse. First, Ferguson announced his intention to satisfy the region's lumbermen by withholding – over Lyons's protests – a 400-square-mile section of the limit for which the newsprint company had applied. A short while later, Ferguson orchestrated an extraordinary deal to deliver another large chunk of the timber tract Fort William Paper sought to Provincial Paper, the government's de facto paper supplier and a firm that was well connected politically. Finally, "the chief" went to remarkable lengths to shave off another slice of Fort William Paper's concession and deliver it to a lumberman who was as notorious as he was well connected. In doing so, Ferguson helped International Paper surreptitiously deepen its involvement in Ontario in a manner that both deleteriously affected the operations of the province's newsprint makers and made it clear once again that political expediency was *the* determinant in how his government dealt with them.

Provincial Paper Mills Company was the Thunder Bay District's only non-newsprint mill; its small facility produced limited quantities of fine

Map 12. Provincial Paper's Pulpwood Situation, 1926

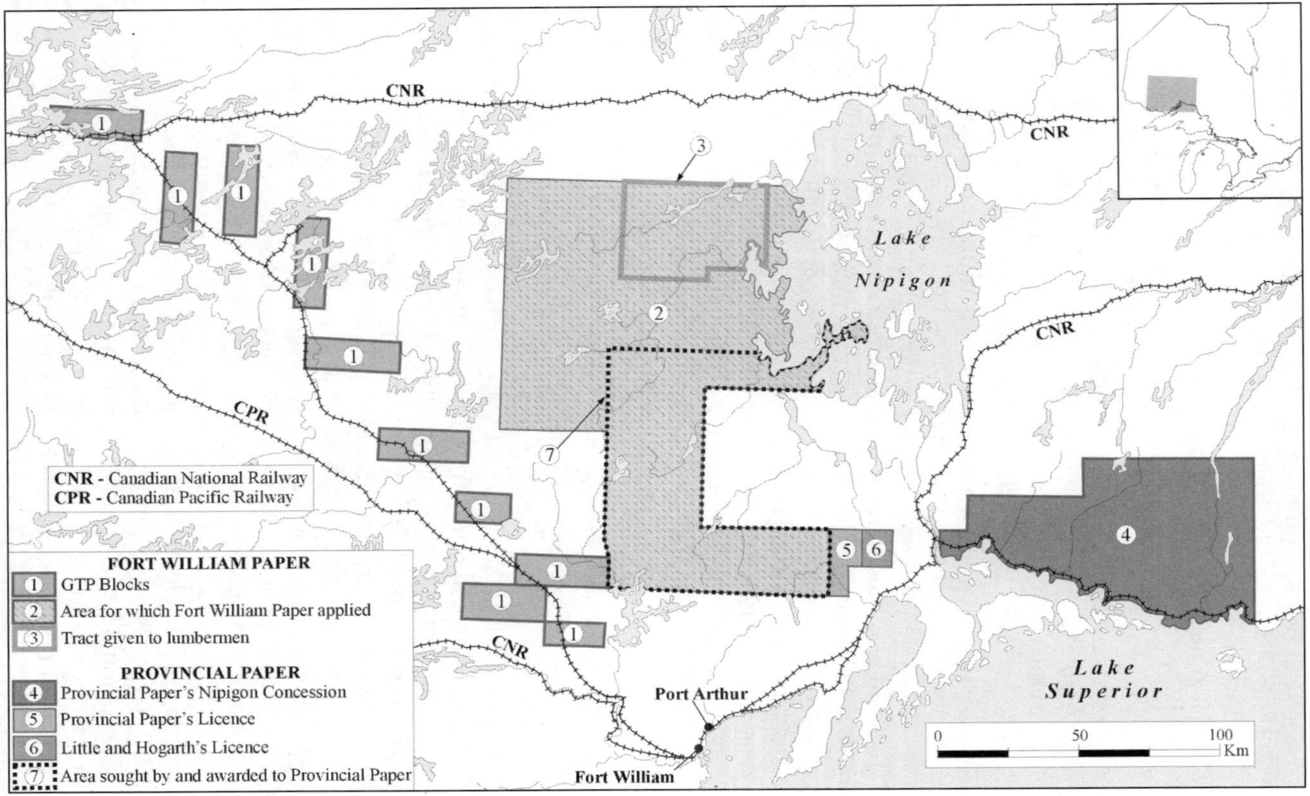

Lake Superior

Lake Nipigon

Port Arthur

Fort William

CNR

CPR

0   50   100
Km

CNR - Canadian National Railway
CPR - Canadian Pacific Railway

FORT WILLIAM PAPER

1   GTP Blocks
2   Area for which Fort William Paper applied
3   Tract given to lumbermen

PROVINCIAL PAPER

4   Provincial Paper's Nipigon Concession
5   Provincial Paper's Licence
6   Little and Hogarth's Licence

7   Area sought by and awarded to Provincial Paper

paper and sulphite pulp. Unlike the local newsprint makers, which did not lease Crown pulpwood concessions prior to 1926, the government had literally given Provincial a prime 1,240-square-mile limit in 1921 on which grew at least 3,000,000 cords of spruce pulpwood. The company also held a licence to a 72-square-mile tract west of the townships of Sterling and Hele. With its mill in Port Arthur requiring only about 150 cords of spruce per day (at most 45,000 cords per year), Provincial had more than enough fibre to meet its needs in perpetuity.[1]

Provincial objected, however, to the price it was obliged to pay for its pulpwood, and James Little and Donald Hogarth were only too happy to provide – at a cost – assistance in addressing this concern. The government charged the company $6.05 on its licence and $2.73 on its concession for each cord of spruce it cut, prices Provincial wished to see lowered to around the more prevalent $2.00 per cord. Little and Hogarth offered to sell Provincial a timber licence they owned to Hele Township, which held over 200,000 cords of pulpwood; it would be cheap to harvest and was a natural fit within the company's existing limits (Map 12). Isaac H. Weldon, the company's president, was prepared to pay Little and Hogarth's price – roughly $650,000 – for this Crown timber, but as with Provincial's own limits, Weldon was averse to paying the high charges (nearly $4.50 per cord) that applied to it.[2]

Little and Hogarth met with Minister Lyons to discuss the matter, and they formulated a stratagem for drastically reducing the prevailing pulpwood prices on Provincial's three areas: its concession, its licence (to the area west of Sterling and Hele Townships), and the licence to Hele Township that it intended to purchase from Little and Hogarth. Provincial would apply for – and the government would grant it – a new substantial concession on which it would pay $2.00 per cord. The government would then recommend amalgamating the new area with Provincial's existing timber holdings into a single Crown lease and calculate an average price it should pay for all this fibre. This computation should have been a straightforward process. Timber estimates for each area would indicate the total volumes available, these data would be multiplied by the prices stated in the agreements with the Crown, and then the total value of all the pulpwood would be divided by the total cordage available. Hele Township, for instance, was known to contain 220,000 cords of pulpwood, and the licence to this timber stated that $6.05 should be paid for each cord; the fibre was thus worth $1,331,000 in Crown stumpage. But applying this formula would not have achieved Provincial's principal aim, namely to reduce dramatically the price it paid for pulpwood. The government thus agreed to use figures that were egregious underestimates for the timber on which the high prices prevailed, thereby dramatically lowering the average price the company would pay for its wood. As abstruse as this scheme sounded, the Tories carried it out with precision.[3]

The first step involved Provincial applying for a tract of timber when Ferguson announced he was tendering the Nipigon pulpwood in the summer of 1925. Citing a "government estimate" that showed only 300,000 cords of pulpwood (or about 1/10 of the actual total) on the large concession it already leased, it asked for another 1,400 square miles of Crown timberland southwest of Lake Nipigon. This block co-incidentally formed a major and integral part of the concession for which Fort William Paper had been lobbying since the early 1920s (Map 12). Moreover, Provincial's modest and unusual tender offer contrasted sharply with the proposals the newsprint companies had submitted. Provincial proposed merely to double the size of its existing facilities, which produced only 35 tons of groundwood and 45 tons of bleached sulphite pulp from spruce per day. Moreover, its offer to construct a new 50-ton soda pulp mill "just as soon as market conditions warrant" also did nothing to strengthen its case for a new limit. Instead of relying on spruce and large amounts of electricity to break down wood fibre, as a newsprint mill did, a soda mill used poplar and expensive chemical solutions in its digestion process. For this reason, since the early part of the century no mills of this type had been constructed in Canada, let alone on the boreal forest, which was dominated by stands of black spruce and harnessable water powers. The fact that soda mills processed poplar also meant that Provincial could have built and operated this type of facility without receiving one stick of additional spruce pulpwood; the limits on which it was already privileged to cut held more than enough poplar to supply several small soda mills forever.[4]

Fort William Paper could not have been faulted for believing that it should have been awarded most if not all of the concession for which both it and Provincial had applied. Provincial already controlled more than enough pulpwood to support its proposed modest expansion program, whereas Fort William Paper had no Crown concession and already operated a 175-ton newsprint mill, and the government had demanded that the company commit to constructing a 425-ton mill within five years in return for receiving a pulpwood limit. Furthermore, this had been a tender, after all, a bidding process that Fort William

Paper had apparently won. It had offered to pay a total of $2.00 per cord, whereas Provincial had bid only $1.95. The limit for which both companies had applied was also a natural fit for Fort William Paper's harvesting operations, as the company could easily drive this wood to its mill near the mouth of the Kamanistiquia River; Provincial's plant was a significant distance away in Port Arthur. Furthermore, this area also made up the only section of the pulpwood tendered on the west side of Lake Nipigon that was directly driveable to Lake Superior. Fort William Paper thus sought control over it to avoid becoming dependent on driving its pulpwood down the Nipigon River, a transportation route that would be very costly and time consuming. Finally, Ferguson had earlier stated his intention to withdraw a 400-square-mile chunk from Fort William Paper's concession, and it thus needed all the remaining timber for which it had applied.[5]

Ferguson did not share this perspective. The department's report on the matter, which must have pleased Provincial Paper mightily, cited its baseless "government estimates" to conclude that Provincial needed another 2,000,000 cords of pulpwood, which was coincidentally the total found on the area for which Provincial had applied, and awarded the firm this tract on this basis. The Tories also used these same data to rationalize their mathematical chicanery that calculated that $2.24 would be a fair price to charge Provincial for all its pulpwood. Finally, the government agreed to merge the company's original licences into its new pulpwood concession agreement in 1926, thereby extending the life of its cutting privileges on these tracts far beyond the five-year deadline by which they should have expired. Provincial's new concession lease, which the government executed in late February, was thus the only contract signed by the mills in the Thunder Bay District that provided a perpetual fibre supply and included terms and conditions that the lessee wished to fulfil. The agreement merely obliged Provincial to undertake a token expansion of its existing small facility and begin construction of its peculiar soda mill "when and as soon as market conditions in the Province of Ontario will justify such expenditure." Not surprisingly, by the end of 1926 Provincial had already fulfilled its contractual commitments and had no problem providing the government with an affidavit attesting to its compliance in this regard. One contemporary observer rightly commented that this deal "was one of the juiciest transactions of that period."[6]

Several factors explain Provincial's success and Fort William Paper's failure in this instance. Provincial's role as supplier of textbook paper to

Ontario's Department of Education undoubtedly proved decisive in helping the firm – and the lieutenants whom it had hired – achieve its aims. On the other hand, Spanish River, which controlled Fort William Paper, had understandably but unwisely chosen to deal with the Conservatives through James Lyons. This seemed reasonable considering he was both the minister and MPP for the riding that centred on Sault Ste Marie, the home of one of Spanish River's mills and its Canadian headquarters. Clearly upset by Ferguson's imperious decision in handling this matter, Lyons protested vociferously and apparently refused to execute Provincial's new lease. Not one to suffer insubordinates, Ferguson installed himself as acting minister, signed Provincial's agreement, and ousted Lyons from cabinet in early March 1926 over an incident that hardly seemed worthy of the scandalous spin the premier gave it.[7]

Even after this setback, however, Lyons continued lobbying on Fort William Paper's behalf, but with little effect. He relayed the company's profound concerns about Ferguson's intention to set aside a 400-square-mile area for the use of the Thunder Bay District's lumbermen within the tract that Fort William Paper sought; the latter would be permitted to harvest the pulpwood in this zone only after the former had cut its jack pine. This arrangement would create an enormous practical problem, Lyons warned the premier, because it would force the company "to take all their timber out through what might be regarded as the neck of the bottle, and makes the operation of the greater part of their limit objectionable and expensive" (Map 12).[8] Nevertheless, Ferguson obdurately confirmed in mid-1926 that his decision would stand. This move, when combined with his government's deal with Provincial, meant that Fort William Paper had lost over one-half of the fibre supply for which it had originally applied.[9]

These developments drove the company to ask the government for compensation, specifically enough pulpwood (a total of roughly 9,000,000 cords) to sustain in perpetuity the 425-ton mill Ferguson was demanding that it build. It thus requested a lease to the remainder of the concession for which it had originally applied and territory west of this area that the government had not tendered but the department's foresters had cruised. When Ferguson sent Fort William Paper a draft of its lease in July 1926, however, this second area was not included in the description of its concession, prompting G.R. Gray, its vice-president, to immediately convey his concerns to the department. He emphasized that the contract committed the government to supply enough pulpwood to the enlarged mill

Map 13. Fort William Paper's Quest for More Pulpwood, 1926–1929

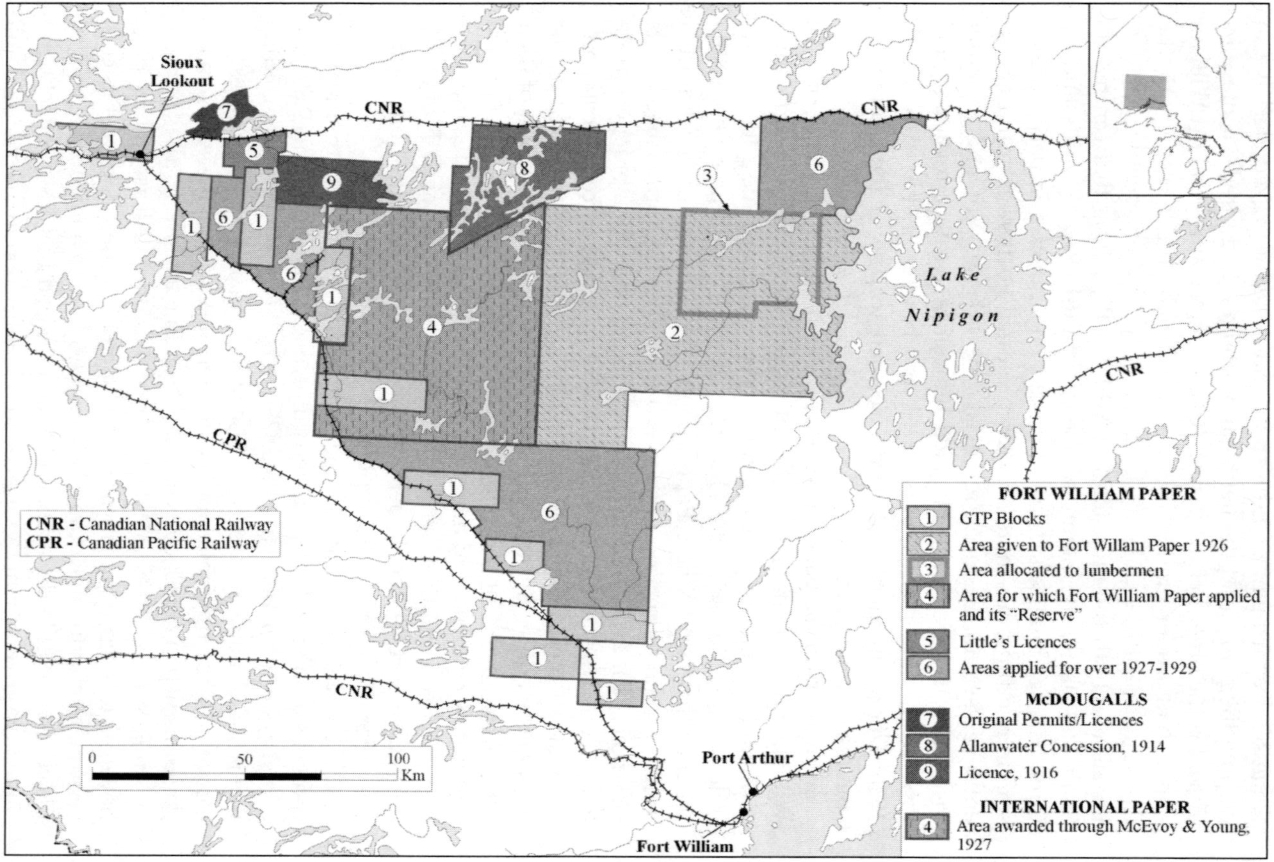

Sioux Lookout
CNR
CNR
CNR
CNR
CPR
Lake Nipigon
Port Arthur
Fort William
CNR - Canadian National Railway
CPR - Canadian Pacific Railway
0
50
100
Km
FORT WILLIAM PAPER
1 GTP Blocks
2 Area given to Fort Willam Paper 1926
3 Area allocated to lumbermen
4 Area for which Fort William Paper applied and its "Reserve"
5 Little's Licences
6 Areas applied for over 1927-1929
McDOUGALLS
7 Original Permits/Licences
8 Allanwater Concession, 1914
9 Licence, 1916
INTERNATIONAL PAPER
4 Area awarded through McEvoy & Young, 1927

for the duration of the contract (one twenty-one-year term renewable once) but that "the territory allotted to the Company is considerably less in mileage than the territory as described in the proposal to the Minister and the Company now finds that the available pulpwood on the territory contained in the Agreement is considerably less than the quantity which the Company felt it should have in order to justify the obligations assumed under its proposal." Gray thus asked the government, at the very least, to reserve this supplemental area for the company. Ferguson refused to provide this assurance in writing, but did so verbally.[10]

With few options available to it, in September 1926, over one year after the tender for the Nipigon limits had closed, Fort William Paper signed its new concession lease, which still contained many terms that it found objectionable. Of all the deals consummated at this time, this one committed a concessionaire to the greatest expansion (from 175 to 425 tons newsprint) in the shortest period (barely two years). Moreover, although Fort William Paper signed the lease on 21 September, it was obliged to spend $1,000,000 on its augmentation program by the end of the year, a task that was practically impossible. And while it had emphasized that its mill expansion depended on being granted about 9,000,000 cords of pulpwood, it received less than half this total. Nevertheless, the government verbally agreed again to set aside its reserve.[11]

This was most troubling news for Fort William Paper. It had commissioned the renowned aerial timber surveyor Frank T. Jenkins to investigate the best means of harvesting both its new pulpwood concession and reserve area. For a host of practical reasons, Jenkins concluded that the efficient operation of its concession area was dependent upon the company being granted cutting privileges on its reserve. If it were able to harvest only the former and not the latter, its wood costs would be prohibitive.[12]

Fort William Paper thus pressed the government to add its reserve to its concession, but the Tories refused. G.R. Gray, the firm's vice-president, brought the new minister, William Finlayson, up to speed on the matter, and pushed for Finlayson's "assurance that there will be no alienation of the [reserve] territory ... until you have fully considered our needs." Boding well for Gray's endeavour were a few steps Ferguson had taken earlier in 1927. In February, the premier had admitted that the newsprint market was glutted, announced a moratorium on the construction of new capacity in Ontario, and postponed the deadline by which Nipigon Corporation was to carry out its contractual obligation to build its plant. Fort William Paper's reserve would presumably not be needed to

)

Within the photograph, the banner reads:

FORT·WILLIAM·PAPER·CO·LTD.
PAPER MILL
DAILY·CAPACITY·WHEN·COMPLETED
300·TONS·NEWS·PRINT.

AUG 14 20

Figure 11. In the Power of the Government: Pulp and paper makers generally devised corporate strategies for establishing, operating, and expanding
their enterprises in Ontario after considering empirical data such as market
demand and industry capacity. For example, Fort William Paper broadcast its
ultimate goal in this photograph taken at the sod-turning ceremony in the late
summer of 1920 for its new mill at the Lakehead. Nevertheless, the provincial
state could control virtually all aspects of the paper makers' business by manipulating the terms under which they leased Crown resources. The reigning
Conservative government poignantly demonstrated its power in this regard
in the mid-1920s in the Thunder Bay District when it dictated to several firms
how and when they would augment their concerns. At the time, Premier
Ferguson ordered Fort William Paper – against its fervent protests – to expand
its existing 175-ton newsprint mill to 425 tons within two years, and refused
to provide the firm with enough fibre to sustain its operation (Thunder Bay
Historical Museum Society, 981.39.320B).

support a new newsprint mill. Nevertheless, Ferguson's government toed a hard line in dealing with the company. It responded to Gray's entreaties in a surly manner, explaining that it disagreed with his "suggestion that the Crown gave anything in the nature of a guarantee as to the quantity of raw material available on the [company's] limit." It also refused to bind itself in writing to grant Fort William Paper this reserve area, let alone lease the firm this tract. While it again trumpeted that "the Department are very anxious to see that your Company is treated properly and it is desired to take care of existing industries," in light of events that were already well underway by this time, the government's pledge had a decidedly hollow ring to it.[13]

This dissonance was a function of Alexander McDougall's determination to avail himself of the advantages accruing from his political connections. It will be recalled that he and his brother Samuel had exploited their celebrated heritage – their father had been Canada's first auditor general – to establish themselves as timber "operators" near Sioux Lookout while the Tories held office during the 1910s (Map 13). The McDougalls had constantly raised the hackles of department officials because of their shoddy practices, and the Drury government had tried but failed to terminate their shenanigans. By the time Ferguson swept to power in 1923, Alexander McDougall had raised his profile even higher. He had deftly exploited his post as head of "Allied" timber operations in Europe during the Great War to cement alliances with the political elite in both Canada and on the Continent; the press remarked at the time that no one in the Canadian Expeditionary Force was "on more intimate terms with King George V." After the conflict, McDougall attempted to capitalize on his elevated status by undertaking a venture to harvest wood from Baltic forests and convert it into ties for Britain's railways. After he ran the project into the ground, he called upon Canada's prime minister, W.L. Mackenzie King, for help. Although not even the Dominion's senior politician could right McDougall's listing ship in international waters, King's willingness to extend a helping hand spoke volumes about how the incorrigible lumberman held sway in high places.[14]

This was especially true in the Legislature in Toronto, as long as Ferguson's hands were on the control levers. McDougall's bitter experience dabbling in European timber drove him back to northern Ontario. In tow, he brought James Calder, the British lumberman who specialized in preserving railway ties with creosote. Even after forming this partnership, however, McDougall had complained to the government in mid-1924 that he was still unable to finance the construction of the tie processing plant that was required under his 1914 agreement for the Allanwater limit (see chapter 3). It was for this reason that he asked the department to return almost the entire $25,000 deposit he had made at the time he had leased the tract, even though this sum was only to be refunded upon completion of his project. In front of only three other cabinet members, one of whom was Lyons, the minister, Ferguson, as acting minister, authored the Recommendation to Council and executed the Order in Council that ensured that McDougall got his money. Seventy-two hours later the provincial auditor informed the department that McDougall still owed the government almost $20,000 in dues and other charges, a condition that, by protocol, precluded refunding his deposit. Nevertheless, by mid-1925 the tie mill was finally up and running in Sioux Lookout.[15]

The Tories granted the McDougalls – Samuel was still associated with Alexander in the Ontario timber ventures – a succession of further favours at this time. Responding to their request, the government amended their lease to the Allanwater limit in order to allow them to export the tract's pulpwood and pay only $1.40 per cord for it.[16] The government's actions apparently came just in the nick of time for Alexander McDougall, who was deeply indebted to and pressed by the department to remit the Crown charges he owed. To remedy this situation, McDougall pledged his revised Allanwater concession agreement and his other Crown timber licences to Montreal Trust, which apparently agreed to clear McDougall's $75,000 debt with the department and grant him annual permits to cut on his limits. And when he needed the premier to bail him out again not long after, Ferguson obliged.[17]

The premier's affinity for assisting McDougall masked the disdain departmental personnel felt for him, but their opportunity to express their views finally arrived in 1926. In May of that year, McDougall asked – as he had numerous times before – for another timber licence even though he had barely cut his existing limits. This time, he requested that the government grant him – without tender – a few hundred square miles of Crown woodlands south of Sioux Lookout. Walter Cain, the deputy minister, pointed out that the area for which McDougall had applied had already been requested by George Farlinger in 1920 to supply a newsprint mill Farlinger intended to construct in the region. In addition, immediately after Ferguson had returned to power in 1923, both Lyons and Frank Keefer, the MPP for Port Arthur, urged Ferguson to facilitate Farlinger's plans. For these reasons, Cain emphasized to

McDougall that "close consideration must of necessity be given to the application formerly made by Mr. Farlinger."[18] When McDougall persisted, Cain proved most unreceptive to his dictatorial tone. McDougall contended that this was an urgent matter because the additional area for which he had applied was necessary for his harvesting operations that winter. Cain categorically rejected McDougall's assertion, replying that he was "rather surprised" by it. "I can scarcely understand," the astonished deputy minister continued, "that after operating on ... [his Allanwater limit] ... where there is some 400 square miles, only for a couple of seasons, an extension to the area is so vital at the present moment as you seem to indicate." Cain informed McDougall that no action would be taken.[19]

Even Ferguson's intervention at this point could not rescue McDougall. Forever teetering on the brink of bankruptcy, his enterprises went over the edge into liquidation in September 1926.[20]

With the 1 December election just around the corner, Ferguson was in need of signs of economic prosperity, not news that a timber operation like McDougall's had just gone under, and so the premier hastily created one. He led Farlinger to believe that the latter would soon be able to commence constructing his newsprint mill in Sioux Lookout by having former premier William Hearst draft leases that conveyed to Farlinger the local pulpwood concession and water powers Farlinger had sought. With these documents ready for execution by the fall of 1926, stories of the proposed new plant swirled in Sioux Lookout, boding well for the Tories' chances as the ballots were being counted. But when Ferguson returned to power a few weeks before Christmas, the leases remained unexecuted.[21]

By early 1927, Archibald Graustein, president of International Paper Company (IP), was already at work on a wily and outrageous plan to ensure that they never would be executed. Sensing McDougall's vulnerability, Graustein pounced. To represent IP, Graustein had shrewdly dumped the Farmers' solicitor, Gordon Waldron, who had acted on IP's behalf with the Drury government. In his stead he hired McGregor Young, the Tories' lawyer of choice and soon-to-be appointee as Ontario's Official Guardian, and his partner, John A. McEvoy. In presenting IP's case to the Conservatives, the firm of McEvoy and Young argued that McDougall did not need another sawlog limit to rejuvenate his now-bankrupt railway tie and lumber operation. Rather, IP's solicitors contended that McDougall was suffering because he was unable to process the pulpwood that grew on his 600 square miles of timber limits (his Allanwater concession and licences). To solve the problem, McEvoy and Young asserted that McDougall would construct a 200-ton newsprint mill to process his spruce, but to do so he needed a nearby 2,000-square-mile pulpwood limit.[22] Incredibly, McEvoy and Young were suggesting that the only means of "rehabilitating" McDougall's tie and lumber business would be to give him – without tender – a large pulpwood concession and oblige him to build a new, multi-million-dollar newsprint mill. As ludicrous as this scheme sounded, the Ferguson government immediately began facilitating its realization. The Tories did so even though the new limit for which McEvoy and Young applied was coincidentally the very tract that had already been requested by and reserved for Fort William Paper and to which Farlinger had been given a draft lease (Map 13).[23]

Departmental officials raised serious concerns about McEvoy and Young's proposal, but their protests went unheeded. The bureaucrats were on solid ground when they challenged the solicitors' low estimate of the pulpwood available on McDougall's existing limits because these woodlands had never been cruised. Moreover, Walter Cain, the deputy minister, pointed out the one major problem he saw with the tract McEvoy and Young sought: it was already "covered by an application of the Fort William Paper Company." Nevertheless, by April 1927 the government had a lease for IP ready to go. The lightning speed at which this contract had been drawn up was understandable considering the Tories had allowed McEvoy and Young to draft it.[24]

Cain's name would be on the document that practically sealed this deal, but its contents hardly bore his signature.[25] In May 1927, he prepared an astounding précis of the situation for the new minister, William Finlayson, in which he painted a sympathetic portrait of the McDougalls' operation. It confused their own ineptitude with bad luck – and euphemisms for proper diction – in stating that "their financial position ... was somewhat precarious, different factors conducing to an inability to economically succeed without regular prospective and real losses." It also argued that the end of their business would be a serious blow to the Crown's revenues, an odd analysis considering the meagre scope of their enterprise and the fact that they were constantly in arrears with the government. Alleging that they were "really stranded and maintain their only salvation is the utilisation of the pulpwood upon their own limits," the document supported granting McDougall the 2,000-square-mile pulpwood concession. Cain had also apparently forgotten that, only one year earlier, he had expressed his incredulity at McDougall's request for another *few hundred*-square-mile limit to supply his tie plant because McDougall had only operated on his concession and licences for a few seasons. Now, in this May 1927 document, the deputy minister contended that from these "old limits ... large quantities of tie and log timber have been taken."

The rest of the memorandum's analyses were truly unbelievable, and it closed by asking one crucial question. The document ignored the government's commitment to tendering timber when it proclaimed that this means of marketing wood was inappropriate in this instance. After pointing out again that Fort William Paper had applied for the same area as McEvoy and Young (i.e., Fort William Paper would have bid on this pulpwood had it been given the chance), the memorandum stated that to "offer the timber by public competition may defeat the very purpose sought, that is, to rehabilitate old industries, up to quite recently going concerns, whose obligations to the Crown cannot possibly, it is claimed, be met except by securing added cordage ... it is the case of old Government patrons trying to extricate themselves from conditions in which they are now placed ... If an agreement satisfactory to the Crown can be effected I do not see from a business point of view why it should not be carried out." The memorandum then ignored Ferguson's public declaration in February 1927 that the newsprint industry's overcapacity necessitated imposing a moratorium on new mills in Ontario and granting an extension of two years for Nipigon Corporation, which IP now owned, to begin building its newsprint plant. Instead, the document proclaimed that the government should allow McEvoy and Young to construct another mill in Ontario to combat a lurking danger that was even greater than a saturated market: an overconcentration of producers. "The question of overproduction," the curious document philosophized, "of course is more or less a moot one but there may be less reason for apprehension in this respect than in the possibility, and I am not sure but it is so shaping, of a consolidating of the pulp and paper industries into a huge monopoly, the results of which might be more disastrous to a consuming public than the drop in price of paper due to increased production." In closing, the memorandum asked the minister, "What is your direction in this?"

Ferguson made certain that he, not Finlayson, rose to answer this question. On 17 June 1927, the premier authorized the execution of a carefully worded Order in Council that appeared innocuous when published in the *Ontario Gazette*. It authorized the minister to sign an agreement with the McDougall lumbering operations "to provide for the re-establishment of the industries hitherto existent but now defunct, *and any new development incidental thereto*" (emphasis added). Considering this transaction involved the construction of a 200-ton newsprint mill and the granting of nearly 2,000 square miles of prime pulpwood limits, this was hardly a "new development incidental" to McDougall's modest timber operations. The next day, McEvoy applied to incorporate the North West Ontario Development Company, and Alexander McDougall and B.R. Hepburn, McDougall's right-hand man during the First World War, long-time crony and former Tory MP, were the only notable names among the firm's five petitioners. With McEvoy urging the government to execute the new pulpwood agreement, on 24 June McDougall and Hepburn transferred their interest in almost every timber asset they still held to North West Ontario, including the unsigned Crown lease for the 2,000-square-mile pulpwood concession, McDougall's saw and tie mills and, most importantly, almost all the 2,000,000 shares (the total that North West Ontario could issue) they held in the new firm. In exchange, North West Ontario would pay McDougall and Hepburn $250,000. The result left North West Ontario under the control of its president, John A. McEvoy.[26]

The pulpwood concession agreement the Tories executed with North West Ontario in late July 1927 was exceptional and reflected their partiality for its proprietors. The government accepted the company's view that the McDougalls' original limits contained only 1,000,000 cords of spruce, that there was no market in Ontario for it, and that much of this fibre was "ripe and should be cut within the next few years." Not only did the document fail to explain how the government knew this pulpwood was "ripe" without having cruised it, but these spruce trees were described as if they were a banana crop on the cusp of going bad instead of a one-hundred-year-old forest that could easily survive for another generation without being cut. The lease declared that the proposed mill would be "of great advantage to the Province and will aid materially in the advancement and development of the districts" involved, that the company needed a large tract of additional fibre to sustain the new industry, and that it was thus "in the public interest" to grant North West Ontario the privilege of harvesting this total of 2,600 square miles of spruce pulpwood (McDougall's original limits and the new concession). Instead of being obliged to construct its 200-ton mill according to a strict schedule consisting of finite expenditures by definite dates, North West Ontario was ordered only to build its facility "with all convenient despatch." Upon its completion, North

West Ontario was required to employ merely 200 hands to operate its 200-ton mill (Thunder Bay Paper was obliged to employ over four times as many workers to operate a plant of the same size). The irony was that North West Ontario – which had no paper plant – controlled over 2,600 square miles of Crown forests containing over 6,500,000 cords of pulpwood, far more fibre than what was available to any of the Thunder Bay District's existing newsprint mills.[27]

While Ferguson and a few political insiders were aware that IP and Graustein were behind North West Ontario, for Fort William Paper, one of Spanish River's mills, this news would have created a crushing sense of déjà vu. Ferguson had promised in 1919 to reserve for Spanish River's mill in Espanola a 4,000-square-mile tract as part of the government's declared policy of retaining the province's pulpwood supply for Ontario's "existing industries." In 1923, however, the government had severed a critical section from Spanish River's reserve for the use of another firm, Continental Wood Products. Not only was this firm one of IP's subsidiaries, but it operated no existing mill and never built the one described in its lease. Now, in 1927, history was repeating itself.[28]

Ferguson ensured that Fort William Paper's problems were far from over. His government demanded that the firm strictly adhere to the construction schedule set out in its 1926 pulpwood agreement, and for the first year at least, Fort William Paper was able to do so. But the concession it leased did not contain enough pulpwood to sustain in perpetuity the 425-ton mill it was obliged to build, and the tract also represented a very expensive fibre source that would be time-consuming to extract. This grim reality had been laid plain in a consultant's report in 1927 and was confirmed the next year by the firm's own foresters. It would take at least two-and-one-half years to transport the pulpwood from its new concession to its mill, at a cost of between $1.50 and $4.00 more per cord than "the cost of pulpwood delivered previously from other limits or outside purchases." During a period of rapidly declining newsprint prices, the cost of tapping this timber was onerous. Facing this quandary, Fort William Paper's vice-president, G.R. Gray, sought a supplemental source of fibre both to augment the mill's supply and to provide cheap fibre to balance the high-cost pulpwood on its Lake Nipigon concession. He purchased a number of relatively tiny pulpwood licences from James Little in 1927, and continued to lobby the government for help. "In order that the necessary wood supply be made available to sustain this mill for even a period of thirty (30) years," Gray asserted, "we should have an allotment of at least 5,500,000 cords of wood," which it did not have. He added that his firm had "always relied on the honour of the Crown in our dealings, hence it is inconceivable that the Fort William Paper Company should in response to expressed wishes of a former Minister, obligate itself by agreement to build and operate a 425-ton mill, without definite assurance as to the wood resources available for such mill." Gray closed by asking for a 260-square-mile limit – which contained roughly 1,000,000 cords – in the vicinity of what was now his mill's former reserve that would have served his firm's needs wonderfully (Map 13).[29]

Finlayson reassured Gray that the Ontario government was anxious to treat his company fairly, but he took no steps to aid it. His carefully worded response to Fort William Paper indicated that his hands had been tied when Ferguson had given its reserve away to IP; he informed Gray that "it was understood that your Company was securing certain additional areas, and it is unfortunate if these have been lost." Finlayson rejected Fort William Paper's application for an additional limit and urged it instead to purchase more pulpwood from settlers. In the minister's view, "it seems unfair to ask for further material from the Crown when Companies are allowing large quantities to be exported."[30]

Over the next few years Finlayson was inclined to help Fort William Paper but was powerless to do so. Gray pleaded with the minister to provide the company with additional areas to supply the enlarged mill it was required to construct, and at the same time alerted Finlayson to another potentially troublesome situation. "They suggested," Finlayson explained in a note to Cain, his deputy minister, in reference to the firm's officials, "that there was a danger of other parties applying for the areas adjoining their limits, and that if they do not get them now it might be impossible to get them when the capacity of the mill was increased." While Finlayson could not possibly have known how the company's concerns would turn out to be self-fulfilling prophecies (over roughly the next dozen years the government would give almost all the areas for which Fort William Paper applied at this time to pulpwood exporters), he recognized that it would be prudent to follow the company's advice. He thus suggested to Cain that the government execute an Order in Council "earmarking the territory applied for" as an extension of Fort William Paper's concession, to be added when required. Ferguson was apparently unimpressed by Finlayson's proposal, as he refused to sanction any action on Fort William Paper's behalf.[31]

A penetrating summary of this chain of events in the Thunder Bay District was provided by several contemporary observers, one of whom merits a lengthy citation. Under the pseudonym "A Forester," *Saturday Night* published a series of articles in late 1928 that described what the author saw as Ferguson's bizarre approach to dispensing this region's pulpwood resources.[32]

The exposé began with a lament. "Politics often means our otherwise intelligent politicians often disregard sound advice because it is expedient. When forest limits were offered for auction by the Government in the greatest profusion and quite regardless of any intelligent application of a policy of permanent forest production," the Forester stated, "the existing mills were forced into undertaking almost ridiculous expansion projects ... With the lease of each new limit went a contract by which the lessee was obligated to a construction project involving the expenditure of so many millions of dollars and the employment of so many hundreds of men. The existing mills, in self protection, were forced to agree to such projects in order to keep these new limits under intelligent control." Turning to the McDougall affair, the author wrote that, just recently, "an area of over 2,000 sq. miles of pulpwood was given without public auction to a bankrupt sawmill company, which already owned 700 sq. miles of excellent timber only 25 per cent. cut over, and whose troubles were entirely due to the most appalling inefficiency and waste ever seen in logging operations in this country. This company had in its midst a man whose political connections were of the strongest kind. The excuse given for the grant was that it was to reinstate a long-established concern whose difficulties were due to post-war depression and lack of accessible timber."

The Forester also decried the troubling situation now facing Ontario's newsprint makers. He revealed that the province's "existing mills ... contrary to general belief, are now left without timber supplies sufficient to ensure permanency" and that this situation would only worsen if the newsprint makers at the Lakehead were forced to expand as required by their recently consummated concession agreements. Consequently, the Forester urged the government to take steps to ensure each plant a supply of spruce sufficient to guarantee it permanent production, specifically 2,250,000 cords per 100 tons of capacity. He added that only one – maybe two – newsprint mills in Ontario controlled enough pulpwood to last sixty years, most had fibre for only thirty or forty years, and the rest had far less.

It is unknown what Ferguson thought of these provocative articles, but C.D. Howe, dean of the University of Toronto's Faculty of Forestry, and Fred Brown, his former student and close friend and veteran forest industry official in Fort Frances, recognized their significance. Howe wrote Brown and forthrightly asked whether his confidant had penned these pieces, which Howe pointed out "must have been written by someone fairly well acquainted with the industries as well as with the internal workings within the government circles." In his reply to Howe, Brown admitted to being well versed in these facts, and understood why Howe had suspected him, but he denied having been the culprit. He opined, however, that he could "hardly see how Ferguson can swing the big stick over the heads of the paper compan[ies], when he and his Department are mostly to blame for the undue expansion of the industry … The papermills have been forced into expansion no doubt. But how Ferguson will save his Face I am curious to know. I am sorry for the Hon. Mr. Finlayson as he will no doubt [be] the goat."[33]

9 "Excluded from the area given to Spruce Falls"

The northern Clay Belt was home to three pulp and paper mills when the Tories won the election of 1923: Spruce Falls Company in Kapuskasing, Mattagami Pulp and Paper in Smooth Rock Falls, and Abitibi Power and Paper in Iroquois Falls. While all these enterprises looked to the Ferguson administration for assistance in procuring Crown resources on favourable terms, the premier decided for a host of political reasons that only one of them would succeed in this endeavour. Kimberly-Clark (KC) had taken over the mill project in "Kap" in 1920, at the very time when the Ontario government desperately needed a white knight to rescue its botched soldiers' colony by providing a local pulpwood buyer and job supplier. KC agreed with alacrity to play this essential role at this critical juncture, and it coaxed the provincial state into picking up most of the tab for developing the local town site, a community whose existence depended almost entirely on KC's enterprise. If ever the Ontario government had a compelling reason to guarantee a mill project, this was it. KC's standing as one of the titans in the American pulp and paper industry, and its canny decision to partner with arguably the world's most important newspaper in its venture, drove Ferguson to lavish the company with the greatest bounty the provincial state could muster. There were only so many cords of pulpwood and horsepower of hydroelectricity to go around, however, and KC's victories – of which there were many – came at the expense of its neighbour, Mattagami Pulp in Smooth Rock Falls. Ferguson went even further, however, denying that company timber in a way that ended up punishing it. Although this was grim news for Mattagami Pulp, the government's actions infused the local market for settlers' pulpwood with significant energy.

This was one reason why Abitibi in Iroquois Falls suffered the same fate in its dealing with the Tories, but there were others as well. Ferguson had besmirched the firm's reputation during the Timber Commission's hearings in the early 1920s, making it politically risky for anyone to assist the company. Not only was a calculating politician like Ferguson not about to take this gamble, he took deliberate steps to demonstrate the provincial state's autonomy vis-à-vis Abitibi, in the process doing the firm more harm than good.

Mattagami Pulp and Paper had leased a pulpwood concession in 1914 that contained enough pulpwood to supply in perpetuity the 100-ton newsprint mill it had planned on constructing in Smooth Rock Falls. The obstructive behaviour of the New Ontario Colonization Company, the local pulpwood exporting firm, however, had prevented it from realizing this end by limiting the quantity of power Mattagami Pulp could generate. This restricted the mill to manufacturing sulphite pulp, which required twice as much spruce as newsprint and meant that it would exhaust its concession's supply of pulpwood in roughly thirty years. The volatile conditions of 1920–1 had pushed the company into receivership, but it remained a viable operation.

Duncan Chisholm was Mattagami Pulp's founder, and he led a group of financiers who were eager to reorganize it. Through W.J. Boland, his lawyer, Chisholm began impressing upon the Ferguson government soon after it won power in 1923 that the mill sought to acquire a supplemental fibre source both to sustain the existing facility and to supply the newsprint mill Boland's clients intended to erect if they won control of the firm's assets. In the spring of 1925, Boland applied specifically for a seventeen-township concession adjacent to his mill's existing limit.[1]

A short while later Kimberly-Clark (KC) submitted its own application, one which paid mere lip service to the truth. It operated a 150-ton bleached-sulphite pulp mill in Kapuskasing through its subsidiary, Spruce Falls Company, and exported its entire output to its converting mills in the United States. Unlike Mattagami Pulp, KC had more than enough pulpwood. Its investigations of its nearly 2,000-square-mile pulpwood concession had found over 7,200,000 cords of spruce, a supply KC had not even begun to tap because, prior to 1928, it purchased almost all its wood from local settlers (Map 14). KC could thus operate its existing bleached-sulphite mill to capacity, and construct and operate the 200-ton newsprint mill its power lease obliged it to build before 1928, confident that its fibre requirements were well looked

Map 14. Mattagami Pulp Battles Kimberly-Clark for Pulpwood, 1923–1926

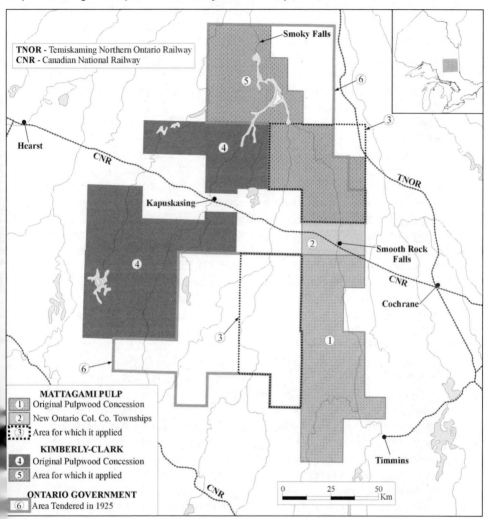

TNOR - Temiskaming Northern Ontario Railway
CNR - Canadian National Railway

Smoky Falls

Hearst

CNR

Kapuskasing

Smooth Rock Falls

CNR

Cochrane

TNOR

Timmins

CNR

MATTAGAMI PULP
1. Original Pulpwood Concession
2. New Ontario Col. Co. Townships
3. Area for which it applied

KIMBERLY-CLARK
4. Original Pulpwood Concession
5. Area for which it applied

ONTARIO GOVERNMENT
6. Area Tendered in 1925

0   25   50
                  Km

after. Nevertheless, Frank J. Sensenbrenner, KC's president, claimed otherwise. He insisted in his correspondence with the new Tory government that, notwithstanding the terms of KC's 1920 lease, his firm was actually obliged to build a 550-ton facility because ex-minister Beniah Bowman had insisted on this condition in 1923 in exchange for granting KC a lease to the Smoky Falls power site.[2] While there was no credible evidence to substantiate Sensenbrenner's case, he pushed for acceptance of his application on this basis.[3]

Sensenbrenner was animated to request additional pulpwood by his pending deal to supply newsprint to the *New York Times*. At least as early as 1923 KC had opened discussions with the venerable daily, whose existing paper contracts were set to expire in 1927. The *Times* was anxious to secure a stable source of fairly priced, high-quality paper, and had agreed to join KC in investing in a 550-ton newsprint mill in Kapuskasing if KC could prove that the venture controlled a perpetual pulpwood supply. Consequently, Sensenbrenner asked the government to grant it cutting privileges on roughly one dozen townships north of the Canadian National Railway (CNR) (Map 14). KC was planning on building a railway to both Smoky Falls – the cascades it would soon develop – and a point on the Mattagami River to which it could drive or haul all the pulpwood on the townships for which it was now applying and then ship this fibre by rail to its mill in Kapuskasing (Map 14).[4]

Ferguson was so enamoured of the prospect of the *Times* joining KC's venture in Kapuskasing that he had already taken steps to market the project. In the summer of 1924, he commanded W.R. Maxwell, Director of the Ontario Provincial Air Service, to place one of the government's planes at the disposal of KC's and the *Times*'s executives, who wished to tour the mill site, Smoky Falls, and the nearby forest. After the party, which included James K. Kimberly, KC's vice-president, and Arthur H. Sulzberger, the *Times*'s vice-president, spent ten days paddling down the Kapuskasing River to Moose Factory, Maxwell was dutifully waiting to fly them out.[5]

Although Ferguson extended no such privileges to Mattagami Pulp's personnel, it appeared that he would grant the requests for pulpwood limits made by Mattagami and KC. These areas overlapped to a small extent but this conflict could be easily resolved. The Tories could allocate the area north of the CNR to the mill in Kapuskasing for the practical reasons Sensenbrenner had outlined. Likewise, they could sell the pulpwood south of the railway to Mattagami Pulp because it could easily drive this timber directly to its mill in Smooth Rock Falls or the CNR, and ship the wood by rail a short distance to its plant. When Ferguson announced in mid-1925 that he would sell two large limits on the northern Clay Belt along with those in the Nipigon watershed, it appeared that this was exactly what he had in mind. The concessions he tendered were, for the most part, those which Mattagami Pulp and KC had requested (Map 14).

There were predictably only two legitimate bidders for this pulpwood. W.D. Ross and Isaac W. Killam, representing the same group that had previously shown an interest in reorganizing Mattagami Pulp, submitted a three-tiered offer. The first proposal sought a small part of the tendered area simply to sustain their existing mill in Smooth Rock Falls. Their next proposition requested a larger chunk of the pulpwood and additional water powers to support a 100-ton newsprint mill they would add within two years to the existing sulphite plant in Smooth Rock Falls. Their third offer asked for all the tendered pulpwood and an additional power supply as part of a plan to build a 250-ton newsprint mill and expand it "if business conditions were conducive." They offered to pay the extravagant price of between $2.95 and $3.15 per cord of pulpwood, depending upon which proposal the government accepted. "Unless we are allotted some of the existing area sufficient to protect the Mattagami enterprise," they pleaded, "the position of the undertaking will be serious because all the nearby wood which could be obtained at a reasonable cost will have been disposed of."[6] Sensenbrenner presented KC's offer, which now asked for the limits *both* north and south of the CNR that the government was tendering (a total of nearly 3,000 square miles). He argued that his mill in Kapuskasing needed at least another 14,000,000 cords of pulpwood to carry out its expansion project, and offered to pay a total of $2.05 per cord. In addition, KC proposed developing the water power at Smoky Falls (something it was already obliged to do), constructing a 550-ton newsprint mill by 1928 and spending upwards of $12,000,000 in the process. Sensenbrenner underscored that the *Times* had made its participation in the undertaking contingent upon, as one of its senior officials explained, "the outcome of these wood negotiations."[7]

The government was at a distinct disadvantage in assessing the relative merits of these offers, but this this did not matter to the Conservatives. They lacked an estimate of the timber found on both KC and Mattagami Pulp's original concessions and the areas they were tendering.[8] Nevertheless, this lack of data did not stop them from making it clear that, from the moment they opened the bids, KC was going to win. The Tories dismissed outright Ross and Killam's first offer on the grounds that Mattagami Pulp could augment its existing pulpwood supply by con- tinuing to purchase settlers' spruce. They deemed unacceptable Ross and Killam's second proposal, to build a 100-ton newsprint mill, on the grounds that the size of the limit for which the two had asked (1,201 square miles) included "far too much timber for a mill this size."[9]

The government assessed the merits of Ross and Killam's third offer (for all the tendered pulpwood in exchange for building a 250-ton news- print mill) in conjunction with that submitted by KC (for all the pulp- wood in exchange for building a 550-ton newsprint mill instead of the 200-ton mill required under the firm's existing leases). The Crown's analysis admitted outright that Ross and Killam had outbid KC by near- ly one dollar per cord ($2.95 versus $2.05), a difference that would trans- late into millions more in stumpage revenues if the government accepted the former offer. Nonetheless, the government produced an estimate – 3,264,000 cords – for the amount of pulpwood on KC's original conces- sion area. Not only had officials in the department just recently admitted that such data did not exist, but KC's cruises in 1924 had revealed that its limit held over twice this total. Lyons then employed a guesstimate from Allan Ferguson, the premier's nephew and departmental deputy minister, which showed only roughly 7,000,000 cords of pulpwood on the tendered areas. The Tories reasoned that KC's planned 550-ton newsprint mill would require about 10,000,000 cords to sustain it for forty years, thereby making it seem like one neat, giant jigsaw puzzle the way the government's above-mentioned data (3,264,000 and 7,000,000) added to this figure. On this basis the Conservatives declared that it should award KC all the pulpwood.

But Ferguson knew that, notwithstanding these creative calculations, all three of Ross and Killam's offers had included bonuses that were far higher than KC's, so the premier stepped into the fray. Prior to an- nouncing the outcome of the tender, Ferguson asked Ross and Killam about their plans for reorganizing Mattagami Pulp, specifically wheth- er they would pay the amounts the firm still owed the area's settlers and merchants for pulpwood and supplies it had purchased prior to its receivership. Ross and Killam's reply explained the situation as they and the courts understood it. The sale of Mattagami Pulp's assets would not even generate enough money to pay the secured creditors, let alone unsecured creditors such as the local claimants. Apparently unim- pressed by this news, the government informed Ross and Killam that it was rejecting their three offers because it did not feel justified in providing additional timber to rehabilitate an enterprise that would not attend to its unsecured creditors. Ross and Killam launched a vociferous campaign to convince Ferguson that he had no right to obtrude into this legal matter, but the chief would not alter his course.[10]

To quash Ross and Killam's continued protests, Ferguson presented another, highly specious reason for rejecting their tenders. An integral part of Ferguson's tender announcement in mid-1925 had been his declaration that "every stick" of Ontario's pulpwood would now have to be manufactured into "finished articles" within the province. Mattagami Pulp made bleached sulphite pulp, some of which it sold in the United States, and Ross and Killam proposed continuing to do so even if they constructed a newsprint mill in Smooth Rock Falls. While the Tories argued that pulps did not qualify as "finished articles," and for this reason they could not accept Ross and Killam's offers, they did not reveal that they applied this policy arbitrarily. KC operated a 110-ton sulphite mill in Kapuskasing, and the lease the Tories would soon give the company for its new pulpwood concessions authorized it to expand its sulphite plant to 250 tons, all of which it would export for conversion into "finished articles" south of the border.[11] Parenthetically, after 1925 the Tories also allowed International Paper's mill in Hawkesbury to continue exporting most of the sulphite pulp it produced even though this mill depended on timber cut from Crown lands in Ontario.[12]

In the end, the premier had made up his mind. He awarded all the pulpwood tendered in this section of the province to KC and gave Mattagami Pulp none of it. This put KC in an extraordinary position (Map 14). After carrying out field investigations throughout 1925, the company's foresters projected that their new tracts held over 12,000,000 cords of pulpwood. When this total was added to the 7,256,000 cords on KC's original concession, it meant that the company now controlled at least 20,000,000 cords of pulpwood, which was more than enough fibre to support its new enterprise for over one century. KC also soon learned of the glaring discrepancy between its and the government's data regarding its timber supply. In March 1927, the department allowed John H. Black, Spruce Falls's vice-president, to review its "official" figures regarding the local concessions, and Black could hardly wait to relay the astonishing news to Sensenbrenner back in Wisconsin. "You will appreciate," Black told Sensenbrenner, "that unquestionably we have at least 50% more [pulpwood] than is estimated by the Government."[13]

Ferguson also favoured KC by providing it with a lease to its new concession which embodied the precise terms it had sought in its negotiations with the government. The company had voluntarily agreed, and was thus obliged, to construct a 550-ton newsprint mill. With the *New York Times* already contracted to purchase over half its output, and with the newspaper willing to pay slightly higher than market prices for a guaranteed supply of high-quality newsprint, KC was left in the enviable position of being able to "dump" a large portion of its newsprint tonnage at below market prices and still come out ahead. Moreover, the government had not compelled KC to adjust its bid of $2.05 per cord despite the fact that Mattagami Pulp's competing offers for this fibre averaged around $3.00 per cord. Most importantly, KC's lease guaranteed the company both a perpetual supply of pulpwood and secure tenure to it. Donald Hogarth learned of these terms and telegraphed the news to a friend that KC's contract with the government "provides for right by company to receive timber from government lands in event area now set aside insufficient," a privilege the Tories refused to extend to any other significant newsprint maker in Ontario. Hogarth's telegram also explained that KC's agreement included unlimited renewals and that the company was "jubilant result negotiations and consider contract best ever issued by province."[14]

KC was still not content, however. Only three months after striking this deal, Strachan Johnston, its lawyer, called upon the premier to amend one critical term in its agreement because KC had encountered a problem in arranging to finance its new mill. Having incorporated Spruce Falls Power and Paper Company (Spruce Falls) to carry out the project, the major subscriber to the securities to be issued – First Trust and Savings Bank of Chicago – had objected to the lease's "employment clause." Johnston pointed out that this provision obliged KC to employ 700 men in its new mill for an average of ten months and 3,500 men in the bush for a minimum of six months for each year of the contract, and that failure to do so would abrogate the agreement. Johnston argued that this condition was absurd and made it impossible to sell the firm's bonds, and he implored the premier to strike this provision from the contract.[15]

Ferguson initially endeavoured to assuage KC's concerns verbally. The premier assured Johnston that investors in Spruce Falls should not worry about this provision, for the government had always interpreted concessionaires' contractual obligations "in the broadest sense and with the utmost elasticity. What the Crown expects is reasonable compliance with the covenants and obligations, and it is always ready and willing to give consideration to difficulties that may arise to prevent the strict observance of the letter of a contract."[16]

Despite the premier's mollifying words, Johnston knew that this pledge, even from the province's most senior elected official, was worthless in legal and financial circles. KC thus insisted upon receiving a legally binding release from the objectionable portion of its agreement, a matter that had become all the more urgent because Arthur H. Sulzberger, vice-president of the *New York Times*, was demanding such a revision. A short time later the Tories quietly acceded to KC's wish when they executed in April 1927 an Order in Council that deleted the employment provision from its lease. The Order explained that the purchasers of $15,000,000 of the $25,000,000 bond issue had insisted upon this amendment, for without it, Spruce Falls "represents that it will be unable to arrange the financing necessary" for its project. Because this was done through an Order and not a new concession agreement that would have been published in the department's *Annual Reports*, none of the province's other newsprint producers were aware that the mill in Kapuskasing had been granted a privilege for which they could only dream.[17]

KC had definitely helped its cause by paying homage to "the chief." First, Sensenbrenner had deferred to Ferguson to handle the publicity for KC's project in Kapuskasing – particularly the *Times*'s involvement in the effort – in a way that redounded to the greatest benefit of his Tory government. As a result, news of this enormous development was splashed across the front pages of the province's major dailies in the few months prior to the December 1926 provincial election. The articles were replete with quotations from the likes of Adolph S. Ochs, the *Times*'s esteemed president, who crowed about the business-like efficiency of Ferguson's government in developing the province's hinterland. Subsequently, Sensenbrenner spared no expense in feting the premier. He invited Ferguson to lay the cornerstone for the new mill in September 1927, for which the latter received a silver trowel and attended – as the guest of honour – a 300-person dinner party in Kapuskasing whose guest list included the senior executives from both KC and the *Times* (Figure 12) (Ferguson responded in kind a short while later by personally overseeing the execution of an Order in Council to name two small lakes situated along KC's new railroad to Smoky Falls after Sensenbrenner's daughters, Gertrude and Margaret). Sensenbrenner even coached Ochs about how to phrase a gracious apology to the premier for missing the event in order to, as Sensenbrenner advised

Figure 12. Cementing a Relationship: Kimberly-Clark, which acquired the pulp and paper mill in Kapuskasing in the early 1920s, adroitly exploited the Ontario government's need for the project to succeed by exacting from the provincial state vast quantities of resources under highly favourable terms. Officials from both KC and the *New York Times*, its partner in the newsprint enterprise in "Kap," also proved adept at publicly feting Howard Ferguson, Ontario's premier during the mid-1920s, treatment that no doubt at least partially explains the remarkable largesse he showered on the project. This photograph captures the laying of the newsprint mill's ceremonial cornerstone (the oversized white brick being lowered by the chain) in the early fall of 1927. Ferguson, who is standing on the platform immediately behind the block, is applying the concrete – with the specially engraved silver trowel KC gave him – just seconds before it was set in place. Among the dignitaries standing behind him are KC's iconic president, Frank J. Sensenbrenner, and Major J.O. Adler, a senior executive with the *Times* (Ron Morel Memorial Museum, Kapuskasing, Ontario).

Ochs, "make a good impression." No doubt Ferguson considered this – and the page-four coverage the *Times* gave the event – at least partial repayment for the debt of gratitude the mill owners in Kapuskasing owed him.[18]

Ferguson's actions in providing for KC allowed it to finance its project in a way that was unmatched in Ontario. It borrowed only roughly one-half the money it needed to pay for its project, ensuring that its debt burden was dramatically lower than that of Ontario's other newsprint makers. More importantly, the unparalleled value of its pulpwood and water power leases permitted it to negotiate a mortgage that was equally unique. Its financiers asked it to pledge as collateral only its Crown agreements to its timber lands and water powers, but not its mill, hydro plants, or any of its capital assets in the Kapuskasing area. This helps explain why Spruce Falls breezed through the Depression while Ontario's other newsprint producers endured trying times.[19]

KC had acquired additional pulpwood and water powers at Mattagami Pulp's expense, but the mill in Smooth Rock Falls had doggedly pushed ahead anyway. During its five-year receivership (1921–6), it had increased its productive capacity by nearly 50 per cent and had operated almost to its potential. It wrapped up its receivership in late 1926 when Isaac Killam purchased its assets, and then in early 1927 he sold them to Abitibi Power and Paper Company, which renamed the enterprise Abitibi Fibre Company. Abitibi was determined to convert Abitibi Fibre from a pulp into a newsprint maker, a goal that the mill's original owners had been unsuccessful in achieving for over one decade. This would necessitate procuring additional Crown pulpwood and water power resources, and even if the mill continued to make only pulp, the company still needed more fibre.[20]

But the Tories were not interested in helping out this – or any other – firm in terms of procuring Crown timber in this area. Ferguson had given KC a colossal volume of wood, and he was aware of that company's long-term plans for ramping up the amount of pulpwood it harvested from its own concessions. He knew that this would dampen the local demand for settlers' spruce, and Ferguson was determined to counter this effect by denying Crown pulpwood to the other mills which sought access to it on the northern Clay Belt.[21]

The Tories took this approach to Abitibi Fibre despite the fact that the firm had emerged from its receivership stronger than ever and that the department had admitted in its *Annual Reports* that the mill in Smooth Rock Falls required more pulpwood. In February 1927, Abitibi Fibre requested that the government tender the timber in two townships just north of its mill (estimated to contain at least 450,000 cords), a privilege for which it had been lobbying for six years because this wood grew only a few miles from its plant. Walter Cain, the deputy minister, prepared an ambivalent summary of the matter for the new minister, William Finlayson. On the one hand, Cain expressed his sympathy for Abitibi Fibre's plight because it had been "excluded from the area given to Spruce Falls" in the recent tender. On the other hand, Cain made an unprecedented recommendation.[22] Although all previous sales of pulpwood licences had stated simply that the spruce was subject to the manufacturing condition, in this case Cain urged that the tender be conditional upon the fibre being made into newsprint or other paper and "not just pulp even though it be bleached sulphite." He did so even though it would, as he put it, "militate against the chances of the Abitibi people [in Smooth Rock Falls] getting it as they do not go beyond the bleached sulphite stage at present." The sale attracted three bids, all of them – including Abitibi Fibre's – from interests that either already made newsprint or had committed to converting their pulp mills to doing so if they won the tender. Even though all the bids were high, the department cancelled the sale of Alexandra and Webster Townships. It is unclear who made this decision, but it was definitely neither William Finlayson nor Walter Cain. "Since these offers were received," read the unsigned memorandum to the minister, "representations have been made to the Department about the possibility of a new industry in the district. Thus I recommend until the details are known that the sale be withdrawn." The nature of this new industry remains as mysterious as the reason why the department favoured its needs over those of "established" mills.[23]

When the Tories finally granted additional cutting privileges to Abitibi Fibre in Smooth Rock Falls, it was a defeat for the company but a victory for the local settlers. In the late summer of 1927 the firm won the bidding for a 155-square-mile tract just northeast of Smooth Rock Falls. The tender's terms had again decreed, however, that the pulpwood had to be processed into a "finished product (i.e., paper) … unless otherwise approved by the Crown." Although the government could have authorized Abitibi Fibre to use the timber in its pulp mill, the provincial state refused and instead took deliberate steps to prevent it from simply walking away from the licence. The department's standard practice was to cash the deposit cheque that winning tenderers submitted and apply this amount against the first Crown charges the licensees owed when they cut the timber. In this instance, however, the government broke with precedent and informed Abitibi Fibre that its $25,000 deposit cheque had been "taken into consolidated revenue." While the company immediately protested, asked what this meant, and pointed out that experience had taught it that "anything taken into 'consolidated revenue' is pretty hard to get out," Cain assured the firm's officials that they need not worry. With its deposit practically impossible to recover, Abitibi had no choice but to post the bonds that the government demanded accompany its new licence. These securities were unlike any other the department had ever required, however. Whereas the government had asked KC in Kapuskasing to post only a $150,000 bond when it awarded the company nearly 3,000 square miles worth of timberlands in 1926, the Tories asked Abitibi Fibre to post bonds totalling $500,000 for the mere 155-square-mile tract the mill in Smooth Rock Falls had won in 1927. This was an extraordinary demand to place upon such an established firm, and it came at a time when funds were especially tight for newsprint companies because the price of their product was falling. The upshot left Abitibi with a prime pulpwood tract that it could not use and for which it was required to pay substantial carrying charges. Commenting on this licence a few years later, C.B. Davis, Abitibi's senior forester, labelled it "a burden to the Company."[24]

For Abitibi and its flagship newsprint mill in Iroquois Falls, an inauspicious omen marked the period just after the Ferguson government had taken office in 1923, and it set the stage for the rest of its dealings with him. Frank Anson, the company's founder, president, and guiding spirit, died in November. He had made Abitibi into one of North America's foremost newsprint producers, and his passing marked a watershed for the company. For the next two decades, Abitibi would not be controlled by an experienced newsprint maker but by a few financiers, beginning with Alexander Smith. He had sat for years as one of Abitibi's directors, representing its investment bankers and the company over which he presided, Peabody, Houghteling and Company. Although superficially little seemed to change as a result of Anson's death, the company's new head lacked the dynamic qualities that had long been Abitibi's trademark.[25]

The death of its patriarch hardly won Abitibi any sympathy from the Tories, for Ferguson was not about to embrace a firm whose reputation with the electorate he had personally destroyed. The Conservatives finally agreed in mid-1924 to execute the agreement that granted Abitibi the pulpwood reserve Ferguson had promised it in 1916, for example, but did so in a manner that rendered it practically worthless to the company. Although Abitibi had asked for a tract between the northern and southern boundaries of its original limit, Ferguson granted it a fundamentally different area in 1924. The bulk of its new concession was located nearly one hundred miles from its mill in Iroquois Falls and on a watershed that flowed away from its plant, and nearly 70 per cent of its supplemental limit was unproductive forest land. Abitibi thus had a new concession whose large size was inversely related to its value, and whose fibre it could harvest only at great cost (Map 15).[26]

Moreover, its lease was marked by ambiguities, which made the concession virtually worthless as collateral. Most notably, the government refused to set a stumpage rate, instead authorizing cabinet to fix these fees "from time to time." The Order in Council Ferguson passed when he executed the contract exacerbated this uncertainty, as it stated that the government would determine the dues it would charge Abitibi each year before any cutting took place. The Tories also inserted an unprecedented preamble into this agreement that not only minimized the extent of Abitibi's operations in Iroquois Falls but did so in a manner that would have made any investor uneasy.[27]

To offset its newly acquired source of high-cost pulpwood, Abitibi asked the government for small but strategically important tracts closer to its mill, but Ferguson would not oblige the company. One such belt of pulpwood ran alongside the Temiskaming and Northern Ontario Railway north of Cochrane, and could have been harvested at relatively minor cost. Another lay just west of Matheson and again adjacent to the railway. Abitibi had repeatedly applied for this swathe of spruce and offered to manage it on a sustained-yield basis according to a forest management plan. On both occasions, Ferguson summarily rejected the company's applications.[28]

Although Ferguson granted Abitibi additional water powers during this period, he ensured that they were of little use to the firm. It will be recalled that Noah Timmins, Hollinger's gold-mining mogul, had sought and won a lease to develop one of the cascades on the Abitibi River – namely Island Falls – from the Farmers in order to escape what he saw as the usurious rates the local power company was charging him for electricity. Abitibi had vehemently protested the government's actions, principally because Hollinger's development would interfere with the paper company's ability to generate power on the same waterway. By 1924, Hollinger's ploy had achieved its aim. The company had constructed a generating station at Island Falls and had exploited its newfound freedom to produce its own power as a bargaining chip to

Map 15. Pulpwood Situation for Abitibi's Mill in Iroquois Falls, 1924

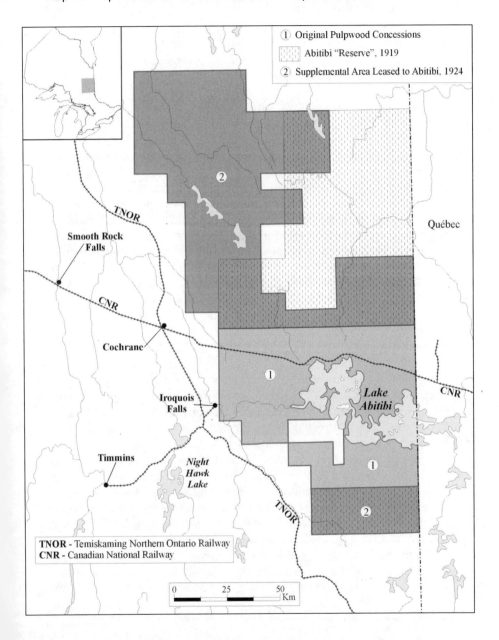

① Original Pulpwood Concessions

▦ Abitibi "Reserve", 1919

② Supplemental Area Leased to Abitibi, 1924

Québec

TNOR

Smooth Rock
Falls

CNR

Cochrane

Iroquois
Falls

Timmins

Night
Hawk
Lake

Lake
Abitibi

CNR

TNOR

TNOR - Temiskaming Northern Ontario Railway
CNR - Canadian National Railway

0   25   50
                        Km

squeeze better terms from its energy provider. Thereupon, Ferguson insisted that Hollinger sell its Island Falls power plant to Abitibi. After lengthy negotiations, Abitibi agreed to Hollinger's exorbitant price of $5,500,000, or roughly four times what Hollinger had spent on the development. Nevertheless, it paid Hollinger's large sum to regain something it held very dear: complete control over the Abitibi River's water powers.[29]

Nevertheless, Ferguson was unprepared to allow Abitibi to carry out its plans. Shortly after the firm purchased Hollinger's Island Falls generating station, it pressed the Tories for three things: its long-promised lease to the Long Sault rapids; approval of the transfer to Abitibi of Hollinger's lease to Island Falls; and inclusion of certain terms in its new leases that would have made them valuable collateral in financing its enterprise. These provisions included at least one term of twenty years and two renewals of fifteen years each, and explicit statements of the rental rates for each period in the agreements. These were, after all, privileges Ferguson had granted KC, Abitibi's not-too-distant neighbour. Abitibi also asked that it – not the government – be authorized to decide if and when the company expanded its plant at Island Falls or harnessed the cascades at Long Sault. Its lawyer, George Kilmer, pointed out that there would be no local market in the near future for large quantities of power and thus stressed that his clients would not have paid such a vast sum to acquire Hollinger's Island Falls station "had they not understood that they would not be called upon to develop Long Sault power until they should need it for their own purposes." For this reason, Kilmer objected to "any provision being put in the lease compelling his clients to develop this power [at either Island Falls or Long Sault] when directed by the Crown to do so and providing for forfeiture if [they did] not develop as directed."[30]

Ferguson insisted on personally handling the file and made it clear that he cared little for Abitibi's views. Its leases to Long Sault and Island Falls included neither renewals nor specific rental rates for each additional term. Far more significant, however, was the clause governing the development of Long Sault Rapids, the cascades Abitibi wished to harness first. Over Kilmer's protests, Abitibi's contract prevented the firm from harnessing this water power "until such time as the Lieutenant-Governor-in-Council may order ... [its] ... development." The agreement also stated that the government was required to give Abitibi only ninety days' notice to develop these rapids, and that failure to comply with this directive would cause Abitibi to forfeit its lease.

Although Abitibi began in early 1925 lobbying for permission to develop Long Sault, the government forbade it from doing so.[31]

The premier took steps to see that the terms of Abitibi's lease to Island Falls were even more drastic. It was de rigueur for the Crown to reserve in such contracts the authority to expropriate a private power development, but the conditions under which it was empowered to do so in this case were anomalous. With only one exception, every other power lease previously executed in Ontario had stipulated that the compensation to be paid in the event of an expropriation would be an "appropriate sum" to be determined by the government or, in case of disagreement, by an arbitrator. In contrast, Abitibi's 1925 lease to Island Falls empowered the state to take over the power plant in as few as twenty years. Furthermore, in determining the compensation Abitibi would receive in this event, the government would "not take into consideration the rights and privileges granted by the lease, or the revenue, or the profits and dividends likely to be derived from the enterprise. Only the actual value of the actual and tangible works connected with and necessary to the development are to be considered." This precluded Abitibi from using this lease as collateral to raise the financing for any project but the construction of this power station, an undertaking that the government refused to allow it to begin. Even former premier William Hearst, who drafted nearly every Crown lease during this period, was struck by this provision's radical nature. He commented that this "special expropriation clause [was] not usually contained in power leases," and that the only other time it had been used was in Hollinger's 1923 contract for the same Island Falls. He stressed, however, that this term "was not a serious matter" for Hollinger, because its mining operation was only expected to last a few decades. In contrast, Hearst asserted that "a like provision in a lease to the Abitibi Company, whose operations are expected to be permanent and constantly expanding, might be serious and embarrassing."[32]

It was. Although Abitibi had gained leases to two power sites, the nature of these contracts made it virtually impossible to use them to raise capital. These circumstances also prevented Abitibi from operating according to its own agenda.

Premier Ferguson's drive to administer Crown resources primarily for political gain during his two terms in office thus had markedly different impacts on the northern Clay Belt's three pulp and paper mills. He had provided KC in Kapuskasing with a veritable war chest of pulpwood and water powers, and inviolable tenure to all its Crown assets. In sharp contrast, he had denied all Mattagami Pulp's requests for resources. And although he had granted Abitibi timber and water powers, he did so on terms that made the company take two steps backward for every one it took forward.

10 "No definite commitment has ever been made by this Department"

One could hardly have faulted newsprint makers E.W. Backus in north-western Ontario and Spanish River Pulp and Paper Mills in the north-east for fretting that the Conservative victory over the Farmers in the 1923 provincial election potentially represented the beginning of their worst nightmares. The Tories had proven inhospitable to these firms during the Conservatives' earlier reign, particularly during Ferguson's tenure as minister (1914–19), and both feared that this icy treatment would continue – if not intensify – now that "the chief" was premier. This foreboding was particularly acute for Backus, who had plugged into the Farmers' patronage network to obtain a remarkable string of Crown resources.

Ferguson made it clear almost immediately after winning power that there was good reason for Backus's and Spanish River's disquietude. The Conservatives reassigned Backus his pariah status in the Ontario government's inner sanctum of power and made him feel less welcome than ever. Undoubtedly, this was partially attributable to the Tories' long-standing allegiance to northwestern Ontario's lumbermen, partic-ularly J.A. Mathieu, the region's leading sawmiller and the freshly re-elected Tory MPP for Rainy River. But far more important was the degree to which Ferguson owed his astonishing political resurrection to his successful campaign to demonize Backus and depict himself as the only leader strong enough to stand up to the wily industrialist to protect the public interest, an effort that he ramped up after regaining office in 1923 (Figure 13).[1] He and his party continued to use their parlia-mentary privilege and power to sully Backus's character with charges that always proved groundless. And for his part, Backus lacked the req-uisite deference in dealing with Ferguson.[2] Whereas a few others, most notably Frank Sensenbrenner, head of the mill project in Kapuskasing, had learned that there was much to be gained by fawning over the premier, Backus instead curried favour among his clients, namely newspaper publishers from the Midwestern United States and western Canada. He spared no expense in wining and dining them with lavish, multi-day extravaganzas, topped off by his legendary "booze cruises" on beautiful Lake of the Woods. But the premier's name was conspicuously absent from the ship's docket, even though Ferguson probably would have declined the invitation anyway because cavorting with Backus was anathema to the premier's political plans.

Slightly different forces caused Spanish River to fare just as badly as Backus during the Tories' reign. The lumbermen were definitely the government's priority in Spanish River's harvesting areas, but Ferguson had also befouled the company's image with Ontarians in the early 1920s, making it highly unlikely he would be seen in its corner any time soon. A competitor, namely International Paper Company, had seized this window of opportunity to set up shop in Spanish River's backyard and best it in competing for the Ontario government's affection. IP – and more specifically its president, Archibald Graustein – demonstrated a brilliant understanding of how to command Ferguson's attention. For its part, Spanish River had endeavoured to win over the Tories by working through James Lyons, the MPP for Sault Ste Marie and Minister of Lands and Forests (1923–6). Within short order, however, it learned that Lyons was virtually powerless to help it. As a result, the Tories actually reduced the volume of pulpwood available to Spanish River during this period.

When the Farmers left office in 1923, Great Lakes Paper Company in Fort William was one of the only newsprint companies in Ontario that enjoyed access to a perpetual supply of spruce. Lewis Alsted, one of the firm's directors, owned leases to three pulpwood concessions (the Pic, Black Sturgeon, and Long Lac) that covered more than 5,000 square miles and held at least 11,000,000 cords of spruce. The Drury government had approved his plan to use these three limits to support the single mill he intended to build in Fort William. Drury had also authorized Ontario Hydro to enter into a contract with Great Lakes Paper that was favourable to the company.

Around the time that Ferguson won power, it became known that E.W. Backus was one of Great Lakes Paper's directors, and thereafter the firm's relations with the Ontario government soured. As most

HIS WALKING TICKET

E. W. BACKUS—"I could get anything I wanted when Drury was here."

HON. G. H. FERGUSON—"Well, I'm here now and you'll get something you don't want if you don't step lively and carry out what you've got."

Figure 13. Ferguson confronting Backus (*Toronto Telegram*, ca 1925).

municipalities in northern Ontario were wont to do, Fort William enticed Great Lakes Paper into its fiefdom by offering tax breaks and other concessions. As the city's ratepayers were set to vote on a by-law that embodied these measures over the winter of 1923–4, however, Ferguson warned civic officials that they should take steps to prevent a "yes" vote. In the process, he raised a series of absurd questions about the terms the city of Fort William was offering the paper maker and threatened serious repercussions if the deal went through.[3] The premier's tactics could not stop the workings of local democracy – the by-law was approved, prompting Ferguson to alter his strategy. He informed fellow Tory MPP Frank Keefer that he had the matter "well in hand, and the less publicity it receives the better for the present." He passed the same directive along to Great Lakes Paper's lawyer, cautioning that "I assume that you prefer to avoid all the publicity that will be involved in an open scrap ... perhaps on the floor of the Legislature." The premier then substituted a new agreement for the one Drury had authorized Ontario Hydro to execute with Great Lakes Paper, one that included several terms that were disadvantageous to the company.[4]

By this time Great Lakes Paper had undergone some dramatic internal changes. In November 1923, Lewis Alsted formally assigned his three pulpwood leases to Great Lakes Paper. In exchange, Great Lakes Paper agreed to supply Alsted's Combined Locks Paper Company in Wisconsin with 30,000 cords of spruce annually for the twenty-one-year term of the three pulpwood agreements. Alsted, and his partner George Seaman, retained a 60 per cent interest in Great Lakes Paper, while Backus, who owned the other 40 per cent, became the driving force behind the firm. The lease Alsted had signed with the Drury government in 1923 obliged him – and now presumably Great Lakes Paper – to construct at least a 150-ton groundwood mill by 1924 and a 100-ton newsprint mill by the following year, and it now appeared that everything was in order for Backus to realize these projects.[5]

The Tories then began doing all they could to erect major obstacles in the path of his enterprise. They refused to recognize Alsted's transfer of the three limits to Great Lakes Paper, a transaction for which gaining the government's approval had heretofore been a mere formality. Nevertheless, Ferguson enjoined Great Lakes Paper to undertake its mill project even though technically it had no timber supply. Backus responded immediately to this demand, but with no timber limits to pledge as potential collateral, he was left with no choice but to personally advance Great Lakes Paper $1,000,000 in cash to complete its first phase – a 150-ton groundwood mill – by the end of 1924. Backus, however, was reluctant to proceed with building a newsprint mill until the government approved the transfer of Alsted's leases to Great Lakes Paper. For the better part of two years he discussed the matter with Ferguson, but the latter would not budge. On 3 February 1926, the department informed Strachan Johnston, Great Lakes Paper's lawyer, that the company had not adhered to the conditions of its concession leases and that it was "hereby notified that the Government will cancel these agreements thirty days from this date." Johnston's pleadings with Ferguson won a reprieve for Great Lakes Paper, but the amnesty period expired when Ferguson's patience ran out in April 1927. At that time the premier drafted a letter to Lewis Alsted which explained that because Alsted was still in default under his three leases (i.e., Great Lakes Paper had not built the newsprint mill), the Ontario government intended "to cancel, and hereby does cancel the said agreement[s], and hereby exercises its rights to repossess the said limits and each of them, and from the date hereof interest in the said limits and each of them is hereby cancelled and forfeited to the Crown."[6]

The Toronto press was most curious about Ferguson's insistence that this particular company fulfil its contractual obligations at this time. The newsprint industry was suffering from excess capacity, the Tories had already declared a moratorium on the construction of new mills, and they had just extended the deadline by which Nipigon Corporation (IP's subsidiary) was to begin building its newsprint plant. In addition, Backus owned a lease through his Transcontinental Development Company to the 2,300-square-mile Nagagami limit and had done little to carry out his obligations under that contract. When a reporter asked Ferguson whether Backus "or any of his companies other than [Great Lakes Paper] is in default?" the premier shot back, "I'm only concerned with this one at the moment ... there has been too much nonsense."[7]

Although it is difficult to piece the story together with the fragmentary evidence that survives, Backus cryptically alluded to why he had not constructed the mill when he explained in April 1927 that "dissensions within his company are responsible for the inaction." In a nutshell, Backus had failed to deliver to the Alsted-Seaman interests even one bolt of the 30,000 cords of spruce he was obliged to ship to Wisconsin each year. Alsted vociferously protested to Ferguson about Backus's breach of contract and hired the prominent Tory lawyer Peter White to represent him in his dealings with the premier. After White had a lengthy discussion with Ferguson in early 1926, White mysteriously became Great Lakes Paper's president and treasurer. When the Ontario government stymied Backus's frantic efforts to procure a source of exportable pulpwood, Alsted and Seaman decided to cut their losses.[8] They sold their 60 per cent interest in Great Lakes Paper to Archibald Graustein, IP's president. Although the province's newsprint makers expressed practically universal concern about Graustein's latest encroachment, Ferguson defended it by arguing that "there is no reason why [IP] should not extend its interests if it desires." Graustein then agreed to approve the construction of the newsprint mill only after Backus purchased Graustein's majority interest in Great Lakes Paper, which Backus did in early 1927 for a cash payment of nearly $2,000,000. Although it was a steep price, Backus now had complete control of Great Lakes Paper, and by mid-1927 the Lakehead was abuzz with reports that he was preparing to break ground on his new newsprint mill.[9]

But the Tories had not yet approved Alsted's assignment of the three concession leases to Great Lakes Paper. It appears that they agreed to do so only after the company pledged its assets – its mill and pulpwood leases – to finance a $10,000,000 bond issue and presented the department with a copy of its mortgage. By 1929, Great Lakes Paper had built its mill, which was capable of producing over 300 tons of newsprint daily. The problem it faced, however, was a shortage of orders, as Ferguson had forced Backus to construct the plant during a period of significant overcapacity in the newsprint industry.[10]

Ferguson proved even less receptive to Backus farther northwest in Ontario. The Farmers had facilitated the establishment of Backus's newsprint mill in Kenora, but it lacked a perpetual supply of pulpwood and sufficient power, and his newsprint mill in Fort Frances was still without a Crown pulpwood concession even though the Ontario government had promised it one several decades earlier. Drury had also given Backus a lease to develop the Seine River's water powers near his newsprint mill in Fort Frances, but Backus had not yet proceeded with this hydro project.

It was over this latter issue that Ferguson and Backus locked horns shortly after the 1923 election, and the drama that ensued showed that the premier was not done toying with Backus just yet. Under Backus's lease to the Seine River, the minister was authorized to permit Backus to export the surplus power he generated from these sites to his pulp and paper mill in International Falls, Minnesota. Backus had repeatedly stated that he would gladly use all the Seine River energy in his mill in Fort Frances if the government granted it a pulpwood limit. The Tories, however, both refused to provide Backus with this timber and rejected his applications to export power he would generate in the future from the Seine River. Backus and Johnston, his lawyer, repeatedly met with the premier to discuss a way to break the impasse, and the latter reassured them that he would protect their interests. It was thus a shock to them when Ferguson cancelled their lease in March 1925, claiming that "no application that he might be heard in the matter of said proposed cancellation has been made by said Edward Wellington Backus." Backus and Johnston pleaded for the premier's forbearance, underscoring the substantial investment – over $200,000 – that Backus had already sunk into the technical studies for the Seine River power project, and their remonstrations seemed to soften Ferguson. The premier informed them in a letter in February 1926 that he would grant Backus a new, revised lease, which the deputy minister promptly drew up, and that Backus could construe this notice as permission to proceed with the project. Backus did, and also added a third machine to his Fort Frances newsprint mill, raising its capacity to 250 tons per day. But Ferguson refused to execute Backus's draft lease, pigeonholing it for over one year, a move his deputy minister, Walter Cain, found most perplexing. Not only did this situation deny Backus potential collateral to fund the undertaking, but Cain was at a loss to explain how the premier could allow Backus to carry out this development although "technically speaking they have no right to be even going on with their construction plans." Only in early May 1927 did the premier execute the agreement.[11]

Ferguson had finally settled this matter, but he refused to provide Backus's mill in Fort Frances with a Crown pulpwood concession, even after Backus had expanded it to 250 tons. When Backus's bankers had asked Ferguson in early 1926 for a brief history of the mill, the premier readily admitted that a draft lease to a pulpwood concession in the Rainy Lake watershed had been prepared in the early 1900s for Backus, but that it had never been executed. "Mr. Backus was entitled to assume," Ferguson declared unequivocally, "that the pulpwood in question would be made available for his mills at Fort Frances by formal agreement." Nevertheless, the premier emphasized that no Ontario government had done anything to fulfil this twenty-year-old pledge, and that "there is not now, and never has been, any agreement between Backus, or any of his Companies, and the Crown, relating to the pulpwood in this District, and he has no pulpwood rights whatever [sic]."[12]

A host of representatives from the mill in Fort Frances were understandably anxious to correct this deficiency. A.D. George, one of

Backus's lawyers, J.A. Alexander, the Crown timber agent for the area, and H.A. Tibbetts, solicitor for the town of Fort Frances, all urged the government to practise what it preached in terms of providing timber to "established industries" by setting aside the pulpwood in the Rainy River and Rainy Lake watersheds for Backus's use. They stressed that the issue was now vital for the mill in Fort Frances. Heretofore, it had relied on purchasing spruce from local settlers and importing timber from Backus's holdings in northern Minnesota, but now these sources were "almost exhausted."[13]

George explained why Backus was particularly vexed by the impact the government's most recent timber policy initiative would have on his mill in Fort Frances. The Tories had begun hand-picking the Rainy Lake region's richest and most accessible patches of spruce and tendering them to local partisan Conservative contractors. In expressing his desire "to strongly protest" this practice, George castigated the government for having "selected spruce areas, easily logged and adjacent to railway or water transportation, put up for sale at the request of anyone who wishes to go into this business. It simply means that when [Backus's] company operates the remaining areas, they will have to take the good with the bad over scattered, inaccessible areas, which will greatly increase operating costs."[14]

In response the government offered Backus its customary platitudes about protecting the interests of existing industries, but it ignored his protests and proceeded along the new course it had charted. He was able to procure only a fraction of the 125,000 cords his mill in Fort Frances needed to operate at capacity in 1928, and he had pleaded with the government for permission to harvest the pulpwood from a roughly 100-square-mile tract centred on Bennett Township that the company estimated contained about 100,000 cords. Reviewing the matter for the minister in September 1927, Walter Cain, the deputy minister, pointed out that there were very good reasons for privately granting Backus this minor tract. There was no guarantee Backus would win it if it were tendered, and given "the enunciated policy of the Government with respect to making reasonable provision to augment the supply of existing concerns it would not be unreasonable to give the Company the right, this coming season, to operate upon the area mentioned, provided a fair and equitable, marketable stumpage price for such pulpwood can be secured." Yet the government still tendered the tract, and Cain's prognosis turned out to be prophetic. Fort William Paper was seeking an alternative pulpwood supply to its own remote and expensive

Crown concession on the west side of Lake Nipigon, and it outbid Backus for the Bennett licence in the fall of 1927. Backus then convinced Fort William Paper to withdraw its tender, presumably compensating it in the process, thereby taking care of his immediate fibre needs.[15]

In the meantime, the Ferguson government curiously chose to publicize Backus's travails and its unwillingness to assist him. The department's foresters completed their cruise of the timber on the Rainy Lake watershed in early 1928, but the government refused to tender a large tract of it for Backus. Instead, the department's 1928 *Annual Report* noted that the Fort Frances newsprint facility had "succeeded for many years in conducting a paper mill at this point of very substantial capacity without having a single limit from the Crown, the first having been acquired during the past year under public competition when under 100,000 cords were secured, less than their requirements for one year." The same *Report* added that the mill's management team was "exercising some concern as to the Government's attitude with respect to additional areas to be offered."[16]

The government also continued to tender tracts of prime pulpwood from within the Crown forest that the mill in Fort Frances believed ought to be reserved for its use. A.D. George, Backus's lawyer, again literally begged the department to desist from doing so. He reminded it that "we have not a cord of pulpwood on Crown lands as yet reserved for the operation of our mill, although we have been assured for over twenty years that if we proceeded with our development ... and erected pulp and paper mills we would be taken care of and that all the pulpwood in the Rainy Lake Watershed would be reserved so that our investment of many millions would be amply protected and our successful operation would be guaranteed." Nevertheless, Charles Greer, a veteran Tory timber operator in the region, sought a large chunk – roughly 200 square miles worth – of this pulpwood, and called upon James Little and Donald Hogarth to lobby the department on his behalf. Reflecting the influence the two Tory henchmen wielded when their clients were lumbermen, Allan Ferguson (the premier's nephew and occasional deputy minister) and Carroll Hele (Ferguson's private secretary) decided in late July 1928 that the government would tender the tract Greer desired.[17]

Predictably, this news elicited an immediate and stern protest from Fort Frances. The town council pleaded with the minister to cancel the sale and reserve this fibre for its newsprint plant. George McLeod, manager of Backus's Fort Frances mill, produced a more forthright remonstration for Finlayson, the minister. "It is my understanding," McLeod began, "that for some time your Department has been convinced that our large Fort Frances mill should be protected with a supply of pulpwood for a long term of years, as is usually the rule in this industry." He was adamant that the massive investment Backus had made in the area was grounds for the government to provide for the mill's needs before selling any of the region's pulpwood to other interests.[18]

Walter Cain, the deputy minister, delivered caustic responses to these latest submissions. He first blasted the municipal officials for their presumptuousness. "The Government of Ontario, through this Department," he stressed, "has not obligated itself in any way to provide that the Fort Frances mill is entitled to the exclusive use of the pulpwood either in the Rainy River or Kenora District, or any portion of either. No definite commitment has ever been made by this Department to the owners of the Fort Frances mill that the pulpwood they require for the supply of the Fort Frances mill should be held in reserve and handed over to the company without public competition." Cain was equally brusque in answering McLeod. "I am a little surprised at the attitude assumed and the arguments advanced by you in your letter," Cain declared. Backus had invested in his Fort Frances project "with eyes wide open and undoubtedly with a full knowledge of the chances of future raw material supplies, and even if it be admitted that your firm must necessarily secure timber for the needs of the mill at Fort Frances, this will not by any means interfere with the policy of the Government that pulpwood timber must be put up for public competition."[19]

Cain's replies convincingly demonstrated the capriciousness of the Ferguson government's attitude towards the different players in the province's pulp and paper industry. In mid-1927, the Tories had privately granted a 2,000-square-mile tract of prime pulpwood in the Sioux Lookout area to North West Ontario Development Company – a shell company that had no mill – even though this tract was eagerly sought by Fort William Paper, a company that operated a large mill at the Lakehead. One year earlier, when the Tories had tendered the pulpwood in the Thunder Bay District and on the northern Clay Belt, they had made a mockery of "public competition" when they rejected the highest bidders for timber tracts and employed untenable rationalizations to explain their actions. In contrast, when it came to Backus asking for minor timber tracts around Fort Frances, the government felt obliged to adhere dogmatically to its long-lost principles.

Concerned by the Tories' attitude and the fear that he would lose the tender for the timber Greer sought, Backus dispatched a personal appeal to Finlayson, but to no avail. Terming the situation regarding his Fort Frances mill's fibre supply "distressing," Backus pleaded with the government not to sell any of the pulpwood within what he defined as the region's fibre basket before the government had met his mill's needs for spruce. Finlayson crafted yet another carefully worded response that showed his hands were tied: "I realise the situation at Fort Frances and appreciate the large investment you have made there," the minister declared sympathetically, "and am anxious to do what I can to secure a supply of raw material for your mills." Nevertheless, Finlayson did not cancel the tender for the pulpwood, which was won by Mashaba Development Company, a firm owned and operated by long-time Conservative Charles Greer.[20]

During this same period Backus had been pressing the government to assist him in overcoming the challenges confronting his newsprint mill in Kenora. While it leased two pulpwood concessions (the Lake of the Woods and English River limits), his own foresters and those in the government's employ agreed that the quantity of spruce found on these tracts was inadequate to support in perpetuity the size of mill his Crown pulpwood leases required him to erect. A forester with the Dominion Forest Service reported in the mid-1920s, for example, that two provincial forest rangers, who had trekked through these woods for twenty years, had produced a "rather startling summary for the whole Kenora Land District" which revealed that "about 90% of it has been burnt off once or oftener [sic] within 50 years! No wonder 'E.W. [Backus]' – as they call him – is scouring every corner for an increase in his 'visible supply.'" Backus also lacked enough power because he was still waiting for the lease to White Dog Falls that the Drury government had promised him in 1920.[21]

Backus raised these concerns – focusing on his timber situation – with Ferguson in April 1925, and although his timing seemed especially propitious, the premier was unmoved. Backus explained that he was in the midst of meeting his contractual obligation to expand his mill in Kenora from 120 to 250 tons but he entertained serious reservations about the project because it lacked access to sufficient resources, particularly pulpwood, and he presented timber cruise reports to buttress his case. He thus asked for a pulpwood concession north of the English River containing roughly 5,000,000 cords of spruce and his long-awaited lease to White Dog Falls. His application seemed well timed because in mid-1925 Ferguson was on the cusp of tendering pulpwood concessions in the Lake Nipigon basin and on the northern Clay Belt for established industries, and Backus's 1920 lease to the English River pulpwood concession obliged the government to tender the timber north of this waterway if his existing supply was found wanting. But the government did not see it that way. It certainly admitted its responsibilities under Backus's 1920 contract, but it pointed out that the Drury government had not found "an insufficiency of timber" on Backus's concession and that the Tories were not about to admit there was one. The government thus declared that the clause in Backus's lease that required it to provide a supplemental fibre source was "null and void" and refused to allot him any more wood.[22]

Backus still fulfilled his contractual obligations by doubling the capacity of his mill in Kenora, and ended up procuring most of his timber in a manner that pleased the government. To conserve his existing fibre supply, he depended primarily upon purchasing settlers' pulpwood. In addition, he acquired from the Dominion government as many timber licences as possible to nearby First Nations' reserves.[23]

During the rest of the decade, Backus continued to lobby the government for more pulpwood, especially because his expanded mill in Kenora required even greater volumes of fibre, but his efforts were for naught. Repeatedly, he and his representatives stressed that both his and the department's officials had drafted his 1920 agreement primarily with the idea of "safeguarding the industry to be established by an assurance of sufficient pulpwood to justify the large expenditures which we contract[ed] to make." They also reminded the government that they and departmental personnel had all agreed that Backus's mill needed – and the government had a legal obligation to provide it with – more timber, and they beseeched the department to carry out the groundwork needed to deliver this fibre to him. In response, the government declared that it did not consider it a priority to address Backus's timber situation, and it never did. Incidentally, International Paper inventoried at this time the tract Backus sought north of the English River and found nearly 5,000,000 cords of pulpwood, precisely the quantity of fibre he had been seeking for his mill in Kenora.[24]

When Backus persisted in applying to Ferguson for pulpwood concessions to support his mills in Fort Frances and Kenora, the premier was driven to wit's end and signalled in 1930, albeit on flimsy grounds, that the matter was closed. As far as the Kenora mill was concerned,

Ferguson argued that it was "reasonably well supplied with raw material" and thus not in need of an additional fibre supply at this time. Conceding that the mill in Fort Frances "occupies quite a different position," he accepted that Backus could rightly "argue with considerable force that the wood supply of this operation is not adequate to maintain the mill over a reasonable period," an obvious understatement. Nonetheless, Ferguson felt it was "impossible for the Government to give favourable consideration to the request that a large quantity of timber such as would be necessary to meet your requirements could be offered for sale at the present time." Ignoring the fact that granting Backus a pulpwood concession would have helped stabilize his Fort Frances mill at a time of increasing uncertainty, Ferguson argued that "in view of the present unsatisfactory position of the newsprint industry and the consequent low price that would be inevitable under the present depression, the Government would not be warranted" in providing the Fort Frances facility with its long-promised timber limit.[25]

Consequently, as the 1920s drew to a close Backus's newsprint mills in the northwest confronted serious challenges. His plant in Kenora faced both pulpwood and power shortages. This latter deficiency forced the mill to curtail production during this period, and eventually compelled it to import high-priced power from Manitoba even though there were many large undeveloped water powers in Ontario that were far closer. In some respects, Backus's mill in Fort Frances was in a more precarious position; it leased no pulpwood concession at all. In fact, it was the only mill in northern Ontario without one, a dubious distinction it held until the early 1940s, long after Backus had been driven from the scene.[26]

Spanish River Pulp and Paper Mills, Canada's largest newsprint maker in the early 1920s, operated plants in Sault Ste Marie, Espanola, and Sturgeon Falls that had been built around the turn of the twentieth century. The pulpwood limits these enterprises originally leased had been poor in terms of spruce, and by the mid-1920s, most of their widely dispersed pockets of pulpwood had been harvested. Spanish River's mill in Espanola was facing an especially bleak fibre situation. In 1919, Ferguson had promised to reserve for its use a 4,000-square-mile supplemental tract if it expanded its capacity. While it upheld its end of the bargain, the Conservative – and then the Farmers – governments had not. Moreover, the latter administration had given a crucial part of this reserve (the Trout-Chapleau pulpwood concession) to Continental

Wood Products, one of IP's subsidiaries, in exchange for an agreement from Continental to build a sulphate pulp mill in Elsas, a small town northwest of Sudbury.

Upon his return to power Ferguson could have exacted revenge on Continental for not having begun building its new mill and having impinged upon Spanish River's turf, but the chief instead treated IP's subsidiary royally. Immediately after the 1923 election, his government allowed Continental to acquire – and then hold – a licence to harvest all the timber in Ossin Township, near Elsas and within the Spanish reserve, in a manner that contravened departmental policy. Soon thereafter, Ferguson personally orchestrated events to deliver a truly unparalleled gift to Continental. The firm already held a "licence of occupation" to a site in Elsas on which it declared it was going to build its kraft pulp mill. Nevertheless, L.E. Bliss, the company's vice-president and erstwhile veteran departmental official, argued that, for "business reasons," Continental needed freehold tenure to this land and a much larger piece of property on which it planned to construct its power station. In May 1924 Ferguson, as acting minister and in front of only three other cabinet members, executed an Order in Council which explained that the matter was pressing for Continental because it was arranging the financing for its mill and had to include this territory in the description of the land "to be covered by the company's bond issue." The Tories thus sold Continental this 971-acre parcel for $1,800. This was a paltry sum considering that Ferguson, for only the second time since 1905 and for the last time in the province's history, had sold outright – instead of leasing – a hydro site to a private concern. This freehold grant contravened departmental policy and exponentially increased the value of Continental's holdings in and around Elsas.[27]

Considering this extravagant gift, Continental ought to have quickly capitalized on its good fortune by breaking ground on its project, but it did not, something with which the Tories proved remarkably comfortable. In mid-1924, Bliss asked for – and received – a one-year extension of the deadline by which Continental was to build its mill and argued that any consideration given his firm would be well rewarded, for, as he explained, it was "Mr. Elsas's [Continental's president] proud boast that our Kraft Mill will be the largest and most up-to-date … in the world." With no sign of a mill one year later, Bliss now contended that the market for kraft pulp products was so flooded that his company wished to delay its plans hoping for improved conditions, specifically because "the impossible and unsettled state of the world markets and

Map 16. Pulpwood Situation for Spanish River's Mill in Espanola, 1923–1926

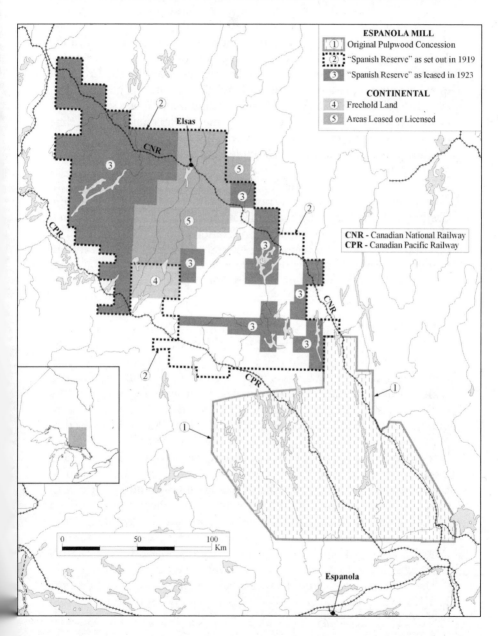

finance" would make it "next to impossible to finance a new venture." Arguing that his company's "very existence" hung in the balance, Bliss gave the government his "personal word that the [extension] privilege, if granted, will be honestly and honorably handled." Not only did the Tories concur with Bliss's analysis and grant the twelve-month respite, but the next year Ferguson personally oversaw granting the firm's request for another extension, this time for three years. Ferguson did so even though he was concurrently demanding that the newsprint firms in the Thunder Bay District undertake massive expansions at a time when everyone agreed their market was flooded; notably, the number of kraft paper firms in Canada doubled between 1925 and 1930 in response to the explosion in demand for consumer packaging.[28]

As a result, what the government had heralded in 1923 as a new industry for Ontario had virtually nothing to show for it by the Depression. Continental had yet to dig the foundation for its mill, and it had even abandoned its pulpwood exporting operation and small sawmill. While it is doubtful whether it had ever intended on constructing a kraft mill at this location, IP's actions through its subsidiary had slyly deprived Spanish River's newsprint mill in Espanola a prime tract of pulpwood which the latter plant needed and had long been promised by the Ontario government.

The Tories finally gave Spanish River a lease to the remnants of its "reserve" in the fall of 1923, but the contract's value was dubious. The firm's pulpwood concession had shrunk from 4,000 square miles containing roughly 4,000,000 cords of spruce to roughly half this size and with just over half as much spruce. The limit was also broken into a number of separate tracts, rendering it expensive to operate. Compounding this problem was the fact that the largest solid block of timber was farthest from the Espanola mill and it was above the height of land (Map 16). This meant that it could only be transported south using the Canadian National Railway line, track that did not even run to Espanola. The terms of Spanish River's lease also rendered it practically worthless as collateral. Whereas the government had set a fixed rate of stumpage dues in Continental's concession agreement, it required that Spanish River pay rates that cabinet fixed "from time to time." There was also no provision for renewing Spanish River's agreement, which was to run for only one twenty-one-year term.[29]

The company received even worse news a short time later. Since the late 1890s, Spanish River's mills in Espanola and Sturgeon Falls had been denied access to thousands of cords of pulpwood on their concessions by the government's insistence that, out of deference to the lumbermen, the paper company abide by the "pine priority" clause, a policy Ferguson's Tories continued throughout their time in office. Spanish River had also been pressing the government to define clearly the boundaries of the two concessions that the mills in Sturgeon Falls and Espanola had initially leased in 1898 and 1899 respectively because this ambiguity had cast into doubt the value of these contracts as collateral. The company had hired a third party to investigate the matter and advise it in its discussions with the government, and Walter Cain, the deputy minister, had counselled Ferguson that the firm's consultant had presented a fair and reasonable position. Nevertheless, the premier, as acting minister, declared in July 1926 that the two mills' concessions were significantly smaller (about 700 square miles) than the evidence indicated they were.[30] Ferguson also demanded that the company begin paying fire protection charges based on the total area of these concessions. Because this included those sections in which the pine timber was licensed to the lumbermen, Spanish River was forced to pay to protect spruce stands that the government prohibited it from cutting. Finally, Ferguson refused to extend or renew these leases even though they were set to expire in only a few years.[31] All the while, the government was handing new licences to the local lumbermen to cut all the large-diameter softwood species – including spruce – from Spanish River's pulpwood concession, thereby further depleting the firm's fibre supply.[32]

Spanish River's mill in the Soo had arguably an even stronger case to buttress its request for more timber. It had been harvesting much of the sparsely scattered spruce on the southern part of its large concession for over three decades and was now managing its limits on a sustained-yield basis, which restricted it to cutting annually only a limited quantity of pulpwood from each watershed. Ben Avery, Spanish River's chief forester, reported to the government during the 1920s that the company's concession could support a yearly harvest of roughly 80,000 cords of spruce, which represented just over half the mill's fibre needs. Moreover, it was cutting from places as far away as Heron Bay over 200 miles northwest of Sault Ste Marie; towing wood this great distance across the open waters of Lake Superior, and then having to store it at the mill, was costly and enormously time-consuming. As a complementary pulpwood source – one that would be relatively cheap and spruce-rich – Avery suggested the government grant the mill cutting privileges along the Algoma Central and Hudson Bay Railway (ACR), along which there were large areas of unalienated lands.[33]

Several factors boded well for Spanish River's chances of success in this instance, but Ferguson cared little for them. Since the late 1890s the Ontario government had been acutely aware that the mill in the Soo sought access to the spruce which grew north of its plant on the boreal forest. The ACR's principal raison d'être, after all, had been to deliver this pulpwood to the mill's grinders, but events had prevented Spanish River from acquiring timber tracts in this area. These events included Ferguson's 1916 rejection of the company's application for cutting privileges on a number of townships along the ACR. Nonetheless, during the 1920s departmental officials continued to recognize Spanish River's claim to the pulpwood along this railway. They denied another applicant the right to export spruce from this area, for example, because "there is the continued demand on the part of ... Spanish River ... for additional raw material and the lands in question are, as it might be said, at the back door of the Sault Ste. Marie mill, into which goes the Algoma Central, contiguous to which is the ... pulpwood in question." Furthermore, in the mid-1920s, Ferguson oversaw the largest tender of pulpwood limits in Ontario's history, and by this time the department had cruised several sizeable pulpwood tracts in the very area in which Spanish River sought additional cutting privileges for its mill in the Soo. But the government turned down the company's applications for these limits without providing a sound reason to explain its actions.[34]

Ferguson put to rest any lingering doubts about his attitude towards Spanish River in August 1926 when he received an intriguing proposal from George H. Mead, the company's president. Mead offered to build a 100-ton pulp mill near Bruce Mines, about thirty miles east of Sault Ste Marie, which would produce bleached kraft sulphite, a relatively new pulp. To supply this facility with fibre, he asked for the privilege of harvesting all species of timber – save for the prized red and white pine that local lumbermen already claimed – between his existing Sault Ste Marie and Espanola concessions; to supply it with energy he requested a lease to develop the major water powers on the Mississagi River. The proposal represented a potential boon on many levels. The new mill would not exacerbate the drain on the province's spruce supplies because it would convert into a valuable pulp several tree species that the province's paper makers had previously underused or completely ignored (such as poplar and balsam fir) and the "waste" slabs and ends from the existing local sawmills; it would be a model of efficient wood utilization. For its part, Spanish River would gain another mill that would fit neatly within the framework of its three existing, local newsprint enterprises, and be able to utilize the spruce from the new concession. Furthermore, because the estimated 65,000 horsepower which could be harnessed from the Mississagi River was far more power than Spanish River's new plant would need, it could transmit this surplus energy to its operations in Sturgeon Falls and Espanola to eliminate the power shortages with which they had grappled for years. Despite these many advantages, the Ferguson government did not approve Spanish River's application.[35]

And so, by the end of the 1920s the Tories' ostensible policy of providing for established industries had proven of little benefit to Spanish River. In fact, as far as access to Crown resources was concerned, its mills were worse off on the eve of the Depression than they had been three decades earlier, when they had leased their original pulpwood concessions and water powers. On the other hand, IP's subsidiary, Continental, had no pulp or paper mill, nor even any timber operations in Ontario at this time. Nevertheless, Ferguson had protected its hold on the resources that Spanish River had sought, and provided it with quantities of Crown resources and leases to them that must have made Spanish River envious.

11 "A policy which had cost Ontario's industry a good and plenty"

By 1927, the operations of Ontario's newsprint makers were being fundamentally altered by the paradoxical forces that were shaping the industry across Canada. After practically a decade of prodigious growth, the Dominion had emerged as the world's largest newsprint producer and most firms were still highly profitable. The country's industry as a whole was operating well below capacity, however, causing some mills to suspend their operations for months at a time. Under these trying conditions, intense conflict began marking relations among the players in the industry. What emerged between the late 1920s and early 1930s was a struggle for survival and supremacy between two combatants: International Paper Company (IP) and the rest of Canada's newsprint makers.[1]

The Ontario government, and specifically Howard Ferguson, were destined to be the ringleaders at the centre of the action. The provincial state, through its jurisdiction over the Crown pulpwood and water powers that the paper makers leased, could potentially exert complete control over the province's newsprint industry. And, in fact, Ferguson had done as much while he had served his terms as minister of lands and forests (1914–19) and premier up until this point. He had allowed his own political priorities to dictate which firms received Crown resources, the terms under which they did so, how much of which pulps and papers they would produce, and when and how they expanded their operations. Ferguson continued to wield this autocratic power over the industry to benefit him and his party during the "the newsprint wars" of the late 1920s and early 1930s. He compelled the companies to follow his directives – despite the clear dangers in doing so – or risk losing their fibre and power supplies.

But Ferguson accorded IP – and Kimberly-Clark to a much lesser degree – special status during this period, treatment that understandably shocked the throngs of observers who had no idea of the privileged rank IP had long occupied in the premier's books. Ferguson permitted Archibald Graustein, IP's lordly leader, to operate free from the fetters the premier placed on Ontario's newsprint makers and chart a course that literally drowned them all. Even though the premier had numerous instruments at his disposal with which he could have reined in IP to protect the province's producers, he refused to use them. Onlookers were stupefied at the special status the premier accorded Graustein's firm because IP had done such an effective job of concealing its wide-ranging activities in Ontario. The preceding chapters have described the manner in which IP gained control over at least 5,000 square miles of the province's prime pulpwood concessions and timber licences.[2] Graustein had shrewdly acquired these properties through subsidiaries whose names – such as the North West Ontario Development Company – bore no relation to the parent firm, and then assigned them in trust to a third party. This surreptitiousness left the department's most senior officials befuddled when cheques began arriving from IP's New York headquarters to cover the annual Crown charges it owed on its timber limits in Ontario, as the department had an account for neither IP nor its Canadian subsidiary.[3] IP had, in fact, pursued this strategy so successfully throughout the country that the *Montreal Herald* was prompted to comment that "few people in Canada have any idea of the manner in which this foreign-controlled corporation has fastened its grip on the forest resources, water powers and the pulp and paper industry of the Dominion."[4]

While Ferguson was too deft a politician to leave a paper trail that would allow historians to determine whether his actions to favour IP (and KC) and damage the interests of Ontario's newsprint makers were deliberate, there is no doubt about the effect his approach had. In addition to IP and KC, Quebec's newsprint producers benefited enormously from Ferguson's willingness to pursue a policy that was seemingly designed by his counterpart in that province and intended to protect its mills, whereas the actions taken by "the chief" were detrimental to nearly all Ontario's newsprint makers. Frederick I. Ker, a veteran newspaper editor and publisher and someone who enjoyed an extraordinary vantage point during these years (he sat on the Newsprint Committees for both the American Newspaper Publishers' Association and the Canadian Daily Newspaper Association), was stunned when he finally realized the error of Ferguson's ways. When Ker began offering advice about the newsprint industry to Mitchell Hepburn's recently christened Liberal government in late 1934, Ker was adamant that the Grits not "follow Ferguson's mistaken policy of hitching Ontario to Taschereau's chariot, a policy which had cost Ontario's industry a good and plenty."[5]

Developments during this period can only be understood in the context of Graustein's cunning, multifaceted strategy to re-establish IP's hegemony in the North American newsprint industry.[6] It had included creating Canadian International Paper (CIP) to build – and purchase – a few massive, state-of-the-art mills in the Dominion during the 1920s at a time when the industry was suffering from overcapacity. Graustein could thereby benefit from the economies of scale accruing from operating plants that averaged nearly 650 tons, whereas many of his competitors, such as Spanish River, operated mills that averaged barely one-third this total. He also maximized his market share by either financing or buying a host of major newspapers in the eastern United States and then forcing them to sign on as IP's long-term customers. More importantly, IP waged a ruthless price war. Heretofore, IP's stature in the industry allowed it to announce each fall the price at which it would sell paper the following year. This would typically become the prevailing "New York price," which other producers would then match in order to retain their customers. Although IP had previously exploited this power to raise the price of newsprint, beginning in the mid-1920s it had systematically slashed prices in an attempt to grab buyers, shaving $15 off newsprint prices between 1924 and 1929. At the same time, IP sought to end the prevailing pricing system in North America whereby newspapers paid to ship their paper from the mills to their presses, an arrangement which inclined them to economize their transportation costs by purchasing from the closest paper maker. Instead, Graustein began offering – simultaneously with IP's price cuts – to pay the cost of delivering paper from his plants to the publishers'. Although IP's scheme pushed its newsprint operations into the red, it could subsidize any deficits from its highly profitable hydroelectric business.

The downward spiral of newsprint prices during the 1920s was thus not a result of a fight in which two foes traded punches. Rather, it was a case of IP unilaterally launching an offensive against which the rest of the industry merely acted in self-defence. A few astute observers recognized the predatory path down which Graustein was steering IP, and how as its ultimate end it sought to leave no rivals standing. In a trenchant commentary on the situation, C.D. Howe, dean of the University of Toronto's Faculty of Forestry, concluded that "the International people are evidently out to control Canadian newsprint production."[7]

The Dominion's major Canadian newsprint producers understandably organized to protect their interests against Graustein's encroachment. Having watched as he drove down newsprint prices in the mid-1920s, eleven mills sought to curb and then reverse this trend by selling their production through a single agency. In May 1927 they jointly incorporated the Canadian Newsprint Company (CNC) and signed a contract a short time later that detailed their arrangement. Spanish River had the largest stake in the CNC with six mills (its three original ones in the Soo, Espanola, and Sturgeon Falls and its branch operations in Fort William, Ste Anne, Quebec, and Pine Falls, Manitoba). Abitibi's mill in Iroquois Falls and several major producers from Quebec were also included in this venture but Backus and CIP were not. This left CNC in control of just over one-half of the country's newsprint capacity.[8]

The CNC's plan was basic enough and it was initially successful. Its executives would oversee the ten-year arrangement to pool their companies' newsprint orders in an effort to stabilize prices. The CNC would also meet IP's pricing challenge by charging its customers the same price for paper regardless of where the newsprint was produced. Each member of the CNC would also pay a levy on every ton of newsprint it made into a fund that would be used to reward those mills that were well placed to serve their customers and whose transportation costs were thus the lowest. The CNC succeeded in late 1927 in striking a huge deal with William Randolph Hearst, the continent's largest newsprint buyer, who agreed to purchase 300,000 tons of newsprint annually from CNC over the next decade; the agreement would be worth over $200,000,000.[9]

This contract was downright crucial to Ontario's newsprint makers. Abitibi and Spanish River had previously provided Hearst with a large quantity of paper each year, and when they joined the CNC, they transferred their proprietary interest in this tonnage to it. This meant that the deal between Hearst and the CNC was not as much a boon to Abitibi and Spanish River as it was a relief for them to learn that they would continue selling to a traditional customer. The CNC's contract with Hearst was also crucial for E.W. Backus. Although he had not joined the cartel, he had secured a large order from Hearst at this time and had agreed to market it through the CNC to maintain a uniform price. As a result of these arrangements, the CNC allocated to Abitibi, Spanish River, and Backus – interests representing the bulk of Ontario's newsprint industry – nearly one-half its business with Hearst. With the CNC having begun supplying Hearst with newsprint in January 1928, and with its contract with him ready for execution by early March, it seemed as if the deal were a fait accompli.[10]

But then it bafflingly unravelled. Just before signing the agreement with Hearst, the CNC inexplicably shuffled its management team. William N. Hurlbut, CNC's president and a veteran director of Spanish River, unceremoniously resigned his office, and in his stead Henry A. Wise became president. Wise was a New York lawyer who had been instrumental in organizing the CNC and had been its de facto adviser since its inception. Curiously, however, he had also represented the American newsprint industry for years and, on the eve of his appointment as head of the CNC, been serving as general counsel to the Import Committee of the American Paper Industry.[11] Immediately upon taking over the CNC, Wise declared that it would not execute the contract with Hearst and provided no explanation for this dramatic about-face. Wise concomitantly drew up a contract setting out the terms under which he had begun working for the CNC, an agreement that indicates that he was not its friend. Wise's deal stipulated that the CNC must pay him $100,000 per year for five years, even if he terminated his relationship with it, and that the astounding $500,000 stipend he was guaranteed over the next one-half decade did not render him the CNC's full-time employee; he was free to continue practising with his esteemed New York law firm of Wise, Whitney, and Parker. Having cancelled the Hearst contract, drawn up his own luxurious employment agreement, and compelled the CNC to execute it in March, five months later Wise abruptly resigned from the Canadian Newsprint Company.[12]

Depending on one's perspective, Hurlbut was either the hero or the goat in this affair. For years he had served as a senior executive with and director of Spanish River. Not surprisingly, his association with the company terminated over this incident, as Hurlbut was a Benedict Arnold to Spanish River and the CNC's other members. To Archibald Graustein, however, William Hurlbut was "Billy," someone who became a lifelong friend, and with good reason. Practically the day after Hurlbut left Spanish's River's employ, Graustein appointed him as one of IP's vice-presidents. No doubt this was in partial recognition of the work Hurlbut was doing on Graustein's behalf at this time, namely ensuring that the Hearst contract, which was to have gone to the CNC, landed in IP's lap instead. For his part, Hearst believed Hurlbut had played him perfectly to IP's advantage.[13]

The loss of the Hearst contract was a huge blow to Ontario's newsprint mills, particularly Abitibi and Spanish River. They had lost 125,000 tons worth of orders they had previously supplied to "the Lord of San Simeon," and Backus had lost 50,000 tons. These setbacks did not release Abitibi and Spanish, however, from their obligation to pay their share of Wise's ransom-like salary over the next five years.[14]

These developments occurred within the context of another round of mergers in the Canadian newsprint industry, the most important of which involved Ontario's mills. While it had been rumoured for much of the decade that Abitibi and Spanish River would consolidate their already tightly knit enterprises, they consummated the deal on 1 January 1928, retaining Abitibi's name. Over the next few years, Abitibi acquired Thunder Bay Paper in Port Arthur and Provincial Paper, the fine-paper maker in the same city, giving it ownership of eight of northern Ontario's thirteen pulp and paper mills.

In the summer of 1928, it appeared the Tories – specifically Ferguson – were poised to take decisive action to aid the province's newsprint makers. At this time, the minister, William Finlayson, rejected Abitibi's calls for the government to appoint a newsprint controller who could force into line companies like IP that had been cutting prices. Dismissing the notion as "absurd," Finlayson declared that "the Government would not consider it as there is not only the question of our power to do it, but it would be extremely dangerous legislation." Although he was convinced that the industry should work out its own problems, he admitted that the government might have an indirect role to play in getting "the outlaws to come in," a perspective shared by L.A. Taschereau, Quebec's premier. But because Finlayson viewed Ferguson as "practically the only cabinet member familiar with the situation," the matter stood until the premier came home from overseas. Upon his return, Ferguson expressed his willingness to employ the state's plenary powers to impose a solution on the newsprint makers if they were unable to resolve their difficulties themselves, namely by threatening to cancel their leases unless they cooperated with his plans.[15]

Graustein's actions a few months later presented Ferguson with an ideal opportunity to practise what the premier preached. IP's president advertised in May 1928 that he would cut the price of newsprint effective the first of the new year, and he announced in the fall that he had executed a deal with the Hearst interests for a large tonnage of paper at prices below those that the CNC had quoted for 1929. More important as far as northern Ontario's mills were concerned, IP also declared that it would henceforth pay practically all charges for delivering paper to its customers, which translated into a reduction of between $7 and $10 per ton depending upon the buyer's location. Achieving this goal had been one of the principal aims of IP's marketing strategy, and it had only succeeded in this regard now that its productive capacity had grown to a point where it could control an appreciable quantity of North America's supply of newsprint.[16]

Graustein's latest thrust precipitated a decisive response from Ferguson, but surprisingly the premier's riposte was directed not at IP but at Ontario's own pulp and paper mills. On 20 November 1928, Ferguson sent notice to all but two of the province's pulpwood concessionaires in which he made it clear that he was taking charge.[17] He insisted that the newsprint industry's leaders participate in a new price-fixing and ton-nage sharing arrangement with their counterparts in Quebec, and warned them that it was "with great regret that the Government finds it necessary to draw your attention to the fact that you are under contract with this Province; that your contracts contain a number of important covenants; that many of the companies are in arrears and default had occurred with respect to a number of the conditions and obligations provided in the contracts." The message was unmistakable.[18]

Ferguson's "wrathful ultimatum," as The Globe labelled it, reflected the premier's unique perspective on the situation. First, Ferguson's threat targeted Ontario's newsprint makers, which had been endeav-ouring to cooperate by sharing tonnage and stabilizing prices through the CNC, not IP, which had been aggressively soliciting orders and un-dercutting prices. Second, those mills in Ontario which were in breach of their Crown leases had, in fact, been ordered by Ferguson against their wishes to commit to undertaking massive expansions only a few years earlier. Although carrying out their obligations at this time would only have exacerbated the industry's overcapacity, Ferguson was now using their refusal and inability to do so against them. Most impor-tantly, the crisis that was developing in the newsprint industry was having only a relatively minor impact on northern Ontario's mills at this time, and most of them had been unable, for one reason or another, to operate at capacity during the 1920s. In other words, there was no crisis in the province's newsprint industry at this point.[19]

Nevertheless, political considerations had spurred Ferguson to issue his most bizarre executive fiat at this time. He emphasized to the press in November 1928 that his threat to intervene in the paper makers' affairs was intended to protect the vulnerable elements in northern Ontario, and that he would not stand by and allow the newsprint industry "to assassinate" hinterland communities. He also charged that the present situation was "causing settlers to suffer" by "restricting the[ir] pulpwood market." Although there was a pronounced disconnect between the premier's comments and the reality in northern Ontario (all of its newsprint mills were still operating and many of them had traditionally purchased large quantities of settlers' pulpwood), Ferguson's actions were predictable coming as they did from an incumbent premier preparing to set out on the hustings. This is precisely what the press surmised. *The Globe* reported that "Ferguson's attitude and motives seemed to puzzle the leaders of the newsprint industry who gathered in conference today ... Whether he had in mind coming Ontario elections when he deplored the fate of the colonists in Northern Ontario in being unable to sell their wood to the pulp and paper mills, or whether he meant that companies should buy more wood so as to aid colonization was not clear."[20]

To strengthen his hand in dealing with the province's newsprint mills, Ferguson passed the Pulpwood Conservation Act a short while later. He claimed that it signalled the beginning of sound management of the province's pulpwood forests, but it dealt only tangentially with silvicultural policy. In the Legislature the government openly admitted that the primary "object of the bill was control of the [newsprint] companies having pulp concessions in Ontario." It would achieve this aim through the provisions that authorized the government, among other things, to dictate the quantity of pulpwood a mill could harvest (and thus the amount of newsprint it could produce) and exact large financial penalties if a concessionaire disobeyed the government's edicts. In attacking the statute, W.E.N. Sinclair, the leader of the Opposition Liberals, underscored that its terms gave the governing party "the power of a dictator" over the province's newsprint makers.[21]

The latter thus bowed to Ferguson's wishes and agreed to cooperate in a new price-fixing scheme with their counterparts in Quebec by joining the newly created Newsprint Institute of Canada (NIC) in late November 1928. Its membership embraced most of eastern Canada's major producers, including Backus's mills. While the NIC would adopt IP's pricing system by paying the cost of shipping newsprint to its customers, there was a new twist to this element of the plan. Each NIC mill would contribute a fee per ton of paper it manufactured to a fund administered by NIC's chief officers, but the money would be used to compensate mills that were located far from their customers and who thus incurred higher shipping costs. This system of advantageously located mills subsidizing remote ones was opposite to the arrangement that the CNC had adopted the previous year.[22]

The NIC's members were also forced to pool their newsprint orders and divide the tonnage according to the relative capacities of their mills, a plan that was simply ruinous to them. A mill's operating costs were lower the closer to capacity it ran, and thus newsprint makers sought to manufacture their tonnage in as few of their plants as possible. Ontario's producers made this point to Ferguson in protesting the NIC's rules about distributing the orders they were allocated among all their mills, but the premier ignored their arguments. With Ferguson contending that his only concern was "to protect the workingman," and with headlines broadcasting that "Government Policy Aids Paper Producing Towns," his aim was to spread employment to every northern mill community because it was politically expedient; he would soon announce a provincial election for October 1929. Just in case there was any doubt about his commitment to enforcing the NIC's regulations, less than seventy-two hours after Abitibi closed its plant in Espanola in an effort to concentrate its production in a few mills, he ordered it to restart its enterprise; the *Toronto Daily Star* reported that this was "the result of the big stick wielded by Premier Ferguson." The origins of the NIC and the provisions that governed its behaviour leave little doubt that Taschereau and Ferguson, with the former leading and the latter following, and not Ontario's newsprint industry, were responsible for it, a conclusion that antitrust investigators in both the United States and Canada also drew after they probed its operations.[23]

As 1929 dawned it was clear that a renewed effort to form a Canadian cartel would only succeed if every major producer, especially IP, were forced to join. If Ferguson had been oblivious to this reality, E.A. Wallberg made him acutely aware of it merely days before the NIC's prorationing agreement was signed. Wallberg, who represented a small mill in Quebec's Saguenay region, thanked the premier for his expressed willingness to assist the newsprint makers. At the same time, Wallberg stressed that their

> main difficulty, however, for some time to come will be to bring and hold the International Paper Company in line with the others. Their ambitions are extraordinary. While they have been hammering prices on the one

hand, they have also been trying to buy Companies that are owned by Canadians. The [situation will] grow even worse as the newsprint end of their business could be held down until Canadian Companies have been ruined and the losses in this department of their Company could be paid from new capital, or from profits in other branches of their paper business, such as kraft, book, magazine, envelope and sulphite which they are also making and the revenues from their power plants. Without holding them in line with the others our plans cannot be effective.[24]

But Ferguson was not about to pressure IP to accept the NIC's rules or join its ranks, and he also unquestioningly accepted Graustein's rationalizations for staying outside its purview. Graustein asserted, for instance, that neither he nor IP could be involved with the NIC because the American government's investigation in 1916–17 into an alleged trust in the newsprint industry had resulted in the guilty parties agreeing to respect a decree that permanently enjoined them from engaging in monopolistic behaviour. But the same decree had also named Alexander Smith (Abitibi's president), George H. Mead (Abitibi's chairman of the board), E.W. Backus, and the newsprint companies with which they were associated, and Ferguson had forced them all to come into line under the NIC. Furthermore, Graustein contended that American antitrust laws prevented IP from joining the Institute because he was an American citizen, that IP had operations in the United States, and that both he and his firm were thus liable to prosecution under antitrust laws south of the border. But again, Smith, Mead, and Backus were in the same boat. All were Americans and either owned or managed newsprint plants in the US, yet Ferguson insisted they and all their plants be subject to the Institute's rules. This meant that these men and their companies were as vulnerable as Graustein and IP to legal action in the United States, if not more so. Even Kimberly-Clark, which refused to join the NIC officially for the reasons Graustein cited, initially agreed to respect its rules.[25]

The premiers of Ontario and Quebec soon granted Graustein another special power. It will be recalled that IP's president had declared in late 1928 that he was unilaterally ending the existing pricing system, a policy that was tantamount to another cut in newsprint prices. Ferguson and Taschereau publicly reprimanded IP's president for his blatant disregard for their joint efforts to stabilize the industry and emphasized that they were going to use their private discussions with Graustein in late 1928 and early 1929 to force him to raise his price. Although the premiers later claimed victory and asserted that Graustein had caved to their demand, in fact they had acquiesced to his wishes. After their meetings, the premiers decreed that the NIC would adhere to IP's new system of quoting newsprint prices based upon a series of arbitrarily drawn "zones" in the United States.[26]

IP's zone pricing system was as simple as its main aim was obvious. Its first incarnation divided the American newsprint market east of the Mississippi into a handful of sections; IP would steadily expand this pricing system until it covered the entire United States (Map 17 illustrates its final version, which was adopted in the early 1930s). Within each zone, buyers would pay a uniform price for their newsprint, regardless of the location of the mill from which the newsprint came. To realize this goal, the producer – initially IP and then practically all the mills in Ontario and Quebec – would absorb a large part of the cost of shipping the paper to their customers. Because most of the newsprint was coming from Canada, presumably the zones should have been drawn to reflect delivery costs from its major production centres, such as northwestern Ontario and the St Lawrence River valley between Trois-Rivières and the Gaspé peninsula; the zones should have been nodal-shaped in concentric rings emanating from these newsprint-producing hubs.[27] Drawing zone boundaries latitudinally did not make sense because proximity to the Canadian border was not the only consideration in terms of shipping costs; east-west distances mattered, too. For example, it cost far less to ship newsprint from Fort Frances across the border to Duluth, Minnesota, instead of Buffalo, New York, even though both American cities are within one hundred miles of the international boundary.

The zones which IP introduced at the time – and later – however, were aimed not at reflecting actual delivery costs but rather at favouring its own mills and, most importantly, obliterating the geographical advantage that accrued to its newsprint-producing competitors in northern Ontario (IP's mills were located alongside many of its rivals in the traditional heartland of Canada's newsprint production, namely southern Quebec, meaning advantages accruing to IP from this system would be shared by its neighbours as well). First, newspapers in New England, which were located nearest IP's paper plants and a substantial number of which IP had coincidentally recently purchased or financed, benefited from being in zones 1 to 3; their paper would be priced up to $1.50 per ton below the prevailing "base rate." While this arrangement made a certain amount of sense, it would have been

Map 17. The Zone Pricing System: The map that illustrated the "zone pricing system" that was implemented during the late 1920s was very similar to this version, which was adopted early in the next decade (*Paper Trade Journal*, 13 June 1935, p. 37).

PRICE ZONE MAP FOR NEWSPRINT

PORT CITIES

1 BELLINGHAM
2 EVERETT
3 SEATTLE
4 TACOMA
5 PORTLAND
6 OAKLAND
7 SAN FRANCISCO
8 WILMINGTON, CAL.
9 SAN PEDRO
10 LONG BEACH
11 SAN DIEGO
12 CORPUS CHRISTI
13 HOUSTON
14 GALVESTON
15 BEAUMONT
16 NEW ORLEANS
17 MOBILE
18 TAMPA
19 JACKSONVILLE
20 SAVANNAH
21 CHARLESTON
22 NORFOLK
23 NEWPORT NEWS
24 BALTIMORE
25 WILMINGTON
26 PHILADELPHIA
27 NEWARK
28 NEW YORK
29 CLEVELAND
30 TOLEDO
31 DETROIT
32 CHICAGO
33 MILWAUKEE
34 DULUTH

ZONE 4 CITIES

35 OMAHA
36 KANSAS CITY, KAN.
36 KANSAS CITY, MO.
37 ST. LOUIS
38 MIAMI
39 ATLANTIC CITY

ZONE 5 CITIES

40 WASHINGTON D. C.
41 PITTSBURGH

NOTE

The minimum price in Zone 10 is the base price less $1.00 at the destination; when delivery is all rail from the mill and the rail freight exceeds $5.00 per ton the price is base price less $6.00 a ton F.O.B. mill plus the actual rail freight. Where delivery is made via a port the price is the base price less $1.00 at such port plus the local freight to destination.

equally logical to have offered the same price breaks to newspaper publishers in the Midwest which were located near northern Ontario's mills.

But IP drew boundaries that ignored such realities. Instead, the most important zone – that in which the base price would prevail (zone 4 on Map 17) – stretched all the way from Minnesota's border with the Dakotas to Atlantic City, New Jersey, thereby eliminating the incentive for newsprint buyers in northern Ontario's "natural market" to buy from the province's mills. Hereafter, newspapers in cities such as Chicago and Milwaukee would pay the same price for their paper whether it came from a few hundred miles away in Backus's mill in Fort William or over one thousand miles away in IP's plant in Trois-Rivières, Quebec. Moreover, the additional zones that IP created for the "deeper" Midwestern market also bore no relation to the true cost of shipping newsprint there from northern Ontario, and the most farcical example was Zone 8. Even though it encompassed places like Bismarck, North Dakota, which was but 600 miles from Fort Frances, it spanned – as a subsequent investigation by the American government put it – "the entire United States from the Canadian border to the southernmost tip of Texas." A string of inquiries undertaken by the authorities in the United States drew the same conclusion after examining the origins of this zone pricing system. "The International Paper Company sought to meet Canadian competition by agreeing to absorb part of the freight," one such study in 1951 concluded. "Moreover," it continued, "International Paper desired to compete in certain areas closer to competitor mills than to its own mills. To ship into the natural distributing areas of another mill, it was necessary to meet the delivered price offered by the closer mill."[28]

Newspaper publishers in Canada were generally dumbfounded by Ferguson's decision to back IP's zone pricing system, and those who defended it because they saw it as establishing a level playing field presented a dissembling case. J.P. Kenney, the *Ottawa Citizen*'s business manager, was bewildered by the practical implications of the new arrangement once he understood them. His presses were propitiously located practically adjacent to two newsprint makers in the capital region, namely E.B. Eddy and J.R. Booth, and the latter had historically supplied his paper. He had assumed that he would continue to be able to purchase his paper from Booth and at a relatively low price, but he realized almost instantly that this was not to be the case. "It seems just a little unfair," he explained in April 1929, that a newspaper publisher in Florida paid nearly $10 less per ton of newsprint than his own daily, all because of the zone pricing system.[29] Fred Ker, publisher of the *Hamilton Spectator*, tried to reassure Kenney that there was both a practical and "higher" purpose to be served by accepting this rather arcane pricing arrangement. For example, Ker assured Kenney, the establishment of the non-discriminatory price principle, whereby all newspapers in the same region paid the identical price for their newsprint, would spell the end of special deals for some and not others. "It is true in your case proximity of the mill works against you in the matter of rebate," Ker explained in addressing the purpose of the zone system to Kenney. "I think this is the case with most Canadian publishers, but I believe that there is a certain noblesse oblige on the part of the Canadian publishers whose consumption of Canadian newsprint is comparatively small compared to that of the United States publishers to refrain from violently opposing an arrangement which means so much to such a large Canadian industry." Had Ker conveyed the entire story, however, Kenney would have seen right through Ker's rationalization. Not only was Ker a major shareholder in IP and outspoken defender of its activities, he was feeding Graustein intimate and confidential information regarding the strategy that the Canadian Daily Newspaper Association was pursuing vis-à-vis the newsprint producers at this critical time. In addition, Ker was requesting and receiving rebates from the company which supplied his newsprint; his ostensible support for the principle of non-discriminatory pricing was hypocritical.[30]

The NIC's policy of subsidizing remote mills, allowing IP to remain outside the NIC's prorationing arrangement and insisting that the Institute adopt IP's zone pricing system, were complex matters for Ferguson to digest. If he misunderstood them or their crucial implications for Ontario's newsprint makers, he was not afforded much time to figure them out for himself. Soon after the Institute began operating in 1929, he was bombarded with complaints about its deleterious impact on the province's mills.

Several came from Backus and his representatives, who provided Ferguson with an incisive dissection of how the NIC was an unmitigated disaster for the province's newsprint makers, especially those in northwestern Ontario. Certainly they supported a plan to stabilize the industry, but not one that restricted producers like Backus to operating his mills at 65 per cent of their capacity while allowing CIP's plants to run at capacity. They pointed out, in fact, that CIP was so oversupplied with customers that it had been forced to sell the NIC orders for 150,000 tons!

Moreover, they attacked the zone pricing system, which prevented Backus from enjoying "the benefit of lower freight rate[s] from International Falls and Fort Frances to [his] natural markets" and was causing him to lose customers in places like Chicago, Milwaukee, and Omaha. Finally, they expressed outrage at the extent to which the NIC's plan to subsidize remote mills completely ignored the advantageous location of his plants. After only six months of operation (January to June 1929), the NIC was already demanding that he remit over $200,000 in equalization payments to less favourably located producers.[31]

Kimberly-Clark (KC), whose mill in Kapuskasing was acting as a de facto member of the NIC, echoed the criticisms levelled by the Backus camp and predicted grave consequences if the present arrangement were continued. KC focused its complaints on Ferguson's willingness to allow IP to operate unrestrained. It was decidedly unfair, Sensenbrenner charged, that "manufacturers in Ontario and Quebec with the exception of International are carrying the whole burden of curtailment ... All of the other manufacturers running full time, get the benefit[s] ... without sharing the burdens of curtailment, and that is a great burden." KC added that it had only agreed to abide by the NIC's prorationing policy assuming that the NIC would rate the firm's mill at its recognized capacity of 550 tons. This was a critical consideration, as KC had predicated its ability to meet its financial obligations on operating its mill to its potential. So when the NIC had underrated its plant's capacity by roughly 15 per cent, KC realized that following the Institute's directive to operate its mill at 70 per cent capacity would translate into significantly lower newsprint sales. It may have sounded like semantics to the premier, but for KC it was a matter of life or death. Manufacturing the smaller volume of paper at the NIC's price would not generate enough revenue to cover KC's costs *and* the interest and dividends owing on its securities. Receivership would result.[32]

While Ferguson ruminated over these analyses, near the end of 1929 he was again presented with an opportunity to bridle the renegade IP. The Institute had announced in December that, effective the first of the new year, it would increase by $5 per ton the industry's prevailing $55 price for newsprint. Just after Christmas, however, Graustein proclaimed that he would continue selling at the old, lower rate. Taschereau frantically conveyed this news to Ferguson a few days after Christmas and expressed his view that Graustein's actions represented a "distinct refusal to accept our suggestion and to follow the price fixed by the

Canadian manufacturers." Quebec's premier asked his Ontario counterpart for suggestions as to how to handle this latest crisis.[33]

Ferguson wholeheartedly agreed with Taschereau's analysis of the problem but pleaded that he was powerless to do anything about it. Ferguson informed Quebec's premier that he had learned that IP had begun reopening and refitting its mills in the United States to produce newsprint, and he classified Graustein's actions as indicating "a combined determination to resist claims of Ontario and Quebec for more generous consideration." But in stark contrast to his willingness to subjugate Ontario's newsprint makers, Ferguson asserted that he was in no position to control Graustein. He dejectedly explained to Taschereau that there was "little we can do to frustrate [IP's] plans," and he preferred instead to consider Graustein's most recent belligerence a function of "the present heated situation" and hoped that "in time, cooler heads will prevail."[34]

Again, it was Ferguson's choice not to bring power to bear upon IP, for he was hardly impotent in this instance. True, he was unable to control Graustein's actions in the United States, but in conceding defeat at this time, Ferguson completely ignored IP's vast timber holdings in Ontario and the fact that it was in breach of all its pulpwood leases. Moreover, he was personally involved during this critical period in acceding to IP's requests for extensions of the deadlines by which it was to fulfil its contractual obligations with the Crown. While Ferguson apparently did not even consider attempting to use this leverage to compel IP to increase its contract newsprint price for 1930 to $60, he suggested to Taschereau that the Quebec premier consider doing exactly what the Ontario premier refused to do. Ferguson advised Taschereau that the latter might be able to deal more effectively with IP and the situation in general by "attaching conditions to the renewals" of the recalcitrant companies' leases with the Quebec government.[35]

One factor made Ferguson's attitude on this occasion particularly noteworthy. Of all the newsprint interests in Ontario against whom the premier could have used the threat of cancelling pulpwood leases, IP was the ideal choice. Terminating the agreement of an existing, operating mill such as Abitibi in Iroquois Falls would have had immediate and grave consequences; hundreds, if not thousands, of northerners would be thrown out of work. On the other hand, Ferguson faced few if any political or economic repercussions in Ontario from cancelling IP's three pulpwood concession leases because Graustein had yet to build the three mills required under these agreements. Ferguson could have rapped Graustein's knuckles without jeopardizing one single job in northern Ontario, but he declined to do so.

Graustein recognized that neither Ferguson nor Taschereau was willing to rein him in, so he maximized his advantage in late 1929 and early 1930. He aggressively solicited new customers using IP's lower $55 price even though he had already sold his mills' entire production for the year. This allowed him to garner an ever greater percentage of the North American newsprint market at the NIC's expense, with the Institute losing 200,000 tons worth of orders over the winter of 1929–30 alone. By early 1930 its largest member in Ontario – Abitibi – was operating at around 50 per cent of its capacity, and it had already closed its mill in Espanola and was about to do the same in Sturgeon Falls. All the while, Ferguson publicly argued that "market forces" and not the NIC were to blame for the distressed newsprint industry, thereby neglecting to mention that unemployment among IP's mill and bush workers in towns such as Gatineau was not a concern at this time because the local plant was operating at – and sometimes over – 100 per cent of its rated capacity. As Ernest H. Finlayson, head of the Dominion Forest Service, lamented at this time, "we might just as well face the fact that one gigantic concern is using all its influence and taking every possible step towards monopolistic control of the pulp and paper industry in this country."[36]

It was at this perilous moment that Ferguson let KC out of his hammerlock. Frank Sensenbrenner, the company's leader, appealed again to the premier for relief in April 1930 on the grounds that the NIC's arrangement was driving his mill towards receivership. Although Ferguson would not sanction Sensenbrenner openly breaking from the NIC, the premier freed KC from its prorationing scheme. Thereafter, its mill in Kapuskasing produced well above its allotted tonnage and refused to remit over $350,000 it owed the NIC's equalization fund. KC did so without penalty, met its interest obligations in the fall of 1930, and actually paid off its bonded debt during the Depression.[37]

Although the NIC disintegrated in September 1930 when a few of its Quebec members broke ranks, the Ontario government still insisted that the province's newsprint producers – except KC – adhere to the NIC's prorationing and pricing policies. Ferguson had resigned as premier in mid-December 1930, but he continued to direct affairs through his appointed successor, George S. Henry, who, the surviving documents reveal, knew very little about either the NIC's existence or its impact on Ontario's newsprint mills. Ferguson steadfastly stuck to his strategy for stabilizing the industry even as it became increasingly apparent that Ontario's mills were sacrificing the most and gaining the least from this arrangement. When Ferguson took up his post as high commissioner in Britain in early 1931, newsprint mills in Espanola, Sturgeon Falls, Fort Frances, and Fort William were closed for want of orders.[38]

If Henry needed a crash course on how the NIC was wreaking havoc on the province's newsprint makers, he received one in early March 1931 from Walter Cain, the veteran deputy minister. Cain's perspicacious analysis of the North American newsprint situation indicated that the Midwestern US consumed about 1,400,000 tons of paper annually, and that this market was "naturally tributary" to northern Ontario because the province's newsprint mills "have a freight advantage to their logical market of from $2.00 to $5.00 per ton over Quebec and eastern Canada." Conceding that firms in the Great Lakes states manufactured about 400,000 tons annually, he calculated that this left "a balance of 1,000,000 tons which economically should be made available for the mills operating in Ontario," a figure that was roughly equal to the province's total capacity. While this meant that Ontario's mills should have been operating near capacity, the NIC's regulations were preventing this from happening. In 1930, for example, they had restricted Ontario to producing under 450,000 tons of newsprint while the rest of the tonnage sold in the Midwestern states had come from "mills less advantageously situated." Moreover, Cain pointed out that all the NIC's mills had declined from operating at 76 per cent in 1929 to 59 per cent in 1930 to 43 per cent during the first seven weeks of 1931, with Backus operating at barely 30 per cent during this latter period; these years had seen the "independents" (i.e., IP) operating near capacity.[39]

The NIC's devastating effects on Ontario's newsprint industry even drove some Conservatives to engage in internecine warfare and speak out against the strategy their "chief" had been pursuing. In an impassioned address to the Legislature, Donald Hogarth, the Tory MPP for Port Arthur, called upon the government to appoint a royal commission or other body to investigate the NIC's activities. He argued that Ferguson had formed it simply as a means of "price-fixing" and that it had "sought to jack up the slipping price. And while the companies of the [I]nstitute were bolstering up prices, other concerns ... began signing up contracts ... while the [I]nstitute clung to its ... price. The International signed contracts here and there and took the market." As a result, Hogarth urged the government to "exert its influence and authority to have the International Paper Company give up some of its excess tonnage," which, he emphasized, IP was selling in "the middle west, our natural market." To achieve this end, Hogarth reminded his fellow MPPs that the "International Paper Company owns three concessions in this district – the Nipigon Corporation, south east of Lake Nipigon, the McDougall concessions west of Lake Nipigon, and the Alsas [sic] concessions north of Chapleau. They are in default in respect to each of these concessions … but the government is not prepared … to proceed against the company and take drastic measures."[40]

One factor that Cain's and Hogarth's analyses had ignored was the manner in which the NIC's price equalization system compelled advantageously situated mills to subsidize remote ones, thereby further damaging Ontario's mills. After two years of operation (1929 and 1930), the tabulations indicated that this scheme was essentially a means by which the mills in Ontario – except KC's – paid considerable compensation to those in Quebec; the former owed nearly $1,600,000 compared with less than $375,000 owed by the latter. Although privy to neither these data nor those prepared by the deputy minister, the *Toronto Mail and Empire* reported in April 1931 that, after executives from the province's newsprint companies met recently with three of the Tories' leading cabinet members, the "predominant opinion was that the co-operation between the Ontario and Quebec Governments in the Newsprint Institute's policy, through Hon. G.H. Ferguson and Hon. L.A. Taschereau, had resulted unhappily for Ontario."[41]

The NIC's prorationing and zone pricing systems had been devastating for Ontario's newsprint makers (except KC), but it still took several exceptional events to send these companies under. Backus's Minnesota and Ontario Paper Company (M&O), through which he controlled his mills in International Falls, Fort Frances, and Kenora, was the first to capsize. Backus's bankers asked him to place the company voluntarily into receivership in early 1931 after they refused to front him the money to meet its interest payments. At this point the courts judged M&O to be solvent, and Graustein's continued offers to pay Backus a steep price for his newsprint empire attested to the value it still held. When Backus refused to sell, his bankers engineered his removal as receiver and his replacement by their hand-picked successors. Backus fought in vain to regain control over his company over the next few years, a battle that left him dead of a heart attack in 1934.[42] When Abitibi went into receivership in mid-1932, the primary cause was its decision to guarantee the financing on a massive hydro project one of its subsidiaries had undertaken at this time.[43]

These developments did not silence the protests against the inherent unfairness of the NIC's zone pricing system. The more courageous receivers who took charge of Ontario's newsprint mills expressed their disapproval of this arrangement. Sir Joseph Flavelle was most outspoken in this regard. As chairman of National Trust, which was managing Great Lakes Paper's receivership, Flavelle objected to the Ontario government's insistence that he abide by the zone pricing system which was so obviously detrimental to Ontario's mills. A fervent proponent of ensuring industry "a living profit," Flavelle favoured charging newspaper publishers "a price ... quoted based on the cost of production and delivery," and stated that "the irritation felt in certain quarters against this method of doing business was because of the artificial system of zone prices in the industry under which selling prices depended on the geographical position of the purchaser and ignored delivery costs of the seller." National Trust's board of directors agreed with its chairman. It argued that an "injustice ... would be done to those interested in the securities of low-cost, well-situated mills if they were to be held back from quoting prices based on their natural advantages in respect of cost and situation."[44]

While Ontario's major newsprint makers were in receivership by the end of 1932, IP avoided this predicament throughout the Depression, an outcome which some Canadians believed was the result of more than mere serendipity. In early November 1932, the *Montreal Herald* informed its readers that "every time there has been a break in the price of newsprint the International Paper Company has been in the vanguard of the movement." While Canadian mills had run at 50 per cent, IP had operated its plants to their capacities, gathering contracts by cutting prices "while professing a desire for co-operation or a merger." It thus asked if IP was "carrying out a long-planned determination to rule with an iron hand the major manufacturing industry of Canada." The *Montreal Star* echoed this perspective in an article entitled "S.O.S." It noted that the Canadian newsprint industry was on the brink of ruin and implied that the premiers of Ontario and Quebec were at least partially responsible for this disaster. "The facts are well known in inner circles," the editorial explained. "A drive engineered in a foreign country, is being made with great skill and daring which will force Canadian newsprint companies into bankruptcy ... some short-sighted Canadians have been foolish enough to help along the attack on Canadian solvency by falling victims to the wiles of the invaders."[45]

Others vented their views by appealing directly to R.B. Bennett, the prime minister and CIP's former director, but with little effect. Having learned that IP charged much less for newsprint than the NIC, Montrealer W.J. Phelps explained to Bennett that it was well known "that this International Co. was being backed by two powerful banks and that no doubt, the intention was to drive our Canadian companies … into liquidation, when this octopus would be able to buy up their assets for a song and then be able to control the entire pulp + paper industry of Canada." Surely, Phelps contended, Dominion officials could "stop this raiding shortly." Louis DeBrisay, an anxious investor from Westmount, asked Bennett why anyone would sink his money into Canadian industry "when any Graustein that comes along is allowed to throttle both ourselves and our governments." Referring to the aforementioned articles in the Montreal dailies, DeBrisay commented that, "if th[ese] paper[s are] telling the Truth is it not time that the Conservative govt at Ottawa tried its Hurculean [sic] strength against Graustein et al?" Despite such appeals, no government in Canada was sufficiently motivated to alter its approach to dealing with either Graustein or IP.[46]

For its part, International Paper seemed to bask in the knowledge that it was free to dictate to Canadian officials the rules by which it would run its business. During the late 1920s and early 1930s, Graustein had been able to convince the premiers of Ontario and Quebec that they should force their newsprint producers – except IP, of course – to form a cartel that was operated according to rules that were damaging – to varying degrees – to these firms. He was acutely aware of the degree to which IP profited from this arrangement, as were some members of the local media; one Toronto newspaper cartoonist drew a caricature of the situation that Graustein liked so much it soon adorned his office wall (Figure 14). IP's reaction to an attempt by Canada's leading bankers to consolidate the country's newsprint firms into one mammoth entity in 1931–2 attested further to Graustein's unbridled confidence regarding his ability to dictate events during this critical period. In commenting on the proposal, IP explained to the Ontario government that it would only agree to this merger if it were carried out according to the "fundamentals" by which IP operated and if "the other policies in which International believes are written into the code of the proposed consolidation." Otherwise, the firm bluntly explained, "we shall continue to paddle our own canoe." While Ferguson had always granted IP the freedom to do so, the fact that the Ontario government continued this policy after his departure left the province's newsprint mills in an especially vulnerable position, one in which their past travails served as an accurate and bleak indicator of things to come.[47]

Figure 14. Shedding Crocodile Tears: This cartoon mocks the ironic situation resulting from the actions taken by the premiers of Quebec and Ontario (Taschereau is on the left and Ferguson on the right). They are seen browbeating Graustein in an attempt to force him to accede to their wishes to raise the price of newsprint, much to the detriment of consumers. All the while the long arm of the (American) legal system is in the background, intently focused on the newsprint combine Taschereau and Ferguson created and to which they insisted all major eastern Canadian producers belong, all except for Graustein's firm (William C. Graustein).

In light of the events which have been described, Graustein's later recognition of the assistance his efforts in Canada received from the country's establishment during the 1920s and 1930s is particularly noteworthy. Testifying in 1950 before the Celler Committee (which was investigating an alleged combine in the North American newsprint industry), Graustein took the highly unusual step of taking time during his deposition to "express ... [his] very deep feeling that these [provincial] Prime Ministers as a group, the responsible heads of the governments of Canada and of its newsprint producing provinces, conducted themselves on the whole with great courage, with wisdom and restraint, and with scrupulous fairness." For reasons which should now be clear, there was plenty for which he owed Canada's politicians – particularly "the chief" of Ontario – his heartfelt thanks.[48]

Conclusion: "The availability of wood for industry is ambiguous"

With Ontario's forest industry in disarray at the depths of the Depression, William H. Finalyson, the minister of lands and forests, called the province's lumbermen to a special meeting in his office. He told them that his goal was to learn their plans for coping with the current crisis and how the Tories could facilitate a solution to it. In his address, Finlayson spoke warmly of "the old lumber industry, which used to be white pine in Ontario and now has developed into other lines. We have the feeling," the minister announced on behalf of his government, "that the lumber industry is peculiarly different from every other industry in that it is a personal family industry." He then took a backhanded swipe at the pulp and paper makers by pointing out that he felt "a great deal of pride and satisfaction in knowing that the lumber industry never exploited the public, never issued paper securities, and in Ontario it has remained intact. I see gentlemen before me who are of the third and fourth generation in one family, carrying on in the lumber industry. I have had one lumberman tell me that his mill was built before Confederation and that he never had any financial operations ... and the mill is still with the family ... There is a personal relationship in the lumber industry that I don't think exists in any other industry."[1]

Finlayson's comments revealed much about the approach the Ontario government had taken over the previous four decades towards the various players in the province's forest industry. Prior to the advent of the pulp and paper industry in Ontario in the late nineteenth century, the provincial government had established clear priorities for northern development, the most important of which was colonization. The lumbermen and pulpwood exporters had crucial roles to play in the state's drive to push farming on the frontier. These two groups enjoyed intimate political and business ties with the government, and the demands they placed upon the state were limited in scope and relatively easy for the politicians to grant. It was hardly surprising, then, that the politicians treated them most favourably.

These circumstances created significant challenges for the pulp and paper mills as they began arriving in northern Ontario on the eve of the twentieth century. The odds of the state offering them its full cooperation were low in light of the fact that the paper makers sought unprecedented quantities of Crown resources and specific terms of access, both of which the state found very difficult to provide. Not only were these requests unique in their nature and scope, but they also interfered with the government's existing priorities and relationships in the hinterland, none of which it was about to abandon. Various bureaucrats and advisers recommended during this period that the state adjust its policies to the rapid rise of the province's pulp and paper industry, but the politicians generally proved unwilling to do so. As Walter Cain, the grizzled, veteran deputy minister of lands and forests admitted to the meeting of Ontario's lumbermen in 1933, "I have nothing to do with governmental policy. I am simply a permanent official of the Government."[2]

Cain and his colleagues were in this position for one simple reason that lies at the core of this story: the provincial politicians in this period clung to their tradition of dispensing Crown resources based upon patronage considerations. This, more than any other factor, shaped the state's attitude towards the pulp and paper makers. Ontario's forest industry matured between 1894 and 1932, transforming itself from a sector consisting overwhelmingly of pine lumber producers to one marked by pulp and paper makers. Moreover, the entrepreneurs engaged in the modern staples industry were certainly eager to see the government adopt a professional, managerial approach to administering northern timber and hydro resources. Nevertheless, the elected officials refused to allow this end to be realized. They preferred to dole out the trees and water powers in a manner that redounded, first and foremost, to the benefit of their political parties and consorts.

The upshot was rather predictable. As the pulp and paper industry came of age, evolving from little more than blueprint drawings on a draftsman's table in the late 1800s to a multimillion-dollar industry employing tens of thousands directly and at least as many indirectly by the eve of the Depression, the provincial state failed to outline and implement a coherent "policy" towards it. Instead, the politicians implemented a haphazard strategy that shifted almost as often as new administrations came to office. To be sure, changing circumstances brought new issues to the fore with each stage of the industry's growth, and occasionally they created conditions in which the provincial state embraced the paper makers. The latter's ability to plug itself into the patronage network or its good fortune in being in the right place at the right time were but a few of the factors that caused the government to welcome certain mills. Likewise, some parties – such as the Liberals (1894–1905) and Farmers (1919–23) – proved, in the main, more helpful to particular players in the pulp and paper industry than the Tories (1905–19 and 1923–32). But, by and large, the Ontario government did remarkably little to further the paper makers' endeavour due to the factors which have been the focus of this story. As a result, between 1894 and 1932 the Ontario government generally exhibited a frosty attitude towards the pulp and paper industry, and a steely determination to keep it on a very short leash.

This approach had a varied impact. In general pulp and paper mills were established in northern Ontario primarily as a function of industrial initiative, not a sympathetic government policy that sought as its goal the creation of a strong pulp and paper industry. In fact, many mills set down roots in the province and significantly expanded their operations despite and not because of the government's actions. Whereas the provincial state reinforced its profound bond with the lumbermen and pulpwood exporters throughout this period, granting them considerable autonomy, the opposite was true for the pulp and paper makers, whose relationship with the government was occasionally characterized by conflict. In fact, the distrust that marked the dealings between the provincial state and most of the players in the modern staples industry compelled the former to keep the latter strictly "in the power of the Government." It was thus a strange paradox that the government's policy of developing northern Ontario's woodlands and water powers between 1894 and 1932 was least responsive to the enterprise that became the most important economic user of those resources, namely the province's newsprint industry.

A comparison of the quantity and quality of the pulpwood supplies the Ontario government leased to various interests during this period bears out this conclusion. Among the state's "unfavoured" mills, only one of them – Great Lakes Paper – had procured what industry and financiers would have defined as a perpetual supply of pulpwood (roughly 2,250,000 cords for every 100 tons of capacity). It had only been able to accomplish this end, however, by merging three concessions to support its one mill. The newsprint plant in Kenora controlled merely twenty years worth of wood, the one in Fort Frances had never held a Crown pulpwood concession in Ontario, and none of Abitibi's mills (including those it absorbed from Spanish River in 1928) leased perpetual supplies of spruce. Moreover, although these firms had continually asked the government for leases that would provide them with secure tenure under reasonable conditions, the preceding chapters have demonstrated that the state never did so. In contrast, the government had leased Kimberly-Clark and Provincial Paper vast quantities of Crown pulpwood under terms that were easy to fulfil and gave them secure tenure. International Paper was in a category unto itself. The government had given it over 14,000,000 cords of spruce pulpwood even though it operated no mill in northern Ontario.

The politicians' approach to dealing with the export of pulpwood exacerbated the situation for the province's pulp and paper makers. Notwithstanding the government's pronouncements to the contrary, the provincial state never intended to implement the manufacturing condition on pulpwood in 1900 to stop the flow of unprocessed spruce to the United States. Instead, it was a calculated measure designed both to facilitate a specific kind of export, one that would sustain the settlers in the harsh northern hinterland, and to assist the coterie of prominent businessmen who were engaged in this enterprise. The volume of pulpwood leaving the province thus skyrocketed between 1894 and 1932, a trend that made Ontario stick out like a sore thumb in this regard. Ernest H. Finlayson, the soon-to-be Dominion Forester and secretary to Ottawa's Royal Commission on Pulpwood, noted in the mid-1920s that the volume of spruce being exported from Canada's traditional centres of such activities – New Brunswick and Quebec – had been dropping for years, whereas there had been "a very decided, and almost continuous, upward trend in the amount of Ontario exports."[3]

Several factors made the government's approach especially damaging to Ontario's newsprint industry. Its actions gave the exporters what was largely the province's most accessible (i.e., cheapest to operate) pulpwood, and made this fibre available to mills in the Great Lakes states that were Ontario's direct competitors in the Midwestern American newsprint market. Moreover, this approach was injurious to the province's – and Canada's – pulp and paper industry even after producers in the Great Lakes states began converting many of their operations from newsprint to higher grades of paper in the mid-1920s. Because the government in the United States protected these product lines with steep tariffs, providing American companies which manufactured them with spruce from Ontario substantially decreased the pressure on the US government to lower these duties and open these markets to the province's mills which produced these same goods. Finally, allowing unprocessed spruce to leave Ontario depressed the price that all mills in the US paid for their pulpwood by decreasing the demand for American spruce. For these reasons, the Ontario government's decision to facilitate the export of pulpwood from the province in the manner that it did amounted to providing a subsidy to the mills south of the border, one that the latter truly cherished. When Ontario threatened to terminate this export trade after the Second World War, the major beneficiaries of this policy in the US pleaded for the province's politicians to reconsider the matter. "Practically every mill ... in the state," Senator Alexander Wiley from Wisconsin declared in an urgent telegram to Premier George Drew in January 1948, "has been to a large extent dependent upon Ontario for its supply of wood for many years in the past." Clearly, the notion of the provincial government managing its Crown pulpwood supply to fulfil a protectionist agenda is a chimerical one.[4]

While most of Ontario's newsprint mills waged practically continuous struggles with the government over the quantity and quality of Crown resources (particularly timber) they leased, there was good reason why, for the most part, they kept their campaigns private. They had little to gain and everything to lose by waging a public battle. There was little hope of tapping latent sympathy for their cause among Ontarians because most of the province's citizens had roots – in terms of both their outlooks and occupations – that were firmly planted in agriculture; their ultraconservative ethos was unlikely to support a corporate agenda of securing large tracts of the public domain for an industry's exclusive use. Mills that fought political battles in the open also risked angering the very elected officials upon whom they depended for access to raw materials, a gamble only the most foolhardy dared take.[5]

There was a more important force that compelled mill managers to keep secret their battles for spruce. Although they lacked perpetual pulpwood supplies, they – and just as often their financial backers – presented a fundamentally different impression to their investors, who insistently sought assurances about the timber available to the newsprint firms whose securities they owned.[6] Most paper company executives who responded to these inquiries became adept at skirting the issue or providing misleading answers. For example, Spanish River had battled unsuccessfully since before the First World War to supplement its fibre holdings, which the company and government both agreed were inadequate; at that time its mill in Espanola controlled a supply of timber that would run out within a half-dozen years. This bleak situation did not, however, stop the firm from trumpeting in its annual reports throughout the 1920s that the pulpwood limits leased by its three flagship mills in Sault Ste Marie, Espanola, and Sturgeon Falls "contain a perpetual supply of the highest grade pulpwood."[7] Likewise, Backus had gingerly tiptoed around the question in his annual reports so as not to set off alarm bells, saying very little about his firm's *actual* pulpwood holdings and focusing instead on their *potential* fibre basket. "The timber supply in Minnesota and Ontario contiguous and tributary to the mills embraces a forest area of approximately 50,000 square miles," one of his typical yearly reviews from the mid-1920s delicately put it, "and contains an almost inexhaustible supply of spruce pulpwood and other papermaking woods."[8]

Instead of broadcasting publicly the state of their insufficient or expensive Crown timber supplies, these companies quietly took steps to compensate for their fibre shortcomings. Spanish River endeavoured to maximize the productivity of its Crown timber limits by managing them on a sustained-yield basis and processing greater quantities of jack pine and balsam fir – instead of relying almost solely on spruce – to manufacture newsprint. By the mid-1920s, it was enjoying marked success in both areas.[9] In addition, where feasible, mills purchased freehold timberlands to supplement their Crown limits. The plant in Smooth Rock Falls, which was especially worried about its fibre supply, had acquired nearly 200 square miles of settlers' lots by the mid-1920s. Most often, Ontario's newsprint makers conserved the timber on their concessions by purchasing as much settlers' and contractors' wood as they could, and this was especially true of those mills that were most concerned about either the quantity and/or the cost of their own spruce supplies. The Dominion's Royal Commission on Pulpwood reported in 1924 that Ontario's mills were unique insofar as they purchased on the open market far more spruce than farmers and settlers could produce, leading it to conclude that this pattern was "an indication that they are endeavouring to conserve their own supplies."[10] Dr James H. White, a forestry professor at the University of Toronto, investigated Ontario's forest industry during the summer of 1929 and drew identical findings. He observed that over half the province's newsprint makers "had been living on settlers' wood."[11]

These facts cast into doubt the argument that historians have made about the pulp and paper industry having been a wanton harvester of the concessions it leased from the government, particularly during the interwar years. The data indicate that the opposite was true. The mills cut only as much timber from their Crown limits as was absolutely necessary, and the intensive harvesting actually occurred on private lands that the provincial government had opened to "homesteading." Ontario's newsprint makers used nearly equal volumes of private and Crown land pulpwood between 1915 and 1932 (and much less than half of their own timber during the mid- to late 1920s), and when the quantity of pulpwood exported during this period is factored in (almost all this timber ought to have come from settlers' lots), the figures reveal that over twice as much spruce was cut from private land as from public forests (Chart 5).

News of the degree to which Ontario's mills relied on settlers' spruce must have been gratifying indeed to the Ontario government. During the period being examined, it had applied increasing pressure on the province's newsprint makers – both directly through coercion and, more importantly, indirectly by depriving them of the timber supplies they sought – to purchase as much homesteaders' wood as possible.[12]

In fact, the government's approach towards Ontario's newsprint makers in this regard gave it even less reason to respond favourably to their needs as far as fibre supplies were concerned. Because the mills maximized their purchase of spruce cut from private lands, this minimized the revenues the government received from the pulpwood the paper mills harvested from their Crown limits. On the other hand, the lumbermen had little choice but to harvest from their Crown timber licences because they alone were authorized to cut pine in commercial quantities from either freehold or public tracts. This meant that the lumbermen's stumpage payments accounted for a disproportionately large part of the department's timber revenues even though the newsprint industry was using a far greater volume of wood during this period. As a result, the longer the government denied a newsprint mill a perpetual supply of pulpwood, the less the mill cut on its Crown concession. In a curious way, this made that mill less important to elected officials who were concerned about balancing the province's books.[13]

While Ontario's pulp and paper industry was, for the most part, still able to procure the pulpwood it required despite its insufficient supply of Crown timber, the government's approach left it few options for financing its operations. Most historians have criticized the Canadian newsprint industry's decision to fund its growth – especially during the 1920s – using fixed-interest-bearing securities such as bonds and

Chart 5. Approximate volume of pulpwood processed by Ontario's newsprint mills that came from Crown and private land, and total pulpwood harvested from private land, 1915–1931

Year	Pulpwood processed by Ontario's newsprint mills (cords)		Exported pulpwood (cords)	Total pulpwood harvested from private land (cords)
	from Crown land	from private land		
1915	153,388	151,747	202,239	353,986
1916	239,808	121,513	149,745	271,258
1917	189,581	184,504	161,625	346,129
1918	238,991	165,176	199,421	364,597
1919	267,055	144,956	196,041	340,637
1920	513,500	134,806	202,171	336,977
1921	458,081	275,777	239,264	515,041
1922	290,530	219,154	269,419	488,573
1923	463,964	289,263	414,288	703,551
1924	411,731	384,802	427,194	811,996
1925	300,615	343,917	439,254	783,171
1926	221,266	306,877	403,651	710,528
1927	353,574	456,846	487,440	944,286
1928	277,088	430,685	633,710	1,064,395
1929	300,491	456,660	459,860	916,603
1930	189,400	352,100	484,943	837,043
1931	55,700	225,678	377,351	603,029
Totals	4,924,683	4,644,184	5,747,616	10,391,800

Note: Data from several mills (Fort Frances, Kenora, and Thunder Bay Paper) are unavailable, but these mills all relied heavily on settlers' pulpwood.
Sources: *Annual Reports of the Department of Lands and Forests, 1915–1931*; AO, RG1-305, Box 2, "Abitibi Power and Paper Company, Limited – Data Required by Pulpwood Conservation Act 1929, *August 1929*"; ibid., RG1-E-5, "Statistical Returns of Manufacturers of Pulp and Paper, 1929–1931."

preferred shares. The evidence presented here demonstrates that the majority of Ontario's paper makers had absolutely no choice in the matter. Reputable financiers considered Crown leases valuable collateral only when these documents included reasonable terms, perpetual supplies of resources, and secure tenure to them; the few companies in Ontario that obtained such prized contracts enjoyed practically complete freedom from their funding partners as a result. In sharp contrast, most of the province's pulp and paper firms obtained Crown leases that held practically no intrinsic value, a secret that only a bold few dared whisper during this period. Frederick Noad, who advised the Opposition Liberals in the early 1930s on forest policy and whom they rewarded after their electoral victory in 1934 by appointing deputy minister, was one such courageous soul. Writing in *Saturday Night* in mid-1933, he offered astute commentary on this subject when he explained that anyone who "carefully [examined] the terms under which those [pulpwood and water power] concessions and rights were granted ... will soon be disillusioned." The reason, Noad pointed out, was that the valuations that the newsprint companies had placed upon "the rights and privileges held under license from the Crown are in no sense property values; they are, in every sense of the word, speculative." This meant that each of the province's pulp and paper makers had capitalized "that to which it has no title either by ownership or control."[14]

And this was the rub. Because their leases were considered such worthless collateral, the mills were forced to mortgage their plants, power houses, logging equipment – in fact, everything they owned including their leases to Crown resources – in order to raise capital for their ventures. This left them highly vulnerable on many fronts. Because they had no other assets available to mortgage if they required additional funding, the province's newsprint mills paid some of the highest interest rates among Canada's industrial borrowers. Most importantly, the financiers were given an irresistible opportunity to obtrude into the mills' affairs, which they did to an enormous extent during the interwar years. The investment houses that agreed to back these enterprises only did so in exchange for being given control over practically every aspect of the newsprint companies' operations. Spanish River's financiers, Peabody, Houghteling and Company, for example, underwrote the bonds that would pay for the expansion of its Espanola mill in 1919–20 only after the company gave it full power over the plant's augmentation program and future financing, and significant representation on its board of directors. This degree of influence allowed the financial wizards to grossly overcapitalize the newsprint firm's assets, especially their Crown leases. When National City Company of New York engineered Abitibi's "merger" with Spanish River in 1928, for example, it estimated the Crown timber and water powers the firm leased from the government to be worth over $50,000,000. Such bloated valuations permitted the financiers to saddle the companies with fixed-interest burdens that reaped the former luxurious profits but encumbered the latter with obligations that were suffocatingly onerous; Spanish River's had just under $11,000,000 worth of bonds and about $8,500,000 worth of preferred shares in 1925, but three years later, after it had been taken over by Abitibi, the figures were $50,000,000 and $36,000,000 respectively. "It was a sad day for the newsprint industry of this country," one observer lamented about the 1920s, "when its control passed from the hands of newsprint manufacturers, who understood both the business and its customers, into the hands of financiers and politicians who understood neither."[15]

The implications for Ontario's newsprint makers of having financiers at the helm were grave. Although the mills kept their production costs under lock and key, documents that survive from this era reveal that Abitibi's plants, when operating at only 75 per cent of their capacity, could manufacture newsprint for between $22 and $31 per ton, not including charges for debt and overhead.[16] Likewise, the receiver for Great Lakes Paper informed the court in the early 1930s that this mill's production costs were only about $36 per ton when it was operating well under capacity.[17] So when newsprint prices plummeted to under $50 in the Depression, these firms were still viable, profitable businesses but they were listing under the weight of the overbearing charges they were forced to pay to finance their enterprises (roughly $10 per ton for Abitibi, a rate which was nearly double what it had paid in fixed charges prior to its 1928 merger). This was the crux of the matter, a point on which William Randolph Hearst, the iconic publishing magnate, picked up when newsprint prices were at their nadir in June 1932. After he had been made privy to this type of inside information on Canadian production costs, he astutely observed that the Dominion's firms could not "make paper at the rates that the present market calls for and pay interest on inflated capitalization, but if they went into bankruptcy and were recapitalized, with all the water squeezed out, they would be able to make a decent profit on paper at a very low price."[18] These circumstances also meant that when these paper companies fell into receivership in the early 1930s, these same financiers gained control over them. For Backus's plants in Kenora and Fort Frances and Abitibi's string of mills across northern Ontario, this translated into long, torturous ordeals.

This analysis has also shown that the criticism levelled at the Canadian newsprint industry for egregiously watering its securities during the interwar period, and thus contributing in a major way to the serious problems it faced during the early 1930s, is largely unjustified. Spanish River, for example, was the province's largest newsprint producer for fifteen years (1913–28) and Canada's for most of this same period, and during these years it never split a single share. Similarly, E.W. Backus was the province's second-largest manufacturer, and he privately held nearly all his firms' shares. Abitibi, on the other hand, was one of the few companies in Ontario that watered its stocks, specifically during the early 1920s and in 1928 when it took over Spanish River. Even its transgressions in this regard, however, pale in comparison to those committed by International Paper, the firm to which the Ontario government gave its warmest reception during this period.[19]

A few observations regarding the behaviour of the main actors in these events are warranted. The province's newsprint companies could have pursued other options in trying to improve their dealings with the government. They could have addressed the state's unwavering commitment to protecting the lumbermen's interests, for instance, by establishing fully integrated operations. This would have involved buying the saw-logging outfits that both operated on their pulpwood concessions and caused some of them so much grief. Although this would have cost a considerable sum, the purchase price would have included exclusive access to the timber on their limits, a privilege that they held dear. Only Backus seems to have attempted this approach, and even then only in Kenora. In the future, a few pulp and paper executives would learn from their predecessors' mistakes by forging these backward linkages.

Moreover, the pulp and paper makers' decision to push ahead with their ventures despite the lack of assistance from the Ontario government raises profound questions about the prudence of their corporate strategies. To be sure, Ontario's natural resources and their proximity to the Midwestern American newsprint market beckoned mill developers. In addition, there were some stark examples of firms in other industries in Canada that outperformed their competitors even though they lacked direct control over their raw materials and instead purchased these resources on the open market.[20] Furthermore, governments in other provinces accepted the rise of the pulp and paper industry during this period and the decline of the lumbermen's traditional sawlog supplies (usually white and red pine) as a signal that it was time to shift allegiances (with varying speeds) to the new modern staples industrialists.[21] In Ontario, however, the government had the opposite reaction to these events, taking vigorous steps to arrest the lumber industry's decline and resist the paper industry's ascent. Nevertheless, Ontario's newsprint makers responded to their successive rebuffs at the politicians' hands with an apparently indomitable faith in the hope that, in the future, things would be different. This transformation in the relations between the provincial state and the pulp and paper industry as a whole would not happen, however, until after the Second World War. In addition, the decision of Ontario's leading newsprint makers to deceive the public about the nature of their timber supplies was an unpardonable miscalculation that directly contributed to the troubles they encountered during the years in question.

By the same token, the expansion of the newsprint industry in Ontario during the mid- to late 1920s was not a function of unsound business planning, as historians have almost universally concluded. Nearly all the province's mills that augmented their enterprises during these years did so only because the Ontario government – namely Ferguson – forced them to do so under penalty of losing their Crown leases. Moreover, Spanish River and Abitibi – the province's two largest producers – did not add any capacity to existing enterprises during the mid- to late 1920s. The only exception to this rule was Kimberly-Clark. And it only proceeded because the government had assured it more than enough resources under highly favourable terms and the company had a guaranteed market – namely the *New York Times* – for more than half its output.

The question remains whether the government's policy of administering Crown timber and water powers between 1894 and 1932 in a manner that was least responsive to the largest user of those resources, namely the province's pulp and paper industry, was a good thing for Ontarians. There was obviously little to be gained from having the state bow before the pulp and paper industry. The Ontario government had, by and large, taken this approach in dealing with the lumbermen, and what could be broadly defined as "the public interest" had suffered as a result. Had the provincial state stood up to the paper makers, granted a few of their requests, and incorporated their needs into a comprehensive policy of resource development in northern Ontario, then it could have been applauded for its performance. But it did not. Instead, it chose to deny most players within the industry, and indulge a select few. This was obviously not a case in which the state decided that, in principle, the things for which the pulp and paper makers were asking were unreasonable or unjustified. Time and time again, the government's actions reflected a desire to do what it believed was politically expedient, not an obligation to implement a rational policy.

That the provincial state was able to behave in this manner speaks to the fallacy in the argument that a government that controls Crown resources can subjugate itself permanently to the supplicants for those trees and water powers. A situation in which elected officials are entrusted with administering "public" resources through leases and licences is simply not conducive to the politicians becoming "clients of the businessmen." Through myriad laws and regulations that define how Crown assets are to be administered, the government retains the power to exercise virtually complete control over them; the rare and glaring exception is the instance in which the politicians decide to sell the resources "freehold," thereby renouncing complete ownership over them. The politicians undeniably bent over backwards to cater to the needs of the lumbermen and pulpwood exporters, and a couple of paper makers, between 1894 and 1932. For these privileged entrepreneurs it threw open the treasure chest of Crown resources, permitting them to exploit practically unfettered the province's trees and water powers at a price that represented but a fraction of what these resources were worth. But in doing so, the state did not remove its hands from the levers that controlled access to nature's bounty. Rather, it chose simply to manoeuvre these instruments to create opportunities for the chosen few to exploit. At the drop of a hat, however, the state could have arbitrarily decided to shift gears, and literally steamroll the resource user by enforcing to the letter of the law all the rules and regulations that governed the administration of Crown assets; it also could have enacted new statutes to legalize an outright expropriation.

Finally, this story also speaks volumes about the contemporary difficulties that pervade the forest industry in Ontario in particular and Canada in general. The historical foundation upon which the province's forest industry rests is, at best, very shaky, and this is clearest when one looks at its fibre allocations. Pulp and paper mills were established in Ontario outside the framework of a logical plan to exploit efficiently the province's timber and water powers. This meant that some mills were established practically within earshot of each other (the future city of Thunder Bay boasted four mills by the mid-1920s), and the politicians often allocated them insufficient supplies of pulpwood that were disadvantageously located. Likewise, many lumber producers survived not because of their ideal location but as a result of a favourable government policy that assisted them at the expense of the pulp and paper industry. The consequences of having set the latter upon such an unstable foundation are still being felt in our contemporary world. Mill closings have become commonplace in our province's hinterland, and one of the contributing factors often cited is the inordinately high cost of wood supplies.[22]

If this is the diagnosis, the chances – until very recently – that the government will take the steps necessary to restore the patient's health are slim, and there are several reasons for this. The assumption that executives from the large pulp and paper firms had merely to stroll into the minister or premier's office and ask for a timber limit in order to receive it is clearly unfounded. Yet the belief that the government has been – and in most cases continues to be – in bed with the large players in the forest industry has become so ingrained in our collective consciousness that it still informs much of the debate when we consider issues involving forest management. Moreover, most Ontarians live far removed from the Crown woodlands, and they have increasingly conceived of the forest as something to be "saved," not sawn, even if the latter is done sustainably. At the same time, the legacy of Crown ownership of natural resources dictates that political considerations and not logic will determine how Ontario's public woodlands are managed. Finally, despite the continued importance of the province's forest industry – it still ranks as our second most valuable exporter behind the automobile sector – the overwhelming majority of votes are cast in "the south," where there is little sympathy for assisting the paper makers and lumber producers. It will take political will to save the sinking ship that is Ontario's forest industry, a situation that does not augur well for its future.

By the same token, there is hope on the horizon that a seismic shift is about to occur in the relations between government and industry in the province's woodlands. The provincial state has seemingly recognized the error of its ways by committing to "modernizing" Ontario's forest tenure system. One of the major goals in this process is "reducing the role of centralized government in wood allocation and replacing the current system with an objective, impartial and de-centralized one." If this ends the influence of patronage in determining how the province's commercial forests are administered, Ontario's wood-using industries would benefit from this monumental breakthrough, one for which progressive minds have been calling for over one century.[23]

Notes

Introduction

1 Memo by T. Southworth, 10 December 1897, in *Preliminary Report*, Royal Commission on Forestry in Ontario, 1897–1898, 14–15.

2 A.R.M. Lower, *Great Britain's Woodyard: British America and the Timber Trade, 1763–1867* (McGill-Queen's University Press, 1973); G. Wynn, *Timber Colony: A Historical Geography of Early Nineteenth Century New Brunswick* (Toronto: University of Toronto Press, 1981); C. Whitton, *A Hundred Years a Fellin'* (Ottawa: Runge Press, 1943); J.W. Hughson and C.C.J. Bond, *Hurling Down the Pine* (Old Chelsea, Quebec: Historical Society of the Gatineau, 1965).

3 G. Carruthers, *Paper in the Making* (Toronto: Garden City Press Co-operative, 1947) is based largely on secondary sources and the author's personal recollections.

4 I. Radforth, *Bush Workers and Bosses: Logging in Northern Ontario, 1900–1980* (Toronto: University of Toronto Press, 1987), 5; M. Bliss, *Northern Enterprise: Five Centuries of Canadian Business* (Toronto: McClelland and Stewart, 1987), 604; B.E. Boothman, "High Finance/Low Strategy: Corporate Collapse in the Canadian Pulp and Paper Industry, 1919–1932," *Business History Review* 74 (Winter 2000): 614. G. Blais, "'Not a Paying Business': The Archival Legacy of the Canadian Forestry Service," *Journal of Forest History* (July 1988), also decries the paucity of forest history documents that have survived.

5 H.V. Nelles, *The Politics of Development: Forests, Mines and Hydro-Electric Power in Ontario, 1849–1941* (Hamden, CT: Archon Books, 1974), ix and 109.

6 P. Oliver, *G. Howard Ferguson: Ontario Tory* (Toronto: University of Toronto Press, 1977), 343. Oliver and Nelles disagree over whether Ferguson's approach to facilitating resource development was in the public interest.

7 I. Drummond, *Progress without Planning: The Economic History of Ontario from Confederation to the Second World War* (Toronto: University of Toronto Press, 1987), 16 and ch. 5: the citation is from 83; W.R. Wightman and N.M. Wightman, *The Land Between: Northwestern Ontario Resource Development, 1800 to the 1990s* (Toronto: University of Toronto Press, 1997); K. Norrie and D. Owram, *A History of the Canadian Economy* (Toronto: Harcourt Brace Jovanovich, 1991), 353–5; Bliss, *Northern Enterprise*, 324 and 400–1; M. Zaslow, *The Opening of the Canadian North, 1867–1914* (Toronto: McClelland and Stewart, 1971), 190.

8 R.S. Lambert and P. Pross, *Renewing Nature's Wealth: A Centennial History of the Public Management of Lands, Forests and Wildlife in Ontario, 1763–1967* (Toronto: Department of Lands and Forests, 1967); P.R. Gillis and T.R. Roach, *Lost Initiatives: Canada's Forest Industries, Forest Policy and Forest Conservation* (New York: Greenwood Press, 1986), ch. 4; B.W. Hodgins, J. Benedickson, and P. Gillis, "The Ontario and Quebec Experiments in Forest Reserves, 1883–1930," *Journal of Forest History* (January 1982); Hodgins and Benedickson, "Resource Management Conflict in the Temagami Forests, 1898 to 1914," *Canadian Historical Papers* (1978); P.A. Pross, "The Development of Professions in the Public Service: The Foresters in Ontario," *Canadian Public Administration* 10 (1967); idem, "The Development of a Forest Policy: A Study of the Ontario Department of Lands and Forests" (PhD thesis, University of Toronto, 1967).

9 J. Hiller, "The Politics of Newsprint: The Newfoundland Pulp and Paper Industry, 1915–1939," *Acadiensis* 19, no. 2 (Spring 1990): 38; idem, "The Origins of the Pulp and Paper Industry in Newfoundland," *Acadiensis* 11, no. 2 (Spring 1982); W.M. Parenteau, "Forests and Society in New Brunswick: The Political Economy of Forest Industries, 1918–1932" (PhD thesis, University of New Brunswick, 1994), 488; L.A. Sandberg, "Forest Policy in Nova Scotia: The Big Lease, Cape Breton Island, 1899–1960," *Acadiensis* 20, no. 2 (Spring 1991): 127; idem, ed., *Trouble in the Woods: Forest Policy and Social Conflict in Nova Scotia and New Brunswick* (Fredericton: Acadiensis Press, 1992); L.A. Sandberg and P. Clancy, *Against the Grain: Foresters and Politics in Nova Scotia* (Vancouver: UBC Press, 2000); R.A. Rajala, *Clearcutting the Pacific Rain Forest: Production, Science and Regulation* (Vancouver: UBC Press, 1998), 84; G. Hak, *Turning Trees into Dollars: The British Columbia Coastal Lumber Industry, 1858–1913* (Toronto: University of Toronto Press, 2000), 65; S. Gray, "The Government's Timber Business: Forest Policy and Administration in British Columbia, 1912–1928," *BC Studies* 81 (Spring 1989); M.L. McRoberts, "When Good Intentions Fail: A Case of Forest Policy in the BC Interior, 1945–56," *Journal of Forest History*

(July 1988); J.P. Charland, *Les pâtes et papiers au Québec, 1880–1980: Technologies, travails et travailleurs* (Quebec: L'Institut Québecois de Recherche sur la Culture, 1990), ch. 2; J. Kendle, *John Bracken: A Political Biography* (Toronto: University of Toronto Press, 1979), 54. B.L. Vigod, *Quebec before Duplessis: The Political Career of Louis-Alexandre Taschereau* (Montreal and Kingston: McGill-Queen's University Press, 1986), 186, disputes the contention that the Quebec premier was "a willing tool of private capital," but the author provides abundant evidence to undermine his case.

10 J.H. Thompson and A. Seager, *Canada, 1922–1939: Decades of Discord* (Toronto: McClelland and Stewart Limited, 1985), 79; R. Cook and C. Brown, *Canada, 1896–1921: A Nation Transformed* (Toronto: McClelland and Stewart, 1985), 86 and 88.

11 I am indebted to Dr Andrew Smith for encouraging me to see Canadian history from a more international perspective; Ha-Joon Chang, *Kicking Away the Ladder: Development Strategy in Historical Perspective* (London: Anthem, 2002); D. Rodrik, *The Globalization Paradox: Democracy and the Future of the World Economy* (New York: Norton, 2011).

12 R. Whitaker, *The Government Party: Organizing and Financing the Liberal Party of Canada, 1930–1958* (Toronto: University of Toronto Press, 1977); J. English, *The Decline of Politics: The Conservatives and the Party System, 1901–1920* (Toronto: University of Toronto Press, 1977); P. Oliver, *Public and Private Persons: The Ontario Political Culture, 1914–1934* (Toronto: Clarke, Irwin, 1975).

13 J. McCallum, *Unequal Beginnings: Agricultural and Economic Development in Quebec and Ontario until 1870* (Toronto: University of Toronto Press, 1980).

14 *The Globe*, 16 February 1900.

15 M.E. Porter and C. van der Linde, "Towards a New Conception of the Environment-Competitiveness Relationship," *Journal of Economic Perspectives* 9 no. 4 (Fall 1995); see also P.B. Evans, *Embedded Autonomy: States and Industrial Transformation* (Princeton, NJ: Princeton University Press, 1995).

16 D. Anastakis, *Autonomous State: The Struggle for a Canadian Car Industry from OPEC to Free Trade* (Toronto: University of Toronto Press, 2014).

Chapter 1

1 The description of Ontario's forests is a synthesis of information extracted from: K. Armson, *Ontario Forests: A Historical Perspective* (Toronto: Fitzhenry and Whiteside, 2001); R.C. Hosie, *Native Trees of Canada* (Ottawa: Canadian Forest Service, 1990); J.S. Rowe, *Forest Regions of Canada* (Ottawa:

Forestry Branch, 1959); *The Forest Resources of Ontario* (Toronto: Department of Lands and Forests, 1931).

2 D. McCalla, *Planting the Province: The Economic History of Upper Canada, 1784–1870* (Toronto: University of Toronto Press, 1993), ch. 4.

3 There is still no thorough study of Ontario's pine lumber industry: A.R.M. Lower, *The North American Assault on the Canadian Forest: A History of the Lumber Trade between Canada and the United States* (Toronto: Ryerson Press, 1938), section I; Radforth, ch. 2; J.R. Trinnell, *J.R. Booth: The Life and Times of an Ottawa Lumberking* (Ottawa: Treehouse Publishing, 1998); K. Armson and M. McLeod, *The Legacy of John Waldie and Sons: A History of the Victoria Harbour Lumber Company* (Toronto: Dundurn Press, 2007); J.P. Bertrand, "Timber Wolves," original manuscript, ca 1961, chs. 1–2; W. Lessie, "The Industrialists," Lake of the Woods Museum Archives (hereafter LOTWMA); Archives of Ontario (hereafter AO), RG1-335, Accession 15155, Box 10, Forest Management Plan by Austin Lumber (Dalton) Limited, 1959; ibid., RG1-549-0-2, "Sale of Burnt and Other Timber," 18 October 1895.

4 Nelles, chs. 1 and 2. In the late nineteenth century the provincial government implemented legislation reserving for the Crown all unalienated water powers in Ontario.

5 *Report of the Director of Forestry for the Province of Ontario, 1903,* 5; *Annual Report of the Clerk of Forestry for the Province of Ontario, 1899,* 6.

6 Ibid., *1897,* 3; ibid., *1899,* 6–7. The lumbermen were so appreciative of their freedom to abandon their licensed tracts once they had cleared them of pine timber that they successfully fended off a movement to begin outright sales of timberlands in the mid-1850s. Nelles, 14–15.

7 Lambert and Pross, 148, write that the province's lumbermen "never found it difficult to influence politicians or to bribe officials whenever loopholes in the regulations were not broad enough to allow them their own way"; *Hansard,* 19–20 April 1894; *Statutes of Ontario, 1894* (hereafter, *SO, year*), ch. 8, 57 Vict.

8 Angus, 229–30.

9 A typical example is found in AO, RG1-246-3, F769, 602/89, 7 May 1889, F. Halliday to A. White.

10 Nelles, 18–19, argues that the ruling party generally held timber sales on the eve of elections to generate proceeds that it could spend on improving its chances of returning to power. A comparison of the dates of elections and timber sales prior to 1905, however, reveals that the largest timber sales were held either soon after elections or in mid-term. The annual reports of the Ontario Department of Crown Lands for this period explain how timber sales were dictated largely by the advance of settlement.

11 *SO, 1868*, ch. 8, 31 Vic.; *Report of the Commissioner of Crown Lands of the Province of Ontario for the Year* (hereafter *Annual Report*) *1878*, vi; AO, RG1-246-3, F1346, 270/15, all documents; A. White, *Forest Resources of Ontario*, reprinted in *Annual Report, 1908*, 133; Hodgins, Benedickson, and Gillis. These measures allowed settlers and lumbermen to coexist much more peacefully in Ontario than in other provinces. For example, the New Brunswick government permitted homesteaders to carve their lots from lumbermen's timber licences, an arrangement that created intense conflicts: Parenteau, ch. 3.

12 Lambert and Pross, 132; AO, RG1-68, Box 3, File 1, 1911 Speech by A. White to Meeting of British Columbia Forest Interests.

13 Lower, *The North American Assault*, chs. 14 and 15; Lower, *Settlement and the Forest Frontier in Eastern Canada* (Toronto: Macmillan, 1936), ch. 4; Lambert and Pross, 84–5.

14 M.L. Branch, "The Paper Industry in the Lake States Region, 1834–1947" (PhD thesis, University of Wisconsin, 1947), 3–39.

15 AO, RG1-545-1-2, Woods and Forests Memos, vol. 2, October 1892, "Permits to Cut Pulpwood," A. White; *Annual Report, 1898*, x–xi; *Annual Report of the Clerk of Forestry, 1896*, passim and 64; *Royal Commission on Forestry in Ontario, Preliminary Report, December 10, 1897*, 14; K. Hearnden, "Black Spruce: The Cinderella Species and the Story of Canadian Forestry," in *Black Spruce Symposium*, G.L.F.R. Centre, Sault Ste Marie, Ontario, Proceedings, 1975.

16 Branch, 62; R.W. Hidy et al., *Timber and Men: The Weyerhaeuser Story* (New York: Macmillan, 1963), chs. 1–7; U.S., *Pulp and Paper Investigation Hearings*, 1908, passim.

17 J.A. Blyth, "The Development of the Paper Industry in Old Ontario, 1824–1867," *Ontario History* 62, no. 2 (June 1970). Details about the failing wood supply in Wisconsin specifically and the United States in general, and the premium prices paid for imported spruce, can be found in U.S., *Pulp and Paper Investigation Hearings, 1908*, 441, 1100–1200, 2120–36, 2157; L.E. Ellis, *Print Paper Pendulum: Group Pressures and the Price of Newsprint* (New Brunswick, NJ: Rutgers University Press, 1948), chs. 2 and 3; *Pulp and Paper Magazine of Canada* (hereafter *PPMC*), June 1903, 33; ibid., September 1903, 13; Branch, 62; Hidy et al., chs. 1–7.

18 In the mid-1920s, E.H. Finlayson, secretary of the Dominion government's Royal Commission on Pulpwood, reflected on how provincial governments had for years endeavoured to draw settlers to lands that were unfit for cultivation by ensuring that they could market the local pulpwood. *Report of the Royal Commission on Pulpwood* (Ottawa: Printer to the King's Most Excellent Majesty, 1924), 124.

19 AO, RG1-545-1-2, 15017/92, October 1892, A. White, "Permits to Cut Pulpwood,"; *Annual Report, 1902*, v; ibid., *1906*, vi; ibid., *1909*, vi; ibid., *1913*, vi; *Sessional Papers for the Province of Ontario* (hereafter *Ontario Sessional Papers*), *1896*, no. 74, 31 January 1895, H. Munro to A. White; *Report of the Survey and Exploration of Northern Ontario, 1900* (Toronto: Printer to the King's Most Excellent Majesty, 1901), xvii.
20 *PPMC*, 14 June 1917, 575.
21 AO, RG1-546-4-2, "P," all entries.
22 AO, MU3114, January 1900, 1 January 1900, J.S. McDonald to J.P. Whitney; ibid., March 1900, 29 March 1900, McDonald to Whitney; *Hansard*, 30 March and 27 April 1900; T.J. Tronrud and A.E. Epp, *Thunder Bay: From Rivalry to Unity* (Thunder Bay: Thunder Bay Museum Historical Society, 1996), 207; Wightman and Wightman, 134. An editorial in the 10 May 1902 edition of the *Toronto Globe* defended the export trade on the grounds that both Liberals and Conservatives were involved, as did a letter to the editor in the 17 May 1902 edition. As a result, when Nelles, 377, uses the term "the old Tory Timber Ring," he does so incorrectly; exporters of all political stripes received the government's wholehearted support.
23 *Sessional Papers, 1896*, no. 74, which includes some typical stories of exporters' illegal cutting activities during this period.
24 *SO, 1892*, 55 Vict., ch. 9; *Hansard*, 25 February and 6 March, 1897.
25 *Fourth Report of the Ontario Bureau of Mines, 1895*, 120.
26 As far as the debate over whether the rapid expansion of the Canadian – and particularly Ontario's – newsprint industry between 1900 and 1920 was due to the elimination of the American tariff over the course of 1911–13 is concerned, the evidence indicates that this change in trade policy was not the crucial factor. Among those sharing this view are: T.J.O. Dick, "Canadian Newsprint, 1913–1930: National Policies and the North American Economy," *Journal of Economic History* 42, no. 3 (September 1982); C.P. Fell, "The Newsprint Industry," in H.A. Innis and A.F.W. Plumptre, eds, *The Canadian Economy and the Great Depression* (Toronto: Canadian Institute of International Affairs, 1934); V.W. Bladen, *An Introduction to Political Economy* (Toronto: University of Toronto Press, 1958); J.A. Guthrie, *The Newsprint Industry: An Economic Analysis* (Cambridge, MA: Harvard University Press, 1941). Those who argue that this tariff adjustment was the primary cause of the Canadian expansion include: Nelles, *The Politics of Development*; N. Reich, *The Pulp and Paper Industry in Canada* (Montreal: McGill University Economic Studies – MacMillan Canada, 1926).

27 N.K. Ohanian, *The American Pulp and Paper Industry, 1900–1940: Mill Survival, Firm Structure, and Industry Relocation* (Westport, CT: Greenwood Press, 1993), 27–8; *PPMC*, 1903–13, passim; Carruthers, 633–5; U.S., *Pulp and Paper Investigation Hearings, 1908*, passim; Forestry Branch, *Forest Products of Canada* (Ottawa: Department of the Interior, 1909), 9.

28 Ontario Hydro Archives (hereafter OHA), OR410.1-143, Nipigon River – Cameron Pool, ca February 1901, Prospectus of the Nipigon Pulp, Paper & Mnfg. Company, Ltd., 6–7; AO, RG22-5800, 1931/2194, 8 February 1933, Affidavit of C. England; ibid., MU1590, Newsprint Statistics, 4 March 1931, Memorandum to Mr. Finlayson; United States – Department of Commerce, *Transportation Factors in the Marketing of Newsprint*, November 1952, 48–9.

29 The category "newsprint mills" will include those plants that were constructed with the intent of producing newsprint even though unforeseen circumstances prevented these plans from being realized. Two others mills constructed during this period – one in Dryden and another in Thorold – are not included in this study.

30 Although the relationship the Ontario government developed with the mining interests during this period is not the focus of this study, it followed the same general pattern. The mining firms were compelled to negotiate with the state for access to Crown resources, and although they were often interested in extracting vast quantities of ore, generally their activities required only small surface areas. They carried out nearly all their work in deep – not wide – open pit mines, or in a labyrinth of tunnels and shafts far underground. This usually limited their visible impact upon the public domain, and their activities barely interfered with the government's push to colonize the north. Consequently, the state granted nearly all their demands. It provided them with patents, not leases, to their claims and subsidies to encourage the processing of ores in the province, and it charged them only nominal fees to extract minerals: Nelles, *The Politics of Development*, 20–30, 87–108, 122–39, 158–81, 327–35, ch. 9, and 426–42.

31 *Report of the Royal Commission on Forestry Protection in Ontario, 1899*, 14–15.

32 A.D. Chandler, Jr, *The Visible Hand: The Managerial Revolution in American Business* (Cambridge, MA: Belknap Press of Harvard University Press, 1977); Rajala, ch. 2; L.A. Sandberg and P. Clancy, "Forestry in a Staples Economy: The Checkered Career of Otto Schierbeck, Chief Forester, Nova Scotia, Canada, 1926–1933," *Environmental History* 2, no. 1 (January 1997); idem, "From Weapons to Symbols of Privilege: Political Cartoons and the

Rise and Fall of the Pulpwood Embargo Debate in Nova Scotia, 1923–33,"
Acadiensis 26, no. 2 (Spring 1997); M. Kuhlberg, "'We are the pioneers in
this business': Spanish River's Forestry Initiatives after the Great War,"
Ontario History 93, no. 2 (Fall 2001).

33 AO, RG1-246-3, 5494, vol. 1, 28 October 1921, N. Hillary to B. Bowman.
34 *Ontario Sessional Papers, 1891*, no. 46; Hak, 109. The same was true when
Price Brothers, a pulp and paper firm in Quebec's Saguenay Valley, first attempted to use its timber licences as security for a bond issue it asked the
Bank of Montreal to back in the early 1900s. The bank refused to do so and
only relented when the Prices agreed to have the bonds underwritten:
Archives nationales du Québec à Chicoutimi (hereafter ANQC), M188,
Series 1, File – S-s 1, 2, 1, 22 December 1949, J. H. Price to A.C. Price, enclosing clipping from *PPMC*, June 1920.
35 One hundred tons of capacity required 120 cords of pulpwood per day
and 36,000 per year. Over a sixty-year crop rotation (the minimum period
needed for spruce to grow from seed to merchantable proportions), this
translated into 2,160,000 cords, a figure that did not allow for any losses
due to fire, insects, and disease.
36 Hak, 109fn50.
37 AO, RG1-246-3, 200A, vol. 1, 10 August 1918, L.L. Horton to G.H. Ferguson.
38 J.E. Hodgetts, *From Arm's Length to Hands-On: The Formative Years of
Ontario's Public Service, 1867–1940* (Toronto: University of Toronto Press,
1995), 22.
39 Ibid., chs. 1 and 7; Pross, "The Development of a Forest Policy"; idem,
"The Development of Professions."
40 Parenteau, passim, but especially Afterword; L.A. Sandberg and P. Clancy,
"Forestry in a Staples Economy"; idem, "From Weapons to Symbols of
Privilege," 35, and footnotes 12 and 35, the latter two references being the
sources from which the citations are taken.
41 AO, RG18-118, Royal Commission into the Affairs of Abitibi Power and
Paper Company, "Official Record of Proceedings," 1273–4.
42 *PPMC*, March 1905, 110; LOTWMA, D. McLeod, "Memorandum re:
Keewatin Lumber Company Limited, Kenora Paper Mills Limited and
Allied Companies and Their Operations at Kenora & Hudson, Ont. & St.
Boniface, Manitoba, 1906 to 1943," (hereafter D. McLeod,
"Memorandum"), 2.
43 *Annual Report, 1913*, vi.
44 Whitaker; English; Oliver, *Public and Private Persons*; Pross, "The
Development of a Forest Policy," and "The Development of Professions,"
concludes that, despite the large number of professional foresters hired by

the department during the first few decades of the twentieth century, they still had little voice in policymaking decisions.

45 Parenteau, 131, remarks that "in contrast to other provinces, where direct negotiations between the provincial government and companies led to immediate developments, the first mills that were built in New Brunswick had done so of their own volition." It will be seen that the same was true in Ontario.

46 Nelles, *The Politics of Development*, 396.

Chapter 2

1 AO, RG1-546-4-2, 9172/00.

2 The Ontario government also made helping the mining industry a higher priority than assisting the pulp and paper makers. Not only did the *Annual Reports of the Commissioner of Crown Lands* during the latter third of the nineteenth century continually crow that mining would be *the* resource-extracting activity in the north, but in the early 1890s the provincial state created both a Bureau of Mines to publicize the industry and Ontario's potential as a host site for it and a School of Mining at Queen's University. When Premier Hardy "predicted a great future" for northern Ontario in 1898, he stressed that it was "rich in mineral and agricultural resources" and said nothing about its potential to support the pulp and paper industry. *The Globe*, 24 February 1898.

3 *The Globe*, 24 October 1898 and 6 March 1900.

4 *Dictionary of Canadian Biography*, vol. 14 (Toronto: University of Toronto Press, 1998),1050–2.

5 Lambert and Pross, 188–9, 263, and 314.

6 AO, RG1-E-4-B, vol. 4, 42-43, 21 November 1894, Agreement between Crown and F.H. Clergue; Nelles, 82–4; D. McDowall, *Steel at the Sault: Francis H. Clergue, Sir James Dunn, and the Algoma Steel Corporation, 1901–1956* (Toronto: University of Toronto Press, 1984), ch. 2; M. Van Every, "Francis Hector Clergue and the Rise of Sault Ste Marie as an Industrial Centre," *Ontario History* 56, no. 3 (September 1964).

7 *Statutes of Canada, 1872*, Ch. XXIII 35 Vict. This "rule" was designed to invalidate property interests which "vested too remotely" and limited the duration of certain restrictions on the use and transfer of property to a perpetuity period of twenty-one years, a length of time that became the norm for pulpwood concession leases in Ontario. Knowing the genesis of this provision demonstrates it was not set, as many have argued, to satisfy institutional investors; the evidence presented here demonstrates

conclusively that financiers demanded terms closer to fifty years, or at least as long as the life of the bonds they were selling. I am indebted to Lisa Douglas, LL.B., for explaining the origins of this common law doctrine.

8   C.W. Humphries, 'Honest Enough to Be Bold': The Life and Times of Sir James Pliny Whitney (Toronto: University of Toronto Press, 1985), 90–1; Carruthers, ch. 36; AO, MU3115, January 1904, 12 January 1904, J.W. Cheeseworth to J.P. Whitney; Sault Ste. Marie Public Library Archives (hereafter SSMPLA), 996.9, Minute Book of the Sault Ste Marie Paper Company, 1896–1903.

9   Hansard, 22 March 1900.

10   Report of the Survey and Exploration of Northern Ontario, 1900 (Toronto: Printer to the King's Most Excellent Majesty, 1901), xvii; B.E. Fernow, An Analysis of Canada's Timber Wealth, reprinted in U.S., Pulp and Paper Investigation Hearings, 2845.

11   University of Toronto Archives (hereafter UTA), B72-0031, Box 15, File – 43, Address by Francis H. Clergue … February Fifteenth Nineteen Hundred and One, 17; Hansard, 29 March 1899; SO, 1900, 63 Vict., Ch. 30; AO, RG4-32, 1899/1913.

12   Van Every, 200–2.

13   Archives of Ontario Library (hereafter AOL), 21 September 1899, Agreement between Crown and the Spanish River Pulp and Paper Company; Carruthers, ch. 35.

14   OHA, OR410.1-143, Water Systems – Nipigon [ca February 1901], Prospectus of the Nepigon Pulp, Paper and Manufacturing Company, Ltd. (hereafter Prospectus); ibid., 16 February 1901, C. McCarthy to J. Whalen and Timber Report of H.B. Blackwood, 1901; AO, RG1-545-1-2, Woods and Forests Memos, vol. 2, File – 7501/95; ibid., RG75-57, OC47/200; AOL, 18 April 1900, Agreement between the Crown and Nepigon Pulp, Paper and Manufacturing Company, Ltd; Annual Report, 1901, vi; ibid., 1902, xii; ibid., 1903, vi; Carruthers, 443; PPMC, January and July 1904, 28; SO, 1902, 2 Edw. VII, Ch. 85.

15   Lake of the Woods Historical Society, Mather House, "John Mather Diary Summary, 1882–1906" (hereafter LOTWHS, Mather Diary Summary), passim; idem, "An Historical Research Inventory of the Mather-Walls Property with a General Overview of Keewatin Developmental History," Reg Reeve, 1979, entries from 1893 to 1896; the following paragraphs are based on the same sources.

16   LOTWHS, Mather Diary Summary, 1903; AOL, April 4, 1901, Agreement between Crown and the Keewatin; AO, RG4-32, File 3807/1921, undated Re: Backus Agreement and Kenora Development; ibid., RG1-E-6, vol. 3,

186–91, 18 January 1906, F. Cochrane Memo Re: Cancelling; *Annual Report, 1902,* xiii.

17 AOL, October 6, 1898, Agreement between Crown and the Sturgeon Falls Pulp Company; AO, RG4-32, 1899/1909, 27 February 1899, Temagami Railway Company to A.S. Hardy; *Toronto Globe,* 20 April 1897 and 7 October 1898; Carruthers, ch. 35.

18 Ibid.; *The Globe,* 27 November 1902; AOL, 15 December 1901, Agreement between the Crown and Sturgeon Falls Pulp Company.

19 Carruthers, ch. 35; *PPMC,* October 1903, 187–9; ibid., 1904, 188.

20 Carruthers, ch. 35 and 669–70; B.W. Hodgins and J. Benedickson, *The Temagami Experience: Recreation, Resources and Aboriginal Rights in the Northern Ontario Wilderness* (Toronto: University of Toronto Press, 1989), ch. 4; *The Globe,* 25 January 1900.

21 M. Kuhlberg, "E.W. Backus," *Dictionary of Canadian Biography,* vol. 16 (Toronto: University of Toronto Press, forthcoming).

22 Hagley Library and Archives, Peabody, Houghteling & Co., *Map showing the location of the Minnesota & Ontario Power Company's mills and their relation to the newspaper industry of the United States,* 1908.

23 Although Backus's detractors at the time and historians since have portrayed him as a sweet-talking "master" in the art of charming governments, the facts do not support this interpretation. Nelles, *The Politics of Development,* 392, for instance, writes that Backus's "generous support of the Conservative party was well known" even though the Tories treated him as their nemesis.

24 AO, MU1353, File – 1934 Jan. 1st – Jan. 22nd, *Save Your Investment;* ibid., RG75-57, OC49/170, OC 50/132 and OC50/454.

25 Ibid., RG75-57, OC50/545, in which is enclosed 13 January 1905, Recommendation-to-Council by A.G. MacKay.

26 Well-known American and Canadian lumbermen also made up the consortiums to which the Liberals granted the Abitibi River and Montreal River pulpwood concessions.

27 *The Globe,* 17 March 1902.

28 *Annual Report, 1903,* v; *Report of the Survey and Exploration of Northern Ontario, 1900* (Toronto: Printer to the King's Most Excellent Majesty, 1901).

29 *The Globe,* 21 March and 13 May 1902; *Hansard,* 11 April 1900 and 4 February 1904.

30 *Annual Report, 1903,* vii; *PPMC,* May 1903, 22; *Hansard,* 21 April 1900; *Annual Reports, 1900–1903; The Globe,* 8 April 1903.

31 *PPMC,* January 1905, 27.

32 This section on exporting pulpwood under the Liberals is based on M. Kuhlberg, "'Pulpwood Is the Only Thing We Do Export': The Myth of Provincial Protectionism in Ontario's Pulp and Paper Industry, 1890–1932," in D. Anastakis and A. Smith, eds, *Smart Globalization: The Canadian Business and Economic History Experience* (Toronto: University of Toronto Press, 2014).

33 *The Globe*, 24 March 1900.

34 *SO, 1900*, 63 Vict., Ch. 11; *The Globe*, 19 May 1902. A very different situation prevailed in Quebec, where exporters owned large Crown licences. This caused them to lobby vociferously (and successfully) against the enactment of the manufacturing condition in 1900. No such campaign was needed or initiated by Ontario's exporters: *PPMC*, 1903–1910, passim. Nelles, *The Politics of Development*, ch. 2, argues that the enactment of the manufacturing condition on pulpwood in Ontario attested to the successful lobby by domestic pulp and paper producers. This view grossly overestimates the paper makers' strength and ignores the central role played by the export of pulpwood in the government's colonization program.

35 *The Globe*, 20 April 1897.

36 *Hansard*, 27 April 1900.

37 *RSO, 1877*, 38 Vict., Ch. 28.

38 *SO, 1896*, 57 Vict., Ch. 8. In addition to those mentioned in the text, other pulpwood concessionaires also undertook to construct railways in an effort to access their pulpwood and acquire freehold timber: *SO, 1902*, 2 Edw. VII, Ch. 69; ibid., *1903*, 3 Edw. VII, Ch. 5; ibid., 2 Edw. VII, Ch. 80; AO, RG1-246-3, 42245, March 9, 1922, M. J. Paterson and E. H. Adams to Minister; ibid., May 22, 1922, Paterson to B. Bowman.

39 *Annual Report of the Director of Forestry for the Province of Ontario, 1900–1901*, 15; *RSO, 1877*, 40 Vict., Ch. 31; *SO, 1868*, 31 Vic. Ch. 8.

40 *SO, 1898*, 61 Vict., Ch. 8; *SO, 1900*, 63 Vict., Ch. 30.

41 The tale of the Montreal River pulpwood limit is instructive. Like the Blanche River concession, it was located in northeastern Ontario and depended upon the granting of a water power lease on the Ottawa River. In 1902, the Liberals had leased this concession to the Montreal River Pulp and Paper Company (Montreal Company), a consortium of five businessmen, three of whom were lumbermen and one of whom had significant experience in the pulp and paper industry. They were to build their 150-ton mill on either the Montreal or Ottawa Rivers and deposited $20,000 to attest to their commitment to the undertaking. They were associated with the backers of the Sault Ste Marie project and suffered from Clergue's financial crisis in 1903 as well as the tight money market of the time. Like

the Blanche River venture, this effort was also delayed by protracted negotiations with the Dominion and Quebec governments regarding the selec-
tion of a power site on the Ottawa River. By the time of the 1905 election,
there was still no mill: AOL, March 3, 1902, Agreement between the
Crown and the Montreal River; AO, RG1-E-6, vol. 3, 59–60, 30 November
1903 Agreement; ibid., 191–2, 7 February 1906, Memo from A.G. Mackay;
ibid., RG75-57, OC47/200, OC50/342, OC47/483 and OC52/90.
42 Gillis and Roach, 94–5; Nelles, *The Politics of Development*, 116.
43 AOL, May 25, 1901, Agreement between the Crown and Blanche River
Pulp and Paper Company.
44 *The Globe*, 16 May 1902.

Introduction to Section II

1 Oliver, *Public and Private Persons*, chs. 2 and 3; Oliver, *G. Howard Ferguson*,
14–30; S. Young and A. Young, *Silent Frank Cochrane: The North's First Great
Politician* (Toronto: MacMillan Canada, 1973), chs. 1–3.
2 *Hansard*, 30 March 1900; ibid., 11 April 1900; ibid., 19 May 1893; AO,
MU3114, File – March 1900, 29 March 1900, Notes re … Spanish River
Agreement; ibid., File – April 1900, letters to J.P. Whitney re … Spanish River
deal; ibid., File – 1–15 March 1901, 8 March 1901, H. Lennox to Whitney.
3 AO, RG3-2, Pulpwood Stumpage, 3 February 1906, Memo for the Minister
from J.F. Clark; ibid., MU1311, Envelope 16, B.E. Fernow, *Forest Resources
and Problems of Canada*, reprinted from Proceedings of the Society of
American Foresters, vol. 7, no. 2, November 1912; ibid., MU3116, 28–31
March 1905, 31 March 1905, T. Southworth to J.J. Foy; ibid., MU3118,
February 1906, 16 February 1906, Clark to J.P. Whitney.
4 Ibid., RG3-2, Rainy Lake Pulp and Paper Company, 3 January 1906,
Statement prepared on application. Montreal River Pulp and Paper
Company had also applied for an extension: ibid., RG1-E-6, vol. 3, 191–2, 7
February 1906, Memo re: Montreal River Pulp.
5 Ibid., RG75-57, OC55/192, enclosed in which is 7 February 1906,
Recommendation to Council by F. Cochrane. The cancelled leases were for
the Rainy Lake, Lake of the Woods, Wabigoon Lake and River, Lake
Nipigon, and Montreal River pulpwood concessions.
6 When the disgruntled concessionaires whose agreements the Tories had
cancelled threatened the government with legal action, the government returned the security deposits these parties had lodged with it: ibid., RG75-
57, OC59/394, OC62/401, and OC63/9; ibid., RG1-246-3, 5520, vol. 1, 6
June 1916, Memo Regarding application by T.A. Gordon … by F.J. Niven.

7 Ibid., RG1-E-6, vol. 3, 186–91; ibid., RG75-57, OC55/192, enclosed in which is 7 February 1906, Recommendation to Council by F. Cochrane.

8 Lower, *Settlement*, 126.

9 AO, RG1-246-3, 3732, vol. 1, 11 July 1919, F.J. Niven to E.E. Knott. The Conservatives also refused to allow industry officials to accompany government cruisers on the few occasions when they investigated limits: ibid., RG18-79, vol. 2, 1643; ibid., RG1-246-3, 1424, vol. 1, 7 June 1917, Memo for the Minister from H.M.R..

10 Ibid., RG75-57, OC55/192, enclosed in which is 7 February 1906, Recommendation to Council by F. Cochrane. Lambert and Pross, 258–60, argue that the retendering of these limits was unsuccessful largely because of a poor market and continued American tariffs on newsprint. This interpretation ignores Cochrane's rejection of bids for two of the limits and the impact the government's inexplicable eight-inch-diameter limit had on the sale of these concessions.

11 AO, RG1-246-3, 5509, vol. 1, 6 January 1925, E.J. Zavitz to W.C. Cain; ibid., May 22, 1917, F.J. Niven to J.A. Oliver.

12 Ibid., RG1-E-4-B, licences between 1890 and 1910; ibid., RG1-411, all subseries, all Timber and Lands Reports; UTA, A72-0025, Box 146, unlabelled, 26 December 1912, B.E. Fernow to R.D. MacKay; Library and Archives Canada (LAC), RG10, vol. 7798, 30001, Timber Resources of Indian Reserves in the Province of Ontario, 1923; OHA, OR410.1-143, Water Systems Nipigon, 16 February 1901, C. McCarthy to J. Whalen; U.S., *Pulp and Paper Investigation Hearings, 1908*, 2369.

13 AO, RG75-57, OC71/571; ibid., RG1-246-3, 1424, vol. 1A, 14 December 1916, Memo re: Application of D.L. Mather; ibid., 10 October 1918, W.B. Raymond to A. Grigg; ibid., 6306, vol. 1, documents between May and October, 1919.

14 AO, RG18-79, Timber Commission Hearings, 9418.

15 Ibid., MU1310, Envelope 10, ca 1908, *Mistakes of the Whitney Government*. It is highly unlikely that Cochrane followed this policy because he wanted to reserve power sites for Ontario Hydro. He was renowned for his vehement opposition to Beck's public power movement and certainly would not have taken steps to assist it. Hydro was also initially established to protect the interests of municipalities in relatively heavily populated southern Ontario by *transmitting* and *distributing* electricity. Not only did Hydro's mandate at this point preclude *generating* its own power, it was not intended for Beck's utility to develop electricity for remote, one-industry towns in northern Ontario. Finally, the Tories went to great lengths to privately grant water powers to mining interests at this time under excessively generous terms. The Canadian Copper Company, which mined

nickel in the Sudbury basin, initially had a *lease* to develop High Falls on the Spanish River. In 1908, the Tories granted the company a *deed* to this power site even though they acknowledged that this contravened the government's expressed policy: ibid., RG75-57, OC61/279.

16 The tender produced only two agreements, one for the Montreal River concession and another for the Wabigoon-Dryden limit. As far as the former is concerned, the terms of sale required the successful bidder to construct a *new* 150-ton mill. The Tories executed a lease for the limit with J.R. Booth in 1907 which only required him to operate his *existing* pulp and paper mills well below their capacities, however. It appears Booth did not even need this limit (he extracted very little timber from it over the next two decades), and he had secured it simply to prevent a competitor from establishing a rival mill within his bailiwick: ibid., RG1-415, 1, Booth, 12 January 1907, Agreement between the Crown and J.R. Booth; ibid., RG1-F-I-5, vol. 2; ibid., RG75-57, OC70/52. The Tories executed an agreement in 1906 for the Wabigoon-Dryden limit with Robert McLauchlin that obliged him to build a mill within three years, but it was not until seven years later that another party constructed it. In the interim the Tories never threatened to cancel the lease despite this breach.

17 Nelles, *The Politics of Development*, 389–90; Lambert and Pross, 261.

18 *PPMC*, January 1906, 4–5; ibid., October 1907, 225, reveals that one year later Whitney announced that he would not be tendering pulpwood concessions again for some time. Except for boasting about the province's pulp and paper industry at election time, the Tories said little about its activities. During the Liberals' tenure prior to 1905, the department's *Annual Reports* had provided yearly updates on the development of Ontario's mills, whereas the Conservatives' reports barely mentioned them.

19 Nelles, *The Politics of Development*, ch. 10, blames the lack of new mill construction in Ontario during the Tories' term in office on extra-provincial factors, such as the tight financial markets caused by the First World War. This explanation ignores the dozens of applications the Conservatives received – and rejected – from genuine pulp and paper makers during the 1910s, particularly during the war, asking them to sell pulpwood to support new mills: AO, RG1-246-3, 3732, vol. 1, is replete with such applications. The department's *Annual Report, 1916*, xii, even boasted about the "constant inquiries being made with respect to pulp bearing lands in the Province of Ontario."

20 The Tories leased pulpwood concessions to the mills that were built in Iroquois Falls (in 1913–14), Smooth Rock Falls (1916), and Dryden (1916), but they refused to accord the same privilege to the plants that were constructed in Thorold (1912), Fort Frances (1914), and Port Arthur (1917).

Chapter 3

1 AO, RG75-57, OC59/311, enclosed in which is 11 October 1907, Memo for the Minister from A. White.

2 Ibid., RG1-246-3, 96480, vol. 1, 9 January 1925, W.C. Cain to J.A. Alexander: when the limit was finally operated for its pulpwood in the mid-1920s, the government agreed that enforcing the nine-inch-diameter limit would render "very little spruce wood on the limit" available for cutting.

3 *Annual Report, 1911*, viii; Thunder Bay Historical Museum Society (hereafter TBHMS), A4/1/1, 6 July 1907, J.T. Horne to A. White; ibid., 27 July, 17 August and 20 November 1907, and 7 January and 8 July 1908, and 3 July 1909, Horne to F. Cochrane; ibid., 13 January 1908, Horne to A.R. Mann; AO, RG1-E-4-B, Burnt Timber Books, vol. 2, 132–3; ibid., RG75-57, OC59/311, enclosed in which is 11 October 1907, Recommendation to Council by F. Cochrane; ibid., OC60/277 and OC61/325: the existence of the guarantee remained secret because it was included in the Recommendation to Council, not the Order in Council that was published in the *Ontario Gazette*.

4 TBHMS, A4/1/1, 25 January, 1909, J.T. Horne to W.W. Sloan; ibid., 1 December 1909, Horne to R.C. Donald; *PPMC*, October 1909, 275; AO, RG1-246-3, 96480, vol. 1, 25 June 1918, Memo for the Minister from F.J. Niven, reveals that Backus obtained permission from the concessionaires just before the First World War to cut the limit's pulpwood. Even though the tract had been partially burned, the department refused to allow him to harvest it.

5 *PPMC*, November 1909, 298.

6 Ibid., May 1911, 213; AOL, General Conditions with Respect to Fort Frances … 10th April, 1911.

7 AO, RG1-E-3-B, 3, A-16, O & M Pulp and Paper Company, Limited, "Early History"; ibid., RG1-246-3, 9476, vol. 1, 11 October 1916, Department to CTA at Fort Frances. Wightman and Wightman, 132–3, confuse the *tendering* of a pulpwood limit with the *execution* of a pulpwood concession lease when they assert that Backus secured the Rainy Lake pulpwood limit at this time.

8 LOTWMA, D. McLeod, "Memorandum," 12–14; AO, RG1-415, 1, K, 19 August 1914, Agreement between Crown and E. W. Backus.

9 Ibid., RG4-32, 1921/3807, History of English River Pulp Limit; ibid., 22 May 1919, D. McLeod to G.H. Ferguson.

10 C. Armstrong, *The Politics of Federalism: Ontario's Relations with the Federal Government, 1867–1942* (Toronto: University of Toronto Press, 1981), 162–3;

AO, RG3-4, Lake of the Woods – Control #1, all documents; ibid., English River Pulp and Timber Limits 1922, all documents; ibid., RG4-32, 1921/3807, ca 1920 History of the English River Pulp Limit; Wisconsin Historical Society – Madison Archives (hereafter WHSMA), MSS279, 2, Minnesota and Ontario Power Company 1913–19, 25 January 1917, E.W. Backus to D.C. Everest.

11 AO, RG3-4, English River Pulp and Timber Limits 1922, 28 and 29 September 1920, F.H. Anson to E.C. Drury and enclosures; ibid., RG4-32, 1921/3807, vol. 3, 15 December 1922, Memo for the Attorney-General re: English River Limits.

12 Chapter 4 explains that on 7 May 1917, the Tories had insisted that the Kapuskasing River concession be cruised before it was sold. In neither case did the government carry out the cruise.

13 AO, RG1-246-3, 14797, vol. 1, 3 May 1917, F.H. Anson and A. Smith to G.H. Ferguson; ibid., 9 and 16 May 1917, Memo for A. Grigg from C.C. Hele; ibid., RG4-32, 1921/3807, vol. 3, 15 December 1922, Memo for the Attorney-General re: English River Limits.

14 Ibid., RG1-BB1, 8, J.A. Mathieu, 29 July 1965, transcript of interview with J.A. Mathieu, by L. Waisberg and V. Nelles.

15 Contemporary observers commented on the Tories' disparate treatment of Backus and Mathieu: AO, RG3-10, 227, Lands and Forests 1934, 4 September 1934, E.J. Callaghan to M.F. Hepburn. Mathieu's machinations are described in J.P. Bertrand, "Timber Wolves", original manuscript, ca 1961, 274; Nelles, *The Politics of Development*, 386; AO, MU3132, November 1911, 22 November 1911, W.A. Preston to J.P. Whitney; *Interim Report of the Timber Commission – Shevlin-Clarke Company of Fort Frances*, 30 October 1920, 6–7; G. Killan, *Protected Places: A History of Ontario's Provincial Park System* (Toronto: Queen's Printer / Dundurn Press: Ministry of Natural Resources, 1993), 42–3.

16 "John Lorn McDougall," *Dictionary of Canadian Biography*, vol. 13 (Toronto: University of Toronto Press, 1994); S. Sinclair, *"Cordial but not cozy": A History of the Office of the Auditor-General* (Toronto: McClelland and Stewart, 1980), 18–29.

17 UTA, A73-0026, 264, 67 – Alexander McDougall.

18 *Tracks beside the Water: Sioux Lookout* (Sioux Lookout: Sioux Lookout and District Historical Society, 1982), 161.

19 AO, RG1-517-0-2, 267; ibid, RG1-517-0-3, 2.

20 Ibid., RG1-246-3, 9582, vol. 1, documents from November and December 1916; ibid., 9 December 1914, Agreement between Crown and A. McDougall; ibid., 5 April 1922, Memo for W.C. Cain re Allanwater from

J.H.H. The McDougalls also probably influenced the drastic redrawing of the concession's boundaries between the time it was tendered and awarded to them: AO, RG1-E-4-B, vol. 3, 164–5.

21 Abitibi-Bowater – Fort William Archives (hereafter FWA), 1 September 1915, Agreement between the GTPR and G.E. Farlinger and S. McDougall.

22 AO, RG1-246-3, 9582, vol. 1, documents from 20 November 1916 to 8 April 1918 dealing with S. McDougall's application: the citation is from 20 January 1917, W. Magrach to A. Grigg.

23 Ibid., vol. 1, passim, particularly 11 October 1918, F.J. Niven to Twin Allan Lumber Company; ibid., RG1-135-3-4, 16 December 1913, J.L. Legris to W. Margach.

24 *In Quiet Ways: George H. Mead, The Man and the Company* (Dayton, OH: Mead Corporation, 1970), 3–55.

25 St Marys Paper Ltd Archives (hereafter SMPA), 14 October 1913, T. Gibson to Shareholders; ibid., *A Decade of Progress* (Sault Ste Marie, ON: Spanish River Pulp and Paper Mills, Limited, 1926) (hereafter *A Decade of Progress*), 8–14; Carruthers, ch. 35.

26 *PPMC*, 1 March 1913, 160.

27 SMPA, 1 March 1911, *Agreement between ACHBR and Lake Superior Paper Company*.

28 AO, RG1-305, *Forest Management Plan for Abitibi Power and Paper Company Limited, 1929*, Sault Ste Marie Division, copy of 17 May 1911, H.E. Talbott to F. Cochrane; ibid., 9 June 1911, F. Cochrane to Lake Superior Paper; SMPA, B-2, 1911–12, 6 October 1911, A. White to J. Maughan.

29 SMPA, *A Decade of Progress*, 8; ibid., Mill Room, Miscellaneous #2, Power Contracts 1911–18, 3 August 1911, G.F. Hardy to H.E. Talbott; *PPMC*, January 1912, 25, and 1913, passim.

30 Because of the great distance and the limited driving season, it took the mill several years to deliver pulpwood by water from its Crown concession to the Soo, and large quantities of wood were also lost en route. Hot logging entailed cutting and shipping the spruce by rail as it was needed, which translated into huge reductions in insurance and storage costs, and prevented the loss of any wood in transit.

31 Alexander House (hereafter AH), Northern Paper Company documents, 1897–1909; AO, RG1-246-3, 59454, Vols 1 and 2, all documents; ibid., 1173, vol. 1, all documents; ibid., RG1-335, ACR, 7 November 1969, L.C. Waugh to A. Herridge; SMPA, A-3, ACR Cut by Townships, 1911–28; TBHMS, A83/2/4, ca June 1930, McComber's notes.

32 AO, RG1-246-3, 12665, vol. 1, 6 June 1916, L.R. Wilson to G.H. Ferguson.

33 The first citation is from ibid., RG18-79, *Final Report of the Timber Commission, 1922*, 61, and the second from ibid., RG1-246-3, 12665, vol. 1,

30 November 1916, L.R. Wilson to G.H. Ferguson; ibid., 8161, vol. 1, 21 July and 17 August 1916, A. Grigg to J.A. Oliver; ibid., 2 and 16 August 1916, Oliver to Grigg; ibid., 28 August 1916, General Conditions with respect to the Pic River.

34 Ibid., 12665, vol. 1, 12 December 1916, Memo for the Minister re. Pic Pulp Concession from A. Grigg; ibid., 29 November 1919, Memo for the Prime Minister from A. Grigg.

35 AO, RG75-57, OC81/31, enclosed in which is 4 January 1917, Memo for the Minister from A. Grigg. It is improbable that Grigg authored this document, as he was an ardent defender of Spanish River's interests and had, apart from this memo, always argued to increase its timber supply.

36 The government also granted Spanish River a privilege for which it had not applied. The Tories now insisted that the company "assume the responsibility" for harvesting balsam fir from its concession and pay dues on this wood. Not only was this species the bane of cutters because of its gummy sap, but when its logs were fresh they were significantly heavier than spruce and sank at a much greater rate when river-driven. As a result, timber cruisers had habitually disregarded balsam in their estimates if a long drive was necessary to deliver the wood to the mill, as was the case with the mill in the Soo. This meant that Spanish River would be forced to harvest this timber and pay for it even though most of it would be lost before reaching its paper plant: SMPA, 1 December 1926, *General Report on 40 Townships, Spanish Concession*, A.J. Auden, 2.

37 AO, RG1-246-3, 12665, vol. 1, 5 February 1917, L.R. Wilson to A. Grigg; *Annual Report, 1916*, xii; AO, RG18-79, 6, vol. XXII, 9395–9400. Wightman and Wightman, 130–1, incorrectly claim that Spanish River simply dictated its wish list to a most compliant government during this affair.

38 AO, RG18-79, *Timber Commission Hearings*, 8419; ibid., RG1-246-3, 9476, vol. 1, 9 and 30 March 1918, G.R. Gray to G.H. Ferguson; ibid., 27 March 1918, Gray to A. Grigg; ibid., 31 October 1916, P.W. Wilson to The Minister; ibid., correspondence between Spanish River and the government, 1917.

39 Ibid., July 1918 correspondence between G.R. Gray and A. Grigg; ibid., 16 October 1918, C. Henderson and J.T. McDougall to Grigg.

40 Hodgins and Benidickson, *The Temagami Experience*, 157.

41 AO, RG1-246-3, 9476, vol. 1, 22 October 1918, Memo for the Minister from A. Grigg.

42 Hodgins and Benedickson, *The Temagami Experience*, 127; ibid., 129–30, reviews another similar episode; AO, RG75-57, OC65/307 and OC70/478; *Ontario Sessionals, 1913*, No. 57.

43 AO, RG1-246-3, 9093, vol. 1, correspondence between 1911 and 1920; ibid., 3785, vol. 1, 23 February 1917, Memo for the Minister from C.C. Hele;

ibid., 18 February 1920, Memo for the Minister from L.H.; ibid., RG1-273-3, 7, 30, ca 1911, Preliminary Report on Water Regulation of the Sturgeon River, W.F.V. Atkinson; SMPA, B-2, unlabelled, 24 July 1934, manufacturing cost data.

44 Ibid., A-2, 6-5 Surveys, 5 December 1917, R.O. Sweezey to G. Mead; AO, RG18-79, *Final Report of the Timber Commission, 1922*, 63–5. It is difficult to reconstruct the Espanola mill's dealings with the government during this period because the department's file dealing with this issue was either destroyed or removed by Ferguson's associates after the Tories' defeat in 1919.

45 SMPA, A-1, Historical, 19 September 1919, G.R. Gray to G.H. Ferguson.

46 AO, RG4-32, 1921/3807, 25 September 1919, G.H. Ferguson to G.R. Gray. Nelles, *The Politics of Development*, ch. 10, makes Ferguson's decision to reserve this tract for Spanish River a cornerstone in his argument that the Tories – specifically Ferguson – were willing to do anything to assist the newsprint companies. Nelles specifically contends that Ferguson flagrantly disregarded the department's requirement to tender timber by privately granting Spanish River this reserve, and that the act of the minister conveying this pulpwood concession to the mill in Espanola was the critical element in the mill's ability to arrange financing for its expansion. This interpretation ignores several crucial facts. The minister had not granted the pulpwood concession to the company; he had simply agreed to reserve it for the firm's future use. Second, it will become clear that Spanish River secured its financing in 1919 on the strength not of Ferguson's actions but rather of Mead's.

47 These are listed in ibid., RG3-7, 1920 Timber Investigation Memoranda.

48 SMPA, Historical Documents, 3 July 1919, A. Smith to G.H. Mead; AO, RG4-32, 1920/674, 2, 21 February 1921, Statement by S. Denison.

49 United States – Federal Trade Commission, *The Final Report of the Commission Relative to the News-Print Paper Industry in the United States* (Washington: Government Printing Office, 1917), 34.

Chapter 4

1 *Annual Report, 1910*, vi; ibid., *1913*, vi; AO, RG6-I-2, 18, DLF, 1914–1932, 25 February 1919, Memo for the Minister from Acting Deputy Minister; ibid., MU1311, ca 1914, *Northern Ontario – Its Progress*, 1; D.E. Pugh, "Ontario Great Clay Belt Hoax," *Canadian Geographical Journal*, January 1975; T.R. Roach, "The Pulpwood Trade and the Settlers of New Ontario," *Journal of Canadian Studies* 22, no. 3 (Fall 1987).

2 The Dominion government enacted the manufacturing condition on Crown pulpwood in 1907, Quebec in 1910, New Brunswick in 1911, and British Columbia in 1913.

3 AO, MU3130, August 1910, 8 August 1910, W. Van Horne to J.P. Whitney; ibid., 10 August 1910, Whitney to Van Horne.

4 Ontario Ministry of Consumer and Corporate Affairs (hereafter MCCR), TC44895, 9 September 1914, Company Prospectus and Return for 1914.

5 This subject is discussed in detail in M. Kuhlberg, "'Pulpwood Is the Only Thing We Do Export.'"

6 OHA, 91.029, OR410.1-143 [Nipigon General], 29 February 1916, C.T. Young to J.A. McAndrew, enclosing "General Preliminary Report ... on Timber Tributary to Nipigon and on the Nipigon Power"; AO, RG3-2, Pulpwood Stumpage, 3 February 1906, Memo for the Minister from J.F. Clark.

7 In fact, the regulations were so strict for this particular forest reserve that they prevented the Hudson's Bay Company's post – Nipigon House on the west side of the lake – from procuring the firewood it needed. I am indebted to Ms Betty Brill, curator of the Nipigon Museum, for this interesting detail.

8 AO, RG1-E-6, 3, 20979/05; *Annual Report, 1913*, xii; B.W. Hodgins, J. Benedickson, and P. Gillis, "The Ontario and Quebec Experiments in Forest Reserves, 1883–1930," *Journal of Forest History*, January 1982, does not explain the Tories' peculiar move to create the Nepigon reserve.

9 Ibid., RG75-57, OC64/532, enclosed in which is 7 July 1910, Recommendation to Council by F. Cochrane; TBHMS, A4/1/1/, 4 January 1908, J.T. Horne to D.G. Stewart.

10 AO, RG18-79, *Timber Commission Hearings*, 5340–51; ibid., RG75-57, OC59/311 and OC64/532; ibid., RG1-E-6, vol. 3, 354–5; ibid., RG1-246-3, 12225, passim, reveals that even the lease the government had given Marks in 1911 was problematic; J. Niosi, "La Laurentide (1887–1928): Pionnière du Papier Journal au Canada," *Revue d'histoire de l'Amerique française* 29, no. 3 (décembre 1975).

11 AO, RG18-79, *Timber Commission Hearings*, 5340–51. It appears that Hearst and Ferguson, who harboured little love for Hydro and its chairman, sought to prevent the Nipigon water powers from falling into Beck's hands by tying them to a mill venture without his knowledge: *Sessionals, 1920*, no. 72.

12 AO, RG1-246-3, 9457, vol. 1, 29 September 1916, A. Fasken to The Minister; ibid., 15 September 1916, A.G. McIntyre to G.H. Ferguson; ibid., 15 September 1916, I.H. Weldon to Ferguson.

13 OHA, 992.132, *Information re Port Arthur and Fort William*, copy of 22 January 1920, Memo to the Minister from A. Grigg; AO, RG1-246-3, 9457, vol. 1, November 1916 to January 1917, inquiries about the tender.

14 Ibid., 14 October 1916, L.E. Bliss to A. Grigg; ibid., 18 October 1916, Grigg to L.E. Bliss, from which the citation is taken; ibid., 6 February 1917, Memo for the Minister re: Black Sturgeon Pulp and Timber Limit from Deputy Minister.

15 Ibid., 22 February 1917, S.A. Marks to A. Grigg.

16 A senior departmental official admitted that Marks's lease called for the government to notify him ten days prior to cancelling his contract, but "the papers show this notice was not given": ibid., 12225, 28 November 1918, Memo for the Prime Minister from Deputy Minister of Mines; ibid., 9457, vol. 1, 9 May 1917, Agreement between Crown and J.J. Carrick; AO, RG18-79, *Timber Commission Hearings*, 5351; *Sessionals, 1920*, no. 72. While Ferguson was minister, his department "lost" crucial correspondence germane to this affair: AO, RG1-246-3, 9457, vol. 1, 16 February 1918, Memo for Mr. Hele from Chief Clerk, Records Branch.

17 AO, RG18-79, *Timber Commission Hearings*, 2514, from which the citation is taken; ibid., RG1-E-10, 157, Great Lakes Paper, vol. 4, 20 October 1961, "Early History of Great Lakes Paper"; Seaman Paper Company Archives (hereafter SPCA), Bermingham & Seaman/Seaman Paper Company Minute Book, 27 December 1918; MCCR, TC24155, 4 July 1919, Summary of State of Affairs as of the 31st Day of December 1919.

18 AO, RG75-57, OC98/119, enclosed in which is 5 November 1919, W.W. Pope to W. Hearst and Draft Agreement between Hydro and Great Lakes Paper.

19 Ibid., RG1-246-3, 18284, vol. 1, 25 October 1917, A. Fasken to The Minister; ibid., 29 October 1917, Memo for the Minister from A. Grigg; ibid., 27 September 1917, A.G. Pounsford to G.H. Ferguson; ibid., 9457, vol. 1, 8 October 1917, J.A. Oliver to A. Grigg; ibid., 1 February 1917, A. Fasken to G.H. Ferguson; ibid., 28303, vol. 1, 17 September 1919, Oliver to Grigg; ibid., 16094, vol. 1, 16 July and 17 September 1917, Oliver to Grigg; Bertrand, "Timber Wolves," 64.

20 AO, RG1-246-3, 18284, vol. 1, correspondence between October 1917 and October 1918; ibid., 11217, correspondence between 1916 and January 1918; ibid., RG1-E-4-B, vol. 4, 98–9, 29 October 1917, Memo for the Minister from A. Grigg.

21 J.B. Beveridge, for example, was a seasoned pulp and paper industrialist who had taken over the stalled mill project in Dryden, Ontario, just before the First World War and had turned it into a successful enterprise. In 1917,

he approached the government about acquiring a pulpwood concession northwest of Fort William to support a newsprint mill he proposed building in that city. He had the expertise to carry out the project and demonstrated that he had lined up backers to finance it, but the Conservatives refused to tender the timber he sought: AO, RG1-246-3, 200, 200A, 3732 and 13773, all documents; ibid., RG1-E-4-B, vol. 2, folio 35, attachments; ibid., RG1-E-3-B, Box 240, W-7-309, all documents.

22 The Tories rejected repeated applications for them to sell the Nagagami River and the Long Lac pulpwood concessions: ibid., RG1-246-3, 21973, vol. 1 and 33582, vol. 1, documents from 1916–19. Within months of taking office in 1919, the Farmers government responded to this demand by tendering and leasing both limits.

23 Ibid., RG1-E-4-B, vol. 3, 146-147, 31 December 1913 and 21 February 1914, D. Chisholm to W.H. Hearst; Abitibi-Bowater – Iroquois Falls Archives (hereafter IFA), Historical Files, 21 February 1913, J.D. McFarlane to Chisholm; AOL, 17 September 1913, General Conditions with Respect to the Metagami Pulp Limit.

24 The government refused to approve this assignment for two years, thereby undermining Chisholm's ability to finance the undertaking. It is impossible to explain the Tories' actions in this instance because Ferguson kept the documents pertaining to the Mattagami concession between 1914 and 1916 in his "private" dossier, which has not survived: AO, RG1-246-3, 1655, 13 March 1916, G.H. Ferguson to D. Chisholm; ibid., 14 March 1916, Memo for Grigg from C.C. Hele; ibid., 31 March 1916, Approval of the Transfer, and 1 April 1916, Macdonell and Boland to The Minister; ibid., RG22-5800, 1921/1339, 9 August 1921, Writ; ibid., RG1-305, 31 March 1916, Agreement between Crown and D. Chisholm.

25 MCCR, TC6544, 4 May 1916, Company Prospectus.

26 When B.E. Fernow's draft of his 1912 report on the northern Clay Belt referred to New Ontario as "an American firm," the company's representatives were outraged. Although their letterhead stated that their firm was based in Buffalo and had offices in Minneapolis and Detroit, its president stressed that his company was Canadian and asked Fernow to edit his references: UTA, A72-0025, 146, unlabelled, 31 December 1912, W.K. Jackson to B.E. Fernow; Lower, *Settlement*, 101; 19 March 1914, *Toronto Sunday World*.

27 *Hansard*, 11 March 1914; AO, RG18-79, *Final Report of the Timber Commission, 1922*, 47–8; ibid., MU1312, 1–10 October 1911, E.S. Wigle to J.P. Whitney; ibid., RG75-57, OC68/570; 14 June 1912, Agreement for Sale of Townships, in *Annual Report, 1912*; ibid., RG22-5800, 1918/2, Examination of W.K. Jackson, 14 March 1918, 20. Wigle also acted for the Detroit

Sulphite Pulp and Paper Company, which had been exporting spruce from Ontario since at least the turn of the century. By 1914, William S. Rushworth, a Toronto businessman and director of New Ontario, was also a director of Driftwood Lands and Timber Company, which became Detroit Sulphite's pulpwood-procuring firm in Ontario.

28 Ibid., RG1-246-3, 4120, vol. 1, 8 and 29 December 1919, W.C. Cain to W.R. Plewman; ibid., 30 March 1916, C.C. Hele to W.K. Jackson; ibid., 18 April 1916, Jackson to G.H. Ferguson; ibid., 15 February 1917, Memo for Cain from Hele; ibid., 2 January 1920, Plewman to A. Grigg; ibid., RG18-79, *Timber Commission Hearings*, 1620; *Sessionals, 1916*, No. 68.

29 For instance, see AO, RG1-246-3, 4120, vol. 1, 18 October 1921, L. Moore to S. Denison.

30 Ibid., 30 July 1920, Bain, Bicknell et al. to the Minister; ibid., 31 July 1920, W.C. Cain to G.A. Bremner; ibid., 7 May 1922, Memo re: Townships of Haggart and Kendrey by S.D.; ibid., RG18-79, *Special Report on the New Ontario*, 47–8.

31 Ibid., RG1-305, 31 March 1916, Agreement between Crown and D. Chisholm; *PPMC*, 1916–19, passim; LAC, RG89, 24, Developed Water Power in Canada – Directory of Pulp and Paper Mills, 1 March 1921.

32 AO, RG1-246-3, 13555, vol. 1, documents from 1917 to 1919.

33 Ibid., 28 February 1917, E. Stewart and S.A. Mundy to G.H. Ferguson, enclosing Memo re: Pulp Limits in vicinity of Kapuskasing; ibid., 18 April 1917, Stewart to Ferguson; ibid., 7 May 1917, A. Grigg to Stewart.

34 When Kimberly-Clark took over the project in 1920, one of the first things for which it asked was permission to cut from the closest township which had been set aside for the colony scheme. Otherwise, the company argued, it would "be very expensive to build [the mill] by bringing in wood from far": AO, RG1-246-3, 13555, vol. 1, 14 July 1920, McPherson & Company to the Minister.

35 AO, RG49-19, *Sessionals, 1921*, No. 68, 23 October 1920, E. Stewart to B. Bowman; P. Butcher, "The Establishment of a Pulp and Paper Industry at Kapuskasing" (MA thesis, University of Western Ontario, 1978), 31–50, provides a keen analysis of how Ferguson's colony scheme impeded Mundy and Stewart's mill plans.

36 Ibid., 48–54, demonstrates that Ferguson had enticed settlers to move to the remote colony by promising them that a mill would soon be built there; AO, RG6-I-2, 18, DLF 1914–1932, 25 February 1919, Memo for the Minister from H.M.R.

37 AOL, 19 September 1917, Conditions with Respect to the Kapuskasing; Tembec – Spruce Falls Archives (hereafter SFA), Regeneration Studies & Surveys, Report of a Cruise of Spruce Falls Company's Limits South of the

C.N.R., 1924, F.R. Wilcox; AO, RG18-66, *Report of the Commission of Enquiry into the Kapuskasing Colony*, 1920, 6; ibid., RG1-246-3, 13555, vol. 1, 17 October 1917, Minister's Notice changing clause 2 of the September 19, 1917 Tender; ibid., documents from late September and early October 1917.

38 SFA, 9 February 1918, Agreement between Crown and S.A. Mundy and E. Stewart; AO, RG75-57, OC105/226, and enclosure; New York Public Library Archives (hereafter NYPLA), *New York Times* Company Records, A.H. Sulzberger Papers, 247(4-10), 9 March 1925, G.F. Hardy, "Report on Spruce Falls Company, Ltd., Kapuskasing, Ontario," 2–3.

39 OHA, OR410.1-114, vol. 1, Water Storage [Kapuskasing River] General, 26 February 1918, H.G. Acres to Chief Engineer; AO, RG1-246-3, 35146, vol. 1, 30 January 1918, G.H. Ferguson to W.W. Pope; ibid., 2 March 1918, Transfer of water power licence from Mundy and Stewart to Spruce Falls.

40 Ibid., 13555, vol. 1, 7 January and 6 May 1919, G.H. Ferguson to F. Telfer and E. Stewart; ibid., 6 June 1919, Deputy Minister to Spruce Falls; ibid., 15 August 1919, Ferguson to Spruce Falls.

41 UTA, A72-0025, Box 138, Aa-Al, 14 November 1924, H.G. Schanche to C.D. Howe: Schanche was Abitibi's chief forester, and he explained to the dean of the University of Toronto's Forestry Faculty that the "timber as a whole [on Abitibi's limit] is small averaging less than eight inches in diameter."

42 AOL, 10 January 1911, General Conditions with Respect to the Abitibi Pulp Limit; AO, RG3-2, Northern Ontario Pamphlets, *The Resources ... Toronto Board of Trade, 1912*, 29; *PPMC*, October 1910, 241; ibid., May 1911, 213; *The Globe*, 11 January 1911.

43 AO, RG75-57, OC68/425.

44 Ibid., F150, File-F-150-8-0-23, Murray, Mather & Co., Circular for Abitibi stock offering, 1914.

45 D.W. Ambridge, *Frank Harris Anson: Pioneer in the North* (New York: Newcomen Society of North America, 1952); AO, RG1-E-4-B, vol. 3, 8–9, 15 August 1912, F. Anson and S. Ogilvie to W.H. Hearst. A series of assignments saw the original pulpwood agreement eventually transferred to this firm: ibid., MU1309, Envelope 1, 23 October 1912, Memo for Mr. Gibson Re: Abitibi.

46 *Annual Report, 1913*, vi.

47 AO, RG75-57, OC70/220; ibid., MU3134, October 1912, 22 October 1912, A. Beck to W.H. Hearst; ibid., MU3135, May 1913, J.P. Whitney to Beck; OHA, OR401.1-193, 124/350, Water Storage Abitibi River #1, 10 May 1912, Beck to Hearst.

48 Despite Abitibi's repeated requests, the Crown refused to remove the offensive TNOR reservation for over thirty years: AO, RG1-246-3, 1418, vol. 3, Power Leases 1860 and 1898 and L.O. 513; OHA, OR401.1-193,

124/350, Water Storage Abitibi River #1, 4 February and 14 March 1913, H.G. Acres to A. Beck. The government tacitly permitted Abitibi to operate above a head of thirty-five feet at Iroquois Falls although it emphasized that the company did so at its peril; it drove home the tenuousness of Abitibi's privileges during the 1930s when it repeatedly reminded the company of this breach of its licence of occupation.

49 AO, MU1309, File – Envelope 1, 11 October 1913, J.A. McAndrew to W.H. Hearst.

50 Ibid., RG1-246-3, 1418, vol. 1, 26 January 1915, Deputy Minister of Mines to CTA at Cochrane; ibid., 29 January 1916, F. Anson to T. Gibson; ibid., 2 February 1916, Memo for the Minister re: Abitibi Lakes.

51 In contrast, the Ontario government categorically refused to permit mining prospectors to stake claims on the areas licensed to lumbermen.

52 Ibid., 47622, vol. 1, 28 June 1918, F. Anson to G.H. Ferguson.

53 Ibid., MG27-II-F-7, Box 24, Timber Commission, 23 May 1916, F.H. Anson to G.H. Ferguson.

54 Ibid., 25 May 1916, F.H. Anson to A. Smith.

55 Ibid., 7 June 1916, F.H. Anson to A. Smith.

56 Ibid., RG1-246-3, 1418, vol. 1, 30 June 1916, Memo for Mr. Grigg re: Abitibi … Application; ibid., 11 August 1916, G.F. Hardy to Hydro; ibid., 25 August 1916, Hardy to G.H. Ferguson, which cites 18 August 1916, H.A. Gaby to Abitibi; ibid., 6 September 1916, P. White to Grigg; ibid., 20 September 1916, F. Anson to Grigg; ibid., September 1916 documents germane to the preparation of the lease.

57 Ibid., correspondence from June to July 1917, with the first citation taken from 27 June 1917, Memo for Mr. Gibson from Surveys Branch, and the second from 31 August 1917, G.H. Ferguson to J. Allard. The lease the government was preparing for Twin Falls would have been of dubious value to Abitibi as collateral. Peter White, whom Ferguson asked to prepare this contract, wrote Ferguson in mid-1918, explaining that he, White, had been waiting over one year to finalize the document and that the minister would "no doubt observe that the lease is radically different from the old form and gives the Minister some very extensive and in some cases somewhat arbitrary powers." White added that he had "practically gone the limit as to its being drastic": ibid., 17 June 1918, P. White to Ferguson.

58 Ibid., 47622, vol. 1, 28 June 1918, F. Anson to G.H. Ferguson; ibid., MG27-II-F-7, 24, Timber Commission, 27 May, 20 August and 28 October 1918, Anson to G.H. Kilmer; ibid., 24 August 1918, Kilmer to Anson; ibid., December 11, 1918, A. Smith to Anson, in which Smith states, "I cannot too

strongly impress upon you the necessity for following this up and I have no doubt you are doing so."

59 Ibid., RG4-32, 1921/3807, Lake of the Woods #1, 14 April 1919, G.H. Ferguson to F. Anson; ibid., 20 August 1919, G.H. Kilmer to Anson. Nelles, *Politics of Development*, ch. 10, contends that Ferguson's handling of this matter demonstrates how the provincial state had been reduced to being a client of industry, but his analysis ignores several crucial facts. Ferguson did not lease Abitibi this timber at this time; he merely promised to reserve it for the firm's use. Secondly, Abitibi never asked Ferguson to grant this limit as a private transaction; Anson only requested that his firm be given a chance to tender on the concession. Most importantly, Nelles argues that the supposed granting of this reserve was crucial to Abitibi securing financial backing for its mill expansion, which was not the case. In 1920, when investors inquired about the status of Abitibi's supplemental pulpwood concession, Anson sent them a copy of Ferguson's commitment to reserve a large tract for the company. While firms such as Royal Securities privately insisted Abitibi finalize these matters forthwith, they went ahead and sold blocks of Abitibi's bonds to the public using circulars that stretched the truth in broadcasting that Abitibi had leases – and not simply promises of leases – to sufficient quantities of pulpwood and water powers. Acting for Royal Securities in April 1920, W.C. Pittfield informed Anson that he was only making the public offering on the presumption that Abitibi would "in due course take up with the Ontario Government the delimiting of the territory to be set aside and settle definitely the question of price and other details in connection therewith, so that leases or licences in the usual form may be issued to your Company." Most of the important documents dealing with this subject – including almost all Abitibi's applications for additional pulpwood (dating back to 1916) – disappeared from the department when Ferguson left office in 1919, and it appears that Abitibi later delivered copies of them to F.R. Latchford, one of the timber commissioners. It is only in his files that these documents survive: ibid., MG27-II-F-7, 24, Timber Commission, 27 April 1920, F. Anson to Royal Securities, and enclosure; ibid., 28 April 1920, W.C. Pittfield to Anson.

60 Ibid., RG1-246-3, 1418, vol. 1, ca May 1919, Memo Re: Lease between Twin Falls and Abitibi, C.C. Hele; ibid., 13 May 1919, G.H. Ferguson to W.W. Pope.

61 Ibid., 1108, vol. 1A, correspondence between May 1917 and June 1918, with the citation from 3 May 1918, A. Grigg to F. H. Anson.

62 *Annual Report, 1915*, ix.

Introduction to Section III

1 Mark Kuhlberg, *One Hundred Rings and Counting: Forestry Education and Forestry in Toronto and Canada, 1907–2007* (Toronto: University of Toronto Press, 2009), 71–3.
2 Ibid.; C.M. Johnston, *E.C. Drury: Agrarian Idealist* (Toronto: University of Toronto Press, 1986), chs. 5–6; UTA, A72-0025, 189, unlabelled, 19 March 1923, C.D. Howe to H.R. MacMillan.
3 The forest fire prevention policy the Farmers implemented made it clear that they placed the settlers' interests ahead of the pulp and paper industry's. For years the industry had argued for tighter restrictions on the settlers' careless use of fire, measures the homesteaders had vehemently opposed. The government had enacted legislation that prohibited burning during the warm weather months but enforced it laxly, hiring merely a handful of grossly under-qualified fire rangers to patrol vast areas. In 1922, the Farmers granted the settlers' request to withdraw these rangers from a series of townships in the Haileybury-Cobalt area, thereby permitting them to burn their debris despite the prevailing dry conditions. Their actions resulted in a conflagration that torched 700 square miles (much of it pulpwood forest), killed 44 persons, and inflicted over $6,000,000 in property damage: AO, RG3-4, Fire … enquiry into cause 1922 and Fire … Fire Marshall's Report, all documents.
4 Kuhlberg, "'Pulpwood Is the Only Thing We Do Export,'" with the citations taken from *Hansard*, 29 May 1920.
5 *Annual Report, 1921–22*, "Report of the James Bay Forest Survey Made in 1922." The government's first cruise results were startling. A 1900 reconnaissance of this 13,500-square-mile tract in northeastern Ontario had estimated that it supported 55,000,000 cords of pulpwood. Twenty years later investigators found less than one-fifth this total.
6 United States – Department of Commerce, *Transportation Factors in the Marketing of Newsprint*, November 1952, passim but especially 94–125; S.N. Whitney, *Antitrust Policies: American Experience in Twenty Industries* (New York: Twentieth Century Fund, 1958), 376.
7 Johnston, chs. 5–7; Oliver, *G. Howard Ferguson*, chs. 6 and 7.

Chapter 5

1 Only after the Farmers' victory did Backus feel safe to speak publicly about how the Tories had stymied his plans for constructing newsprint mills in northwestern Ontario: *Toronto Telegram*, 30 September 1920.

2 This section on Backus draws heavily on Kuhlberg, "'Eyes wide open': E.W. Backus and the Pitfalls of Investing in Ontario's Pulp and Paper Industry, 1902–1934," *Journal of the Canadian Historical Association* (2005): passim.

3 AO, RG49-19, *Sessional Papers, 1922*, No. 68, 20 September 1920, Memo for the Minister from E.J. Zavitz; ibid., RG6-2, E.C. Drury, 17 September 1920, Memo for the Minister from G. Grant.

4 Ibid., RG3-4, English River … 1922, ca 1921, B. Bowman; ibid., 28 and 29 September 1920, F.H. Anson to E.C. Drury, and enclosures; ibid., RG4-32, 1921/3807, File 3, 4 September 1920, P. Heenan to Drury; ibid., 24 September 1920, Conditions with Respect to the English River Pulp and Timber Limit; *Annual Report, 1921–1922*, 30 September 1920, Agreement between Crown and E.W. Backus et al. regarding Lake of the Woods pulp-wood limit; ibid., 15 and 22 December 1920, Memo for the Minister from E.J. Zavitz; ibid., 14 February 1923, Memo to the Attorney-General from Zavitz.

5 *Annual Report, 1921–1922*, 7 January 1921, Agreement between Crown and E.W. Backus et al.; AO, RG6-2, 20, H.C. Nixon 1920–3, 31 December 1920, Memo for Mr. Smith from the Provincial Secretary; ibid., RG49-19, *Sessional Papers 1922*, No. 68, 7 January 1921, Minister to Backus.

6 TBHMS, A83/1/2, 14 February 1923, J.A. Little to D.M. Hogarth.

7 Johnston, 180; *Toronto Telegram*, 6 and 8 November 1920 and 2 October 1922; AO, RG4-32, 1921/3807, notes germane to Ferguson's attacks.

8 Ibid., RG1-246-3, 14797, vol. 1, 5 November 1919, Memo re: English River, Pulp Limit from F.J. Niven; Oliver, *Public and Private Persons*, ch. 3. Nelles and Oliver have, for the most part, accepted Ferguson's portrayal of these events. Johnston, 175–80, presents a more accurate analysis when he explains that this was "vintage Ferguson" who "shrewdly exploited" the situation. Undoubtedly the terms of the tender favoured Backus's agenda, but they did not preclude other parties from either bidding for or winning the limit. Abitibi and Spanish River were the only other major pulp and paper producers in Ontario at the time, and neither was interested in undertaking the project in Kenora.

9 Armstrong, *The Politics of Federalism*, 162–4.

10 AO, 16799, vol. 1, correspondence between 8 June 1921 and 4 January 1923; ibid., RG75-57, OC124/162.

11 Ibid., RG1-246-3, 21973, vol. 1, documents from 11 April 1918 to 11 June 1921; ibid., RG3-4, Nagagami … 1920, 6 August 1920, Day, Ferguson & Co. to the Premier and enclosure; *Annual Report, 1922*, 15 September 1921, Agreement between Crown and Transcontinental Development Company;

MCCR, TC23132, 10 June 1921, Petition for Letters Patent; ibid., 4 November 1939, C. England to F.A. Hicks.

12 AO, RG1-246-3, 21973, 2 March and 10 September 1922, Tilley et al. to B. Bowman; ibid., 10 March 1922 and 3 July 1923, Bowman to Transcontinental; ibid., 2 October 1922, Memo for the Minister from Bowman; ibid., 25 May 1923, Memo to the Minister … Transcontinental; ibid., 15 June 1923, Memo for the Minister from W.C. Cain.

13 Ibid., RG75-57, OC119/58, 119/246 and OC126/297; ibid., RG3-4, Timber Limits 1920, 8 September 1920, A.T. Mackie to Department; ibid., RG1-246-3, 33582, vol. 1, documents from 9 September 1920 to 13 April 1923; *Annual Report, 1922*, 9 August 1921, The Long Lake Pulp … Agreement. Critics may suggest those who stood behind the Great Lakes Paper project were simply holding out for the richest bid before "flipping" their pulpwood concessions, but the evidence does not support this view. The "Wausau group" of paper makers in Wisconsin offered Seaman and Alsted $1,000,000 in the fall of 1920 for the three timber leases that Seaman and Alsted owned. The pulp and paper industry was crashing at this time, and this offer represented an ideal opportunity for Seaman and Alsted to cash in their timber holdings before the value of these tracts dropped. But the two businessmen rejected the offer and proposed to the Wausau group instead that it become involved in their project, an invitation the Wausau group declined. The crucial factor that delayed Great Lakes Paper's undertaking throughout the early and mid-1920s was their inability to agree on a development strategy, a subject about which more will be said in subsequent chapters: WHSMA, MSS279, 14, 1 William Scott 1920, correspondence between July and December 1920, particularly 12 October 1920, W. Scott to G.M. Seaman.

14 This paragraph represents a synthesis of information drawn from these files: AO, RG3-4, Great Lakes Pulp … 1920, Timber Limits 1920, Nipigon Power … 1920, and Great Lakes Pulp … 1923; ibid., RG4-32, 1920/3840; OHA, OR-53, Direct Customers Great Lakes Paper Company; TBHMS, G3/6/1–G3/6/2, Government of Fort William – Great Lakes Paper … 1919.

15 *PPMC*, 23 November 1922, 1028–9; AO, RG3-6, Great Lakes Pulp … 1924, 18 January 1924, I.B. Lucas to G.H. Ferguson; ibid., RG4-32, 1920/3840, 28 April 1920, L. Alsted to E.C. Drury; ibid., RG3-4, Great Lakes Pulp … 1920, 11 February 1920, Great Lakes Paper to Drury. Hydro's standard contract obliged it to provide only "commercially continuous power" (i.e., the supplier was responsible for any interruption) not "continuous electrical power" (i.e., the supplier was liable for any interruption). To lawyers and financiers, these two concepts were as different as night and day.

16 Shortly after Ferguson's electoral victory in 1923, he charged that "Mr. Backus had discreetly kept in the background during negotiations" with the Drury government regarding Great Lakes Paper and the Nagagami and Long Lac limits: *Hansard*, 19 March 1924.

17 MCCR, TC24155, Great Lakes Paper ... Return for 1923; AO, RG75-57, OC128/41½, OC130/127, OC130/142; ibid., RG3-4, Great Lakes Pulp ... 1923 #3, all correspondence; ibid., RG1-246-3, 33582, vol. 1, 10 July 1923, L.L. Alsted to The Minister; ibid., 12 July 1923, Minister to Alsted.

18 *Fort William Times-Journal*, 19 December 1922.

19 *PPMC*, 30 September 1920, 1024.

20 AO, RG1-246-3, 3785, vol. 1, 18 February 1920, Memo for the Minister from L.H.; ibid., 5 May 1920, Memo re: application by Spanish River by L.V. Rorke; ibid., 9093, vol. 1, documents from 1920.

21 This paragraph and the one preceding it are based on ibid., RG18-79, *Timber Commission Hearings*, May 1921 to January 1922, and *Final Report of the Timber Commission*, 63–5; ibid., RG4-32, 674/1920, 25 June 1921, S. Denison to W.E. Raney; Oliver, *G. Howard Ferguson*, 68–9; May 1920 to June 1922, *The Farmers Sun*, with the citation taken from 2 February 1921.

22 AO, RG3-4, Spanish River Lumber [*sic*] Company 1923, note and map indicating area for which Spanish River applied; SMPA, Forestry – 1921, 21 February 1921, Espanola Great War Veterans' Association to Minister; *Hansard*, 9 March 1923.

23 This paragraph represents a synthesis of information drawn from: AO, RG1-246-3, 3734A and 3734B, correspondence between 1916 and 1919; ibid., 28567, vol. 1, correspondence between 16 September 1919 and 11 November 1920; "Continental Paper and Bag Mills, 1899–1921," *Paper Trade Journal*, April 1921; Thomas Heinrich, "Product Diversification in the U.S. Pulp and Paper Industry: The Case of International Paper, 1898–1941," *Business History Review* 75 (Autumn 2001).

24 AO, RG1-246-3, 5322A, 19 October 1926, L.E. Bliss to W.C. Cain.

25 This paragraph is a synthesis of information drawn from: ibid., 12334, vol. 1, passim; ibid., 46370, vol. 1, correspondence from June 1922 to January 1923; ibid., RG1-E-3-B, 244, W-8-113. Waldron also asked to lease two water powers, cut the pine on the patented land Continental now owned, and purchase lots along the Loon River, where it hoped to develop another water power.

26 Ibid., RG1-246-3, 46370, vol. 1, correspondence from January to June 1923; ibid., RG75-57, OC127/286; ibid., RG1-E-4-B, vol. 6, 16 April 1923, Conditions with Respect to the Trout-Chapleau Pulp and Timber Limit; *PPMC*, 26 April 1923, 439.

27 These matters included the grants the Ontario government owed two transcontinental railways: ibid., RG1-353, 2/8, 17, 29 June and 4 July 1923, B. Bowman to W.E. Raney.

28 Ibid., RG1-246-3, 46370, vol. 1, correspondence from June 1923; ibid., 10 July 1923, Agreement between Crown and Continental Wood Products Company, Ltd. Continental's lease required it to cut at least 75,000 cords of pulpwood annually from its limit even though it was obliged to construct a kraft mill which produced only 75 tons of pulp each day. This type of mill would use, at most, 150 cords of pulpwood each day (2 cords per ton of chemical pulp) and it would operate roughly 300 days per year. Continental would thus annually need only 45,000 cords from its concession to supply its new mill and would presumably export the other 30,000 cords.

29 Ibid., 6 June 1923, Memo for the Prime Minister from B. Bowman.

Chapter 6

1 *PPMC*, 15 July 1920. Wightman and Wightman, 183, contend that during the early 1920s mill developers in the Thunder Bay District entered lavish agreements for power and pulpwood but "dragged their heels on the erection of promised mills," a conclusion the evidence does not support.

2 FWA, binder T-1-1 to T-4-5, 20 August 1920, Agreement between GTPR, G. Farlinger and S. McDougall and the Mead Investment Company. The mysterious workings of Mead Investment Company (MIC) are given only cursory attention in *In Quiet Ways*, 87, 108–14, 136, and 179. This in-house history claims that Mead formed MIC to protect his American operations and aid in their future acquisitions, and that Mead only entered the Canadian newsprint industry to further his interests south of the border. These explanations seem unconvincing in light of the fact that, by the mid-1920s, his Canadian operations dwarfed his American activities.

3 AO, RG1-246-3, 32405, 24 September 1920, A.H. Dennis to B. Bowman.

4 Ibid., 7410, 23 February 1921, B.M. Wylie to A. Grigg; ibid., 32405, 10 June 1922, Application of Fort William Paper Co. Ltd., enclosed in 10 June 1922, G.W. Kilmer to B. Bowman; Kuhlberg, "'We are the pioneers,'" passim.

5 This paragraph represents a synthesis of documents found in: AO, RG1-246-3, 32405, vol. 1, especially 22 December 1922, B. Bowman to T. Gibson; ibid., 23 December 1922, Gibson to Bowman; ibid., RG3-4, Pulpwood 1923, passim; *PPMC*, 30 September 1919, 1031.

6 AO, RG1-E-3-B, 242, W-8-8, Timber Licence sheet; ibid., RG4-32, 1920/674, 22 February 1921, Timber Investigation; ibid., RG1-246-3, 44482,

documents from 1922; WHSMA, M80-616, 31 October 1950, "Reminiscences,"
G.W. Mead.

7 AO, RG3-4, Great Lakes Pulp … 1923 #1, 1 February 1922, G.W. Mead to
W.C. Cain.

8 Ibid., RG1-246-3, 44482, 9 August and 11 November 1922, F.N. Youngman
to B. Bowman; ibid., October 1922, correspondence between Youngman
and E.C. Drury; ibid., 13 November 1922, Bowman to Youngman; ibid.,
9 August 1923, Youngman to F.H. Keefer; ibid., RG3-4, H.E.P.C. Re:
Nipigon … 1923, 14 March 1923.

9 Ibid., RG1-246-3, 44482, 19 October 1922, E.C. Drury to B. Bowman; ibid.,
20 October 1922, Bowman to Drury; ibid., 46025, 24 October 1922,
Bowman to E.J. Zavitz; ibid., 2 November 1922, Memo for Zavitz from
W.C. Cain.

10 Ibid., RG3-4, H.E.P.C. re. Nipigon … 1923, 23 February 1923, A.
McNaughton to E.C. Drury; ibid., 26 February 1923, C.B. Devlin to Drury;
ibid., RG1-246-3, 32405, vol. 1, February 1923, Agreement between Crown
and Fort William; *Hansard*, 15 March 1923; *PPMC*, 22 March 1923, 319.

11 AO, RG3-4, Thunder Bay Paper … 1923, 17 March 1923, F.R. Youngman to
Minister; ibid., RG1-246-3, 44482, vol. 1, 13 March 1923, G.P. Berkey to B.
Bowman; ibid., 15 March 1923, Bowman to Berkey.

12 Ibid., RG3-4, H.E.P.C. re. Nipigon … 1923, 9 April 1923, E.C. Drury to E.E.
Johnson.

13 Ibid., RG75-57, OC127/406; ibid., RG1-246-3, 44482, 13 April 1923,
Conditions with respect to The Humboldt Bay and Nipigon Pulpwood
Limits.

14 More will be said in chapter 7 about a third pulp and paper mill which
was also constructed in the Thunder Bay District at this time and to which
the Farmers refused to lease a pulpwood concession. This paragraph is
based on ibid., 5 May 1923, F.N. Youngman to B. Bowman; ibid., 32405,
16 April 1923, Memo to Bowman from E.C. Drury; ibid., 24 April 1923,
Memo from Prime Minister's Secretary to Bowman; ibid., 39865, vol. 1,
correspondence between 1920 and 1923, especially 6 June 1923, Bowman
to W.E.C. Day.

15 Ibid., RG1-246-3, 18284, vol. 1, 28 September 1920, Tender for Timber West
of Hele and Sterling Townships; ibid., 28 October 1920, Memo for the
Minister from E.J. Zavitz.

16 Ibid., RG3-4, Pulpwood 1920 #1, 18 September 1920, [H.T.] Gagnier to E.C.
Drury; ibid., 22 September 1920, Drury to Gagnier; ibid., RG1-246-3, 12156,
vol. 1, 4 December 1919, Deputy Minister to A. Fasken; ibid., 8 and
30 December 1919, Fasken to A. Grigg; ibid., 6, 8, 16 and 21 January 1920,

correspondence between Grigg and J.A. Oliver; ibid., 16 January 1920, Grigg to Fasken; *The Forest Resources of Ontario* (Ontario Department of Lands and Forests, 1930), table 3, 57.

17 AO, RG1-E-4-B, 21 October 1920, Conditions with Respect to the Nipigon Pulp and Pine Limit 1920; ibid., RG1-246-3, 21973, vol. 1, 18 April 1921, J.E. Day to B. Bowman; ibid., 12156, 3 March 1920, Memo for Mr. Grigg from F.J. Niven and enclosure; ibid., 7 January 1921, Memo for the Minister from E.J. Zavitz; ibid., 32405, 24 September 1920, A.H. Dennis to Bowman; ibid., 25 September 1920, Nipigon Fibre to Bowman; ibid., 12156, 23 November 1920, H.J. Wehman to Bowman.

18 Ibid., 22 March and 12 October 1921, Deputy Minister to A. Fasken, drafts enclosed; ibid., 20 July 1921, C.C. Calvin to Deputy Minister, draft enclosed; ibid., 20 October 1921, Fasken to Department, agreement enclosed; *Annual Report, 1923*, 15 July 1921, Agreement between Crown and Provincial Paper Mills, Limited; SMPA, A-1, Forestry 1924, Report on the Central Part of Nipigon Limits, 1924.

19 LAC, RG20, 38, 17412, 24 February 1920, T.C. Norris to G. Foster; ibid., 27 February 1920, Foster to Norris; ibid., RG33, 1, Correspondence 3, 25 April 1919, G.T. Clarkson to R.A. Pringle; Humphries, 160–1; AO, RG1-246-3, 12156, 8 October 1920, I.H. Weldon to B. Bowman. Provincial Paper's lease obliged it to sell the Ontario Department of Education all the paper it needed at "market prices."

20 Ibid., RG3-4, Water Power Crown Leases 1920, 29 November 1920, E.C. Drury to A. Beck; *PPMC*, 13 May 1920.

21 *Globe*, 11 October 1921; AO, RG1-246-3, 47622, vol. 1, 20 and 22 November 1922 and May 30, and 12 and 17 July 1923, B. Bowman to G.H. Kilmer; ibid., 15 November 1922 and 15 May 1923, Kilmer to Bowman; ibid., 12 July 1923, Agreement between Crown and Abitibi; ibid., 1108, vol. 1, 20 May 1921, A. Grigg to S. Denison; ibid., 27 May 1921, F. Anson to Bowman. Bowman also refused to grant Abitibi another small limit for which it had applied and ignored its offer to build another mill well north of the National Transcontinental Railway: ibid., 47622, vol. 1, 22 November 1922, Anson to Bowman; ibid., 30514, vol. 1, all documents.

22 Kuhlberg, "We have 'sold' forestry to the management of the Company"; AO, RG1-305, Abitibi ... Data Required by Pulpwood Conservation Act, 1929, August 1929, Iroquois Falls Division.

23 Hollinger's battle with Northern Canada can be followed in AO, RG22-5800, 1921/405.

24 Ibid., RG1-246-3, 1108, vol. 1, 16 December 1920, L.V. Rorke to Holden and Murdoch; ibid., 19 April 1921, W.W. Pope to Rorke; ibid., 7 June 1921,

Holden to Minister; ibid., 48171, vol. 1, 7 April 1922, J.G.G. Kerry to Rorke; ibid., 2 June 1922, Memo for the Minister from Rorke; ibid., 5 June 1922, Summary re: Northern Canada Power ... from Rorke; Hollinger's *Annual Report, 1922*, 2, admits that Abitibi had a prior claim to Long Sault; OHA, OR401.1-169, 124/350, Water Storage – Abitibi River 2/5, 3 May 1921, A. Beck to E.C. Drury.

25 Bowman probably did this without Drury's approval and was later forced to rescind this Order when the premier learned of its existence: AO, RG1-246-3, 34983, vol. 1, 8 May 1923, Ruling Records Branch; ibid., 10 May 1923, L.V. Rorke to G.H. Kilmer; ibid., 47256, vol. 1, 29 May 1923, Minister to G.W. Lee; ibid., 48171, vol. 1, correspondence from August 1922 to July 1923; ibid., 59129, vol. 1, 4 March 1922, G.H. Kilmer to B. Bowman; ibid., 48181, vol. 1, documents from March to May 1923; ibid., RG3-4, Long Sault Rapids 1923, correspondence between January and April 1923; ibid., RG75-57, OC128/114; ibid., RG75-57, OC130/141; ibid., RG75-57, OC128/206.

26 Ibid., RG1-246-3, 34983, vol. 1, 4 May 1923, G.H. Kilmer to B. Bowman; ibid., 7 May 1923, Memo for Mr. Rorke from Bowman; ibid., 10 May and 8 June 1923, Rorke to Kilmer and enclosure.

27 Ibid., RG3-4, New Ontario Colonization Company: Report by A.W. Roebuck 1922, all documents.

28 Ibid., RG1-246-3, 1655, vol. 1, 26 February 1916, Memo for the Minister re ... Crown Lease 1908; ibid., 5 June 1916, H.G. Acres to T.W. Gibson; ibid., 29 June 1916 and 17 February 1917, L.V. Rorke to Macdonell and Boland; ibid., 1 November 1916, G.H. Ferguson to W.K. Jackson; ibid., 20 March 1918, Memo ... by Rorke; ibid., 17 January 1917, A.C. Macdonell to Ferguson; ibid., 17 February 1917, Rorke to D. Chisholm; ibid., 15 March 1918, J.W. Bain to Ferguson; ibid., 5 December 1918, P. White to Ferguson.

29 Ibid., RG22-5800, 1920/712, 19 May 1920, Writ; ibid., 1920/885, 25 June 1920, Statement of Claim; ibid., RG3-4, New Ontario Colonization Company: Report by A.W. Roebuck, 1922, passim; ibid., RG1-246-3, 3267, vol. 1, documents from June 1920 to April 1922.

30 Nelles, 458fn42, states that an Order in Council passed in 1941 by the government of Mitchell F. Hepburn "provides one of the few documented cases of the 'walking order,' an order-in-council not passed at a meeting of cabinet, but rather circulated among the required number of ministers for signature." An examination of Orders in Council that deal only with Crown timber and hydro resources reveals that "walking orders" were repeatedly the instrument of choice for the Ontario government (especially under G.H. Ferguson and Hepburn) when it addressed important matters in questionable ways.

31 AO, RG75-57, OC128/430½; ibid., RG3-4, New Ontario Colonization Company 1923, 6 June 1923, W.C. Cain – Memo re: New Ontario ... ; ibid., RG1-246-3, 3267, 5 June 1922, G.T. Clarkson to B. Bowman; ibid., 4120, vol. 1, 5 June 1922, Clarkson to Bowman; ibid., 18 January 1923, Memo from Cain; ibid., January-April 1923, correspondence between the Crown and New Ontario's lawyers.

32 Ibid., 3267, vol. 1, 27 November 1922, D. Chisholm to the Minister; ibid., 47959, vol. 1, 19 and 28 April 1923, Chisholm to the Minister; ibid., 25 April 1923, Minister to Chisholm; ibid., 3 May 1923, Chisholm to Department; ibid., RG3-4, Mattagami Pulp ... 1923, 7 May 1923, W.J. Boland to E.C. Drury.

33 U.S., *Pulp and Paper Investigation Hearings, 1908*, 1867–86; T. Heinrich and B. Batchelor, *Kotex, Kleenex, Huggies: Kimberly-Clark and the Consumer Revolution in American Business* (Columbus: Ohio State University Press, 2004); J.R. Kimberly, *Four Young Men Go in Search of Profit: The Story of Kimberly-Clark Corporation, 1872–1957* (New York: Newcomen Society of North America, 1957); NYPLA, *New York Times* Company Records, A.H. Sulzberger Papers, 247(4-10), 9 March 1925, G.F. Hardy, "Report on Spruce Falls Company, Ltd., Kapuskasing, Ontario," 3.

34 AO, RG18-66, *Report of the Commission of Enquiry into the Kapuskasing Colony*, 1920, 13.

35 Ibid., RG1-246-3, 31637, 21 June 1920, L.V. Rorke to B. Bowman; ibid., 13555, vol. 1, 14 July 1920, McPherson & Company to the Minister; ibid., ca April–May 1920, Memo from Spruce Falls; ibid., RG3-4, Spruce Falls ... 1920, 29 May 1920, E.C. Drury to McPherson.

36 Ibid.; ibid., 31 May 1920, W.D. McPherson to E.C. Drury; ibid., 1 June 1920, F.J. Sensenbrenner to Drury; ibid., 8 June 1920, Drury to Sensenbrenner; AO, RG1-246-3, 13555, vol. 1, 11 June 1920, Agreement between Crown and Spruce Falls Pulp and Paper; ibid., 14 July 1920, McPherson & Company to the Minister; ibid., RG75-57, OC103/382 and OC105/226; E.C. Drury, *Farmer Premier: Memoirs of the Honourable E.C. Drury* (Toronto: McClelland and Stewart, 1966), 96–7 and 131; Johnston, 170.

37 J.C. Kimberly was chairman of the board of the First National Bank of Neenah, Wisconsin, and F.J. Sensenbrenner was vice-president of the First National Bank of Appleton: AO, RG1-246-3, 13555, vol. 1, 16 June 1920, McPherson & Company (M&C) to W.E. Raney; ibid., 21 June 1920, L.V. Rorke re: Kapuskasing Pulp Limit; ibid., 17 June 1920, F.E. Ballister to Minister; ibid., 18 June 1920, R.S. Powell to Minister; ibid., 17 June 1920, First Wisconsin National Bank to Minister; ibid., 2 July 1920, M&C to F.E. Titus.

38 Johnston, 167–71
39 AO, RG1-246-3, 13555, vol. 1, 13 September 1921, Declaration of F.J.
    Sensenbrenner; ibid., 24 August 1921, Memo to the Minister from W.C.
    Cain; ibid., RG1-246-3, 35146, vol. 1, 19 May 1923, W.D. McPherson to the
    Minister; ibid., 47959, vol. 1, 26 April 1923, Sensenbrenner to the Minister;
    AO, RG75-57, OC116/128, 124/145 and 128/204; ibid., RG3-4, Kapuskasing
    Townsite 1923, 26 April 1923, Sensenbrenner to E.C. Drury and enclosure.
40 NYPLA, *New York Times* Company Records, A.H. Sulzberger Papers,
    247(4-10), 9 March 1925, G.F. Hardy, "Report on Spruce Falls Company,
    Ltd., Kapuskasing, Ontario," 10.
41 Ibid., RG1-246-3, 47959, vol. 1, 7 May 1923, W.J. Boland to B. Bowman.
42 Ibid., 3267, vol. 1, 27 November 1922, D. Chisholm to the Minister; AO,
    RG75-57, OC124/145.

Introduction to Section IV

 1 *Canada Lumberman*, 4 January 1924; Kuhlberg, "'Pulpwood Is the Only
    Thing We Do Export.'"
 2 Oliver, *Public and Private Persons*, 46; Lambert and Pross, 199–201; Pross,
    "The Development of Professions," 394–5; Gillis and Roach, 101–2.
 3 AO, RG18-79, vol. XXII, 9152-9156; ibid., RG75-57, OC67/377; ibid.,
    MU1354, 26 May–31 May 1934, 28 May 1934, C.C. Hele to The Prime
    Minister; Oliver, *G. Howard Ferguson*, 262.
 4 AO, MU1580, Pigeon River 1919–1929, 31 March 1927, B. Alexander to E.E.
    Johnson.
 5 Other examples of this ruse from this period, including at least one which
    Ferguson oversaw while acting minister, are found in: ibid., RG1-246-3,
    8919, vol. 1; ibid., 86613; ibid., 16064.
 6 Kuhlberg, "'Nothing but a cash deal': Crown Timber Corruption in
    Northern Ontario, 1923–1930," Thunder Bay Historical Museum Society,
    Papers and Records, 2000.
 7 During this period Little and Hogarth were constantly fretting about their
    ability to achieve their goals. Hogarth confided to Little in 1924 that "one
    can never tell what will intervene to upset ones [*sic*] plans when dealing
    with governments no matter how friendly they may be." They were so un-
    certain about their standing in this regard that, in the spring of 1925, Little
    urged Hogarth to investigate matters to see "whether or not ... our friends
    on the hill would double cross us." Hogarth asked Charles McCrea, the
    veteran Tory MPP from Sudbury, to assuage their concerns. A relieved

Hogarth telegraphed Little in mid-1925 that McCrea "insists has no
knowledge chief wants us out way": TBHMS, A83/1/3, 16 January 1924,
D.M. Hogarth to J.A. Little; ibid., A83/1/3, 4 April 1925, Little to Hogarth;
ibid., 6 April 1925, Hogarth to Little.

8   Ibid., 4 July 1925, D. Hogarth to J.A. Little; ibid., 6 July 1925, Little to
Hogarth; AO, RG1-246-3, 48171, documents from 1924 and 1925.

9   UTA, A72-0025, 147, W to Wa, 9 December 1924, C.D. Howe to R.M. Watt;
ibid., 144, Rog-Rz, 10 December 1925, Howe to Antoine Lacasse
[Confidential]; Ellis, 132; AO, RG1-246-3, 57426, 17 December 1924, J.
Lyons to J.E. Weatherhead; TBHMS, A83/1/2, 6 June 1924, J.A. Little to D.
Hogarth.

10   *PPMC*, 7 February 1924, 173–4; *Toronto Mail and Empire* and *Globe*, 1
August 1923; *Annual Report, 1924*, 12; *Hansard*, 28 March 1924.

11   *PPMC*, 30 July 1925, 865; AO, RG1-246-3, 1108, vol. 1, 23 February 1925,
L.R. Wilson to J. Lyons; ibid., 7 March 1925, Minister to Abitibi; ibid.,
59650, vol. 1, 12 August 1925, D. McLeod to Lyons; *Globe*, 10 August 1925
[Letter to the Editor from F. Noad]; ibid., RG75-57, OC146/196.

12   The document was simply a form letter in which the blanks – regarding
the number of new jobs to be created by the industry – had been filled in.
Moreover, it was neither signed by A. Smith, Abitibi's president, addressed to Ferguson, nor written on Abitibi's easily recognizable
stationery.

13   Ibid., RG3-6, Abitibi Power … 1926, all correspondence related to this supposed project; Branch, 136–7; Oliver, *G. Howard Ferguson*, 275. On the eve
of the 1926 election, the Tories also unveiled plans for a massive new hard-
wood lumber mill on the north shore of Lake Huron, an enterprise that
never got past the planning stages. The strategy of announcing new pulp
and paper mill developments on the eve of a provincial election proved so
successful that the Liberals adopted it in 1937.

14   Oliver, *G. Howard Ferguson*, 193, 365, and 372, argues that Ferguson "was
determined to lessen dependence on the United States" and his "persistent
endeavour [was] to formulate strategies to resist American encroach-
ments." The evidence strongly suggests that the opposite was true.

15   Kuhlberg, "'In the Power of the Government': The Rise and Fall of
Newsprint in Ontario, 1894–1932" (PhD thesis, York University, 2002),
285–91, serves as the basis for this and the next paragraph.

16   While most Canadian newsprint firms had a representative from one of
Canada's major banks on their board of directors, CIP's inaugural board
included the heads of the country's three largest.

Chapter 7

1   AO, RG1-246-3, 32405, 5 June 1924, T. Gibson to G.H. Ferguson; ibid.,
    7 September 1923, Gibson, Fort William Paper Application; ibid., 20 June
    1924, Gibson to J. Lyons, enclosing copy of 6 June 1924, Gibson to A. Beck;
    ibid., 44482, documents germane to Thunder Bay Paper's application be-
    tween August 1923 and May 1924.
2   TBHMS, A83/1/3, 10 July 1925, J.A. Little to D.M. Hogarth; ibid., 9 and
    16 March and 8 July 1925, Hogarth to Little; ibid., 9 July 1925, Hogarth to
    E.A. Cuff; ibid., A83/1/4, 13 July 1925, Hogarth to Little; ibid., 15 July
    1925, Little to Hogarth; A83/1/2, 7 July 1923, Hogarth to Little.
3   Ibid., A83/2/2, 8 April 1926, Agreement between Thunder Bay Paper ...
    and J.A. Little; ibid., 24 January 1924, J. Lyons to D.M. Hogarth; ibid.,
    A83/1/2, 25 September and 10 October 1923, J.A. Little to Hogarth; ibid.,
    A83/1/3, 26 February and 11 March 1925, Little to Hogarth [2]; ibid., cor-
    respondence from February and March 1925 between Hogarth and
    Thunder Bay Paper; ibid., 19 March 1925, Hogarth to F.N. Youngman;
    ibid., 12 June 1925, G.W. Mead to Hogarth; ibid., A83/1/5, 27 January
    1926, W.H. Hearst to Hogarth; ibid., 29 January 1926, Mead to Hogarth.
4   Details regarding Nipigon Fibre's origins are summarized from: ibid.,
    32405, vol. 1, ibid., 25 September 1920, Nipigon Fibre to Bowman; ibid.,
    1 March 1923, J.A. Little to B. Bowman; ibid., RG18-83, *Interim Report*,
    15 November 1922, 8–10; ibid., RG1-E-4-B, W-8-61; *PPMC*, 13 May 1920,
    529; Bertrand,"Timber Wolves," 102–3; TBHMS, A83/2/1, 19 January 1922,
    Memo of Agreement; ibid., A83/1/2, 10 February 1922, Little to D.
    Hogarth; MCCR, TC17628, passim.
5   Immediately after signing the deal with Timmins, Hogarth and Little felt
    obliged to take steps to portray it as one which had absolutely nothing to
    do with, as Hogarth aptly put it, "our ability to bring influence to bear on
    the Government of the day to give us a timber concession": TBHMS,
    A83/1/3, 20 March 1925, J.A. Little to D.M. Hogarth; ibid., 4 July 1925,
    Hogarth to Little.
6   Ibid., A83/1/2, 4 December 1923 and 10 and 11 March 1924, D.M. Hogarth
    to J.A. Little; ibid., 28 November 1923 and 12 March 1924, Little to
    Hogarth; MCCR, TC48322, all documents; *PPMC*, 4 October 1923, 992.
7   TBHMS, A83/1/2, ca 4 December 1923, D.M. Hogarth to J.A. Little.
8   Ibid., A83/1/2, 20 August 1924, D.M. Hogarth to J.A. Little, enclosed in
    which is 20 August 1924, Re: Timber Policy; AO, RG1-246-3, 44482, vol. 1,
    6 September 1924, Hogarth to J. Lyons; ibid., 8 September 1924, Minister to
    Hogarth.

9 TBHMS, A83/1/3, 24 June 1925, D. Hogarth to G.W. Mead.

10 Ibid., 17 March 1925, F.N. Youngman to D.M. Hogarth; ibid., 26 February 1925, J.A. Little to Hogarth; ibid., 23 and 24 February 1925, E. Rossiter to Hogarth.

11 Ibid., A83/1/2, 16 January 1924, D.M. Hogarth to J.A. Little [2].

12 *Annual Report,1924*, 10–11; ibid., *1925*, 11; TBHMS, A83/2/2, 23 May and 15 September 1924, D.M. Hogarth to J.A. Little.

13 *Annual Report, 1925*, 10; AO, RG1-246-3, 58915, vol. 1, 28 July 1925, Deputy Minister to J.S. Gillies.

14 Ibid., RG3-6, Timber Limits 1925, 5 October 1925, G.H. Ferguson to C. McCrea [c/o F.H. Keefer] and to J. Lyons; ibid., 25 November 1925, Ferguson to F.A. Drake; ibid., 10 December 1925, M. Francis to Ferguson; ibid., 14 December 1925, Ferguson to Francis; AOL, General Conditions with respect to Pulp and Timber Limits, 10 September 1925.

15 It is noteworthy that the premier portrayed Keefer's new role as one designed to further industrial and social development in the north even though Keefer had been closely identified for over two decades with the pulpwood exporters and zealously pushed their agenda after he was named legislative secretary. Northern MPPs of all stripes were unimpressed by his appointment, and while his demeanour and politics were so vexatious that his Tory colleagues found him intolerable, Ferguson stuck by him. Ferguson even supported him as the Conservative candidate in the 1926 election, whereas Hogarth was so disgusted by Keefer's activities that he opposed him as an Independent-Conservative in the contest, which Hogarth won: TBHMS, A83/1/2, 17 March 1924, J.A. Little to D.M. Hogarth; ibid., A83/1/8, undated, Hogarth to Little; *Hansard*, 15 March 1924; A83/1/4, 24 November 1925, Hogarth to Little.

16 AO, RG1-256, MR Reconnaissance 1930, 30 September 1930, Dept. Forester to J.E. Rothery; ibid., RG1-246-3, 16084, vol. 1, 23 April 1929, W.C. Cain to D.A. Clark; TBHMS, A83/2/2, 31 December 1923, D.M. Hogarth to J. Lyons; Bertrand, "Timber Wolves," 102–3.

17 AO, RG1-246-3, 44482, documents between 31 December 1923 and 17 March 1924; ibid., 16084, vol. 1, documents from the late 1910s and early 1920s.

18 TBHMS, A83/1/3, 8 January and 17 March 1925, D.M. Hogarth to J.A. Little; ibid., 11 March 1925, Little to Hogarth; ibid., A83/1/2, 11 December 1923 and 3 September and 5 December 1924, Little to Hogarth.

19 Ibid., A83/1/4, 3 September and 23 and 24 November 1925, D.M. Hogarth to J.A. Little; ibid., 19 and 25 November 1925, Little to Hogarth: Little explained to Hogarth that this news completely undermined Nipigon

Corporation's plans for its mill. "If this easily accessible and good timber be taken away from us," Little lamented, "we can't possibly afford to pay the price named in our tender inasmuch as a great deal of our area is thinly timbered and difficult to log."

20 AO, RG1-246-3, 58915, vol. 1, 25 December 1925, F.N. Youngman to J. Lyons; ibid., 25 November 1925, Minister to Provincial Paper, Fort William Paper, Thunder Bay Paper, and Nipigon Corporation.

21 LAC, RG39, 344, 47409-1, 20 June 1925, G.M. Seaman to Minister Stewart; TBHMS, A83/1/4, 30 and 31 December 1925, D.M. Hogarth to J.A. Little.

22 AO, RG1-246-3, 61305, 10 September 1925, Fort William Paper to J. Lyons; ibid., 61302, vol. 1, 10 September 1925, G.W. Mead to Minister; ibid., 61303, vol. 1, 10 September 1925, E. Rossiter to Minister.

23 In 1925 Abitibi employed 1,440 men in its 500-ton newsprint mill in Iroquois Falls. By 1928, although the mill had increased its capacity to over 550 tons, Abitibi needed only 1,020 mill workers: UTA, A72-0025, 143, unlabelled, 16 June 1925, C.B. Davis to C.D. Howe; AO, RG1-E-5, vol. 1, Statistical Returns of Manufacturers of Pulp and Paper, Abitibi – Iroquois Falls, 1928.

24 Ibid., RG1-246-3, 61303, vol. 1, 4 and 19 January 1926, W.H. Hearst to J. Lyons.

25 Ibid., 61301, 18 March 1927, F.M. Gordon to F.J. Sensenbrenner; ibid., 61304, vol. 1, 20 May 1926, I.H. Weldon to Department; ibid., 61303, vol. 1, 19 January 1926, W.H. Hearst to J. Lyons. Ferguson's intransigence in this instance was exceptional in light of his actions only a few months later. In March 1926, as acting minister of lands and forests, he personally executed a lease for a pulpwood concession for Howard Smith Paper Mills in Cornwall and acceded to its request that the employment provisions in its contract be qualified by the word "approximately": ibid., 61186, vol. 1, all documents from 1925–6.

26 Oliver, *G. Howard Ferguson*, 209–10; Lower, *Settlement*, 126–8.

27 AO, RG1-246-3, 61303, vol. 1, 19 January 1926, W.H. Hearst to J. Lyons.

28 Ibid., 61302, vol. 1, 22 July 1927, G.W. Mead to W.H. Finlayson; ibid., 27 August 1927 and 1 February 1928, Mead to D.M. Hogarth; ibid., 29 August 1927, Finlayson to Mead; ibid., 29 August 1927, S.A. Russell to Finlayson; ibid., 8 February 1928, W.C. Cain to Thunder Bay Paper; ibid., 30 April 1928, Newaygo to Deputy Minister; ibid., RG1-256, MPF Nipigon Provincial Forest, 16 November 1929, A.J. Auden to Forestry Branch.

29 *Annual Report, 1927*, 30 January 1926, Agreement between Crown and Nipigon Corporation; AO, RG1-246-3, 16084, vol. 1, 18 August 1922, J.H. Milway to W.C. Cain; ibid., 14 January 1926, E. Rossiter to J. Lyons; ibid.,

15 January 1926, Lyons to Rossiter; ibid., 22 September 1926, Rossiter to the Minister; ibid., 61303, vol. 1, 22 September 1926, Rossiter to the Minister; ibid., 29 September 1926, Cain to Nipigon Corporation; AO, RG75-57, OC150/235.
30 *Moody's Industrials, 1928*, International Paper Company; TBHMS, A83/2/3, 2 March 1928, J.I. Rankin to D.M. Hogarth; ibid., A83/3/1, Daily Journal 1929 – Cash Account, Entry of $257,812.50 for 11 December.
31 AO, RG1-246-3, 61303, vol. 1, 7 February 1927, J.J. Rankin to Mr. Finlayson; ibid., 9 February 1927, Department to Rankin.
32 Ibid., 27 June 1927, Minister to Nipigon Corporation; ibid., 16 April and 25 June 1927, E. Rossiter to Mr Finlayson; ibid., 29 July 1927, J.H. Milway to W.C. Cain; ibid., 11 August 1927, Deputy Minister to Milway; ibid., 19 August 1927, Cain to Nipigon Corporation; ibid., 19 August 1927, W.W. Pope to Finlayson; ibid., 1 September 1927, Minister to Nipigon Corporation; ibid., RG75-57, OC159/350 and OC160/342.

Chapter 8

1 Provincial also held a licence to the Sibley Forest Reserve, but this area was relatively insignificant.
2 AO, RG1-246-3, 18284, vol. 1, 10 January 1923, Memo for the Minister from W.C. Cain.
3 TBHMS, A83/1/4, 15 July 1925, D.M. Hogarth to J.A. Little; ibid., 17 July 1925, Little to Hogarth; ibid., A83/1/3, 6 April, 11 June and 10 July 1925, Hogarth to Little.
4 AO, RG1-246-3, 61304, vol. 1, 10 September and 21 December 1925, I.H. Weldon to J. Lyons.
5 Ibid., 39865, Tenders on West Side Lake Nipigon, 1925.
6 Ibid., 61304, vol. 1, 31 December 1926 and 18 February 1928, I.H. Weldon to W.C. Cain; ibid., 28 January 1928, Memo for Cain from F.E. Titus; ibid., 31 January 1928, Cain to Provincial Paper; ibid., 3 February 1926, Minister [unsigned] to W.H. Hearst; ibid., 4 March 1926, J.W. Pickup to Cain; ibid., 16 March 1926, Cain to Provincial Paper; Bertrand, "Timber Wolves," 102. Provincial openly admitted a few years later that at "the time of making the lease in 1926, we accepted the Government's estimate of the quantity of wood" even though the company knew that its limits held about 5,000,000 cords of pulpwood: AO, RG1-246-3, 18284, vol. 1, 11 September 1929, S.F. Duncan to W.C. Cane [*sic*]; Mutual Life Company Archives (hereafter MLCA), 81.20-150, 18 August 1932, Report to the Bondholders Protective Committee by the Chairman of the Committee [Strictly Confidential].

7 In January 1926, the provincial auditor found that Lyons's hardware firm in the Soo had done just over $2,800 worth of business with the government, which violated the Tories' recently announced policy of prohibiting MPPs from selling wares or services to the government. Compared to the improper activities in which Ferguson was involved at this time, Lyons's transgression was relatively innocent and trivial, and the premier could easily have smoothed it over had he wished to do so: AO, RG3-6, Lyons Fuel … 1926, 29 January 1926, G.A. Brown to W.H. Price; ibid., Resignation of Jas. Lyons … 1926, 1 March 1926, Minister Lyons to Mr. Ferguson and Ferguson to Lyons.

8 Fort William Paper would not be permitted to harvest within this section until the jack pine had been sold: TBMHS, A83/1/3 and A83/1/4, documents germane to the partitioning of this tract.

9 AO, RG3-6, Timber Limits 1925, 3 May 1926, J. Lyons to G.H. Ferguson; TBHMS, A83/1/4, 2 December 2, 1925, D.M. Hogarth to J.A. Little. Even Hogarth was shocked at Ferguson's extreme actions in this instance.

10 AO, RG1-246-3, 66423, vol. 1, 23 July 1926, G.R. Gray to W.C. Cain.; ibid., 28 July 1926, Deputy Minister to Fort William Paper; FWA, Binder T-1-1 to T-4-5, 3 February 1926, B.F. Avery to W. Greer.

11 Ibid., Agreements Binder #1, 10 December 1928, General Report on the Nipigon Limit; TBHMS, A83/2/3, ca 1926 Draft of Fort William … Agreement; AO, RG75-57, 158/426; ibid., RG1-246-3, 61305, 27 February 1926, J. Lyons to W.C Cain; ibid., 8 March 1926, Memo to L.V. Rorke from Cain.

12 FWA, Agreements Binder #1, 10 December 1928, General Report on the Nipigon Limit; SMPA, A-1, Report on Aerial Forest Reconnaissance … for Fort William Paper … 30 November 1927, James D. Lacey & Company, 6–7. Ferguson refused requests from politicians in both Port Arthur and Fort William to subsidize the construction of a railway to facilitate the development of the timber resources on the west side of Lake Nipigon. They reminded the Tories that the public purse had been tapped to exploit northeastern Ontario's minerals through the construction of the Temiskaming and Northern Ontario Railway (TNOR) in the early part of the century. Moreover, during the mid-1920s Ferguson poured millions of dollars into extending the TNOR to the gold finds in the Rouyn-Noranda region: AO, RG3-6, H.E.P.C. re: Duluth … 1926, 25 February 1926, A.M. McNaughton to G.H. Ferguson and 2 March 1926, Fort William Board of Trade to Ferguson; ibid., Pulpwood Industry 1926, 12 February 1926, T.F. Milne to the Crown; A. Tucker, *Steam into Wilderness: Ontario Northland Railway, 1902–1962* (Toronto: University of Toronto Press, 1978), ch. 8.

13 AO, RG1-246-3, 66423, vol. 1, 22 October 1927, G.R. Gray to W. Finlayson; ibid., 24 October 1927, Department to Fort William Paper.

14 UTA, A73-0026, 264, 67, Alexander McDougall; LAC, MG26-J, C2256, 76009-76013 76010-11, 15 February 1923, A. McDougall to J. Pope; ibid., 76012, 20 February 1923, F.A. McGregor to W.L.M. King; ibid., 76009, 3 March 1923, McDougall to King; ibid., 76013, 5 March 1923, King to McDougall; ibid., C2267, 88389, 4 June 1924, McGregor to McDougall; ibid., 88390-1, 2 August 1924, W.H. Walker to McDougall; ibid., 88392-3, 3 August 1924, Memorandum for the Prime Minister regarding the claims of Messrs. McDougall and Hepburn Against the Latvian Government, Walker; AO, RG1-246-3, 9582, vol. 1, documents from 1921-2, especially 26 January 1921, Memo for Mr. Zavitz.

15 Ibid., RG75-57, OC141/184; ibid., RG1-246-3, 9582, vol. 1, 1 March 1924, Assignment by A. McDougall to Calders (Canada), Ltd; ibid., 17 September 1924, McDougall to Minister; ibid., 4 December 1924, Statutory Declarations of J. Calder and A. McDougall; ibid., 8 December 1924, Memo for Mr. Cain from Provincial Auditor.

16 The manufacturing condition was only operative if a concession lease explicitly stated that the contract was subject to it. If the lease did not, as was the case here, the spruce was exportable.

17 Ibid., RG75-57, OC153/150; ibid., RG1-246-3, 9582, vol. 1, 23 November 1925, Affidavit of A. McDougall; ibid., 24 November 1925, J.F. Hobkirk to W.C. Cain; ibid., 25 November 1925, Cain to Young & McEvoy (Y&M); ibid., 3 December 1925, Y&M to Deputy Minister. Details of Ferguson's final bailout of McDougall are found in AO, RG3-6, Timber Limits 1926, and ibid., RG75-57, OC153/150.

18 Ibid., RG1-246-3, 39865, vol. 1, correspondence from July 1923 to January 1924, and 14 May 1926, W.C. Cain to A. McDougall; ibid., 61307, 11 May 1926, McDougall/Twin Allan Lumber and Pulp Company to Minister; ibid., RG3-4, H.E.P.C. Nipigon Development 1923, 5 April 1923, G.F. Doan to E.C. Drury, enclosing 2 April 1923 resolution from Sioux Lookout.

19 Ibid., RG1-246-3, 39865, vol. 1, 17 June 1926, W.C. Cain to Twin Allan Lumber & Pulp Coy. Ltd.

20 Ibid., 9582, vol. 1, 20 September 1926, G. Scott, Liquidation Notice.

21 Ibid., 25095, 20 April 1932, History of Farlinger's Negotiations, by H.C. Draper, explains that Ferguson had "promised on several occasions to have the lease[s] executed but owing to pressure of work, this was not done"; ibid., 1926 Agreement for pulpwood in Sioux Lookout area; ibid., 9 February 1927, G.E. Farlinger to W. Finlayson; ibid., 60457, vol. 1,

23 March 1926, Farlinger to Ferguson; ibid., 11 August 1926, L.V. Rorke to W. Hearst; ibid., 19 November 1926, Rorke to Minister.

22 The press reported that IP had men investigating this pulpwood concession during the early part of 1927 as part of the firm's "prospecting in every possible place in Ontario and Quebec where a new mill may be located or where power and pulp incidence suggest such possibility": *Toronto Telegram*, 25 February and 19 July 1927.

23 Ibid., RG1-246-3, 39865, vol. 1, 21 January 1927, Y&M to W.C. Cain; ibid., 7 February 1927, Y&M to the Minister; ibid., 10229, vol. 1, 15 December 1928, Y&M to Cain.

24 Ibid., 39865, vol. 1, 26 January 1927, W.C. Cain to Y&M; ibid., 11 April 1927, Y&M to W. Finlayson; ibid., Draft Agreement between the Crown and [blank] Limited, April 1927; ibid., 12 and 22 April 1927, J.A. McEvoy to Cain.

25 Ibid., 13 May 1927, Memo for the Minister from W.C. Cain. This is another document that C.C. Hele probably prepared for Cain's signature.

26 Ibid., RG75-57, OC158/426; ibid., RG1-246-3, 39865, vol. 1, 24 June 1927, J.A. McEvoy to W.C. Cain; MCCR, TC30385, 18 June 1927, McEvoy to W.W. Dennison and enclosure; ibid., 27 June 1927, Agreement between North West Ontario … A. McDougall and B.R. Hepburn; AO, RG1-246-3, 39865, vol. 1, 12 October 1927, Option agreement from Alexander McDougall … to International Paper Company. Under this contract IP advanced McDougall roughly $40,000 in exchange for an option on North West Ontario's pulpwood concession. There was little chance, however, that McDougall would ever clear his debt because IP already controlled McDougall's timber operations and limits through North West Ontario. McDougall failed to repay his loan in February 1928, but IP permitted him to sign over several more promissory notes, including one dated 28 June 1928, for $500,000. This appears to have been the cost of buying McDougall's silence, for although he never repaid his loans, IP waited until the late 1930s to launch legal actions against him: AO, RG22-5800, 1937/2037 and 1938/1800.

27 Ibid., MU1591, Statistics Timber Limits, Summary of Woodlands in Quebec, New Brunswick and Ontario, Owned or Controlled by I.P. and Subsidiaries, ca 1931.

28 *Hansard*, 28 March 1928; *PPMC*, 5 January 1928, 16. The Tories soon carried out another, almost identical scheme on International Paper's behalf, this one involving a large pulpwood tract in northwestern Ontario that Fort William eagerly sought: AO, RG1-246-3, 5509, vols. 1 and 2, all documents;

MCCR, TC28127, all documents; AO, RG75-57, OC163/235; ibid., MU1591, Timber Limits Statistics, 17 February 1931, J.H. Hinman to E.E. Johnson.

29 FWA, Agreements Binder #1, 10 December 1928, General Report on Nipigon Limit; AO, RG1-246-3, 61305, vol. 1, 17 January 1927, G.R. Gray to Department; ibid., 66423, vol. 1, 10 November 1927 and 16 January 1928, Gray to W. Finlayson; ibid., 7608, all documents from 1927–8; TBHMS, B11/1/1, 21 December 1926, W.C. Lillie to Phoenix Assurance.

30 AO, RG1-246-3, 66423, vol. 1, 25 January 1928, Minister to G.R. Gray.

31 Ibid., 4 December 1929, G.R. Gray to The Minister, enclosed in which is 3 December 1929, Memo re Fort William Division wood resources; ibid., 11 December 1929, Memo for Mr. Cain from W. Finlayson. For the next two decades, the Ontario government refused to augment the company's pulpwood supply; when it finally adjusted the mill's concession in the mid-1930s, it reduced the amount of fibre available to the operation.

32 *Saturday Night*, 24 November, and 1 and 8 December 1928.

33 UTA, A72-0025, 138, Bro-Bry, 28 November 1928, C.D. Howe to F. Brown; ibid., 10 December 1928, Brown to Howe.

Chapter 9

1 AO, RG3-6, Mattagami Pulp … 1925, 25 April 1925, W.J. Boland to G.H. Ferguson and J. Lyons; ibid., 11 May 1925, Boland to Lyons.

2 Ibid., RG1-246-3, 13555, vol. 2, 8 June 1925, B. Bowman to F.J. Sensenbrenner. W.C. Cain noted on this letter that it had been handed to him on that day "to be placed on the public records, as evidence of what Mr. Beniah Bowman, while Minister of Lands & Forests, in the Drury Government, intended for the Spruce Falls Company Ltd., had they remained in power." Neither Bowman nor Sensenbrenner mentioned this larger newsprint mill when Bowman had granted the lease to Smoky Falls in 1923, and nothing in the files germane to this matter even hints that this was the understanding at that time. Sensenbrenner had also scrupulously ensured that his arrangements with the Ontario government were matters of public record.

3 Butcher, 99–104; SFI, Regeneration Studies and Surveys, Report of a Cruise of Spruce Falls Company's Limits, 1924, F.R. Wilcox; AO, RG1-246-3, 13555, vol. 1A, 18 December 1924, F.J. Sensenbrenner to Minister.

4 Butcher, 107–13; M. Berger, *The Story of the New York Times, 1851–1951* (New York: Simon and Schuster, 1951), 246 and 333; AO, RG1-246-3, 13555, vol. 1A, 18 December 1924 and 15 January 1925, F.J. Sensenbrenner to Minister; ibid., 61301, vol. 1, 2 June 1925, J.H. Black to J. Lyons; ibid., 24 June 1925, Minister to Spruce Falls.

5 Ibid., RG1-116, box 1, Memoranda – Director 1924, 26 September 1924, J.K. Kimberly to W.R. Maxwell; ibid., 8 October 1924, Maxwell to H.D. Wilshire; ibid., 9 October 1924, Maxwell to Kimberly.

6 Ibid., 58915, vol. 1, 10 September 1925, W.D. Ross and I.W. Killam; ibid.; RG3-6, Timber Limits 1925, 25 November 1925, Memo from W.J. Boland.

7 Ibid., RG1-246-3, 61303, vol. 1, 10 September 1925, F.J. Sensenbrenner to J. Lyons [2]; NYPLA, *New York Times*, A.H. Sulzberger Papers, 247(4), 3 August 1925, A.H. Sulzberger to Dear Father. KC also asked for an agreement lasting much longer than twenty-one years on the grounds that this short term "may prove a serious hindrance to our financing," a wish the Tories granted.

8 AO, RG1-246-3, 3267, 6 May 1925, Memo for Mr. Cain from J. Lyons; ibid., 11 May 1925, Memo for Cain from W.F.T.; ibid., 13555, vol. 2, 9 January 1925, Memo to Cain from Lyons; ibid., 14 January 1925, Memo for Cain from J.H.H.; ibid., 58915, vol. 1, 23 July 1925, Memo for Lyons from A. Ferguson; ibid., 10 July 1925, I.W. Killam to Lyons; ibid., 17 and 24 July 1925, Minister to Killam.

9 Ibid., RG3-6, Timber Limits 1925, 26 September 1925, Memo for G.H. Ferguson from J. Lyons.

10 Ibid., 24 November 1925, W.J. Boland to G.H. Ferguson, Ferguson to Boland, and Ferguson to J. Lyons; ibid., Mattagami Pulp … 1925, passim; ibid., Mattagami Pulp … 1926, all documents; ibid., RG1-246-3, 58915, vol. 1, 5 and 16 November 1925, Minister to W.D. Ross and I. Killam; ibid., 12 November 1925, Ross and Killam to Lyons.

11 Ibid., RG3-6, Timber Limits 1925, all documents, especially 27 November 1925, G.H. Ferguson to W.J. Boland; ibid., RG1-246-3, 58915, vol. 1, 11 November 1925, J.H. Black to J. Lyons, and 16 November 1925, Minister to I.W. Killam and W.D. Ross; ibid., 13555, vol. 4, 22 March 1937, Mortgage from Spruce Falls to National Trust Company, Limited, enclosed in which is 12 May 1926, agreement between Spruce Falls and Kimberly-Clark for sale of sulphite pulp.

12 Ibid., RG1-E-5, vol. 19, Mill Returns, 1928–1932.

13 SFI, Regeneration Studies and Surveys, 9 March 1927, J.H. Black to F.J. Sensenbrenner; Butcher, 114–15.

14 TBHMS, A83/1/4, 29, 30 and 31 December 1925, D. Hogarth to J. A. Little: the citations are from December 31; AO, RG75-57, OC149/395 and OC153/47; ibid., RG1-246-3, 34202, documents from 1925–6. Ferguson granted Spruce Falls a string of additional favours, including a release from its contractual obligation to build a sawmill to utilize the large timber on its limits. More importantly, he addressed fears KC's investors

expressed about the firm's power lease to Smoky Falls by extending the contract for over fifty years and permitting KC to choose the order in which it developed its hydro sites: ibid., RG3-6, Spruce Falls ... 1926, 22 September 1926, Memo for the Prime Minister from W.C. Cain; ibid., 4 October 1926, G.H. Ferguson to J.H. Black; ibid., RG75-57, OC151/483.

15 Ibid., RG3-6, Spruce Falls ... 1926, 17 April 1926, S. Johnston to G.H. Ferguson. Nelles, 384, argues that the financial backers did not understand the provisions of the agreement because they were Americans. This interpretation ignores the fact that American investment houses had been deeply involved in the Canadian pulp and paper industry for several decades, and the particular investor in this instance, First Trust and Savings Bank of Chicago, had a long history of financing pulp and paper ventures in Ontario, specifically Backus's mills (including Great Lakes Paper). In chapter 10, it will be shown that in 1926–7 Ferguson notified Great Lakes Paper that it had defaulted on its leases and that his government was going to cancel them. Thus, the American financiers were not unfamiliar with Crown agreements, and had an acute understanding of these leases and the extent to which Ferguson was prepared to enforce the provisions in these contracts.

16 AO, RG3-6, Spruce Falls ... 1926, 21 April 1926, G.H. Ferguson to S. Johnston. Nelles, 382–4 and 396–8, cites this letter from Ferguson to substantiate his contention that the interests of the state and industry had become practically congruent. Nelles asserts that "no better illustration of the interdependence of government and industry could be given than Howard Ferguson's explanation of the role of government, as he conceived it, written for the benefit of the Spruce Falls ... shareholders." Nelles's argument hinges on the fact that investors were reassured by Ferguson's words, which they clearly were not.

17 NYPLA, *The New York Times* Company Records, A.S. Ochs Papers, 112(10), 15 March 1927, F.J. Sensenbrenner to A.H. Sulzberger; ibid., 19 and 23 March, Sensenbrenner to Sulzberger; AO, RG75-57, OC157/411.

18 *The Globe*, 1 October 1926 and 14 February 1928; SMPA, A-1, 26 November 1917, Petition – In District Court of United States for Southern District of New York, United States of America against George H. Mead et al., 4; *New York Times*, 27 September 1927; *Cooperation*, November 1927; NYPLA, *The New York Times* Company Records, A.S. Ochs Papers, 112(10), 2 August 1926, F.J. Sensenbrenner to A.S. Ochs; ibid., 28 August 1926, Ochs to Sensenbrenner.

19 Butcher, 123–5.

20 AO, RG22-5800, 1921/1339, all documents, particularly ca November 1926, Memo re: Mattagami Pulp, by G.T. Clarkson.

21 *Toronto Mail and Empire*, 26 September 1923; *The Globe*, 16 December 1925.
22 This analysis substantiates the contention that Cain did not write the crucial mid-1927 memo that had argued in favour of privately granting North West Ontario a massive pulpwood concession near Sioux Lookout. In that instance, as well as here, there were equally "keen rivalr[ies]" for the pulpwood in question, and Cain habitually argued for selling Crown timber in a manner that maximized the price the buyer paid for it.
23 AO, RG1-246-3, 3267, vol. 1, 26 February 1927, G.H. Kilmer to W. Finlayson; ibid., 28 February 1927, Memo for W.C. Cain from Minister; ibid., 4 March 1927, Memo for the Minister from Cain; ibid., 72456, vol. 1, 12 September 1927, G.C. Hurdman to W. Finlayson; ibid., 12 August 1927, Tender for Alexandra and Webster; ibid., bids from Beaver Wood Fibre [2], Hawk Lake Lumber Company and Ontario Paper; *Annual Report, 1928*, 14. Abitibi Fibre in Smooth Rock Falls lobbied unsuccessfully for permission to harvest this pulpwood throughout the 1930s and early 1940s, and the department only relented after the Second World War.
24 AO, RG1-246-3, 53229, vol. 1, all documents from 1926–7; ibid., 10 and 15 August and September 20 1927 and 24 March and July 20 1928, W.C. Cain to Abitibi Fibre; ibid., 17 August 1927, L.R. Wilson to Cain; ibid., 7 August 1928, G. Kilmer to Cain; ibid., vol. 2, March 29, 1935, C.B. Davis to H.G. Schanche.
25 G.R. Horne, "The Receivership and Reorganization of The Abitibi Power and Paper Company, Limited" (PhD thesis, University of Michigan, 1954), 41; SMPA, A-1, unlabelled, 28 May 1945, T.H. Stone to C.B. Davis.
26 AO, RG75-57, OC138/60; ibid., RG1-305, August 1929, Data Required by "Pulpwood Conservation Act, 1929," Abitibi Power and Paper Company, Limited (hereafter Data Required by ...), Iroquois Falls Division. Abitibi never tapped much of the far northwestern section of this new limit because it would have been egregiously expensive, but only in the mid-1950s did the government agree to delete it from the mill's concession: ibid., RG1-E-10, 144, Abitibi P/P Co. vol. I, 10 November 1952, Memo to F.A. MacDougall; ibid., 1 April 1953, J.F. Sharpe to J.B. Matthews; ibid., 24 April 1953, Memo to J.S. Yoerger from Sharpe.
27 The first paragraph of Abitibi's lease outlined a situation that any company would have been loath to broadcast, namely that its authorized capital was composed solely of hundreds of thousands of no-par-value shares. The contract then explained that Abitibi owned and operated only a 400-ton mill in Iroquois Falls, even though the company had built generating stations whose capacity exceeded 50,000 horsepower and its paper mill manufactured over 550 tons of newsprint and 30 tons of wrapper paper

each day: ibid., RG75-57, OC138/60; ibid., RG1-246-3, 47622, vol. 1, 15 May 1924, Memo for the Minister from W.C. Cain; ibid., 16 May 1924, Memo for Mr. Zavitz from Cain; ibid., 23 May 1924, Zavitz to Cain.

28 Ibid., 30 July 1926, G.H. Kilmer to the Minister; ibid., 11 August 1926, Memo for Mr. Cain from J.H.H.; ibid., 31592, vol. 1, 1 December 1926, L.V. Rorke to L.R. Wilson; ibid., RG3-6, Forest Conservation 1925, 4 November 1925, G.H. Ferguson to J. Lyons; ibid., Abitibi Power ... 1926, 22 April 1926, Ferguson to Wilson; ibid., RG1-305, August 1929, Data Required by ..., Iroquois Falls Division.

29 Ibid., RG1-246-3, 48171, vol. 1, correspondence from winter 1923–4; ibid., 34983, vol. 1, correspondence from September 1923 to February 1924; ibid., RG3-6, Long Sault ... 1925, correspondence between August 1924 and April 1925; ibid., RG22-5800, 1932/2994, 1 April 1941, Order – Relative to supply of electric power; ibid., MU8664, Island Portage, 25 June 1923, Sir William Arrol & Company Limited to Kerry & Chacey Limited re: Island Portage.

30 Ibid., MU2490, HEPC Abitibi Power – Abitibi Canyon, 18 July 1925, W.H. Hearst to W.F. Nickle, which cites Kilmer; ibid., 6 and 14 July 1925, Nickle to G.H. Ferguson; ibid., 14, 16 and 20 July 1925, Ferguson to Nickle; ibid., 16 July 1925, W.C. Noxon to Nickle; ibid., 20 July 1925, Nickle to Ferguson, which reads "Kilmer objects provision giving Crown discretion regarding necessity development"; ibid., RG3-6, Long Sault Rapids 1925, all documents.

31 Ibid., RG75-57, OC155/48. Numerous questions remain regarding this episode, including why Abitibi's new power leases were dated 1 August 1925 even though Ferguson only executed them by Order in Council on 11 November 1926.

32 Ibid., RG1-246-3, 48171, vol. 2, undated Memo re: lease of Island Falls, initialled by W.H.H.. In addition, Abitibi's licence of occupation for Island Falls was only valid "during the pleasure of the Crown": ibid., 34983, 15 April 1926, L.V. Rorke to W. Hearst; ibid., 8 June 1926, Memo for Minister from Rorke.

Chapter 10

1 Unless otherwise indicated, the information in this chapter about Backus is drawn from Kuhlberg, "Eyes wide open."

2 In addition to the examples cited in the text, Backus did not endear himself to Ferguson in 1928 when the premier asked Backus to contribute $20,000 a year for five years as seed money to the Ontario Research

Foundation (ORF). Whereas Archibald Graustein, IP's president, had immediately remitted the contribution to the premier without any caveats about future contributions, Backus delayed sending in his initial payment for over six months. When he finally forwarded his cheque, he cast doubt on his ability to donate again because of the deteriorating conditions in the newsprint industry. Ferguson was undoubtedly unimpressed by Backus's demurring, as was Sir Joseph Flavelle, the ORF's chairman. Flavelle derisively referred to Backus as "a slippery old man" and congratulated Ferguson on "finally hooking this fish": AO, MU1025, Minnesota and Ontario Paper Company, 17 July 1928, E.W. Backus to G.H. Ferguson; ibid., MU1024, Ontario Research Foundation, 5 February 1929, J.W. Flavelle to G. Grant.

3 For one of the only times in his career, Ferguson donned the environmentalist's cap in taking issue with the municipal politicians for having promised Great Lakes Paper that it could dump its waste liquids into the Kaministiquia River. The premier reminded the civic officials that the provincial board of health would have the final say in this issue, and he left no doubt that it would not look favourably upon Great Lakes Paper polluting this waterway: AO, RG3-6, Great Lakes Pulp ... 1924, 6 September 1923, G.H. Ferguson to N. Edmeston.

4 Ibid., MU1027, Kaministiquia Power ... 1924, 3 January 1924, G.H. Ferguson to F. Keefer and to S. Johnston; ibid., 28 December 1923, Keefer to Ferguson; ibid., RG75-57, OC135/353; TBMHS, A55/8/1, G.R. Duncan Misc., Address by city solicitor, 31 August 1923. The new contract raised the price of the electricity to $21 per horsepower, stipulated that the mill would be provided with "commercially continuous" and not "continuous" power, and dubiously claimed that the previous lease had been cancelled by "mutual consent."

5 Alsted, Seaman, and Backus had incorporated Interlake Securities, Limited, to hold the three leases: MCCR, TC24155, 15 August 1924, Statement in lieu of Prospectus; LAC, RG95-1, Box 1549, Interlake Securities; AO, RG1-E-3-B, 1, A-10, 8 November 1923, Agreement between Great Lakes Paper and Combined Locks Paper Company and Affidavit of Lewis Alsted.

6 Ibid., 8 November 1923, Reference Outline concerning ... Great Lakes Paper; ibid., RG1-246-3, 33582, vol. 1, 4 September 1924, F.H. Keefer to W.C. Cain; ibid., 2 February 1925, Cain to J.H. Black; ibid., 9457A, vol. 1, 9 October 1942, E. Rowe to N.O. Hipel, and attachment; ibid., vol. 2, 3 February 1926, Minister to S. Johnston; ibid., 13 March 1926, Johnston to Cain; ibid., 27 February 1926, Johnston to J. Lyons; ibid., 1 March 1926,

Minister to Johnston; ibid., 10 March 1926, Cain to Johnston; ibid., April 20, 1927, Minister to Lewis L. Alsted; *Toronto Mail*, 4 May 1927.

7 *Toronto Daily Star*, 8 April 1927.

8 Backus had purchased the Algoma Eastern Railway lands in 1926 through the Transcontinental Paper Company. Although the manufacturing condition applied to the pulpwood on these tracts, he endeavoured to persuade the Tories to allow him to export this spruce, presumably to satisfy the terms of his contract with Alsted and Seaman. The government refused to cooperate: AO, RG1-246-3, 1173, vol. 1, 1 and 4 October 1926, Memoranda for Mr. Cain from F.E. Titus.

9 SPCA, Seaman Paper Company Minute Book, 5 May 1924 and 20 April 1927; *PPMC*, 12 May 1927, 616; *Toronto Mail*, 4 May 1927; AO, RG1-246-3, 33582, vol. 1, 22 May 1935, L.L. Alsted to P. Heenan; ibid., 23 September 1936, P. White to Heenan; ibid., 9457A, vol. 1, 9 October 1942, E. Rowe to N.O. Hipel, and attachment; MCCR, TC24155, Statement or Return, 1924 to 1928; LAC, RG95-1, 1549, Interlake Securities Limited, 18 April 1927, Bain et al. to Secretary of State; *Fort William Daily Times Journal*, 16–21 May, 31 August and 7 September 1927.

10 AO, RG1-246-3, 9457, vol. 1, 11 April 1928, Crown approval of transfer; ibid., 11 April 1928, S. Johnston to Minister; ibid., RG22-5800, 1933/1012, 13 July 1931, Affidavit of F.R. MacKelcan. While National Trust was acting as Great Lakes Paper's receiver, its officials asked the department for details about the paper company's affairs. They were astonished to learn that the Tories had only approved Alsted's transfer on 11 April 1928 even though Alsted had assigned his concessions to Great Lakes Paper on 8 November 1923. Assuming that this discrepancy was due to a typographical error, National Trust's officials asked the department for clarification, to which departmental personnel promptly replied that this information was accurate: ibid., RG1-246-3, 33582, vol. 1, 18 October 1934, R.W. Finlayson to W.C. Cain; ibid., 30 October 1934, Deputy Minister to Finlayson.

11 Ibid., RG75-57, OC143/409 and OC158/3; ibid., RG3-6, Foley Mine 1925, 10 and 18 February and 6 March 1925, H.G. Acres to G.H. Ferguson; ibid., 17 and 26 February 1925, Ferguson to Acres; ibid., RG1-246-3, 16799, vol. 1, 13 February 1925, W.C. Cain to E.W. Backus and S. Johnston; ibid., vol. 2, 7 April 1925, Johnston to Ferguson; ibid., 61486, vol. 1, 10 February 1926, Ferguson to Johnston; ibid., 17 February and 17 March 1927, Memo for W. Finlayson from Cain; ibid., May–June 1926 correspondence between S. Johnston and Department; ibid., 18 June 1926, Memo for Ferguson from Cain; ibid., vol. 1A, July 1926 Johnston's submissions to the Department; ibid., 18 April 1927, Minister to J.A. Mathieu; ibid., RG3-6, Fort Frances

Pulp ... 1925, 28 April 1925, Ferguson's notes from his meeting with J.H. Black, Backus, and Johnston. After reinstating Backus's lease to the Seine River water powers, Ferguson initiated a legal action on behalf of the Ontario government against Backus for the timber his flooding had damaged. The premier did so even though Backus had applied for permission to cut this wood prior to proceeding with his project and the department had allowed Backus to complete it without mentioning the matter. The story can be traced in these files: ibid., RG1-246-3, 200, 200A, and 34928.

12 Ibid., RG3-6, Control of ... 1926, 4 February 1926, G.H. Ferguson to E.W. Decker; ibid., 4 February 1926, Ferguson to S. Johnston.

13 Ibid., 797, vol. 1, 4 November 1926, J.A. Alexander to W.C. Cain; ibid., 68396, vol. 1, 12 February 1927, H.A. Tibbetts to the Minister, and enclosure; ibid., 6 June 1927, A.D. George to W. Finlayson.

14 Ibid., 3 February 1927, A.D. George to W. Finlayson; ibid., 37584, vol. 1, 8 July 1925, D. McLeod to J. Lyons; ibid., 39983, documents germane to timber north and south of Hematite Station.

15 Ibid., 7 March 1927, Minister to J.W. Walker; ibid., 5 February 1927, Memo for W.C. Cain from W. Finlayson and from Department to A.D. George; ibid., 15 February 1927, Memo for E.J. Zavitz from Cain; ibid., 17 February 1927, Minister to H.A. Tibbetts; ibid., 18648, vol. 2, 9 September 1927, Memo for the Minister from Cain; ibid., 23 September 1927, Tender for Bennett Township; ibid., RG1-E-3-B, W-8-492, all documents.

16 *Annual Report, 1928*, 13–15; *The Forest Resources of Ontario, 1930*; H.H. Parsons, "Aerial Timber Sketching Memoirs" (Toronto: unpublished manuscript, 1976), map between 107 and 108.

17 AO, RG1-246-3, 18648, vol. 3, 17 November 1927, A.D. George to W. Finlayson; ibid., 37584, vol. 1, 4 March 1926, Memo for Mr. Cain from W.F.T.; ibid., 6 June 1927, George to Finlayson; ibid., 10 May 1928, Mashaba to Department; ibid., 25 July 1928, Authorization for "Sale of Pulpwood."

18 Ibid., 14 August 1928, G. McLean to W. Finlayson; ibid., 16 August 1928, J.W. Walker to Finlayson.

19 Ibid., 21 August 1928, W.C. Cain to J.W. Walker and to G. McLean.

20 Ibid., 68396, vol. 1, 28 August 1928, E.W. Backus to W. Finlayson; ibid., 31 August 1928, Minister to Backus; ibid., 28 February 1929, Minister to J.W. Walker; ibid., 31 August 1928, Memo to W.C. Cain from Finlayson; ibid., 37584, vol. 1, 21 December 1928, Memo to the Minister from Cain; ibid., vol. 2, November to December 1928, documents germane to this tender.

21 LAC, RG39, 352, Ontario Research, 14 October 1922, J.R. Dickinson to R.D. Craig.

22 AO, RG3-6, Fort Frances Pulp ... 1925, 28 April 1925, Ferguson's notes from his meeting with J.H. Black, E.W. Backus, and S. Johnston; ibid., MU1591, Statistics Timber Limits, 9, 24, and 29 July 1925, G. McLeod to Backus; ibid., RG1-246-3, 14797, vol. 1, 25 April 1925, Memo for J. Lyons from W.C. Cain; *Toronto Mail &.Empire*, 25 April 1925 and 2 May 1925.

23 LAC, RG10, vol. 30144-7 Part 2, 9 May 1929, F. Edwards to Assistant Deputy; ibid., vol. 7052, Whitefish Bay Reserves 32-34A 1929-49; ibid., vol. 7848, 30129-8 Pt. 2; ibid., vol. 7850, 30130-5A.

24 AO, RG1-246-3, 1956, vol. 2, 12 December 1927, D. McLeod to W. Finlayson; ibid., 17 January 1928, W.C. Cain to Keewatin Lumber; ibid., 16 December 1927, Cain to McLeod; ibid., RG1-256, MR – Reconnaissance 1930 [English River], 27 September 1929, B.F. Avery to J.F. Sharpe; ibid., 10 October 1929, Sharpe to Avery.

25 Ibid., RG1-246-3, 18648, vol. 3, 29 August 1930, G.H. Ferguson to E.W. Backus.

26 Backus would soon encounter more problems. He had incorporated Kenora Paper Mills Company in 1925 to operate his newsprint plant in that town, and he had assigned his two pulpwood leases (English River and Lake of the Woods) to it. Kenora Paper then mortgaged the leases to finance its activities. Backus had not, however, received the department's approval for these moves, and the Tories were outraged when they got wind of them. On the minister's behalf, H.C. Draper explained to Backus's lawyers in November 1931 that disclosure of these transactions "comes as a very great surprise to the Department, in that, notwithstanding that the documents were executed over six years ago, the Department has never been advised of the assignments comprised therein nor has the Department consented to such assignments." Draper added that the department was not about to approve them, either: ibid., 14797, vol. 2, 1 April 1925, Assignment from Backus ... to Kenora Paper Mills; ibid., 6 November 1931, H.C. Draper to Tilley et al. In contrast, the Tories learned long after the fact that IP's subsidiary – Continental – had done exactly the same thing with its leases to the Crown resources in the Elsas area (i.e., mortgaging them without the government's consent), but they turned a blind eye to Continental's transgressions. After the Tories were defeated in the 1934 election, the new deputy minister investigated this matter and was shocked to discover what Continental had done: ibid., 104142, 27 December 1934, Minister to Continental.

27 Ibid., 51744, germane documents; ibid., RG1-246-3, 28567, vol. 1, 7 December 1923, L.E. Bliss to J. Lyons; ibid., 4 May 1923, Assignment by

Continental to Montreal Trust; ibid., RG75-57, OC136/290; ibid., RG1-E-4-B, W-8-209, all documents.

28 Ibid., RG1-246-3, 28567, vol. 1, 25 October 1923 and 28 June 1926, L.E. Bliss to W.C. Cain; ibid., 9 June 1925, Bliss to J. Lyons; ibid., 31 August 1925, Minister to Bliss; ibid., 200A, 28 October 1924, V.A. Sinclair to Cain; Canada – Department of Labour, *Investigation into an Alleged Combine in the Manufacture and Sale of Paperboard and Shipping Containers and Related Products: Report of the Commissioner, 14 March 1939* (Ottawa: King's Printer, 1939), section II.

29 AO, RG75-57, OC131/332.

30 The government admitted that its position was based upon a map that an official within the department had reportedly drawn up in 1917 but that, like so many other crucial documents from this period, mysteriously disappeared. The government conceded that the concession boundaries it drew in 1926 were "thought by the Department officers to be measurably correct": ibid., OC153/196, and enclosed undated Memo for the Minister from W.C. Cain, which Cain probably did not write.

31 Ibid., RG1-246-3, 9476, vol. 1, documents from 1920 to 1923; ibid., vol. 2, documents from 1926–7, particularly 12 May 1926, F.J. Niven to W.C. Cain; SMPA, A-1, 8 March 1921, Report on Spanish River ... Montreal Engineering Limited; ibid., Forestry 1924, 25 March 1924, F.R. Phelan's analysis; ibid., 3 April 1924, Forester's Report for 1923–1924. Hodgins and Benedickson, *The Temagami Experience*, 168, do not include in their analysis the events leading up to this settlement and thus depict it as one that enlarged these concessions.

32 AO, RG1-246-3, 25114, correspondence from 1920s and 1930s; *SO, 1927*, Chap. 24 17 Geo. V.

33 SMPA, W-4, R-1-64, Algoma Central Railway Study Report ... 1929, 13 September 1929, B.F. Avery to H.R. Soderston.

34 AO, RG1-246-3, 1173, vol. 1, 2 June 1922, Memo for Mr. Mills from W.C. Cain; ibid., 12 and 18 October 1921, Memoranda for Mr. Titus from Cain; ibid., 2 drafts of legislation to amend ... 1922; ibid., 7 June 1922, Memo re proposed legislation; ibid., 5937, 13 August 1926, G.R. Gray to the Minister; ibid., 42245, vol. 1, 23 June 1926, R.H. Smith to G.H. Ferguson; ibid., 8712, correspondence between February 1927 and September 1929; SMPA, A-1, Forestry 1924–1927, Forester's Reports for 1924 to 1927.

35 AO, RG1-246-3, 5937, 13 August 1926, G.H. Mead to Minister. Ferguson had rejected a similar offer from Mead in 1919: ibid., 17 September 1919, Application of Mead and J.O. Heyworth; ibid., 24 November 1919, Mead

to Ferguson; ibid., 24 August 1926, Deputy Minister to Spanish River. The Tories thwarted Spanish River's alternative efforts to resolve its energy shortage in Espanola and Sturgeon Falls by rejecting its applications for additional water powers even though departmental officials saw "no objection to favorably entertaining the application[s]": ibid., 69711, vol. 1, all documents, with the citation taken from 21 March 1927, Memo for W.H. Finlayson from L.V. Rorke; ibid., 75531, documents regarding Spanish River's application to develop Ragged Chutes on the Sturgeon River.

Chapter 11

1 Most accounts of this period have criticized the newsprint industry for having reacted to the growing crisis in the late 1920s by engaging in a merger drive that only further exacerbated its problems: Lower, *Settlement*, 127–9; E.A. Forsey, "The Pulp and Paper Industry," *Canadian Journal of Economics and Political Science* 1 (1935); Guthrie, 71; A.E. Safarian, *The Canadian Economy in the Great Depression* (Toronto: University of Toronto Press, 1970 [1959]), 44; Boothman, 74. While R.W. Hay, "Mergers and the Expansion of the Productive Capacity in the Canadian Pulp and Paper Industry, 1926–1932," Atlantic Canada Economics Association, *Papers* 14 (1985), challenges this view, the pages that follow indicate that neither of these explanations accounts for the events that occurred during this period.

2 In addition to IP's acquisitions in Ontario which have been mentioned in the preceding chapters, the company also gained control over the pulp mill in Hawkesbury, the few hundred square miles of timber licences which were owned by Central Paper Company northwest of Fort William, the International Fibreboard mill in Penetang, and a new fibreboard plant it built in the Ottawa Valley. Details of these acquisitions can be found in AO, RG1-246-3, 200 and 200A; ibid., RG1-E-4-B, vol. 2, Folio 35; ibid., RG75-57, OC165/305 and OC181/86; *Moody's Industrials, 1930*, International Paper Company.

3 AO, RG1-246-3, 61303, vol. 2, 6 December 1933, Memo for the Minister from W.C. Cain. Frank A. MacDougall, who had been employed by the department since the early 1920s and served as deputy minister from 1941 to 1967, was also shocked to learn in 1950 that IP had been so deeply involved in Ontario since the mid-1920s: ibid., vol. 4, 16 October 1950, Memo to F.A. MacDougall; ibid., 9582, vol. 1, documents from 1929–30.

4 *Montreal Herald*, 3 and 4 November 1932.

5 AO, F1198, 1, 22, 16 November 1934, F.I. Ker to L.B. Palmer.

6   Graustein also spearheaded the drive to form an international newsprint cartel in the late 1920s, although it is unclear whether a deal was ever reached: Archives nationales du Québec à Montréal (hereafter ANQM), P149, 6, 41, 7 August 1928, Minutes of Directors' Meeting; United States – Senate, Document 214, *Newsprint Paper Industry*, 71st Congress, Special Session of the Senate, 1930, 106–7.

7   *FTC Report, 1930*, 40–1; US Department of Commerce, *Transportation Factors*, 105; ANQM, P149, 5, 26, Minute Book of Canadian Export Paper Company Limited, Minutes from 6 May 1925; ibid., 5, 29, Minutes of Meetings of Advisory Committee, 15 February 1924 and 3 July 1925; *Financial Post*, 7 September 1928; UTA, A72-0025, 144, Su-Sy, 19 March 1930, C.D. Howe to W.L. Sykes.

8   LAC, RG95-1, 534, Canadian Newsprint Company, 2 May 1927, Letters Patent; SMPA, Historical Files, 1 June 1927, Agreement between Canadian; ANQM, P149, 6, 41, Papers re: sales agreement and Minute Book of Canadian Newsprint Company, Limited.

9   The CNC incorporated Canadian Paper Sales Company (CPS) to handle its contract with Hearst: ibid., 7, 49, Minute Book of Canadian Paper Sales Company, Limited.

10 *Toronto Globe*, 18 June 1928.

11 There is little in the minute books of either the CNC or the CPS to explain the dramatic turn of events. The CPS's Minute Book simply states that, at a meeting on 30 March, Hurlbut resigned from all his positions and that after a brief adjournment, the one share of stock standing in his name had been transferred to Wise, who was then elected a director of CPS as well as its president and member of its executive committee: ANQM, P149, 7, 49, Minute Book of Canadian Paper Sales, Limited, 30 March 1928, Minutes of Meeting.

12 *PPMC*, 20 October 1927, 1343; US – Senate, *Newsprint Paper Industry* … 1930, 36–8; *Toronto Globe*, 18 June 1928; ANQM, P149, 6, 41, Minute Book of Canadian Newsprint Company, 28 July 1927, Minutes of Directors' Meeting [2]; ibid., 472, 6, 15 June 1927, F.B. Common to H. Wise; ibid., 20 June 1927, Wise to Common; ibid., 7, 49, Minute Book of Canadian Paper Sales, Limited, April 1928 to May 1929: CPS's affairs were wrapped up in May 1929.

13 Correspondence and discussions with W.C. Graustein, September–October 2004; *Fourth Estate*, 24 November 1928; Bancroft Library, University of California at Berkeley (hereafter BLUCB), MS19B3, 199 (Newsprint 1928–34), 23 April 1928, confirmation of telephone message today to Col. Knox and Mr. Neyland, J. Willicombe [from W.R. Hearst].

14 SMPA, Document drawer, 21 July 1937, "Compilation of Statements and Information Obtained by the Bondholders Representative Committee [in the receivership of Abitibi Power & Paper Company]," 23.
15 AO, MU1020, Newsprint Industry II, 20 August 1928, L.A. Taschereau to G.H. Ferguson; ibid., 19 July and 3 August 1928, W. Finlayson to Ferguson; ibid., 28 August 1928, Ferguson to Taschereau.
16 US – Senate, *Newsprint Paper Industry … 1930*, 40–1.
17 In 1928–9 Graustein told the American government's investigation into the newsprint industry's alleged cartel that Ferguson's threat had been directed solely at Graustein's Nipigon Corporation to force him to raise his newsprint prices. This was hardly the case, as ironically this was the *only* interest Graustein controlled in Ontario that received this warning. Ferguson did not send it to either North West Ontario or Continental Wood (IP's subsidiaries), which leased large pulpwood limits in Ontario and were in default under their agreements: US – Senate, *Newsprint Paper Industry … 1930*, 42–3. Historians have accepted Graustein's claim at face value: Whitney, 349; Bladen, 194.
18 AO, MU1020, Newsprint Industry II, 19 November 1928, G.H. Ferguson to Ontario's pulpwood concessionaires except those mentioned in footnote 17; *Toronto Telegram*, *Toronto Globe*, and *Toronto Mail and Empire*, 19 November 1928. In 1926, Ferguson had assured Kimberly-Clark that the government would never strictly interpret the company's new pulpwood concession lease. Moreover, Oliver, *G. Howard Ferguson*, 346–7, and Vigod, 127–8, argue that the provincial governments could not use pulpwood concession agreements to enforce a price-fixing arrangement, but this is exactly what Ferguson did in this instance and others that followed.
19 *Toronto Globe*, 20 November 1928. For example, Spanish River's mill in Sturgeon Falls had shut down intermittently for want of power between 1910 and 1930, and other plants had also occasionally closed their doors for the same reason. The newsprint industry was, after all, highly cyclical, and occasional work interruptions were a normal and accepted part of this business.
20 *Toronto Telegram*, 19 and 20 November 1928; *Toronto Globe*, 19 and 21 November 1928.
21 *Fort William Daily Times-Journal*, 12 February 1929; *Toronto Globe*, 21 March 1929; *SO, 1929*, chap. 13, 19 Geo. V. Representatives from all sectors of Ontario's forest industry were aghast at the act's non-forestry provisions, particularly section 3, which required newsprint companies to provide summaries of their authorized and paid-up capital, and their bond or debenture issues: AO, RG1-246-3, 81701 and 81701A, passim.

22 Ibid., MU1020, Newsprint Industry II, ca November 1928, Rules and Regulations.

23 *Toronto Mail and Empire*, 27 November 1928; *Toronto Daily Star*, 24 and 26 November 1928 and 18 and 21 January 1929; also see note 24; US – Senate, *Newsprint Paper Industry* ... 1930, 4 and 86–7; Canada – Department of Justice, *Canadian and International Cartels: An Inquiry into the Nature and Effects of International Cartels and Other Trade Combinations*, Report of Commissioner, Combines Investigation Act (Ottawa, 1945), 37–8.

24 AO, MU1020, Newsprint Industry II, 26 November 1928, E.A. Wallberg to H. Ferguson; ibid., 27 November 1928, Ferguson to Wallberg; *PPMC*, 5 December 1929, 860.

25 SMPA, Historical Documents, 26 November 1917, Final Decree ... U.S.A. vs. George H. Mead and others; *PPMC*, 6 December 1928, 1751; *Ottawa Citizen*, 2 October 1930; AO, MU1020, Newsprint Industry II, ca November 1928 Rules and Regulations. Even though Graustein refused to operate according to the NIC's regulations, he succeeded in having one of his men, Victor M. Drury, appointed chairman of the NIC's executive committee, a position which empowered Drury to shape the cartel's policy. Drury had been appointed president of E.B. Eddy after IP had taken control of it in 1926–7. It was incomprehensible that Drury would be given this pre-eminent position with the Institute considering he headed a relatively small newsprint maker in Hull, had but a few years of experience in the industry, and was intimately tied to Graustein, the NIC's nemesis: ANQM, P149, 476, 476-8, 7 March 1929, P.B. Wilson to G. McKee.

26 The zone system IP introduced at this time had only four sections, but its goal was identical to the ten-zone arrangement (which is illustrated in Map 17) that the company adopted a short time later.

27 US – Department of Commerce, *Transportation Factors*, 95–105. The map on p. 73 of this report clearly illustrates how, for newsprint at least, it would have made sense to use such nodal-shaped zones to reflect transportation costs.

28 US – Senate, *Special Committee to Study Problems of American Small Business ... A Report Prepared in 1939 by Federal Trade Commission for Attorney General of the United States and Presently Released for Public Use*, 79th Congress, 2nd Session, 2 January 1947, 22; United States – House of Representatives, Report 505, *Newsprint. Report of the Subcommittee on the Study of Monopoly Power of the Committee of the Judiciary, Submitted by Mr. Celler*, 82nd Congress, 1st Session, 28 May 1951, 73–4, with the first citation from p. 74; Whitney, 345, 376, and 384; US – Department of Commerce, *Transportation Factors*, 95, from which the final citation is taken.

29 AO, F1198, Box 1, 12, 1 April 1929, J.P. Kenney to F.I. Ker.
30 Ibid., 3 April 1929, Ker to Kenney; ibid., 3 December 1929, Ker to S.B.
   Preston; ibid., 2 January 1929, Ker to A.R. Graustein; *Hamilton Spectator*,
   20 November 1929, contains an editorial that resoundingly defends IP's
   position in the newsprint wars.
31 AO, MU1020, Newsprint Industry III, 17 July 1929, T.W. McGarry to G.H.
   Ferguson; ibid., 30 July 1929, E.W. Backus's memo enclosed in ibid.,
   1 August 1929, McGarry to Ferguson; ANQM, 476, 8, 7 March 1929, P.B.
   Wilson to G. McKee, enclosing copy of memo from Anglo-Canadian to NIC.
32 AO, MU1343, Jan. 21st – 31st 1931, 9 November 1929, F.J. Sensenbrenner to
   G.H. Ferguson; ibid., 21 January 1929, J.H. Black to P.B. Wilson; ibid.,
   19 February 1929, Black to Ferguson.
33 Ibid., MU1020, Newsprint Industry I, 28 December 1929, L.A. Taschereau
   to G.H. Ferguson.
34 Ibid., 11 January 1930, G.H. Ferguson to L.A. Taschereau.
35 Ibid., RG1-246-3, 9582, vol. 1, 21 July 1930, Memo for Acting Deputy
   Minister; ibid., 12334, 13 April 1928, J.H. Hinman to W.C. Cain; ibid.,
   28 April 1931, Deputy Minister to Continental; ibid., MU1020, Newsprint
   Industry I, 11 January 1930, G.H. Ferguson to L.A. Taschereau.
36 Ibid., RG3-6, Newsprint 1930, 19 May 1930, G.H. Ferguson to N.B. Darrell;
   ibid., MU1020, Newsprint Industry I, data on production for 1930; *PPMC*,
   28 November 1929, 832, and 20 February 1930, 305; LAC, RG39, 84, 42401
   vol. 2, 20 December 1929, E.H. Finlayson to W.W. Cory; UTA, A72-0025,
   139, Ce-Cl, 2 July 1930, C.D. Howe to H.R. Christie.
37 AO, MU1343, Jan. 21st – 31st 1931, 4 April 1930, F.J. Sensenbrenner to G.H.
   Ferguson.
38 *Ottawa Citizen*, 2 October 1930; ANQM, P149, 478, 2, 24 September 1930,
   J.H. Price to Board of Governors, NIC; ibid., 477, 31, 25 September 1930, E.
   Rossiter to Secretary, NIC; AO, MU1343, Jan. 1st – 20th 1931, 12 January
   1931, G.H. Ferguson to G.S. Henry, enclosing copy of 10 January 1931,
   Ferguson to F.J. Sensenbrenner; ibid., Jan. 21st – 31st, 13 January 1931,
   Sensenbrenner to Ferguson.
39 Ibid., MU1590, Newsprint Statistics, 4 March 1931, Memo to the Hon.
   Mr. Finlayson.
40 *Toronto Globe* and *Toronto Mail and Empire*, 6 March 1931; *Fort William Daily
   Times-Journal*, 14 April 1931; AO, RG1-246-3, 61302, 1930 protests from Port
   Arthur.
41 Archives nationales du Québec à Québec (hereafter ANQQ), Superior
   Court of Quebec, 1931/17687, 27 February 1931, Plaintiff's Declaration;
   Toronto Mail and Empire, 25 April 1931.

42 Kuhlberg, "E.W. Backus," *DCB*, vol. 16 (Toronto: University of Toronto Press, forthcoming).

43 Abitibi went on to suffer a torturous receivership (1932–46), which can be followed in AO, RG22-5800, 1932/2994.

44 LAC, MG28-II-14, Minute Book of the National Trust Company, vol. 17, 5 October 1932, Minutes of Board Meeting, 5005; ibid., vol. 18, 3 May 1933, Minutes of Directors' Meeting, 5236. While proximity to its Midwestern market was one such "natural advantage," National Trust's chief accountant explained that Great Lakes Paper's newsprint orders could be "more profitably filled by delivering [them] by water rather than by rail," a competitive edge that the NIC's zone policy also vitiated: AO, RG22-5800, 1931/2194, 8 February 1933, Affidavit of C. England; ibid., 30 March 1933, R.G. Meech, Report to Bondholders.

45 *Montreal Herald*, 3 and 4 November 1932; *Montreal Star*, 21 October 1932.

46 LAC, MG26-K, M1416, 456762-456765, 22 October 1932, W.J. Phelps to R.B. Bennett; ibid., M1111, 295634, 5 November 1932, L. DeBrisay to Bennett.

47 AO, RG3-8, Newsprint Situation 1931, 19 December 1931, *Newsprint Situation in Canada: A National Problem* [IP's publication], enclosed in 28 December 1931, N.C. Head to G.S. Henry.

48 Ibid., RG1-E-10, 4, [Celler] Investigation of Newsprint Industry 1950, Statement of A.R. Graustein, 575.

Conclusion

1 AO, RG1-246-3, 97493, vol. 2, Verbatim Report of the Meeting of the Lumbermen of the Province of Ontario Held at the Parliament Buildings, Toronto, September 7, 1933.

2 Ibid.

3 *Report of the Royal Commission on Pulpwood* (Ottawa: Printer to the King's Most Excellent Majesty, 1924), 55.

4 LAC, MG32-C3, 143, Senator Alexander Wiley, 12 January 1948, A. Wiley to G. Drew; *Report of the Ontario Royal Commission on Forestry*, 1947, 151.

5 Even today, pulp and paper companies speak out rarely against the provincial government. During the mid-1990s, for example, on at least one occasion the Ontario government unilaterally shrank the size of a major newsprint firm's timber limit without any mention in the media: confidential source.

6 The few minute books that survive from Canada's newsprint companies that operated prior to the Second World War are revealing. Laurentide Paper Company hired forester Ellwood Wilson in the early 1900s to manage its woodlands, and he began Canada's first commercial-scale

reforestation effort on Laurentide's private lands in an effort to augment the firm's supply of Crown timber. The company was compelled to emphasize these facts in responding to its shareholders' persistent inquiries about the state of its available wood supply: ANQM, P149, 9, 62, Minute Book of Laurentide Company, Limited, 1910s–1920s.

7　*Moody's Industrials 1919,* Annual Report for Spanish River; ibid., *1928,* Annual Report for Fort William Power Company, 1928. When shareholders grilled G.H. Mead about the quantity of fibre available to his mills, he replied that "surveys conducted indicated that the company could be assured of an abundant supply for all time, provided present plans for safeguarding timber resources were carefully worked out and followed": *PPMC,* 4 October 1923, 992; ibid., 4 September 1924, 913.

8　"Minnesota & Ontario Paper Company," *Annual Financial Review,* 1926.

9　Kuhlberg, "We are the pioneers." Abitibi also launched a silvicultural program to develop the means by which it could maximize the productivity of its woodlands: Kuhlberg, "We Have 'Sold' Forestry to the Management of the Company": Abitibi Power & Paper Company's Forestry Initiatives in Ontario, 1919–1929, *Journal of Canadian Studies* 34, no. 3 (Fall 1999).

10　*Report of the Royal Commission on Pulpwood,* Ottawa, July 1924 (Ottawa: Printer to the King's Most Excellent Majesty, 1924), 61–2.

11　UTA, B83-0022, 12, J.H. White's Notebook from his 1929 summer trip across northern Ontario. Hearings conducted by the Dominion's Royal Commission on Pulpwood (1923–4) revealed that Ontario's newsprint makers would have purchased even more settlers' timber but there were many factors that mitigated against them doing so. Mills employed woodlands managers who formulated multi-year plans for harvesting Crown concessions, but settlers and farmers were seldom able to guarantee either the time or the size of their pulpwood deliveries. It was in their best interests to refrain from committing to sell at a set price to domestic mills in the autumn because they might be able to garner higher prices for their wood from American purchasers in the spring's "spot" market. Freight rates also discriminated against domestic mills purchasing private pulpwood; railways charged more to ship timber a short distance to the local processing plant than the much greater distance to the United States. Finally, the provincial governments in both Ontario and Quebec demanded that the pulp and paper companies that leased Crown concessions harvest timber that burned on their limits. This made it extremely difficult for these firms to purchase private pulpwood on a long-term basis: LAC, RG39, 594, Royal Commission on Pulpwood, vols. 8 and 11.

12　*Kenora Examiner,* ca 1924; *Mail and Empire,* 26 September 1923; *PPMC,* 24 December 1925, 1517; AO, RG1-246-3, 5322A, 15 December 1928, G.H. Ferguson to D.M. Hogarth.

13 Gillis and Roach, Ch. 4. The *Annual Reports* provide only rudimentary data regarding the sources of Crown timber revenues for this period, but it is apparent that harvesting sawlogs produced far more income than harvesting pulpwood.

14 *Saturday Night*, 13 May 1933.

15 NYPLA, *The New York Times* Company Records, 49(16), 10 December 1929, American Newspaper Publishers' Association, Bulletin No. 5704; AO, F1198, 1, 22, 8 November 1934, F.I. Ker to The Editor, *Financial Counsel*; ibid., 30 October 1936, Ker to L.B. Palmer; LAC, MG28-II-14, Minute Book of National Trust Company, 1914–30: the fixed securities that financed Ontario's newsprint firms paid up to 8 per cent annually, whereas electric utilities paid roughly half that rate; SSMPLA, 992.10, Series 2 – Annual Reports, 4 March 1929, *Abitibi Power & Paper Company, 15th Annual Report for Fiscal Year Ending December 31, 1928*; C.A. Schenck was a German forestry professor and confidant of C.D. Howe, dean of the University of Toronto's forestry school (1919–41). Schenck believed that the pulp and paper firms' silvicultural initiatives were designed "to obtain for the Co[mpanies] better terms on their outstanding bonds": UTA, A72-0025, 144, Sch-Scy, 29 November 1927, C.A. Schenck to C.D. Howe.

16 These figures were not merely reflections of the Depression's low labour costs. The data for the Canadian newsprint industry in 1928 show production costs ranged between $20 and $38 per ton prior to charges for debt and overhead: ANQM, P149, 473, 2, Confidential cost data for 1928 for Canadian mills from the Newsprint Service Bureau.

17 AO, RG22, 1931/2194, 13 July 1931, Affidavit of F.R. MacKelcan.

18 BLUCB, MS19B3, 199 (Newsprint 1928–34), 7 June 1932, W.R. Hearst to D.E. Town.

19 Safarian, 201; Horne, 81; Boothman, passim; Guthrie, 71.

20 Craig Heron, *Working in Steel: The Early Years in Canada, 1883–1935* (Toronto: McClelland and Stewart, 1988), 13–32. Heron explains the difficulties that fully integrated firms such as Algoma Steel and Dominion Iron and Steel Company endured even though they controlled the natural resources they processed. In contrast, the Steel Company of Canada bought its raw materials on the open market and enjoyed far more success.

21 For example, see Sandberg and Clancy, *Against the Grain*, 13–15.

22 *The Minister's Council on Forest Sector Competitiveness* (Toronto, 2005), Executive Summary.

23 *Strengthening Forestry's Future: Forest Tenure Modernization in Ontario* (Toronto: Queen's Printer, 2011), 5.

Sources

Primary Sources

Abitibi-Bowater
  Fort William Archives (FWA), Thunder Bay, Ontario – all fonds
  Iroquois Falls Archives (IFA), Iroquois Falls, Ontario – all fonds
Alexander House (AH), Port Edwards, Wisconsin
  Northern Paper Company binder
  Nekoosa-Edwards Papers
Archives nationales du Québec à Chicoutimi (ANQC), Chicoutimi, Quebec
  P1 – Dubuc Collection
  P146 – Price Brothers Company
  P666 – La Compagnie Price
Archives nationales du Québec à Montreal (ANQM), Montreal, Quebec
  P149 – Repertoire du fonds Consolidated-Bathurst Incorporated
Archives nationales du Québec à Québec (ANQQ), Quebec City, Quebec
  Records of Quebec Superior Court – 1931 #17687 – Price Bros. Ltd. vs. Abitibi
Archives of Ontario (AO)
Private Collections
  F5, J.P. Whitney
  F6, W.H. Hearst
  F7, E.C. Drury
  F8, G.H. Ferguson
  F9, G.S. Henry
  F10, M.F. Hepburn
  F12, G.D. Conant
  F30, P. Heenan
  F45, A.W. Roebuck

F50, I.B. Benson
F150, Gillies Lumber Company
F197, W. Delahey
F208, E.E. Johnson
F210, J.A. McPhail
F242, A.E. Wicks Ltd.
F1014, F.A. MacDougall
F1055, F.A. Gaby
F1056, R.L. Hearn
F1095, A.H.D. Ross
F1274, F.E. Moore
F1335, Hollinger Mines, Limited
F1432, P. Dewan
F4332, P.O. Rhynas
Government Collections
RG1, Department Crown Lands/Ministry of Natural Resources
Series – Special Collections [Maps], A-I-10, BB-1, E-3-A, E-3-B, E-4-B, E-5, E-6, E-9, E-10, E-12, F-IV, J-1, J-2, 122, 246, 256, 305, 335, 408, 415, 416, and 425
RG3, Office of the Premier: Series 2, 3, 4, 5, 6, 7, 8, 9, 10, 17, and 23
RG4, Office of the Attorney General: Series 2, 32, and 36
RG6, Department of the Treasury: Series 2, 6, 14, and 15
RG8, Department of the Provincial Secretary: Series 5, 13, and 29
RG18, Royal Commissions: Series 66, 79, 83, 118, 120, and 125
RG22, Supreme Court of Ontario: Series 5800
RG49, Select Committees: Series 12 and 115
RG53, Recording Office: Series 17 and 57
RG55, Companies Branch: Series 27
RG75, Executive Council Office: Series 2, 42, 56, 57, and 59
Library
Copies of Crown Pulpwood Concession Agreements, 1894–1926
Avenor [now part of Abitibi-Bowater]
Avenor Inc., Archives (AIA), Corporate Headquarters, Montreal, Quebec – all fonds
Thunder Bay Division Archives (ATBA), Thunder Bay, Ontario – all fonds
Bancroft Library, University of California at Berkeley (BLUCB), Berkeley, California
MS19B3 – William Randolph Hearst
Dalhousie University Archives (DUA), Halifax, Nova Scotia
MS4-68 – Scott Paper Company
MS4-116 – Driftwood Lands and Timber Company

Dryden Historical Museum Archives (DHMA), Dryden, Ontario
  Minute Book of the Dryden Paper Company, Limited
Hagley Museum and Library, Wilmington, Delaware
  Pamphlets
Lake of the Woods Historical Society (LOTWHS), Kenora, Ontario
  Mather House, "John Mather Diary Summary, 1882–1906"
  Mather House, "An Historical Research Inventory of the Mather-Walls
  Property with a General Overview of Keewatin Developmental History,"
  Reg Reeve, 1979.
Lake of the Woods Museum Archives (LOTWMA), Kenora, Ontario
  "The Industrialists," W. Lessie
  "Memorandum re: Keewatin Lumber Company Limited, Kenora Paper
  Mills Limited and Allied Companies and Their Operations at Kenora &
  Hudson, Ont. & St. Boniface, Manitoba, 1906 to 1943," D. McLeod
Lakehead University Archives (LUA), Thunder Bay, Ontario
  MG1 – Robinson Papers
  MG7 – Oscar Styffe
Library and Archives Canada (LAC), Ottawa, Ontario
Private Collections
  MG26-G, W. Laurier
  MG26-H, R.L. Borden
  MG26-J, W.L.M. King
  MG26-I, A. Meighen
  MG27-II-D13, N.W. Rowell
  MG27-III-B-7, R.J. Manion
  MG27-III-B-20, C.D. Howe
  MG28-II-14, National Trust
  MG30-A-51, J.H. Dunn
  MG32-C3, G.A. Drew
  MG32-C85, N. Lambert
Government Collections
  RG10, Department of Indian Affairs
  RG39, Dominion/Canadian Forest Service
  RG110, Combines Investigation Branch
Mutual Life Company Archives (MLCA), Waterloo, Ontario
  81.20, Abitibi Power and Paper Company
New York Public Library Archives (NYPLA), New York, New York
  The New York Times Company Records, A.H. Sulzberger Papers; A.S. Ochs
  Papers.

Nipigon Museum
    Historical photos
Ontario Hydro Archives (OHA), Toronto, Ontario
    Files germane to the pulp and paper industry
Ontario Ministry of Consumer and Corporate Affairs (MCCR), Toronto, Ontario
    Files germane to northern Ontario's forest industry
Queen's University Archives (QUA), Kingston, Ontario
    Joseph Flavelle Papers
Ron Morel Memorial Museum, Kapuskasing, Ontario
    Historical Photos
Sault Ste Marie Public Library Archives (SSMPLA), Sault Ste Marie, Ontario
    MG7-992.10 – Abitibi Power and Paper
    996.9 – Algoma Steel Collection: Lake Superior Corporation, Lake Superior
    Power Company, Sault Ste Marie Pulp and Paper and Tagona Water and Light
Sault Ste Marie Historical Society (SSMHS), Sault Ste Marie, Ontario
    Various files, the most important of which was the 410.1 Series
Seaman Paper Company Archives (SPCA), Baldwinville, Massachusetts
    Bermingham & Seaman Paper Company Minute Books
    Seaman Paper Company Minute Books
St Marys Paper Ltd Archives (SMPA), Sault Ste Marie, Ontario
    All fonds
Tembec
    Spruce Falls Archives (SFA), Spruce Falls Inc., Kapuskasing, Ontario – all fonds
Thunder Bay Historical Musuem Society (TBHMS), Thunder Bay, Ontario
    A4, J.T. Horne
    A28, B. Black
    A55, G.R. Duncan
    A83, Donald M. Hogarth/James A. Little
    B11, Young and Lillie
    B14, Abitibi Power and Paper Company, Limited
    B22, Newaygo Timber Company
    G3, City of Fort William Records
    Unprocessed – Donald A. Clarke Papers
University of Toronto Archives (UTA), Toronto, Ontario
    A1972-0025, Faculty of Forestry
    A1973-0026, Department of Graduate Records
    B1983-0022, J.H. White
Wisconsin Historical Society – Madison Archives (WHSMA), Madison, Wisconsin
    MSS279, D.C. Everest Papers

C.C. Yawkey and A.P. Woodson Papers
Hixon and Company Papers
M80-616, G.W. Mead Papers

Government Documents

CANADA

Forestry Branch
Forest Products of Canada. Ottawa: Department of the Interior, 1909.
Department of the Interior
H.G. Acres, *Water Powers of Canada – The Province of Ontario*. Dominion
   Water Powers Branch, Department of the Interior, 1915.
Department of Justice
*Canadian and International Cartels: An Inquiry into the Nature and Effects of In-
   ternational Cartels and Other Trade Combinations*. Report of Commissioner,
   Combines Investigation Act. Ottawa, 1945.
Restrictive Trade Practices Commission. *Report Concerning the Manufacture,
   Distribution and Sale of Boxboard Grades of Paperboard*. Ottawa, 1956.
Department of Labour
*Investigation into an Alleged Combine in the Manufacture and Sale of Paperboard
   and Shipping Containers and Related Products: Report of the Commissioner,
   14 March 1939* (Ottawa: King's Printer, 1939).
Royal Commissions
Report of the Royal Commission on Pulpwood. Ottawa: Printer to the King's
   Most Excellent Majesty, 1924.
Select Committees
Proceedings of the Select Committee of the House of Commons on Banking
   and Commerce, 6 March 1934 to 14 June 1934. 1934.
Sessional Papers
1917 – No. 114 – Copies of Orders in Council regarding the manufacture,
   sale, etc., of newsprint.
1918 – No. 64 – Interim Report of P. A. Pringle, Commissioner inquiring
   into the manufacture, sale, price and supply of newsprint in Canada,
   20 March 1918.
1919 – No. 196 – Return to an Order 31 March 1919 – for all correspondence
   between N.W. Rowell, President of the Privy Council and Commissioner
   Pringle, re Pulp and Paper Inquiry.
Statutes of Canada, 1872–1940

ONTARIO

Department of Crown Lands / Lands and Forests / Ministry of Natural Resources

Annual Reports and *Reports of the Commissioner of Crown Lands* [*Annual Reports*], *1894–1950.*

Annual Reports of the Director/Clerk of Forestry for the Province of Ontario, *1885–1903.*

The Forest Resources of Ontario, 1930. Toronto: Department of Lands and Forests, 1931.

The John R. Booth Story. Forest Resources Group Publication [Reprinted from *YourForests*, Volume 11, Number 2, Summer 1978], ca 1979.

List of Water Powers in the Province of Ontario. King's Printer, 1925.

Settlers' Lands, Roads, Timber, Pulpwood, Water Power in Northern Ontario. 1930.

The Minister's Council on Forest Sector Competitiveness. Toronto: Queen's Printer, 2005.

Strengthening Forestry's Future: Forest Tenure Modernization in Ontario. Toronto: Queen's Printer, 2011.

Hansard [Newspaper]

Royal Commissions or Select Committees

Report of the Royal Commission on Forestry Protection in Ontario, 1899 [1900].

Report of the Survey and Exploration of Northern Ontario, 1900.

Report of the Royal Commission into the Kapuskasing Colony, 1920.

Report of the Royal Commission on Timber, 1922.

Report of the Royal Commission on Hydro, 1924.

Report of the Royal Commission on Forestry, 1947.

Sessional Papers, 1890–1940

Statutes of Ontario, 1880–1940

UNITED STATES

Department of Commerce

Transportation Factors in the Marketing of Newsprint. November, 1952.

Federal Trade Commission

News-Print Paper Industry: Letter from the Federal Trade Commission Transmitting Pursuant to a Senate Resolution of April 24, 1916. The Final Report of the Commission Relative to the News-Print Paper Industry in the United States. Washington: Government Printing Office, 1917.

House Documents [General]

Numbers 860 and 867. *Responses to Inquiry ... re: International Paper*. 60th Congress, 1st Session, 1907–1908.

House of Representatives

Select Committee of House of Representatives. *Pulp and Paper Investigation Hearings*. Washington: Government Printing Office, 1908.

Report 505. *Newsprint. Report of the Subcommittee on the Study of Monopoly Power of the Committee of the Judiciary, Submitted by Mr. Celler*. 82nd Congress, 1st Session, 28 May 1951.

Senate

Document 28. *Timber Legislation ... in Canada*. 62nd Congress, 1st Session, 1911.

Document 31. *Report of the Tariff Board on Pulp and Newsprint Paper Industry*. 62nd Congress, 1st Session, 1911.

Document 56. *Reciprocity with Canada ...* [Hearings]. 62nd Congress, 1st Session, 1911.

Document 92, Part 14. *Utility Corporations* [Testimony of A.R. Graustein]. 70th Congress, 1st Session, 1929.

Document 11, Parts I and II. *Newspaper Holdings of the International Paper & Power Company*. 71st Congress, 1st Session, 1929.

Document 214. *Newsprint Paper Industry*. 71st Congress, Special Session of the Senate, 1930.

Document 84. *Report of Tariff Commission on Wood Pulp and Pulpwoods*. 72nd Congress, 1st Session, 1931–32.

Hearings Before a Special Committee on Investigation of Bankruptcy and Receivership Proceedings in the United States Courts. 73rd Congress, 2nd Session, 1934.

Special Committee to Study Problems of American Small Business. Survival of Free Competitive Press. Newsprint Industry – A Report on Wartime Conditions in Paper and Paper-Products Industry and Newsprint Paper Decree Investigation: A Report Prepared in 1939 by Federal Trade Commission for Attorney General of the United States and Presently Released for Public Use. Seventy-Ninth Congress – Second Session. January 2, 1947.

Newsprint. Report of the Subcommittee on the Study of Monopoly Power of the Committee of the Judiciary. 82nd Congress, 1st Session, House Report No. 505, Part 1. Submitted by Mr. Celler, 28 May 1951.

Newspapers/Periodicals

Annual Financial Review
B.C. Lumberman

Canada Lumberman
Canadian Forestry Journal
Financial Post
Forestry Chronicle
Fort William Times-Journal
Hamilton Spectator
Kenora Examiner
Montreal Gazette
Montreal Herald
New York Times
Ottawa Citizen
Port Arthur News Chronicle
Pulp and Paper Magazine of Canada
Saturday Night
Toronto Daily Star
Toronto Evening Telegram
Toronto Globe
Toronto News

Interviews

Graustein, W.C., email correspondence and telephone conversations, September–October 2004 and December 2012–January 2013.

Secondary Sources

Published Monographs

Amigo, E., and N. Mark. *Beyond the Adirondacks: The Story of the St. Regis Paper Company*. Westport, CT: Greenwood Press, 1980.
Anastakis, D. *Autonomous State: The Struggle for a Canadian Car Industry from OPEC to Free Trade*. Toronto: University of Toronto Press, 2014.
Angus, J.T. *A Deo Victoria: The Story of the Georgian Bay Lumber Company, 1871–1942*. Thunder Bay, ON: Severn Publications, 1990.
Armson, K. *Ontario Forests: A Historical Perspective*. Toronto: Fitzhenry and Whiteside, 2001.
Armson, K., and M. McLeod. *The Legacy of John Waldie and Sons: A History of the Victoria Harbour Lumber Company*. Toronto: Dundurn Press, 2007.
Armstrong, C. *The Politics of Federalism: Ontario's Relations with the Federal Government, 1867–1942*. Toronto: University of Toronto Press, 1981.

Armstrong, C., and H.V. Nelles. *Monopoly's Moment: The Organization and Regulation of Canadian Utilities, 1830–1930*. Toronto: University of Toronto Press, 1986.

Berger, M. *The Story of the New York Times, 1851–1951*. New York: Simon and Schuster, 1951.

Bertrand, J.P. *Highway of Destiny: An Epic Story of Canadian Development*. New York: Vantage Press, 1959.

Bladen, V.W. *An Introduction to Political Economy*. Toronto: University of Toronto Press, 1958.

Bliss, M. *A Canadian Millionaire: The Life and Business Times of Sir Joseph Flavelle, Bart., 1858–1939*. Toronto: McClelland and Stewart, 1978.

Bliss, M. *Northern Enterprise: Five Centuries of Canadian Business*. Toronto: McClelland and Stewart, 1987.

Bothwell, R. *Loring Christie: The Failure of Bureaucratic Imperialism*. New York and London: Garland Publishing, 1988.

Bothwell, R., and W. Kilbourn. *C.D. Howe: A Biography*. Toronto: McClelland and Stewart, 1979.

Burley, K.H. *The Development of Canada's Staples, 1867–1939*. Toronto: McClelland and Stewart, 1971.

Burtch, L. *Great Lakes Power: 75 Years of Continuous Progress*. Sault Ste. Marie: Great Lakes Power, 1992.

Carruthers, G. *Paper in the Making*. Toronto: Garden City Press Co-operative, 1947.

Chandler, A.D., Jr. *The Visible Hand: The Managerial Revolution in American Business*. Cambridge, MA: Harvard University Press, 1977.

Chang, Ha-Joon. *Kicking Away the Ladder: Development Strategy in Historical Perspective*. London: Anthem, 2002.

Charland, J-P. *Les pâtes et papiers au Québec, 1880–1980: Technologies, travail et travailleurs*. Quebec: Institut québecois de recherche sur la culture, 1990.

Cleveland, H. van B., and T.F. Huertas. *Citibank, 1812–1970*. Cambridge, MA: Harvard University Press, 1985.

Cook, R., and C. Brown. *Canada, 1896–1921: A Nation Transformed*. Toronto: McClelland and Stewart, 1985.

Dales, J.H. *Hydroelectricity and Industrial Development: Quebec, 1898–1940*. Cambridge, MA: Harvard University Press, 1957.

Denison, M. *The People's Power: The History of Ontario Hydro*. Toronto: McClelland and Stewart, 1960.

Drummond, I. *Progress without Planning: The Economic History of Ontario from Confederation to the Second World War*. Toronto: University of Toronto Press, 1987.

Drury, E.C. *Farmer Premier: Memoirs of the Honourable E.C. Drury*. Toronto: McClelland and Stewart, 1966.

Ellis, L.E. *Print Paper Pendulum: Group Pressures and the Price of Newsprint*. New Brunswick, NJ: Rutgers University Press, 1948.

English, J. *The Decline of Politics: The Conservatives and the Party System, 1901–1920*. Toronto: University of Toronto Press, 1977.

Evans, P.B. *Embedded Autonomy: States and Industrial Transformation*. Princeton, NJ: Princeton University Press, 1995.

Flader, S.L., ed. *The Great Lakes Forest: An Environmental and Social History*. Minneapolis: University of Minnesota Press, 1983.

Freeman, N.B. *The Politics of Power: Ontario Hydro and Its Government, 1906–1995*. Toronto: University of Toronto Press, 1996.

Gillis, P.R., and T.R. Roach. *Lost Initiatives: Canada's Forest Industries, Forest Policy and Forest Conservation*. New York: Greenwood Press, 1986

Gray, J.H. *R.B. Bennett: The Calgary Years*. Toronto: University of Toronto Press, 1991.

Gray, J.R. *The Trees behind the Shore: The Forests and Forest Industries of Newfoundland and Labrador*. Ottawa: Economic Council of Canada / Minister of Supply and Services, 1981.

Guthrie, J.A. *The Newsprint Industry: An Economic Analysis*. Cambridge, MA: Harvard University Press, 1941.

Hak, G. *Turning Trees into Dollars: The British Columbia Coastal Lumber Industry, 1858–1913*. Toronto: University of Toronto Press, 2000.

Harris, R.C., and J. Warkentin. *Canada before Confederation: A Study in Historical Geography*. Toronto: Oxford University Press, 1974.

Heinrich, T. and B. Batchelor. *Kotex, Kleenex, Huggies: Kimberly-Clark and the Consumer Revolution in American Business*. Columbus: Ohio State University Press, 2004.

Heron, C. *Working in Steel: The Early Years in Canada*. Toronto: McClelland and Stewart, 1988.

Hidy, R.W. *Timber and Men: The Weyerhaeuser Story*. New York: MacMillan, 1963.

Hodgetts, J.E. *From Arm's Length to Hands-On: The Formative Years of Ontario's Public Service, 1867–1940*. Toronto: University of Toronto Press, 1995.

Hodgins, B.W., and J. Benedickson. *The Temagami Experience: Recreation, Resources and Aboriginal Rights in the Northern Ontario Wilderness*. Toronto: University of Toronto Press, 1989.

Hosie, R.C. *Native Trees of Canada*. Ottawa: Canadian Forestry Service, 1990.

How, D. *Canada's Mystery Man of High Finance: The Story of Izaak Killam*. Hantsport: Lancelot Press, 1986.

Hughson, J.W., and C.C.J. Bond. *Hurling Down the Pine*. Old Chelsea, Quebec: Historical Society of the Gatineau, 1965.

Humphries, C.W. *'Honest Enough to Be Bold': The Life and Times of Sir James Pliny Whitney*. Toronto: University of Toronto Press, 1985.

In Quiet Ways: George H. Mead, The Man and the Company. Dayton, OH: Mead Corporation, 1970.

Jacques, S.A. (Priebe). *Smooth Rock Falls, 1916–2004*. Field, ON: WFL Communications, 2004.

Johnston, C.M. *E.C. Drury: Agrarian Idealist*. Toronto: University of Toronto Press, 1986.

Kauffmann, C. *Logging Days in Blind River: A Review of the Events That Established a Town*. Sault Ste Marie, ON: Carl Kauffmann, 1970.

Kendle, J. *John Bracken: A Political Biography*. Toronto: University of Toronto Press, 1979.

Killan, G. *Protected Places: A History of Ontario's Provincial Park System*. Toronto: Queen's Printer / Dundurn Press, Ministry of Natural Resources, 1993.

Kuhlberg, M. *One Hundred Rings and Counting: Forestry Education and Forestry in Toronto and Canada, 1907–2007*. Toronto: University of Toronto Press, 2009.

Lambert, R.S., and P. Pross. *Renewing Nature's Wealth: A Centennial History of the Public Management of Lands, Forests and Wildlife in Ontario, 1763–1967*. Toronto: Department of Lands and Forests, 1967.

Linteau, P-A. et al. *Quebec: A History, 1867–1929*. Toronto: James Lorimer, 1983.

Lower, A.R.M. *Great Britain's Woodyard: British America and the Timber Trade, 1763–1867*. Kingston and Montreal: McGill-Queen's University Press, 1973.

Lower, A.R.M. *The North American Assault on the Canadian Forest: A History of the Lumber Trade between Canada and the United States*. Toronto: Ryerson Press, 1938.

Lower, A.R.M. *Settlement and the Forest Frontier in Eastern Canada*. Toronto: Macmillan Canada, 1936.

Marchak, P. *Green Gold: The Forest Industry in British Columbia*. Vancouver: University of British Columbia Press, 1983.

Marchildon, G.P. *Profits and Politics: Beaverbrook and the Gilded Age of Canadian Finance*. Toronto: University of Toronto Press, 1996.

Marshall, H., F.A. Southard, and K.W. Taylor. *Canadian-American Industry: A Study in International Investment*. New York: Russell and Russell, 1936.

Mauro, J.M. *Thunder Bay: A History*. Thunder Bay: Lehto Printers, 1981.

McCalla, D. *Planting the Province: The Economic History of Upper Canada, 1784–1870*. Toronto: University of Toronto Press, 1993.

McCallum, J. *Unequal Beginnings: Agricultural and Economic Development in Quebec and Ontario until 1870*. Toronto: University of Toronto Press, 1980.

McDowall, D. *Quick to the Frontier: Canada's Royal Bank*. Toronto: McClelland and Stewart, 1993.

McDowall, D. *Steel at the Sault: Francis H. Clergue, Sir James Dunn, and the Algoma Steel Corporation, 1901–1956*. Toronto: University of Toronto Press, 1984.

McKay, D. *Empire of Wood: The MacMillan Bloedel Story*. Vancouver: Douglas and McIntyre, 1982.

McKay, D. *Heritage Lost: The Crisis in Canada's Forests*. Toronto: Macmillan Canada, 1985.

McKay, P. *Electric Empire: The Inside Story of Ontario Hydro*. Toronto: Between the Lines, 1983.

McQuillen, M.J., and W.P. Garvey. *The Best Known Name in Paper: Hammermill, A History of the Company*. Hammermill Paper Company, 1985.

Neatby, H.B. *William Lyon Mackenzie King, 1924–1932: The Lonely Heights*. Toronto: University of Toronto Press, 1970.

Nelles, H.V. *The Politics of Development: Forests, Mines and Hydro-Electric Power in Ontario, 1849–1941*. Hamden, CT: Archon Books, 1974.

Newman, P.C. *Flame of Power: Intimate Profiles of Canada's Greatest Businessmen*. Toronto: Longmans, Green, 1959.

Norrie, K., and D. Owram. *A History of the Canadian Economy*. Toronto: Harcourt Brace Jovanovich, 1991.

Ohanian, N.K. *The American Pulp and Paper Industry, 1900–1940: Mill Survival, Firm Structure, and Industry Relocation*. Westport, CT: Greenwood Press, 1993.

Oliver, P. *G. Howard Ferguson: Ontario Tory*. Toronto: University of Toronto Press, 1977.

Oliver, P. *Public and Private Persons: The Ontario Political Culture, 1914–1934*. Toronto: Clarke, Irwin, 1975.

Plewman, W.R. *Adam Beck and Ontario Hydro*. Toronto: Ryerson Press, 1947.

Prang, M. *N.W. Rowell: Ontario Nationalist*. Toronto: University of Toronto Press, 1975.

Radforth, I. *Bush Workers and Bosses: Logging in Northern Ontario, 1900–1980*. Toronto: University of Toronto Press, 1987.

Rajala, R.A. *Clearcutting the Pacific Rain Forest: Production, Science and Regulation*. Vancouver: UBC Press, 2000.

Rea, K.J. *The Prosperous Years: The Economic History of Ontario, 1939–1975*. Toronto: University of Toronto Press, 1985.

Reader, W.J. *Bowater: A History*. London: Cambridge University Press, 1981.

Regehr, T.D. *The Beauharnois Scandal: A Story of Canadian Entrepreneurship and Politics*. Toronto: University of Toronto Press, 1990.

Reich, N. *The Pulp and Paper Industry in Canada*. Montreal: McGill University Economic Studies / Macmillan Canada, 1926.

Reynolds, L.G. *The Control of Competition in Canada*. Cambridge, MA: Harvard University Press, 1940.

Robson, R. *Forest Dependent Communities in Canada: An Interpretative Overview and Annotated Bibliography*. Brandon, MB: Brandon University, Rural Development Institute, 1995.

Rodrik, D. *The Globalization Paradox: Democracy and the Future of the World Economy*. New York: Norton, 2011.

Rowe, J.S. *Forest Regions of Canada*. Ottawa: Forestry Branch, Department of Northern Affairs and Natural Resources, 1959.

Rumilly, R. *Histoire de la province de Québec*. Ottawa: Fide, 1958.

Safarian, A.E. *The Canadian Economy in the Great Depression*. Toronto: University of Toronto Press, 1970 [1959].

Sandberg, L.A. *Trouble in the Woods: Forest Policy and Social Conflict in Nova Scotia and New Brunswick*. Fredericton, NB: Acadiensis Press, 1992.

Sandberg, L.A., and P. Clancy. *Against the Grain: Foresters and Politics in Nova Scotia*. Vancouver: UBC Press, 2000.

Saywell, J.T. *'Just Call Me Mitch': The Life of Mitchell F. Hepburn*. Toronto: University of Toronto Press, 1991.

Schindler, F.F. *Responsible Government in Ontario*. Toronto: University of Toronto Press, 1969.

Sinclair, S. *"Cordial but not cozy": A History of the Office of the Auditor-General*. Toronto: McClelland and Stewart, 1980.

Sisam, J.W.B. *Forestry Education at Toronto*. Toronto: University of Toronto Press, 1961.

Swanberg, W.A. *Citizen Hearst: A Biography of William Randolph Hearst*. New York: Charles Scribner's Sons, 1961.

Swift, J. *Cut and Run: The Assault on Canada's Forests*. Toronto: Between the Lines, 1983.

Taylor, G.W. *Timber: History of the Forest Industry in B.C.* Vancouver: J.J. Douglas, 1975.

Thompson, C.D. *Confessions of the Power Trust: A Summary of the Testimony Given in the Hearings of the Federal Trade Commission on Utility Corporations Pursuant to Resolution No. 83 of the United States Senate Approved February 15, 1928*. New York: E.P. Dutton, 1932.

Thompson, J.H., and A. Seager. *Canada, 1922–1939*. Toronto: McClelland and Stewart, 1985.

Tracks beside the Water: Sioux Lookout. Sioux Lookout: Sioux Lookout and District Historical Society, 1982.

Traves, T. *The State and Enterprise: Canadian Manufacturers and the Canadian Government, 1917–1931*. Toronto: University of Toronto Press, 1971.

Trinnell, J.R. *J. R. Booth: The Life and Times of an Ottawa Lumberking*. Ottawa: Treehouse Publishing, 1998.

Tronrud, T.J., and E.A. Epp. *Thunder Bay: From Rivalry to Unity*. Thunder Bay, ON: Thunder Bay Historical Museum Society, 1996.

Tucker, A. *Steam into Wilderness: Ontario Northland Railway, 1902–1962*. Toronto: Fitzhenry and Whiteside, 1978.

Vigod, B.L. *Quebec before Duplessis: The Political Career of Louis-Alexandre Taschereau*. Montreal and Kingston: McGill-Queen's University Press, 1986.

Whitaker, R. *The Government Party: Organizing and Financing the Liberal Party of Canada, 1930–1958*. Toronto: University of Toronto Press, 1977.

Whitney, S.N. *Antitrust Policies: American Experience in Twenty Industries*. New York: Twentieth Century Fund, 1958.

Whitton, C. *A Hundred Years a Fellin'*. Ottawa: Runge Press, 1943.

Wiegman, C. *Trees to News: A Chronicle of the Ontario Paper Company's Origin and Development*. Toronto: McClelland and Stewart, 1953.

Wightman, W.R., and N.M. Wightman. *The Land Between: Northwestern Ontario Resource Development, 1800 to the 1990s*. Toronto: University of Toronto Press, 1997.

Winkler, J.K. *The First Billion: The Stillmans and the National City Bank*. New York: Vanguard Press, 1934.

Winkler, J.K. *William Randolph Hearst: A New Appraisal*. New York: Hastings House, 1955.

Wood, J.D., ed. *Perspectives on Landscape and Settlement in Nineteenth Century Ontario*. Toronto: McClelland and Stewart, 1975.

Wynn, G. *Timber Colony: A Historical Geography of Early Nineteenth Century New Brunswick*. Toronto: University of Toronto Press, 1981.

Young, S., and A. Young. *Silent Frank Cochrane: The North's First Great Politician*. Toronto: Macmillan Canada, 1973.

Zaslow, M. *The Opening of the Canadian North, 1870–1914*. Toronto: McClelland and Stewart, 1971.

Published Articles, Booklets, and Pamphlets

Abitibi – A Story in Pictures: An Illustrated Story of the Development of the Newsprint Paper Mill of the Abitibi Power and Paper Co. Limited, Iroquois Falls, Ontario. Montreal: [s.n.], 1924.

Ambridge, D.W. *Frank Harris Anson: Pioneer in the North*. New York: Newcomen Society in North America, 1952.

Black Spruce Symposium, G.L.F.R. Centre, Sault Ste Marie, Ontario, Proceedings, 1975.

Blais, Gabrielle. "'Not a Paying Business': The Archival Legacy of the Canadian Forestry Service." *Journal of Forest History* (July 1988).

Blyth, J.A. "The Development of the Paper Industry in Old Ontario, 1824–1867." *Ontario History* 62, no. 2 (June 1970).

Boothman, B.E.C. "High Finance/Low Strategy: Corporate Collapse in the Canadian Pulp and Paper Industry, 1919–1932." *Business History Review* 74 (Winter 2000).

Dick, T.J.O. "Canadian Newsprint, 1913–1930: National Policies and the North American Economy." *Journal of Economic History* 42, no. 3 (September 1982).

Fell, C.P. "The Newsprint Industry." In H.A. Innis and A.F.W. Plumptre, eds, *The Canadian Economy and the Great Depression.* Toronto: Canadian Institute of International Affairs, 1934.

Fernow, B.E. *Lectures on Forestry.* Delivered at the School of Mining, Kingston, Ontario, 26–30 January 1903. Reprinted in 1905 *Sessional Papers* as part of the *Report of the Bureau of Forestry.*

Forsey, E.A. "The Pulp and Paper Industry." *Canadian Journal of Economics and Political Science* 1 (1935).

Gillis, R.P. "The Ottawa Lumber Barons and the Conservation Movement, 1880–1914." *Journal of Canadian Studies* (February 1974).

Girard, M.F. "The Commission of Conservation as a Forerunner to the National Research Council, 1909–1921." *Scientia Canadensis* 15, no. 2 (1991).

Goltz, E. "Espanola: The History of a Pulp and Paper Town." *Laurentian University Review* 6, no. 3 (June 1974).

Gray, S. "The Government's Timber Business: Forest Policy and Administration in British Columbia, 1912–1928." *BC Studies* 81 (Spring 1989).

Haskell, W.E. *The International Paper Company, 1898–1924.* New York: International Paper Company, 1924.

Hay, R.W. "Mergers and the Expansion of Productive Capacity in the Canadian Pulp and Paper Industry, 1926–1932." Atlantic Canada Economics Association, *Papers* 14 (1985).

Heinrich, Thomas. "Product Diversification in the U.S. Pulp and Paper Industry: The Case of International Paper, 1898–1941." *Business History Review* 75 (Autumn 2001).

Hiller, J. "The Origins of the Pulp and Paper Industry in Newfoundland." *Acadiensis* 11, no. 2 (Spring 1982).

Hiller, J. "The Politics of Newsprint: The Newfoundland Pulp and Paper Industry, 1915–1939." *Acadiensis* 19, no. 2 (Spring 1990).

Hodgins, B.W., J. Benedickson, and P. Gillis. "The Ontario and Quebec Experiments in Forest Reserves, 1883–1930." *Journal of Forest History* (January 1982).

Hodgins, B.W., and J. Benedickson. "Resource Management Conflict in the Temagami Forest, 1898 to 1914." Canadian Historical Association *Historical Papers* (1978).

Hull, J.P. "Research at Abitibi Power and Paper." *Ontario History* 79, no. 2 (June 1987).

Hydro-Electric Commission of Fort William. *Electricity and Fort William: History of the Development of Electricity in the City of Fort William, 1898–1967.* Hydro-Electric Commission of Fort William, 1967.

The Instructor. Gardenvale, PQ: The Community Study Club of Ste Anne de Bellevue, November 1934.

International Paper Company: After Fifty Years, 1898–1948. New York: International Paper Company, 1948.

Kellogg, R.S. *Newsprint Paper in North America.* New York: Newsprint Service Bureau, 1948.

Kimberly, J.R. *Four Young Men Go in Search of a Profit: The Story of Kimberly-Clark Corporaton (1872–1957).* New York: Newcomen Society of North America, 1957.

Kuhlberg, M. "'By just what procedure am I to be guillotined?': Academic Freedom in the Toronto Forestry Faculty between the Wars." *History of Education* 31, no. 4 (July 2002).

Kuhlberg, M. "E.W. Backus." *Dictionary of Canadian Biography*, vol. 16. Toronto: University of Toronto Press, forthcoming.

Kuhlberg, M. "'Eyes wide open': E.W. Backus and the Pitfalls of Investing in Ontario's Pulp and Paper Industry, 1902–1934." *Journal of the Canadian Historical Association*, vol. 16 (2005).

Kuhlberg, M. "'Pulpwood is the Only Thing We Do Export': The Myth of Provincial Protectionism in Ontario's Pulp and Paper Industry, 1890–1930." In D. Anastakis and A. Smith, eds, *Smart Globalization: The Canadian Business and Economic History Experience.* Toronto: University of Toronto Press, 2014.

Kuhlberg, M. "'Nothing but a cash deal': Crown Timber Corruption in Northern Ontario, 1923–1930." In Thunder Bay Historical Museum Society, *Papers and Records* (2000).

Kuhlberg, M. "Ontario's Nascent Environmentalists: Seeing the Foresters for the Trees in Southern Ontario, 1919–1929." *Ontario History* 88, no. 2 (June 1996).

Kuhlberg, M. "'We are the pioneers in this business': Spanish River's Forestry Initiatives after the First World War." *Ontario History* 93, no. 2 (Autumn 2001).

Kuhlberg, M. "'We have "sold" forestry to the management of the company': Abitibi Power and Paper Company's Forestry Initiatives in Ontario, 1919–1929." *Journal of Canadian Studies* 34, no. 3 (Fall 1999).

Layton, W. *Newsprint: A Problem for Democracy.* London: P. O'Donogue, 1946.

Liberty, Equality and Fraternity. Three Addresses Delivered by Employees of the Spanish River Pulp and Paper Mills Limited at the 8th Annual President's Banquet. Sault Ste Marie, ON: [s.n.], 1924.

McGibbon, D.L. *The Pulp Industry in Canada*. Paper Presented at the Canadian Forestry Convention, 7 March 1902.

McRoberts, M.L. "When Good Intentions Fail: A Case of Forest Policy in the BC Interior, 1945–56." *Journal of Forest History* (July 1988).

Merchant, E.O. "The Government and the News-Print Paper Manufacturers." *Quarterly Journal of Economics* 32 (February 1918).

Moody's Manual of Investments: American and Foreign Industrial Securities. New York: Moody's Investors Services, 1920–1932.

Murray, W.S. *Government Owned and Controlled Compared with Privately Owned and Regulated Electric Utilities in Canada and the United States*. New York: National Electric Light Association, 1922.

Nelles, H.V. "Empire Ontario: The Problems of Resource Development." In D. Swainson, ed., *Oliver Mowat's Ontario*. Toronto: Macmillan Canada, 1972.

Newsprint Prorationing: An Account of Governmental Policy in Quebec and Ontario for the Honorable P. E. Cote, K.C., Minister of Lands and Forests, Province of Quebec. Montreal: Newsprint Association of Canada, 1940.

Niosi, J. "La Laurentide, 1887–1928: Pionnière du papier journal au Canada." *Revue d'histoire de l'Amérique française* 29, no. 3 (1975).

Northern Ontario: Its Progress and Development under the Whitney Government. Liberal-Conservative Party, ca 1911.

Parenteau, W. and L.A. Sandberg. "Conservation and The Gospel of Economic Nationalism: The Canadian Pulpwood Question in Nova Scotia and New Brunswick, 1918–1925", *Environmental History Review* 19, no. 2 (Summer 1995).

Piedaiue, G. "Les groupes financiers au Canada, 1900–1930." *Revue d'histoire de l'Amérique française* 30, no. 1 (1976).

Piedaiue, G. "Les groupes financiers et la guerre du papier au Canada, 1920–1930." *Revue d'histoire de l'Amérique française* 30, no. 2 (1976).

Porter, M.E., and Claas van der Linde. "Towards a New Conception of the Environment–Competitiveness Relationship." *Journal of Economic Perspectives* 9, no. 4 (Fall 1995).

Pross, P. "The Development of Professions in the Public Service: The Foresters in Ontario." *Canadian Public Administration* 10 (1967).

Pugh, D.E. "Ontario's Great Clay Belt Hoax." *Canadian Geographical Journal* (January 1975).

Pulpwood and Its Problems [Reprinted articles]. Globe Printing Company, 1907.

Roach, T.R. "The Pulpwood Trade and the Settlers of New Ontario." *Journal of Canadian Studies* 22, no. 3 (Fall 1987).

Sandberg, L.A. "Forest Policy in Nova Scotia: The Big Lease, Cape Breton Island, 1899–1960." *Acadiensis* 20, no. 2 (Spring 1991).

Sandberg, L.A., and P. Clancy. "Forestry in a Staples Economy: The Checkered Career of Otto Schierbeck, Chief Forester, Nova Scotia, Canada, 1926–1933." *Environmental History* 2, no. 1 (January 1997).

Sandberg, L.A., and P. Clancy. "From Weapons to Symbols of Privilege: Political Cartoons and the Rise and Fall of the Pulpwood Embargo Debate in Nova Scotia, 1923–1933." *Acadiensis* 26, no. 2 (Spring 1997).

Southworth, C. "The American-Canadian Newsprint Paper Industry and the Tariff." *Journal of Political Economy* 30 (1922).

Thompson, W.G. "The History and Status of Forestry in Ontario." *Canadian Geographical Journal* (September 1942).

Van Every, M. "Francis Hector Clergue and the Rise of Sault Ste. Marie as An Industrial Centre." *Ontario History* 56 (September 1964).

Zavitz, E.J. "Reforestation in Ontario." *Canadian Geographical Journal*, April 1947.

Unpublished Secondary Sources

Bertrand, J.P. "Timber Wolves." Original manuscript, ca 1961.

Branch, M.L. "The Paper Industry in the Lake States Region, 1834–1947." PhD dissertation, University of Wisconsin, 1954.

Butcher, P. "The Establishment of a Pulp and Paper Industry at Kapuskasing." MA thesis, University of Western Ontario, 1978.

Cummins, J.G. "Concentration and Mergers in the Pulp and Paper Industries of the United States and Canada, 1895–1955." PhD dissertation, John Hopkins University, 1960.

Hall, K. "The Sweet Smell of Success: A Study of the Origins and Development of the Pulp and Paper Industry in Dryden, Ontario." Undergraduate dissertation, Lakehead University, 1992.

Horne, G.R. "The Receivership and Reorganization of the Abitibi Power and Paper Company, Limited." PhD thesis, University of Michigan, 1954.

Hull, J.P. "Science and the Canadian Pulp and Paper Industry, 1903–1933." PhD dissertation, York University, 1986.

Kuhlberg, M. "In the Power of the Government: The Rise and Fall of Newsprint in Ontario, 1894–1932." PhD dissertation, York University, 2002.

Parenteau, W.M. "Forests and Society in New Brunswick: The Political Economy of Forest Industries, 1918–1932." PhD thesis, University of New Brunswick, 1994.

Parsons, H. "Aerial Timber Sketching Memoirs, 1922–1976." Unpublished manuscript, Toronto, 1981.

Pross, P. "The Development of a Forest Policy: A Study of the Ontario Department of Lands and Forests." PhD thesis, University of Toronto, 1967.

Index